D1186748

THE PAINTINGS IN
THE ROYAL COLLECTION

A THEMATIC EXPLORATION

Books by the same author

A Catalogue of the Earlier Italian Paintings
in the Ashmolean Museum (1977)
Camille Pissarro (1981)
Studies on Camille Pissarro (editor) (1986)
The Queen's Pictures: Royal Collectors through
The Centuries (1991)
Masterpieces in Little: Portrait Miniatures
from the Collection of
Her Majesty Queen Elizabeth II (1997)

THE PAINTINGS IN
THE
ROYAL COLLECTION

A THEMATIC EXPLORATION

Christopher Lloyd
Surveyor of The Queen's Pictures

Foreword by HRH The Prince of Wales

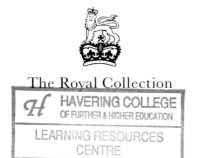

The Royal Collection

HAVERING COLLEGE
OF FURTHER & HIGHER EDUCATION

LEARNING RESOURCES
CENTRE

7082

155571

Revised, paperback edition published in 1999 by

Royal Collection Enterprises Limited,
St James's Palace,
LONDON
SW1A 1JR

http:/www.royal.gov.uk

© 1999 Royal Collection Enterprises Limited

Text by Christopher Lloyd and reproductions of all items in
The Royal Collection © Her Majesty The Queen

All rights reserved. Except as permitted under current
legislation no part of this work may be photocopied, stored in a
retrieval system, published, performed in public, adapted,
broadcast, transmitted, recorded or reproduced in any form or
by any means, without the prior permission of the copyright
owner.

The right of Christopher Lloyd to be identified as author of this
work has been asserted by him in accordance with the
Copyright, Designs and Patents Act 1988.

ISBN 1 902163 59 1

British Library Cataloguing in Publication Data

A record for this book is available from the British Library.

Original design by Design/Section Frome, Somerset

Produced with the assistance of
Book Production Consultants plc, Cambridge

Printed and bound by Kyodo Printing Co. (S'pore) PTE Ltd,
Singapore

Distributed by Thames and Hudson Ltd

Hardback edition originally published as *The Royal Collection* in
1992 by Sinclair-Stevenson

Front cover: Sir Anthony van Dyck, '*The Great Peece*', 1632
(detail of FIG. 130)
Back cover: Canaletto, *View of London: the Thames from
Somerset House towards the City*, 1750–1 (detail of FIG. 194)

Contents

Looking can be a form of worship and also an exact science. The great thing is to be able to look correctly and with attention, with as much objectivity as possible. This is not only pleasurable as a contemplative process but it also provides the basis for feeling.

CHRISTOPHER NEVE
Unquiet Landscape 1990

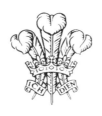

The Royal paintings form a remarkable collection. It would have been even more remarkable had the Civil War in England in the seventeenth century not resulted in the dispersal of many of its finest paintings. Some of these great works of art can now be seen in the world's greatest museums, including the Louvre in Paris. Fortunately for the Royal and national heritage, King George IV, that most perceptive and extravagant of collectors, eventually redressed the balance by buying many important works of art from France during its Revolution.

Perhaps you can imagine what a great joy it has been for someone like myself, with a particular love of history and of painting, to be surrounded through my life by such wonderful examples of man's artistic creativity. I remember as a child gradually becoming aware of the fascinating pictures which adorned the walls - especially the Canalettos in the Grand Corridor at Windsor Castle. The longer I lived with the pictures, the more I became aware that they represented, above all, the individual tastes and interests of successive sovereigns. Despite its great riches and variety, the Royal Collection, we should remember, is not like an art gallery; it is not a representative collection and it has not been put together by a committee of art historians.

Although the paintings were bought over centuries to decorate the homes and official residences of sovereigns, they are not the private property of the sovereign. They are national heirlooms which are an integral part of the institution of monarchy and of which each sovereign in turn is the guardian, adding to them as she, or he, thinks fit and is able, and looking after them with all possible love.

The Royal Collection Trust has, since its establishment in 1993, made strenuous efforts to ensure that the Collection can be seen by as many people as possible. Many of the paintings in this book are hanging in Royal residences which are open to the public - including Buckingham Palace, Windsor Castle, Hampton Court and Kensington Palace. We also send well over one hundred major works of art every year on loan to exhibitions in this country and abroad.

What so fascinates me about the Collection is the way in which successive monarchs have commissioned contemporary artists to record important aspects of their lives - family occasions, great statesmen, national events, children, friends, dogs and horses. In my own modest way, I try to continue this tradition, for its value both to today's artists and to posterity, by inviting painters whose work I admire to accompany me on official visits abroad and to record other aspects of life today. I hope that by so doing, I can help maintain the vitality of the Collection, ensuring that it continues to bring joy to the increasing numbers of people who are coming to know it. This book will, I know, spread that knowledge much more widely and with it, I hope, the enthusiasm for this great Collection which I have always felt.

Charles

Author's Acknowledgements

The Royal Collection is a project which has been undertaken by gracious permission of Her Majesty The Queen. The purpose is to bring the paintings in the Royal Collection before a wider public and this could not have been done without the forbearance and cooperation of Members of The Royal Family and of the Royal Household.

This book has been written in conjunction with the television series of the same name. Andrew Hewson of John Johnson Ltd played a critical role in introducing the various parties and it is largely because of his efforts that the project has been brought to fruition. As the first documentary to have been made using the high-definition television format, the six programmes may be described as epoch-making. The credit for this contribution to television history falls jointly to Channel 4 and NHK (Japan): Michael Grade, Managing Director of Channel 4, and Waldemar Januszezak, Commissioning Arts Editor of Channel 4, and Chizuko Kobiyashi and Noriyuki Kurosawa of NHK. I am grateful for the confidence both Channel 4 and NHK placed in me as writer and presenter.

The series was co-produced by Antelope and Icon Films Ltd without whose enthusiasm and professional skills nothing at all would have been achieved. Mick Csaky (Executive Producer) steered the project through from start to finish, while Harry Marshall (Producer) was an inspirational force at all stages; Kenneth Corden (Director) brought a wealth of experience to the task and, with Jonathan Cooke (Editor), spent long hours in cutting rooms in London and Japan. The wisdom of Adrian House (Consultant) was an essential ingredient. We were extremely fortunate that Carl Davis agreed to compose the music which was such a vital contribution, adding an extra and unforgettable dimension to the series. The participation of Dr Marco Chiarini (Director of the Palazzo Pitti, Florence), Richard Ormond (Director of the National Maritime Museum, London) and Don McCullin (Photographer) is also gratefully acknowledged. On location I benefited enormously from the experience of Michael Miles (Cameraman), Keith Desmond (Sound), Fiona Freed (Production Manager), Charlotte Moore (Research). Others, such as Peter Montagnon and Chris Ralling, were generous in giving advice at critical moments. As a neophyte in the world of television, I found it a singular pleasure to work with people who to a rare degree combine wisdom and wit with patience and understanding. It was a memorable experience for me and I hope that for them *The Royal Collection* was more than just another assignment.

One of the distinguishing features of the television series was the access granted to Royal Residences and Palaces. Thanks are extended to all those who facilitated the time spent in Buckingham Palace, Windsor Castle, St James's Palace, Balmoral Castle, Sandringham House, Osborne House, Hampton Court Palace, the Banqueting House and The Queen's Gallery. The National Gallery in London, the Palazzo Ducale in Urbino and the Galleria degli Uffizi in Florence also kindly permitted filming.

I am deeply conscious of my debt to those colleagues in the Royal Household with whom both the series and the book have been discussed, particularly members of the Royal Collection department. Their understanding and consideration were exemplary. It cannot, in addition, be sufficiently emphasised to what extent anyone working on the paintings in the Royal Collection is dependent upon the contributions over the years of Sir Oliver Millar, Surveyor Emeritus of The Queen's Pictures. A cursory glance at the section on Further Reading (page 306) will indicate exactly what is meant by that statement.

For particular research and help at various stages I am indebted to Major David Rankin-Hunt, Gerard Vaughan, David Baldwin, Lisa Matthews, Michael Upton and especially Anne Thorold. Edward Platt checked the references and typed the manuscript with great care and accuracy. I hope that they will not be disappointed by the results as presented in this book, although, of course, they should not be held to blame for my errors, misrepresentations, misappropriations or eccentricities. A profound debt is owed to the publisher Christopher Sinclair-Stevenson. Penelope Hoare has been an outstanding editor. Lorraine Estelle and Graham Webb have brought flair and expertise to the overall design of the book. Emily Mallaby and Roger Cazalet have coordinated the production process.

No publication of this sort is achieved in isolation as I know my family will corroborate. My parents, Hamilton and Suzanne Lloyd, read the type-script diligently and constructively. It is to them that I owe my love of history and literature. My wife, Frances, supported me throughout, even typing the scripts in their original form. Her comments were constructive and much appreciated. My children, Alexander, Benedict, Oliver and Rupert, looked on with gentle amusement. For all of this I am eternally grateful and I fervently hope that they will be pleased with the television series and the book.

CHRISTOPHER LLOYD,

SURVEYOR OF THE QUEEN'S PICTURES,

LONDON, 1992

Preface to the Revised Edition

The paintings in the Royal Collection are a source of constant fascination. The combination of historical association and aesthetic quality makes the collection one of the greatest in the world. Added to this is the vast number of pictures distributed throughout numerous royal residences.

Over the years the paintings have become better known through exhibitions and scholarly publications, but the present book was written with a different purpose in mind. Now available in paperback, it remains the most comprehensive survey of the paintings in the Royal Collection in print. Arranged thematically, it aims to discuss as broad a range of pictures as possible and by adopting this approach it has been possible to examine the paintings in a new light and to make some revealing comparisons. The book illustrates familiar works, as well as less well-known ones, and so provides what is hopefully an enjoyable and illuminating introduction to a large and wide-ranging collection formed over several centuries. Above all, I am pleased that this paperback edition provides an opportunity for more readers to share the enjoyment of looking at and examining paintings in the Royal Collection.

CHRISTOPHER LLOYD,

LONDON, 1999

Introduction

Clio, the muse of history, presides over the Royal Collection. The paintings reflect history in the lives of monarchs and their peoples, in the evolution of institutions and in the record of events. They mirror political, military, religious and social developments.

The Royal Collection is held in trust by each sovereign in turn for those who will succeed to the throne. It is, therefore, a private collection, although its sheer size (some 7,000 pictures) and its display in palaces and royal residences (several of which are open to the public) give it a public dimension.

It is not the purpose of the Royal Collection to be comprehensive. The evolution of the British Royal Collection has depended upon the choice of the reigning monarch. The paintings are an expression of the sovereign's personal taste, which is why this collection is so distinctive and does not share the obligations of a national gallery or museum. The National Gallery in London, for example, which has about 2,300 paintings, is concerned to collect pictures that provide a survey of the development of Western painting, ideally by acquiring the finest examples of an artist's or a school's work. Although, in theory, monarchs have been in a position to obtain paintings of a similar standard, by no means all of them have aspired to do so. Queen Anne, George I, George II, William IV, George V and Edward VII cannot be described as collectors in the real sense, but, equally, they could not afford to be totally uninterested, because painting retained a political potency in disseminating the image of the monarch. Also, unofficially during these reigns, painting continued to embody a certain social status or to fulfil a private whim. It is, of course, regrettable that George II did not have a more harmonious relationship with William Hogarth, just as it is sad that George III and Queen Charlotte so despised Sir Joshua Reynolds, but this does not in itself represent a total abdication of interest in painting.

Few sovereigns can stand comparison with Charles I, George IV or Queen Victoria (with Prince Albert), who were the principal collectors and greatly extended the boundaries of the Royal Collection. It is due to their taste and energy that the paintings in the collection are so heterogeneous.

Diversity of quality is another hallmark of the Royal Collection. While there are outstanding groups of paintings by Hans Holbein the Younger,

Van Dyck, Canaletto, Thomas Gainsborough and Sir Edwin Landseer, for example, there are also large gaps. In recent years, although acquisitions have been made, the emphasis has, of financial necessity if nothing else, been on the more practical aspect of administering and consolidating the collection. On the walls of royal residences masterpieces frequently jostle for space with pictures that are of far less significance.

Throughout the evolution of the collection iconography has always been as important as style or quality. Very often the subject matter of the painting is of especial value and overrides other considerations. In this context, as in no other, the numerous portraits and narrative compositions which illustrate significant moments in British history are in their way just as relevant as the masterpieces.

The British Royal Collection is of greatest interest because of its very survival as a private collection; this has sometimes been against considerable odds, notably the execution of Charles I in 1649. In France, Germany, Spain, Austria, Holland and the Scandinavian countries, former royal collections have usually been ceded to the state and now form the nucleus of national collections in European capitals. By contrast, the British Royal Collection has more or less remained intact within those buildings long associated with the monarchy – Windsor Castle, Hampton Court Palace, St James's Palace, the Palace of Holyroodhouse, Kensington Palace, Kew Palace, Frogmore House, Buckingham Palace, Balmoral Castle, Osborne House and Sandringham House, to name only those that have survived into the twentieth century.

Each of these royal residences varied in significance from dynasty to dynasty and even from monarch to monarch. Sometimes the buildings were appreciated, enlarged or altered by more than one sovereign. Hampton Court, for instance, extends from the Tudors through the Stuarts (specifically William III and Mary II) to the early Hanoverians, but was not favoured by Queen Victoria. Windsor Castle was built by the Normans, extensively modernised by Charles II and handsomely redesigned by George IV. Kew Palace and Buckingham House are basically thought of in terms of George III and Queen Charlotte, until Buckingham House was gradually converted into a palace by George IV, William IV, Queen Victoria and finally George V. Kensington Palace is primarily associated with William and Mary, until it is remembered that it was here that Queen Victoria spent her childhood and in 1837 received the news of her accession to the throne. It is the numerous permutations of this kind that make the Royal Collection a living historical entity, which, as far as the pictures are concerned, spans a period of 500 years from the establishment of the Tudor dynasty to the present House of Windsor.

The paintings in the Royal Collection are extremely well documented. It may not be easy to visualise how the Tudors arranged their pictures at Whitehall Palace and Hampton Court Palace, or how Charles I divided his exceptionally fine collection between Whitehall Palace, Somerset House and the Queen's House at Greenwich, but there are inventories that date back to the sixteenth and seventeenth centuries describing the paintings and their distribution room by room. There has also survived from the time of George III a series of schematic drawings of the arrangement of the paintings in Buckingham House.

For more recent reigns there exists a certain amount of visual evidence in the form of watercolours, prints and photographs. The most elaborate of such visual records is *The History of the Royal Residences* by William Henry Pyne, published with detailed descriptions in three volumes in 1819. This includes a series of images of Carlton House where George IV lived in considerable style and kept his magnificent collection until in 1827 he chose to have the building demolished (FIG. I). As important as Pyne's publication, but more limited in scope, was Joseph Nash's *Views of the Interior and Exterior*

FIG. I
Charles Wild: *The Blue Velvet Room, Carlton House*,
c. 1818

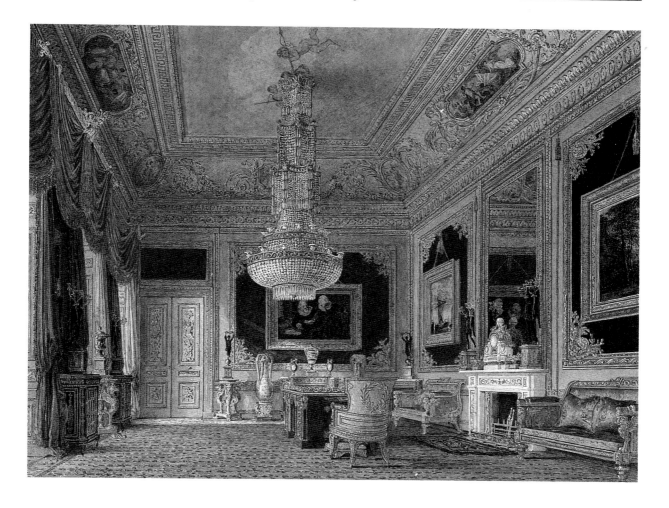

of Windsor Castle (1848) (FIG. II). Both publications serve not only as invaluable tools of reference, but also as sources of inspiration for honouring the traditional arrangement of pictures in some of the more formal rooms in the royal residences.

This kind of evidence indicates changes of taste over the years. The Picture Gallery in Buckingham Palace, for instance, which was planned by George IV but properly established by his successors William IV and Queen Victoria, is recorded in a watercolour that shows how the smaller pictures were originally strung like beads to form the lower line of the hang (FIG. III). Later, however, during the reign of King George V, the same Picture Gallery had been totally rehung with the paintings seemingly obscured by dark varnish that makes the gallery appear badly lit and dingy (FIG. IV). A similar transformation can be discerned in the Private Apartments at Windsor Castle where, at the beginning of Queen Victoria's reign, the Queen's Sitting Room contains a residual flavour of Regency taste – a spacious distribution of pictures, works of art and furniture in a light airy atmosphere (FIG. V). Yet by the end of the reign the same room

FIG. II
Joseph Nash: *The Van Dyck Room, Windsor Castle*, 1846

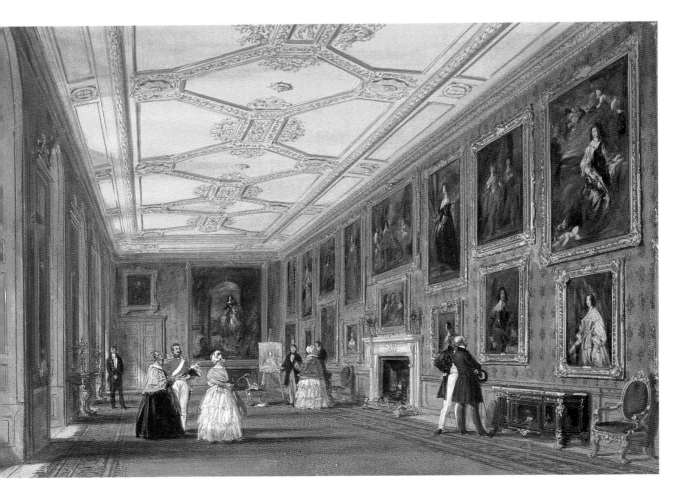

14

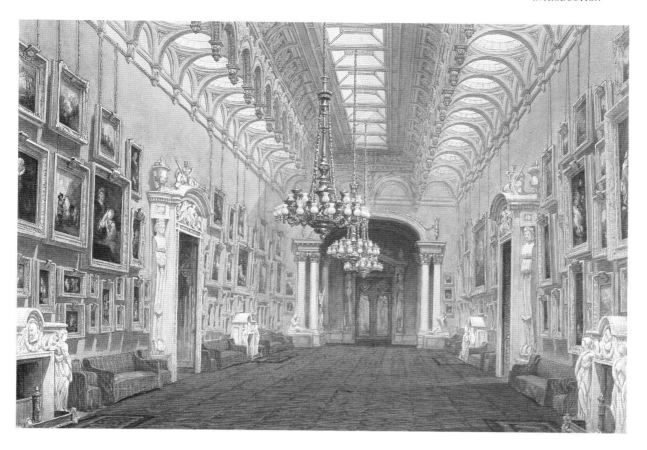

FIG. III
Douglas Morison: *View of
the Picture Gallery,
Buckingham Palace*, 1843

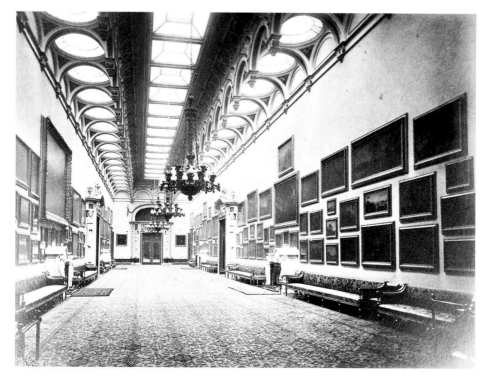

FIG. IV
Alexander Hood: *The
Picture Gallery, Buckingham
Palace*, c. 1914

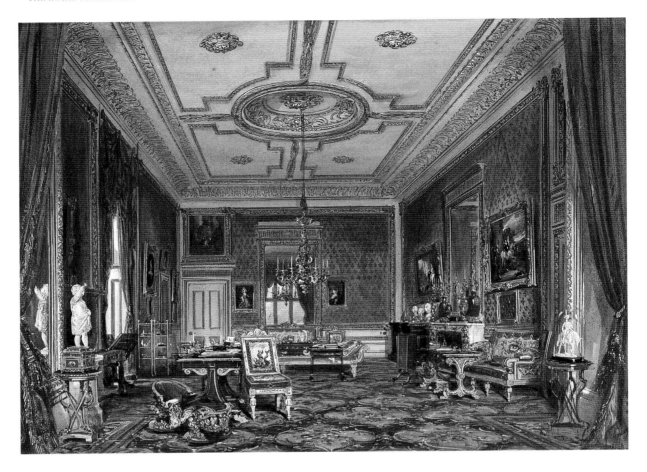

FIG. V
Joseph Nash: *The Queen's
Sitting Room, Windsor Castle*,
c. 1848

had been transformed into the cluttered array of items that is the epitome of Victorian interior decoration (FIG. VI).

By this date the lavish publications of Pyne and Nash had given way to more serious and scholarly appraisals of the collection, undertaken by pioneer art historians whose achievements helped to establish the subject as an academic discipline: Gustav Waagen, the first director of the Royal Museum in Berlin (1835 and 1854); Johann David Passavant, the great Raphael scholar and Director of the Staedelisches Kunstinstitut in Frankfurt-am-Main (1833); and the writer and iconographer Anna Brownell Jameson (1844).

For this book I have chosen a thematic arrangement. The purpose is to combine the strengths and weaknesses of the Royal Collection in order to demonstrate its unique qualities and to stress its continuing significance both for the specialist and for a wider public.

The titles of the chapters are self-explanatory and are intended to be all-embracing. 'The Genius of Italy' (Chapter 2) touches on such topics as the history of the Order of the Garter, the influence of the Reformation on

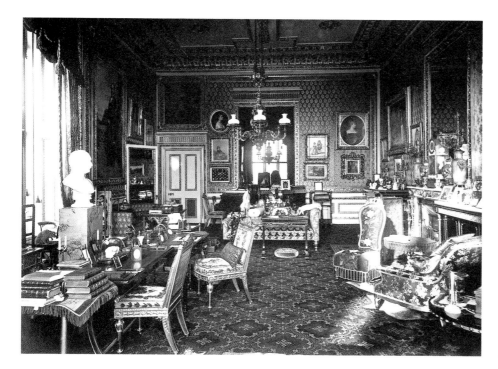

FIG. VI
Mary Steen: *The Queen's
Sitting Room, Windsor Castle,*
1895

art and the popularity of the Grand Tour, culminating in a discussion of the paintings by Canaletto in the Royal Collection – the largest group of works by this popular artist in existence. 'The Kingdom of Nature' (Chapter 3) examines animal painting and the art of landscape. The Collection has a particularly good holding of equestrian pictures, including numerous examples by George Stubbs, while for animals in general and attitudes to hunting in particular, the paintings of Sir Edwin Landseer are still relevant. For landscape painting, works by John Wootton, Claude Lorrain, Gainsborough, Hobbema, Ruisdael and Cuyp serve to demonstrate changing approaches to nature. 'The Sword and the Sceptre' (Chapter 4) discusses those pictures representing State Visits and related diplomatic events, beginning with the Field of the Cloth of Gold in 1520 and extending to the British Empire in India. Contrasting with diplomacy is warfare, and it is understandable that the collection should be rich in battle paintings – both naval and military. The depiction of such battles as Crécy, the Plains of Abraham at Quebec, Trafalgar, Waterloo and Inkerman reveal varying attitudes to war. 'Private View' (Chapter 5) has a certain duality. It traces the evolution of a type of composition known as the royal conversation piece, which is intended to show the sovereign on an informal basis, but at the same time the subject matter of many of the pictures in the collection provided monarchs themselves with insights into the private lives of ordinary people. The final chapter, 'The Regal Image', concentrates on the State Portrait, which was given such impetus by the achievements of Van

Dyck, and analyses ceremonial paintings which reach a climax with scenes of the Coronation.

The link between these chapters is the fact that the Royal Collection would not have been formed without the enthusiasm for art nurtured by Charles I, George IV, Queen Victoria and Prince Albert. The opening chapter, 'The Collectors', emphasises their roles in the development of the Collection; but it is also stressed that other figures such as Henry, Prince of Wales, the elder brother of Charles I, and Frederick, Prince of Wales, the father of George III, were successful and influential as collectors, although not on quite the same scale.

This book is written from a privileged position. To be responsible as I am for such an outstanding group of paintings as can be found in the British Royal Collection is challenging and daunting. The sheer number of items, the range of subjects represented, the problems of display in several palaces or royal residences and, not least, all the aspects of conservation give some idea of the magnitude of the task.

It was Charles I who appointed the first Surveyor in May 1625. The post was given to Abraham van der Doort, a specialist in the applied arts rather than paintings, and a man of Dutch origins. His salary was £40 per annum. His tenure was not happy, and he committed suicide in 1640. Since then the post of Surveyor has varied over the centuries. Some of those appointed have been artists such as George Knapton, Benjamin West, Augustus Callcott, Richard Redgrave, perhaps the greatest Surveyor, and Sir J. C. Robinson. More recently, the tendency has been to appoint art historians: Sir Lionel Cust, Lord Clark, Anthony Blunt, Sir Oliver Millar. What is certain is that the duties of the Surveyor have not really changed since they were defined by Charles I for Abraham van der Doort:

> . . . to prevent and keepe them [the paintings] (soe much as in him lyeth) from being spoiled or defaced, to order marke and number them, and to keepe a Register of them, to receive and deliver them, and likewise to take order for the makeing and coppying of Pictures as Wee [Charles I] or the Lord Chamberlaine of Our Household shall directe, And to this end . . . hee shall have Accesse at convenient Times unto Our Galleries Chamber and other Roomes where Our Pictures are.

THE PAINTINGS IN
THE ROYAL COLLECTION

A THEMATIC EXPLORATION

CHAPTER 1

The Collectors

All British monarchs have acquired paintings, but few have been genuine collectors. The status and quality of the Royal Collection derives principally from the efforts of three sovereigns: Charles I, George IV and Queen Victoria (with Prince Albert). These monarchs were true connoisseurs whose enthusiasm for art transformed the exercise of official patronage and by the same token extended the boundaries of the Royal Collection. What unites these three very different sovereigns is a shared sense of quality. The Royal Collection is essentially their creation.

The fact that the three significant reigns are spread over a period of almost 300 years is interesting, because what emerges from studying these three royal collectors is not just a sense of changing taste, but different patterns of collecting. Such patterns include the establishment of a traditional picture gallery, as in Whitehall Palace in the seventeenth century or in Buckingham Palace at the beginning of the nineteenth; the growth of the art market, which was given such impetus by the sale of Charles I's collection after his execution in 1649 and which many years later was the source of many of George IV's more spectacular purchases; and what might be called the invasion of the artist's studio, which was a tactic employed by Queen Victoria and Prince Albert, partly out of the queen's interest as a fellow practitioner, and partly to encourage those particular stylistic characteristics that she expected to find in a painting.

Charles I had the most refined taste of any British monarch and the collection he formed at the beginning of the seventeenth century was the finest – in terms both of quality and of quantity – ever assembled in this country. The quality was such that the collection influenced the whole course of British painting; the quantity so great that its dispersal helped to promote the art market in the modern sense. The sale of Charles I's collection also meant that many important pictures left Britain never to return. Anyone visiting the major museums of Europe – in Paris, Madrid, Vienna, Berlin, Amsterdam – will see paintings that once belonged to Charles I.

His collection numbered nearly 1,500 pictures and included several masterpieces – in the true sense – by Renaissance artists such as Leonardo da Vinci, Raphael, Titian, Correggio and Dürer, as well as outstanding works by contemporary artists such as Rubens and Van Dyck. Here at last was a British monarch whose cultural achievements could rival those of French, Spanish, Habsburg and Italian princes. Indeed, it might well have been this competitive spirit that sharpened Charles I's collecting instincts. Yet, whatever reasons he may have had for forming a collection, the king's sense of quality was paramount. Lucy Hutchinson, the wife of the Puritan regicide Colonel John Hutchinson, wrote:

> King Charles was temperate, chaste, and clever. Men of learning and ingenuity in all arts were in esteem and received encouragement from the king who was a most excellent judge and a great lover of paintings, carvings, engravings and many other ingenuities, less offensive than the bawdry and profane abusive wit which was the only exercise of the other court [James I].[1]

FIG. 1
Sir Anthony Van Dyck:
Charles I in Three Positions,
1635–6

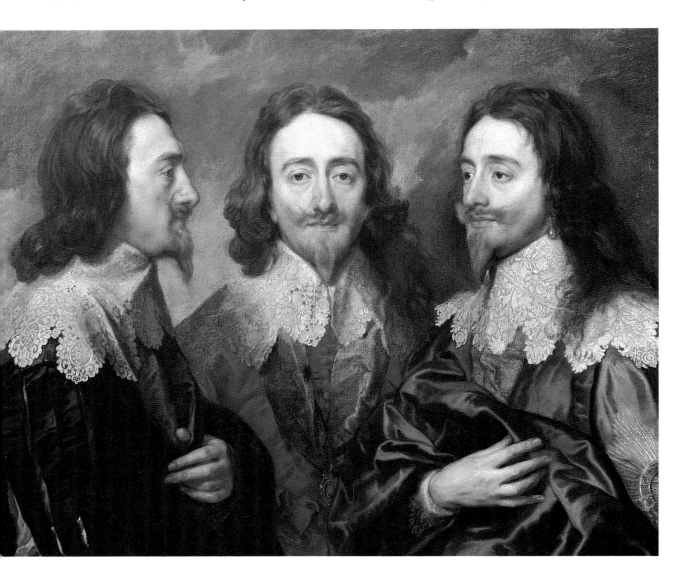

Even the political and religious divisions of the Civil War do not obtrude upon a contemporary judgement on Charles I's love of art.

The most eloquent testimony of the king's temperament and interests is found, not unexpectedly perhaps, in a painting – *Charles I in Three Positions* (FIG. 1). Painted by Van Dyck in 1635–6, it was depicted specifically to be sent to Rome to the sculptor Gian Lorenzo Bernini, who, encouraged by Pope Urban VIII, had been commissioned by the queen, Henrietta Maria, to carve a portrait bust of Charles I. The triple position of the head was a conventional way of conveying a person's character and appearance. Titian had given the convention an allegorical twist (London, National Gallery), but another Venetian precedent lay in Charles I's own collection, in a portrait by Lorenzo Lotto (Vienna, Kunsthistorisches Museum), then thought to be by Titian. After Van Dyck, the French painter Philippe de Champaigne adopted the same formula for his portrait of Cardinal Richelieu (London, National Gallery) which was also despatched to Rome for a similar piece of sculpture, and Sir Godfrey Kneller performed the same service (London, National Portrait Gallery) for the sculptor John Michael Rysbrack in the context of a sculpted bust of the second Earl of Nottingham.

Van Dyck's chief skill as a portrait painter was to penetrate beneath the surface and to reveal hidden aspects of the sitter's personality. Here, therefore, the viewer is made aware of Charles I's elegance, refinement, sensitivity, intelligence, dignity and shyness, but also of his single-mindedness, obtuseness, aloofness, stubbornness and the surprising mental and physical strength that was to be so severely tested during the Civil War. Gesture plays as important a part as physiognomy: the fingering of the ribbon of the Order of the Garter on the left denotes a certain nervousness or tension, and the enfolding of the hand within great swathes of drapery on the right suggests a certain love of luxury.

The bust was carved in the summer of 1636 and arrived at Oatlands Palace in Surrey in July the following year, where it was universally admired. It was the first bust that Bernini had carved for someone outside the orbit of his Roman patrons and it simply outclassed everything of its kind in Britain. As the English sculptor Nicholas Stone the Younger informed Bernini, the success of the bust rested 'not only for the excellence of the work, but the likeness and neat resemblance it had to the king's countenance'.[2] Plans were set in motion for Bernini to carve a companion bust of Queen Henrietta Maria, but this was never brought to fruition. The king's bust was first installed in Greenwich Palace, but later moved to Whitehall Palace, where it was destroyed by fire in 1698. It is known now only through a somewhat pedestrian copy thought to have been made by Thomas Adye.

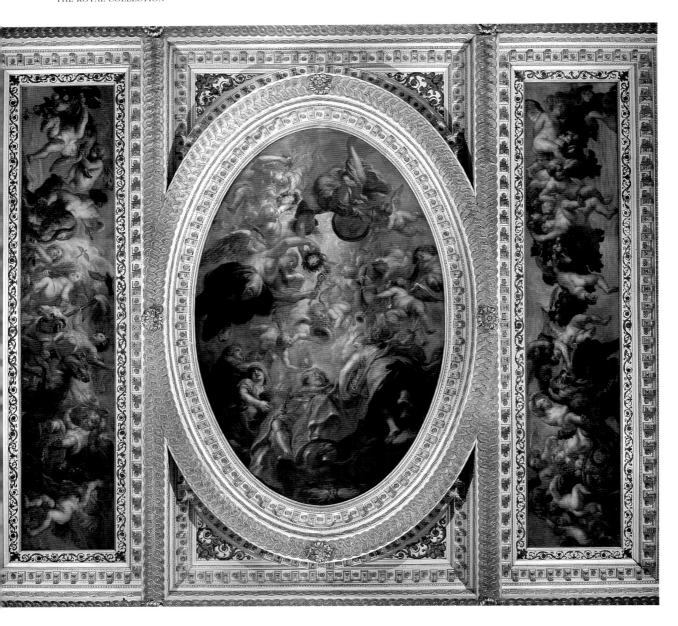

FIG. 2
Sir Peter Paul Rubens: *The Apotheosis of James I, flanked by Processions of Putti*, c. 1634

The commissioning of the bust of Charles I should not be seen simply from the point of view of portraiture. Van Dyck and Bernini were artists of the highest calibre and their participation in such projects vividly demonstrates the level on which Charles I's connoisseurship was exercised, influencing the development of British art and transforming British taste. In his patronage of these artists, and of Rubens, Charles I showed himself to be in the forefront of European cultural thinking. Indeed, his decision to be sculpted by Bernini, the leading sculptor in Rome, the artistic capital of the world, resulted in a veritable procession of luminaries with similar intentions: Cardinal Richelieu, Duke Francesco d'Este and Louis XIV.

Charles I's love of art was not – indeed could not have been – nurtured in a vacuum. Partly it was inherited from his parents. His father, James I, was an intellectual; his grasp of political theory – summarised in his books, *Basilikon Doron* (1599) and *The True Law of Free Monarchies* (1603) – became the basis of Charles I's advocacy of the divine right of kings. James also conducted a successful foreign policy, maintaining peace with Holland, France and Spain throughout his reign.

Charles acknowledged his father's political skills in the ceiling decorations in the Banqueting House in Whitehall – the only part of the palace that has survived. The building was designed by Inigo Jones in the Italian Renaissance style of Andrea Palladio for James I in 1619–22. The ceiling was specially commissioned later from Rubens by Charles I and finished by 1634 (FIG. 2). It is the largest decorative scheme by Rubens still to be seen in its original setting. The central oval of the ceiling was devoted to the *Apotheosis of James I* and the two rectangular sections on the same axis represent the *Unification of the Kingdom* (Scotland and England) which resulted from James I's succession, and the *Peaceful Reign of James I*. The theme was unmistakably the glorification of Charles I's father and the smaller scenes reinforced the message in allegorical terms.

The Banqueting House was a building of great significance, and not just in an architectural sense. It was here, for instance, that many court entertainments were enacted, in the form of masques written by Ben Jonson and staged by Inigo Jones. The masques, too, were replete with allegorical meanings that the learned Stuart court enjoyed disentangling. Once Rubens' ceiling was in place, however, Charles I instructed that no more court entertainments could be produced in the Banqueting House in case the smoke from the spluttering torches and candles damaged the paintings. It is extraordinary to reflect that Charles I passed through this very room before mounting the scaffold on the day of his execution in Whitehall on that cold morning in January 1649.

Although clever, James I was not attractive. He was notoriously self-indulgent, physically repulsive, sexually deviant and remarkably unprepossessing in his personal habits. His wife, Anne of Denmark (FIG. 3), the sister of Christian IV, preferred pictures to men, according to a contemporary source. Shortly before her death in 1619, she is reported often to have walked alone in her picture gallery. Earlier she had associated herself not only with new architecture and garden design, but also with the innovative style of portraiture found in the work of Isaac Oliver and Marcus Gheeraerts the Younger.

The impetus for developing the Royal Collection really came from Anne of Denmark. In Tudor times, tapestries were generally preferred to paintings. The sovereigns, especially Henry VIII, had favoured portraits,

FIG. 3
Paul van Somer: *Anne of Denmark*, 1617–18

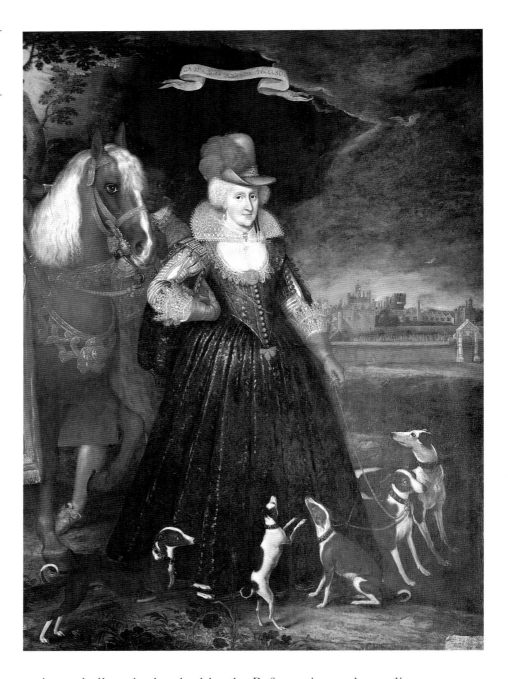

FIG. 3
Paul van Somer: *Anne of Denmark*, 1617–18

FIG. 4
Paul van Somer: *James I*, c. 1620

anti-papal allegories inspired by the Reformation and grandiose representations of important occasions such as the meeting with Francis I at the
Field of the Cloth of Gold. The achievements of Hans Holbein the Younger
stand out as exceptional, but the scope of the collection was limited and
the quality varied.

The pictures collected by Anne of Denmark were more wide-ranging,
showing a far greater awareness of artistic potential. Beyond portraits,
which were so important for dynastic and political reasons, her collection

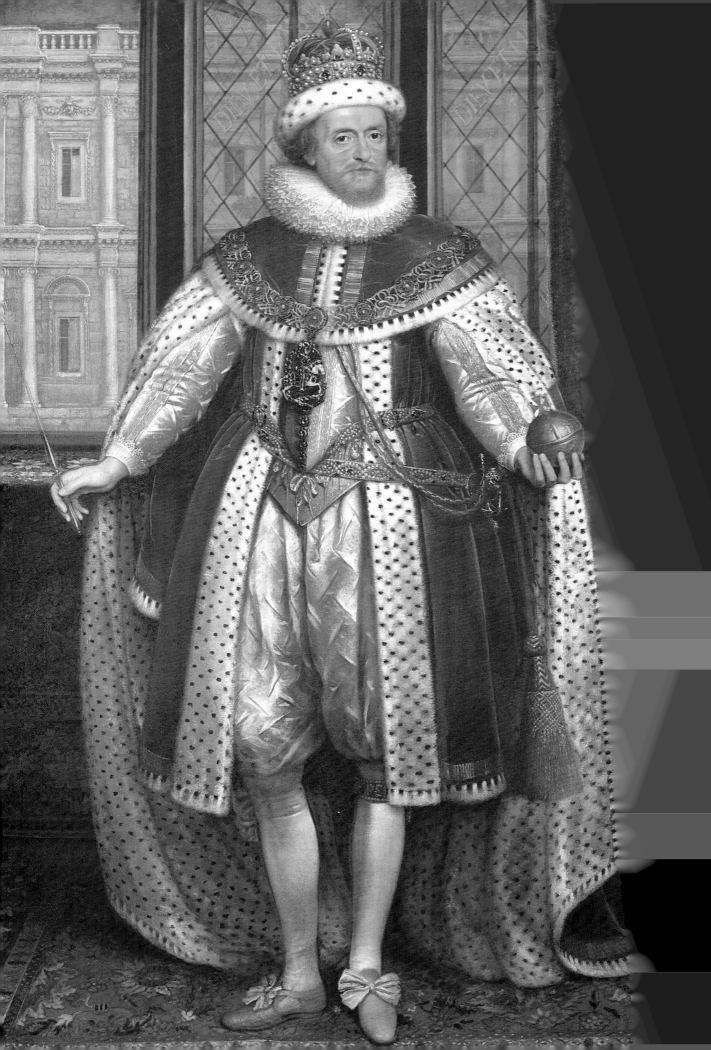

included religious, mythological and topographical pictures, as well as still lifes.

James I is depicted by Paul van Somer standing before the Banqueting House (FIG. 4) whereas the queen is shown *à la chasse* in front of Oatlands Palace (FIG. 3), the new entrance to which was designed by Inigo Jones (1616–18). Her eldest son, Henry, Prince of Wales (FIG. 5), was also a patron of Inigo Jones and during his short lifetime came to personify the Renaissance in Britain, even though he never travelled on the Continent. Not only was he scholarly and interested in all the arts, he was also a warrior prince of the kind associated with the Italian Renaissance – ships, horses, arms and armour, tournaments and military exercises absorbed his attention. He was well-advised and had distinguished friends such as Robert Devereux, third Earl of Essex; John Harington, second Baron Harington of Exton; and William Cecil, second Earl of Salisbury, all of whom were carefully selected and had similar interests.

The collection of paintings formed by Prince Henry is notable for its diversity. There appear to have been religious paintings, allegorical subjects and military and marine pictures by artists such as Hendrik Vroom and Jan Porcellis. The *Portrait of a Boy Looking through a Casement* by a painter of the Cremonese school suggests the idiosyncratic nature of his collection, which, although promising and largely imported from Italy, still fell far short of its continental counterparts.

Henry, Prince of Wales, died of typhoid fever in 1612, aged only eighteen. It was a great loss and contemporary eulogies were for once sincere in their expressions of grief. One correspondent in a private letter referred to the prince as 'the Flower of his House, the Glory of his Country, and the Admiration of all Strangers'.[3] His younger brother, Charles, was created Prince of Wales in 1617 and a great deal must have been expected of him.

In the realm of art, at least, the future Charles I easily exceeded his brother. Indeed, it must have emerged quite early on that he had a discerning eye for pictures and would set different standards. A courtier, Lord Danvers, sought in 1620 to acquire a painting by Rubens as a gift for the twenty-one-year-old Prince of Wales. The *Lion Hunt* (Rome, Galleria Corsini) was sent over by the artist, but it had to be rejected by Danvers because 'in every painters opinion he hath sent hither a piece scarce touched by his own hand, and the postures so forced, as the Prince will not admitt the picture into his own gallery'.[4] The *Lion Hunt* was duly returned.

Three years later Danvers was encouraging Rubens to rectify his mistake by sending a self-portrait in an attempt to seek the Prince of Wales' patronage. The self-portrait (FIG. 6) was bold, and reveals that Rubens was

FIG. 5
Robert Peake (attributed to): *Henry, Prince of Wales, in the Hunting-Field*, c. 1606–7

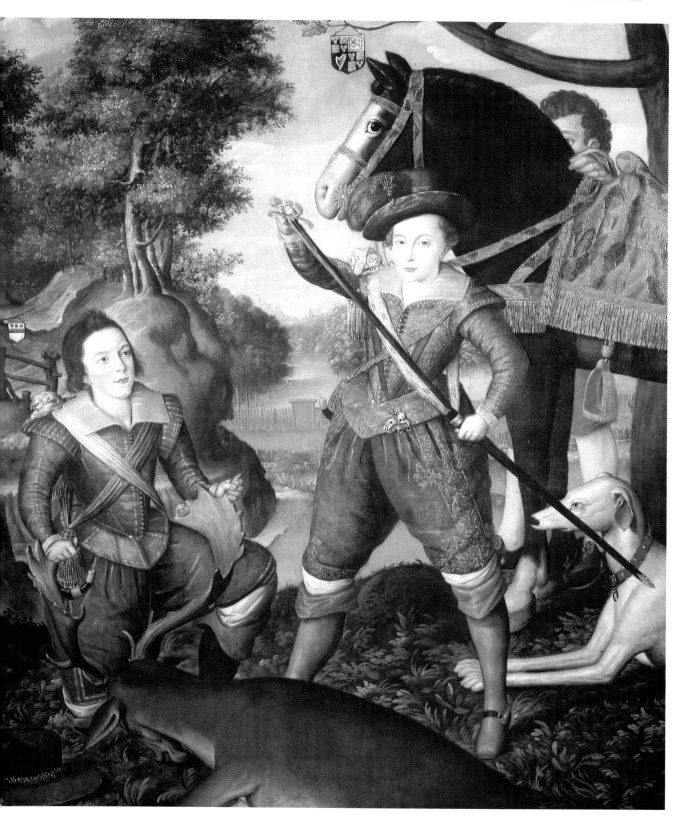

fully at home in royal circles: the artist wears a hat and places himself against a rocky background, creating an image that implies Rubens is more an equal than a suppliant. The gift of the self-portrait proved successful and thereafter Rubens was frequently employed at the English Court. On the eve of Charles I's accession in 1625 the artist wrote in a letter that 'The Prince of Wales . . . is the greatest amateur of paintings among the princes of the world.'[5]

In writing this Rubens could have been accused of flattery, but the truth of the statement was soon to become evident. The collection formed by Charles far outstripped those formed by his mother and elder brother, and that of his father's favourite, Robert Carr (later the Earl of Somerset). Significantly, it was another of James I's favourites, George Villiers (created first Duke of Buckingham in 1623), who exercised a decisive influence over the future Charles I.

Villiers had a meteoric rise to power (and an equally dramatic death in 1628 at the hands of an assassin in Portsmouth), and by the early 1620s he was forming a distinguished and wide-ranging collection of paintings. He owned, for example, the *Ecce Homo* by Titian (Vienna, Kunsthistorisches Museum), as well as several works by contemporary Italian painters as varied as Guido Reni, Bartolommeo Manfredi and Giovanni Baglione. Politically speaking, Buckingham was a parvenu who used art as a means of bolstering his social position. He probably introduced into Britain the concept – perhaps one that can only be fully appreciated retrospectively – by which an outstanding art collection gained for its patron prestige, influence, and wealth. As his adviser Sir Balthazar Gerbier wrote to him in 1625:

FIG. 6
Sir Peter Paul Rubens:
Portrait of the Artist, 1622.

> Let enemies and people ignorant of painting say what they will, they
> cannot deny that pictures are noble ornaments, a delightful
> amusement, and histories that one may read without fatigue. . . .
> Our pictures, if they were to be sold a century after our death,
> would sell for good cash, and for three times more than they have
> cost. I wish I could only live a century, if they were sold, in order
> to be able to laugh at those facetious folk who say, It is money cast
> away for baubles and shadows.[6]

A turning point in Charles I's initiation as a collector occurred in the company of the Duke of Buckingham. In 1623 the two men were travelling together in Spain. The purpose was to woo the younger sister of Philip IV as a bride for the Prince of Wales. The episode, complete with false names and disguises, was conducted in an atmosphere worthy of Mozart's *Così fan tutte*. The Infanta Maria did not marry Charles I, but the visit to Spain

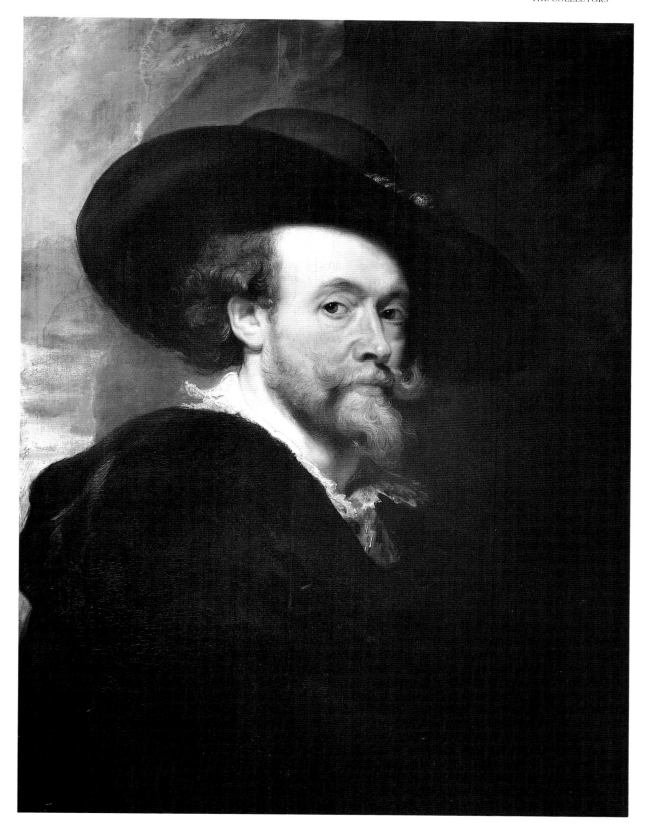

had a dramatic affect on his artistic consciousness, since it brought him into contact with the greatest collection of paintings in Europe, namely that inherited by Philip IV from Charles V and Philip II.

Philip IV was only eighteen when Charles I and Buckingham reached Madrid – younger than either of his visitors – but he was undoubtedly aware of his artistic heritage and was soon to become the patron of Rubens and of Velazquez, who painted a now lost portrait of the Prince of Wales during this visit to Spain. The collection, housed in the Alcazar Palace in Madrid, was strong in Netherlandish painting, particularly works by Hieronymus Bosch, but its chief glory was the work of Venetian High Renaissance artists, especially Titian. While the prospect of the marriage lasted, the English prince was given the *Venus del Pardo* (Paris, Louvre) and the *Portrait of Charles V with a Hound* (Madrid, Prado), both by Titian. He was offered some of the finest mythologies painted by the same artist for Philip II, but these pictures were eventually withheld when the negotiations over the marriage ran into difficulties. Charles also made his own purchases while in Spain, including the painting by Titian entitled *Nude Girl in a Wrap* (Vienna, Kunsthistorisches Museum), which he acquired from a private collection.

More spectacular still was the acquisition of the set of seven cartoons by Raphael prepared in 1515–16 in connection with the tapestries that were woven in Brussels for the Sistine Chapel in Rome. Charles I bought the cartoons in Genoa for £300 through an agent. These cartoons were not intended for display, but rather to be used for practical purposes in the factory established by James I at Mortlake in 1618 as patterns to be followed in the production of tapestries. For this reason the cartoons were cut into vertical strips. It was only in subsequent reigns that they were reassembled and hung as works of art in Hampton Court Palace and Buckingham Palace. Later, in 1865, they were given by Queen Victoria to the South Kensington Museum (now the Victoria and Albert Museum), which was founded to encourage the arts of design and manufacture. Charles I had therefore presided over the acquisition of one of the crucial examples of the principles of classical design. Illustrating incidents from the early history of the church, Raphael had reduced complicated configurations into carefully unified compositions. There is no visual confusion or ambiguity, as each individual in the scene reacts spontaneously to a given moment. The clarity of the narrative, the balancing out of the essential components, and the close relationship between the settings and the backgrounds reveal Raphael as a supremely articulate artist in full command of his powers resulting in a level of achievement that was to reverberate down the centuries (FIG. 7).

The visit to Spain triggered Charles I's collecting instincts and introduced him to the highest standards of artistic excellence. On his return to England it was apparent that during the 1620s and 1630s a number of other major collections were being formed in London. Apart from the Royal Collection, which was itself mainly divided between St James's Palace, Whitehall Palace, Somerset House and Greenwich Palace, there were the establishments of the third Marquis (later first Duke) of Hamilton at Wall-

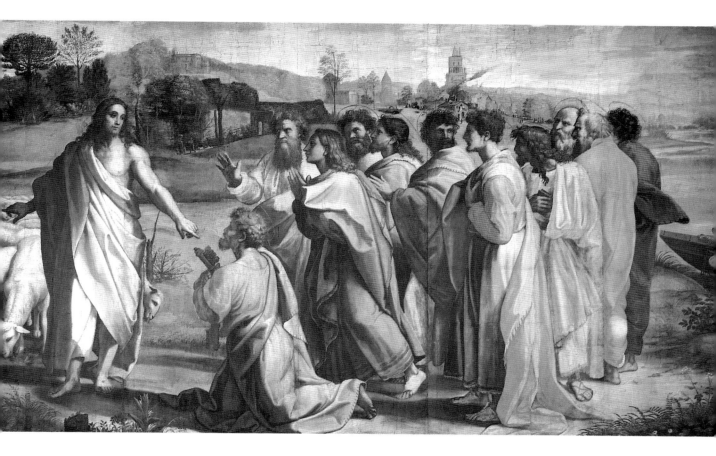

ingford House (on the site of the Admiralty), the Duke of Buckingham at York House and the Earl of Arundel at Arundel House, both along the Strand.

The Marquis of Hamilton was ambitious, cunning and vain. He proved to be an inadequate military commander fighting for Charles I in the north during the Civil War. His collection amounted to some 600 paintings, among which were the *Three Philosophers* and *Laura* by Giorgione (both now in Vienna, Kunsthistorisches Museum) and the altar-piece by Antonello da Messina from the church of S. Cassiano, Venice (also in Vienna, Kunsthistorisches Museum). It is likely that the collection reflected the Marquis of Hamilton's desire for advancement; but the Earl of Arundel was a genuine connoisseur – as was his wife Aletheia – whose

FIG. 7
Raphael: *The Charge to St. Peter*, c. 1515–16

33

interests extended well beyond paintings to embrace antique sculpture, drawings and prints. He was patrician, taciturn, moody, and withdrawn, and their marriage was not altogether happy. The Earl of Arundel travelled extensively in Germany and the Netherlands, and in Italy, where he died. His taste spanned the richly coloured coruscated surface of Titian's *Flaying of Marsyas* (now in the Kroměříz, Statnzamek) as well as the intensely linear images of Hans Holbein the Younger and Dürer. In many ways, though he was not a member of Charles I's immediate circle, the Earl of Arundel served as a role model for the king. In an atmosphere in which it was fashionable to collect great art, Charles I as a collector emerges as *primus inter pares*.

The desire among a core of individuals based in London avidly to collect pictures promoted a network of contacts. Collectors of aristocratic status during the seventeenth century depended upon agents, and Charles I benefited from the system. At one level there were the ambassadors or special envoys, who either acted directly on behalf of collectors or else purchased paintings for themselves while abroad and sold them on arrival back in London. Cities such as Venice and The Hague, where an incipient art market flourished, were important diplomatic postings and it was in these two places that career diplomats such as Sir Henry Wotton and Sir Dudley Carleton operated – only two of several ambassadors so employed by Charles I.

Even more influential were the knowledgeable middlemen. Both Endymion Porter, who often negotiated in Spain and was a patron and friend of poets, and Sir Balthazar Gerbier, who was a painter and architect, were at first closely associated with the Duke of Buckingham. Nicholas Lanier, a keen collector of drawings employed at court as Master of the King's Music, and Daniel Nys, a merchant, were also in close touch with artists. These romantic, somewhat shadowy figures were permanently on the lookout for paintings for the king and awaiting his instructions to enter into negotiations on his behalf.

They were, in addition, zealous in soliciting gifts to be presented to the king and, indeed, made such gifts themselves so that their services would be retained. The two most distinguished paintings by Dürer owned by Charles I (*Portrait of the Artist's Father*, now in London, National Gallery, and *Self-Portrait*, now in Madrid, Prado) were presented through the Earl of Arundel as gifts from the city of Nuremberg in 1636. From the States-General of the United Provinces in the same year, the king received two fine early religious panels by Geertgen tot Sint Jans (*Lamentation* and *Burning of the Bones of St John the Baptist*, both now in Vienna, Kunsthistorisches Museum). Such gifts were, of course, prompted by political motives, or as expressions of loyalty following Charles I's accession in 1625. It was, how-

ever, as private individuals that Sir James Palmer presented the king with
the *Wilton Diptych* (London, National Gallery) and Sir Robert Kerr (later
the Earl of Ancrum) gave him the *Portrait of the Artist's Mother* (FIG. 8), an
early painting by Rembrandt acquired in 1629 directly from the artist's
studio in Leiden.

The leading collectors also made exchanges between themselves, in
the desire to obtain more works by artists that they particularly liked or
sought. Practices like this reflect fluctuations in personal taste. Charles I
gave away or exchanged major works by northern artists in favour of
paintings by Italians: for instance, a volume of portrait drawings by Hans
Holbein the Younger was presented to the Earl of Pembroke in exchange

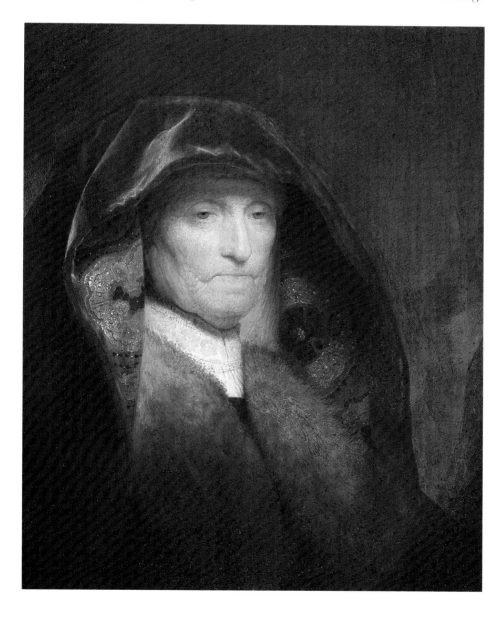

FIG. 8
Rembrandt van Rijn:
Portrait of the Artist's Mother,
c. 1629

for *St George and the Dragon* by Raphael (Washington, National Gallery), and the *Portrait of Erasmus* (now in Paris, Louvre) by Holbein was given in part exchange to the Duc de Liancourt for *St John the Baptist* by Leonardo da Vinci (Paris, Louvre).

The most dramatic moment in the formation of Charles I's collection was the acquisition *en bloc* of the Gonzaga collection in Mantua. This was a veritable coup and Charles I through his agents outwitted his principal French and Italian rivals. The Gonzaga family had ruled in Mantua since the fourteenth century and had made the city into one of the greatest art capitals in Europe. By the early seventeenth century, however, the fortunes of the Gonzagas were dwindling rapidly and the dynasty was collapsing

FIG. 9
Andrea Mantegna: *The Triumphs of Caesar*, c. 1485–94

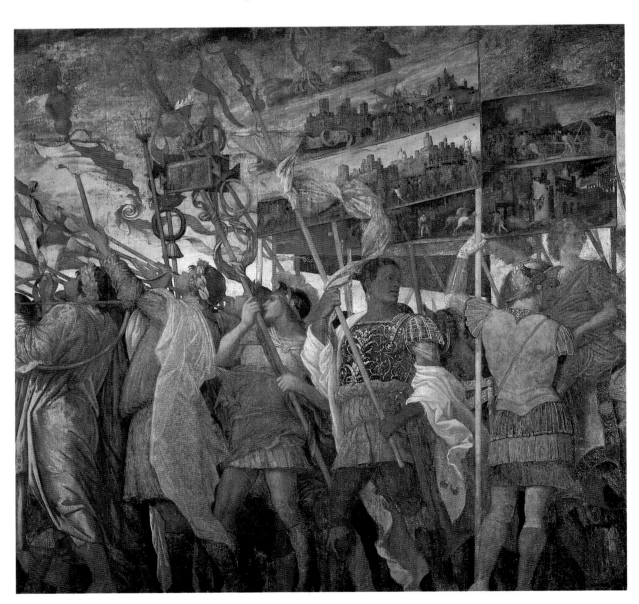

under a surfeit of good living and debauchery, misdirected religious zeal and an unhealthy interest in dwarfs and parrots. The collection was legendary, and was described by the agent Daniel Nys as 'so wonderful and glorious a collection that the like will never again be met with'.[7] Major works by Mantegna, Raphael, Andrea del Sarto, Giulio Romano, Titian, Tintoretto, Correggio, Annibale Carracci, Caravaggio, Guido Reni, Domenico Fetti and Rubens were reported.

Negotiations with Vincenzo II, the ruling member of the Gonzaga family, began in earnest at the end of 1626 and were conducted in secrecy by Nicholas Lanier and Daniel Nys. A preliminary sale was clinched in 1627 for a total cost of £15,000 and most of the paintings, including *The Twelve Caesars* by Titian (since destroyed by fire), the *Butcher's Shop* by Annibale Carracci (Oxford, Christ Church) and the *Death of the Virgin* by Caravaggio (Paris, Louvre), were transported by sea. More delicate items, such as the *Allegory of Vice* and the *Allegory of Virtue* by Correggio (both now Paris, Louvre), which were painted in tempera, travelled overland.

News of the sale caused a furore. As Nys remarked, 'Since I came into the world, I have made various contracts, but never a more difficult one than this and which has succeeded so happily. In the first place, the City of Mantua, and then all the Princes of Christendom, were struck with astonishment that we could induce the Duke to dispose of them. The people of Mantua made so much noise about it . . .'.[8] But worse was to come, for Nys reported, 'The best informed persons told me that I had left the most beautiful behind and, that, not having The Triumph of Julius Caesar, I had nothing at all'.[9]

The famous group of canvases by Andrea Mantegna, *The Triumphs of Caesar* (FIG. 9), had been excluded from the initial sale. After the death of Vincenzo II, the Gonzaga family encountered further financial difficulties, and they were eventually persuaded to sell in 1628 for £10,000. This set of nine canvases had been painted by Mantegna for Francesco II over a period of ten years (c. 1485–94), for display in the Palazzo Ducale in Mantua. Although frequently restored, they remain the largest and most significant works of their kind by a Renaissance artist outside Italy. Furthermore, they are unrivalled examples of Mantegna's ability to recreate with almost archaeological accuracy the remote world of antiquity. He was a slow, methodical worker with a precise, linear style and he relied on dramatic foreshortening and complicated perspective to achieve striking visual effects. In the *Triumphs of Caesar*, Mantegna paints a composite of several of Caesar's victory parades; his purpose being to present the clamour and the sense of movement of such an occasion. This is achieved so successfully that the modern viewer becomes a spectator watching the parade pass by, with its attendant noise and bustle eventually becoming reduced to a distant echo.

Charles I now possessed about 1,500 pictures and the Gonzaga sale had enhanced his reputation as a collector, but there were other, less happy consequences: he had diverted money from other more pressing and serious political purposes. His agent, Nys, overreached himself in the negotiations and was himself beset by financial difficulties. The citizens of Mantua had lost their art treasures, a fact bewailed by Rubens, who, like Mantegna before him, had been court painter to the Gonzaga family. The Gonzaga deal ushered in the age of the modern predatorial collector, epitomised slightly later in the seventeenth century by Queen Christina of Sweden, roaming the cities of Europe and securing vast numbers of works of art in the wake of military success or changing political affiliations. The centre of Charles I's activities, Whitehall Palace, was now at its most resplendent with the walls enlivened by masterpieces painted by the hands of Leonardo da Vinci, Raphael, Titian, Correggio, Rubens and Van Dyck, to name only the most prestigious artists. By then, Charles I must have felt that his collection could at last rival that of Philip IV.

The king's attempts after this date to acquire other collections *en bloc* (the Ludovisi collection in Rome and the Bartolomeo della Nave in Venice) failed because the political circumstances changed. Even so, while in London in 1629, Rubens could already remark:

> I must admit that when it comes to the pictures by the hands of first-class masters, I have never seen such a large number in one place as in the royal palace in England and in the gallery of the late Duke of Buckingham.[10]

Charles I had a penchant for Italian art. He admired graceful compositions, warm colours and elegant brushwork as exemplified by artists of the High Renaissance. He was particularly drawn to the varied application of paint and glowing colours of Titian, apparent in both the religious and the often more sensual secular works. He was less successful in securing the attentions of contemporary Italian artists, although attempts were made to do so. Instead of Guido Reni, Guercino or Albani – all leading masters of the Bolognese school – he had to employ the itinerant Orazio Gentileschi (FIG. 38), who was an interesting, but not a major, follower of Caravaggio. Although Charles I owned outstanding examples of the work of Dürer and Holbein the Younger, such paintings were not his favourites and it is apparent that the two northern contemporary artists whom he most admired – Rubens and Van Dyck – both had a stylistic panache and vividness of colouring that stemmed in large part from Titian.

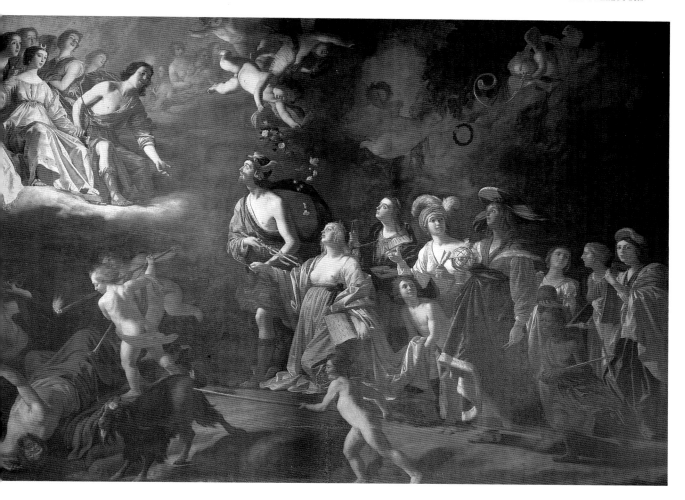

FIG. 10
Gerrit van Honthorst:
Apollo and Diana, 1628

The scale and speed of Charles I's acquisitions were matched only by their dispersal. Our contemporary knowledge of the collection is based upon the documents prepared by the first Surveyor of the King's Pictures, Abraham van der Doort. As the king continued to search for and to buy more paintings, the country edged closer towards Civil War, which broke out in 1642. Charles I's fortunes as a political and military figure began to fluctuate dramatically, but his reputation as a connoisseur remained intact. He possessed neither the political aptitude nor the military competence to sustain the ideals of kingship that he expounded in theory and clung to so tenaciously. And the crisis in which he found himself was to a certain extent compounded by his love of art and the drain that this had put on his financial resources.

That the atmosphere of the court was becoming more and more rarefied and withdrawn from reality is amply demonstrated by a large allegorical painting devised in the manner of a masque by a Dutch follower of Caravaggio, Gerrit van Honthorst, dating from 1628 (FIG. 10). It shows

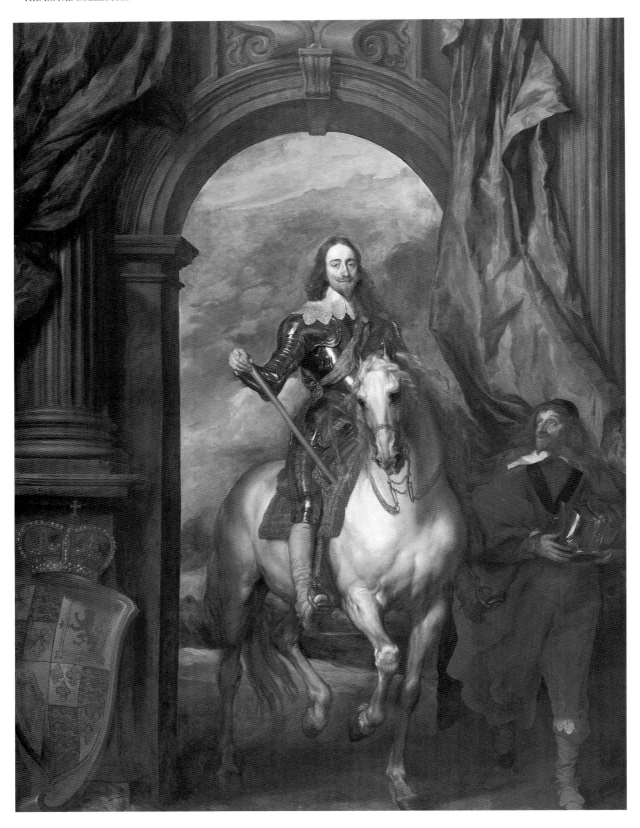

Apollo and Diana enthroned top left. Apollo has been given the features of Charles I and Diana those of his French wife, Henrietta Maria, the daughter of Henri IV and Marie de' Medici. Below is Mercury introducing the Liberal Arts led by Grammar holding a book. These two figures are given the features of the Duke and Duchess of Buckingham. They are followed by Logic, Rhetoric, Astronomy, Geometry, Arithmetic and Music. The king and queen are about to receive the homage of the arts, and in doing this, vices such as Ignorance, Envy and Lust are put to flight in the lower left-hand corner. Such obvious personifications and dry intellectual allusions were standard practice at the time. The fun was esoteric and somewhat obscure. The painting symbolises the isolation of the court and illustrates how it offered an escape from the mounting financial, religious and political problems threatening its very existence.

The artist whose work most exactly mirrors the plight of the early Stuart court in its dying moments is Van Dyck. The painter came from Antwerp, having been born into a prosperous middle-class family. He had been a pupil of Rubens and as an artist he achieved success easily both in his own country and in Italy. His self-portraits reveal good looks and an undeniable self-confidence. He was suave, opinionated, neurotic and vain. When he settled in London in 1632 he lived at Blackfriars, a part of the city which has been described as 'wealthy, cosmopolitan, and just a little disreputable'.[11] Van Dyck lived in some comfort and had a beautiful but excitable mistress. The king, who shared Van Dyck's admiration for Titian, allowed him to build a special landing stage from the Thames to his house so that there would be easy access for his sitters.

FIG. 11
Sir Anthony Van Dyck:
Charles I with Monsieur de St. Antoine, 1633

Such are the expectations of successful portrait painters. In return, for the last nine years of his life (1632–41), Van Dyck provided definitive images of the king, his family and his court. It was important, for example, for there to be an official equestrian portrait of the king seen in armour being led through a triumphal arch by his equerry M. de St Antoine (FIG. 11). This is how Titian, Rubens and Velazquez painted princes: it provided a context for the monarch's power, albeit one that in this case proved to be an illusion. Van Dyck's skill lay in depicting his sitters as they saw themselves, but in doing this he reveals for the viewer their real character or situation. His purpose, therefore, was not so much flattery as veiled criticism. Here we see an image replete with the trappings of absolute power, but, at the same time, the attenuated face, the tinge of melancholy in the expression, the touch of weariness in the complexion, the uncertainty in the flicker of the eyes all hint at weaknesses. This is how Van Dyck transmits the truth to us.

One of the most beautiful paintings undertaken by Van Dyck for Charles I, *Cupid and Psyche* (FIG. 12), encapsulates both the artist's debt to

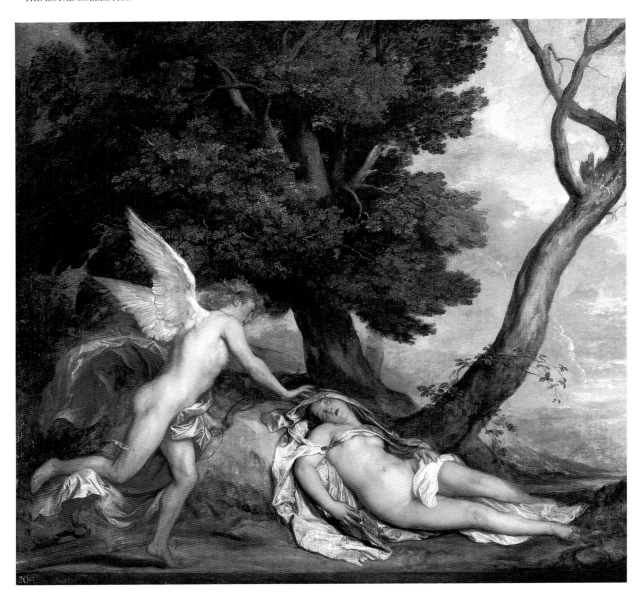

FIG. 12
Sir Anthony Van Dyck:
Cupid and Psyche, 1639–40

Titian and the alembicated existence of those in attendance at the Caroline court. On the other hand, his numerous portraits (FIG. 13) have been seen as the perfect expression of a section of society on the verge of extinction, at a time comparable in some respects with France before the Revolution or Europe before the 1914–18 war. The people he depicts seem to lead a charmed existence: they are well-dressed, beautifully coiffured, lofty in mind, seemingly oblivious of circumstances, introspective, keen to maintain the status quo and determined to enjoy themselves. These were the courtiers who fled from London in 1642 and followed the king to Oxford where they lolled and strolled in college gardens, desperately hoping that the Royalist cause would prevail. Events, however, would soon overtake them

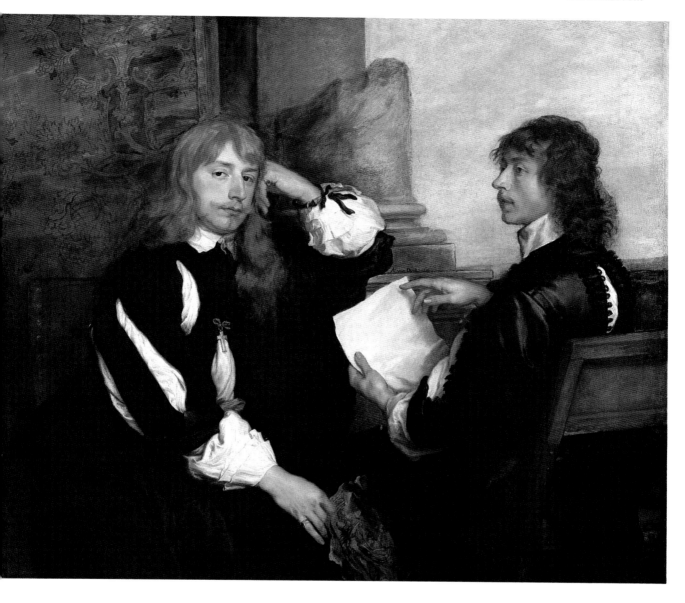

and crush the gilded fragility of that existence. As the historian G. M. Trevelyan wrote in a famous passage,

> Given over to the use of a Court whose days of royalty were numbered, its [the garden of St John's College, Oxford] walks and quadrangles were filled, as the end came near, with men and women learning to accept sorrow as their lot through life, the ambitious abandoning hope of power, the wealthy hardening themselves to embrace poverty, those who loved England preparing to sail for foreign shores and lovers to be parted for ever. There they strolled through the gardens as the hopeless evenings fell listening, at the end

of all while the siege guns broke the silence with ominous iteration. Behind the canon on those low hills northward were the inexorable men who came to lay their hands on all this beauty hoping to change it to strength and sterner virtue.[12]

Van Dyck was a perfect courtier. His portraits are so telling precisely because he himself shared this lifestyle, and it is hardly surprising that what he created in paint finds an echo in contemporary poets such as Herrick, Lovelace, Suckling and Waller. His death as the Civil War broke out was almost symbolic; it was left to the more muscular William Dobson to depict the passage of the court through Oxford.

The Civil War led to the defeat and capture of the king by that wide range of anti-monarchical factions led by the future Lord Protector, Oliver Cromwell. Charles I was brought to trial in Westminster Hall (FIG. 14) and beheaded on 30 January 1649. His execution resulted in the enforced sale of his collection and other possessions in order to pay off his debts. The sale was arranged in considerable haste and was on an unprecedented scale.

FIG. 14
Edward Bower: *Charles I at his Trial*, 1648

Commissioners were first appointed to draw up lists and value the paintings, which featured, for example, £2,000 for the *Madonna della Perla* by Raphael (Madrid, Prado), £1,000 each for the *Allegories of Virtue and Vice* (Paris, Louvre) and *Venus and Cupid with a Satyr*, formerly known as *Jupiter and Antiope* (Paris, Louvre), both by Correggio, and £800 for the *Education of Cupid* (London, National Gallery) by the same artist. The bust of Charles I by Bernini was also valued at £800; the set of the *Labours of Hercules* (Paris, Louvre) by Guido Reni at £400; *St John the Baptist* by Leonardo da Vinci (Paris, Louvre) at £140; Caravaggio's *Death of the Virgin* (Paris, Louvre) and Raphael's *St George and the Dragon* (Washington, National Gallery) at £150 each. The value of £1,000 was put on the *Triumphs of Caesar*, whereas Rembrandt's *Portrait of the Artist's Mother* (FIG. 8) was valued at only £4, and Van Dyck's *Portrait of Nicholas Lanier* (Vienna, Kunsthistorisches Museum) at £10, although Van Dyck's *Cupid and Psyche* (FIG. 12) was marked down at £110. Paintings by Titian varied between £600 (*Entombment* and *Last Supper*, both in Paris, Louvre) and £250 (*Alfonso D'Avalos Allegory*, in Paris, Louvre, and *Allocution of Alfonso D'Avalos* in Madrid, Prado). As many as 1,570 pictures are listed with a total value of about £37,000. The sales began in October 1649 and lasted into the mid-1650s.

After the initial rush the pace slowed. It was realised early on that the paintings alone would not generate enough cash to pay off all the creditors, and so payments were organised partly in money and partly in kind. This created a further buoyancy in the art market, since most of the creditors,

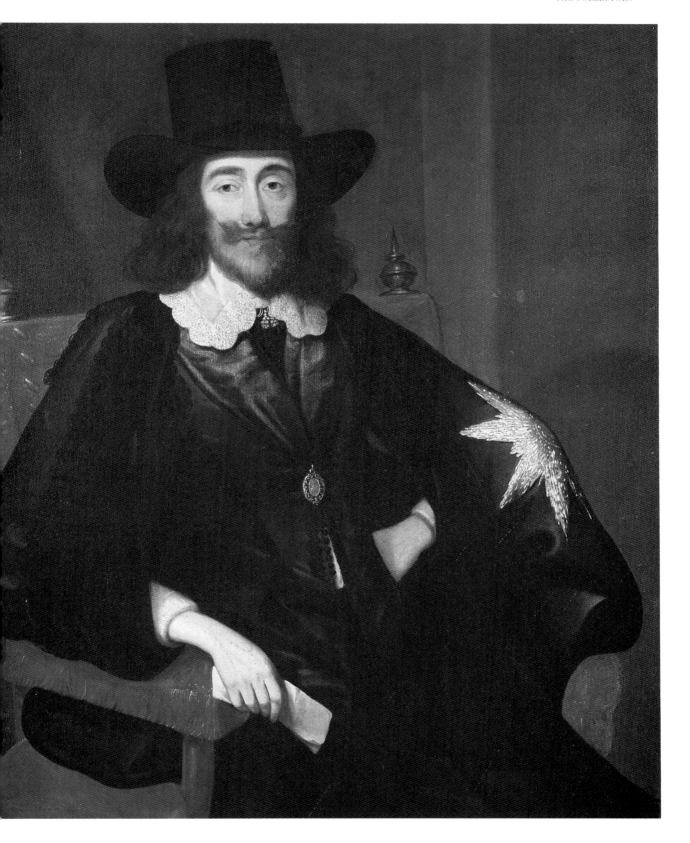

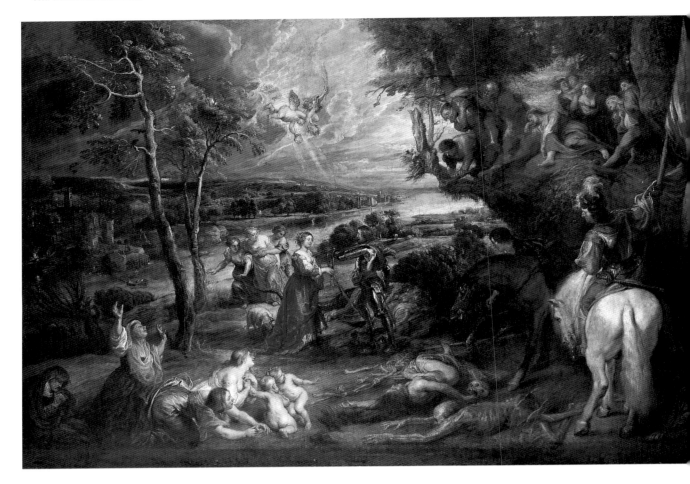

FIG. 15
Sir Peter Paul Rubens:
Landscape with St. George,
1629–30

either as individuals or as members of a syndicate, eagerly resold their allocation of pictures so that they could realise the money. Those who most benefited from this situation were the experts and agents such as Gerbier, or artists such as Emanuel de Critz (who bought the bust by Bernini) and Peter Lely (who bought Van Dyck's *Cupid and Psyche*), as well as enlightened army officers favoured by Cromwell such as Hutchinson. The new government under Cromwell retained for itself the *Cartoons* by Raphael and Mantegna's *Triumphs of Caesar* – both being large works of art that could suit the purposes of a republican government just as well as the monarchy. The sale of Charles I's collection gave a huge impetus to the burgeoning art market.

The Royalist cause in the Civil War ended in ignominy and the dispersal of Charles I's collection symbolised the political situation. Several of the paintings so carefully acquired by the king were spread far and wide. The pictures no longer adorned the walls of palaces, but passed into the possession of a more democratic cross-section of society – craftsmen, artists and soldiers.

When the monarchy was restored in 1660, many of those paintings that had remained in Britain were returned to the crown, but it had already become impossible to reassemble Charles I's collection in its entirety. Agents representing France, Spain and the Spanish Netherlands had carried off the important works by Raphael, Titian, Correggio and Caravaggio. It is the final irony that those royal or aristocratic collections which had first inspired Charles I were the ultimate beneficiaries of his unfortunate death, so that his finest paintings were used to augment the reputations and to enrich the holdings of his main rivals. Philip IV even managed to buy back the paintings by Titian that he had given the then Prince of Wales in 1623. However, in the long run, the British Royal Collection has outlasted its continental counterparts, even though the dispersal of Charles I's collection was an irreparable loss.

The only royal collector who stands comparison with Charles I is George IV. Conscious of his predecessor's achievements, he bought back such key paintings as *Charles I in Three Positions* by Van Dyck (FIG. 1), and the *Landscape with St George* (FIG. 15) by Rubens. But George IV did not set out to recreate Charles I's collection. Such an endeavour would have been an act of piety and not the aim of a man who was an eager collector in his own right. George IV had enthusiasm and an eye for art, and he was acquisitive.

George IV (FIG. 16) acceded to the throne on 29 January 1820. By a singular quirk of history this was the eve of the anniversary of Charles I's execution. Since 1811 he had been acting as Prince Regent while his father, George III, sank further into old age and ill-health; and by the time he became king at the age of fifty-eight he had already indulged to the full his apparently insatiable appetite for life. The character and habits of George IV obsessed his contemporaries, absorbed the energies of numerous literary figures and exercised the caricaturists. The novelist William Makepeace Thackeray was particularly effective in his condemnation of the Hanoverians and it is difficult to negate the influence of his book *The Four Georges*. Of George IV Thackeray writes:

> To make a portrait of him at first seemed a matter of small difficulty. There is his coat, his star, his wig, his countenance simpering under it: with a slate and a piece of chalk, I could at this very desk perform a recognisable likeness of him. And yet after reading of him in scores of volumes, hunting him through old magazines and newspapers, having him here at a ball, there at a public dinner, there at races and so forth, you find you have nothing – nothing but a coat and wig and a mask smiling below it – nothing but a great simulacrum.

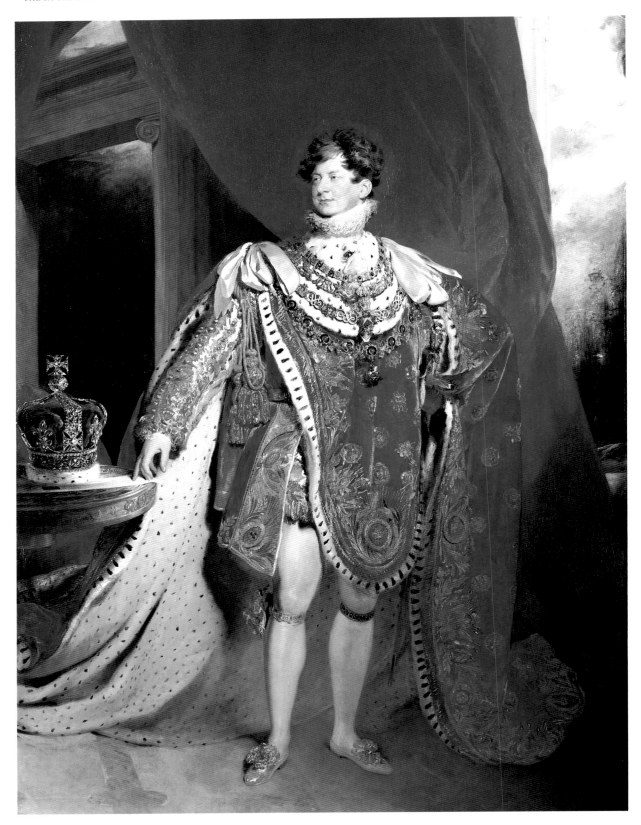

His sire and grandsires were men. One knows what they were like: what they would do in given circumstances: that on occasion they fought and demeaned themselves like tough good soldiers. They had friends whom they liked according to their natures; enemies whom they hated fiercely; passions, and actions, and individualities of their own. . . . But this George, what was he? I look through all his life, and recognise but a bow and a grin. I try and take him to pieces, and find silk stockings, padding, stays, a coat with frogs and a fur collar, a star and blue ribbon, a pocket-handkerchief prodigiously scented, one of Truefitt's best nutty brown wigs reeking with oil, a set of teeth and a huge black stock, under-waistcoats, more under-waistcoats, and then nothing.[13]

This is clever, but cruel. Yet it skilfully captures the floridity of the king's character which is so evident in his portraits. George IV inspired extreme feelings in his contemporaries, either adulation or contempt, but he was also a man who could exercise great charm. Similarly, he had an enduring capacity for friendship, reinforced by acts of remarkable generosity. His unpopularity was due as much to the changing political scene fuelled by a growing social awareness in the wake of the French Revolution and his unfortunate marriage to Caroline of Brunswick, as to the extravagant lifestyle which led to quarrels with his family and excessive demands on Parliament for money to repay his huge debts. He was plagued by financial problems, but continued to spend prodigiously, almost recklessly, on buildings, clothes, horses and works of art.

George IV was a creator of fashion. As Prince of Wales and even as Prince Regent he set out to enjoy himself. The Royal Pavilion at Brighton and Carlton House in London were perfect expressions of his taste: gilded, expensive, ornate, lavish, slightly unpredictable. The interiors of Carlton House (Introduction Fig. 1) represent a rich harmonising of furniture, fabrics and pictures that overawed visitors. Carlton House, however, was pulled down in 1827 because George IV regarded it as an unsuitable residence for a monarch. Most of the objects were transferred to Windsor Castle and Buckingham Palace, both of which he transformed into official residences. Here proper provision was made for the display of paintings in the traditional manner of the Long Gallery which had been an architectural feature of grand houses in Britain since the sixteenth century: the Grand Corridor at Windsor Castle and the Picture Gallery in Buckingham Palace (Introduction Fig. III). Changes of direction such as this were typical of George IV. Ultimately he achieved a sense of proportion and an awareness of responsibility, but, fortunately for posterity, he never lost his enthusiasms, one of which was for collecting paintings, and this he did with relish.

FIG. 16
Sir Thomas Lawrence:
George IV, 1821

His parents, George III and Queen Charlotte, must often have despaired of their eldest son's extravagant and dissolute behaviour, but in matters of art they were an important, although possibly unconscious, formative influence. This is best reflected in works by the German artist Johann Zoffany, who came from Frankfurt-am-Main, entered royal service after reaching London in 1760, and during his final years sought patronage in India.

Queen Charlotte at her Dressing Table (FIG. 17) was painted c. 1765. The queen is seated in a room overlooking the garden of Buckingham House.

FIG. 17
Johann Zoffany: *Queen Charlotte at her Dressing Table,* c. 1765

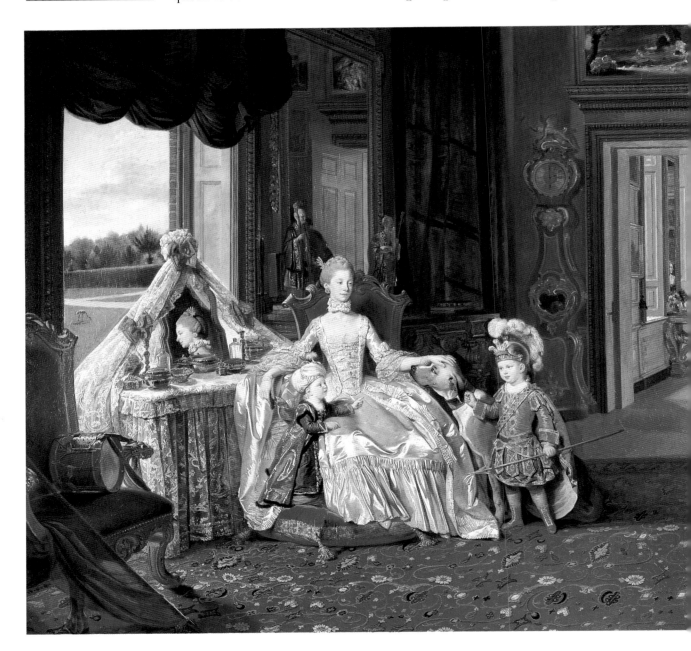

The young Prince of Wales is dressed in a Telemachus uniform as a Greco-Roman soldier holding a spear, with his helmet adorned by Prince of Wales feathers. His brother, Frederick, Duke of York, is dressed as a Turk. The drum and the standard have been abandoned and are composed as a still life on the chair in the lower left-hand corner of the composition. In many respects the painting is a dress rehearsal for the older George IV's life. The children are grouped with their mother and a dog, forming a pyramid of domestic harmony in the centre. The painting demonstrates George III's and Queen Charlotte's love of the applied arts. The carpet is in the Persian style, two chinoiserie figures stand guard behind the queen, but are dominated in turn by the tall long-case clock. On the dressing table is an elaborate silver-gilt toilet service. The crisp handling of the paint, the careful observation and the precise mapping of the spatial divisions and the path of light are the essence of Zoffany's style and, indeed, of George III's taste. The reflections – Queen Charlotte's face in the mirror and the figure of the lady-in-waiting or maid in the long mirror above the console table in the room beyond – reveal Zoffany's visual dexterity. The pictures that decorate the room are those which had recently been bought on the king's behalf in Venice from Consul Joseph Smith, who had been the patron of Canaletto.

Smith's collection included not only a variety of paintings, prints and drawings, but also books and gems. Having been resident in Venice for so long, he had accumulated a large collection of paintings by contemporary Venetian artists (with the regrettable omission of Giovanni Battista Tiepolo) and his collection of works by Canaletto was incomparable. Smith had banking connections with northern Europe and to a lesser degree he had an interest in small Dutch and Flemish paintings, one of his acquisitions being *A Lady at the Virginals with a Gentleman* by Vermeer (FIG.168), which during the eighteenth century was thought to be by Frans van der Mieris.

The visual accuracy that George III respected in Canaletto's or Zoffany's paintings, the mechanical precision that he admired in clocks and scientific instruments and the firm, purposeful sense of design that he recognised in pieces of furniture must have served as a good introduction to the arts for George IV, who must also have felt sympathy with his mother's taste for silver, jewellery and porcelain. As John Adams, the first American ambassador to the Court of St James's and the second President of the United States, remarked after his visit to Buckingham House in 1783:

> In every apartment of the whole house, the same taste, the same judgement, the same elegance, the same simplicity, without the smallest affectation, ostentation, profusion or meanness. I could not

but compare it, in my own mind, with Versailles, and not at all to the advantage of the latter . . . .[14]

By contrast, George IV set out to outshine Versailles.

France had always played a dominant role in George IV's appreciation of the arts and when he began collecting in earnest during the 1790s it was a propitious moment. The upheaval of the French Revolution and the Napoleonic campaigns that followed, particularly in Spain, Italy and the Netherlands, resulted in the release of literally thousands of works of art on to an art market that was by now firmly established. Great European collections – royal, dynastic and ecclesiastical – were being broken up as a result of plundering and financial duress. Where Charles I had been served by agents, George IV and his fellow collectors had recourse to a network of dealers who were adept at moving pictures across national frontiers and finding new sources of supply. The doyen of these extending commercial empires was a Scottish lawyer, William Buchanan, whose book *Memoirs of Painting, with a chronological history of the Importation of Pictures by the Great Masters into England since the French Revolution* (1824) gives a vivid account of the discovery of numerous masterpieces and their subsequent movements. As one writer wittily expressed it,

> . . . bliss indeed was it to be a collector in that dawn, but to be a dealer was very heaven.[15]

George III, on the other hand, sarcastically remarked that all his noblemen had become picture dealers. The flood of pictures was heralded by the sale in 1792 of the collection belonging to Louis-Philippe-Joseph, Duke of Orléans ('Philippe Egalité'), which was the finest in Europe at that date and royal in origin. The Italian and French pictures were bought by a syndicate of British noblemen headed by the Duke of Bridgewater, who was also investing heavily in coal mining and canal building.

The purchases made by the syndicate were exhibited in London in 1798 and those not reserved for members' own collections were sold to other connoisseurs. The critic William Hazlitt was one of those who were profoundly influenced by the experience of viewing the Orléans collection in London.

> We had heard the names of Titian, Raphael, Guido, Domenichino, the Carracci – but to see them face to face, to be in the same room with their matchless productions, was like breaking some mighty spell – was almost an effect of necromancy.[16]

It was, in fact, the finest display of pictures in Britain since the dispersal of Charles I's collection. The houses of the rich – not just aristocrats, but industrialists and financiers as well – were turned into art galleries, and it is significant that during these years connoisseurs from the continent made visits specifically to see British collections.

The future Director of the Royal Museum in Berlin, Gustav Waagen, first came to Britain to travel extensively and to view paintings in 1835; in 1854 he published a revised account of his visits to collections couched in the form of a series of letters to his wife. In one he writes:

> You will now have been able to form an idea of the astonishing treasures of admirable works of art of all descriptions which this island contains. . . . I often feel some apprehension of my being unable to master the whole. I am therefore, literally, in an embarras de richesses and frequently wish for the hundred eyes of Argus all of which would find ample employment here. . . . I cannot refrain from again praising the refined taste of the English for their adorning the rooms they daily occupy, by which means they enjoy from their youth upwards the silent and slow but sure influence of works of art.[17]

Britain was again, as under Charles I, the centre of the art world and London once more had a concentration of outstanding collections in close proximity to one another in magnificent houses such as Stafford House, Bridgewater House, Lansdowne House, Hertford House and Grosvenor House. Many of these collections have now been disbanded. Indeed, the exportation of works of art during the middle decades of the twentieth century is the exact reversal of what happened during the nineteenth century.

George IV, like Charles I before him, was acting in concert with contemporary collectors. The scale of his collecting differed, but his taste concurred with theirs. He had neither the patience nor the inclination to seek out bargains and so he tended to buy with the market trend and consequently to pay high prices. He was not a particularly audacious or innovative collector of paintings. For him the touchstone was always quality, meaning a high finish characterised by compositional verve and painterly opulence. Two such contrasting works as *The Shipbuilder and his Wife* by Rembrandt (FIG. 18) and *David Garrick and his Wife* by William Hogarth (FIG. 19), although united by theme, are nonetheless stylistically divorced from one another in a revealing way. The former – an early and comparatively rare double portrait by the artist – exemplified the awakening of Rembrandt's compositional power, transforming a standard Renaissance treatment into the baroque idiom. This is achieved by emphasising the

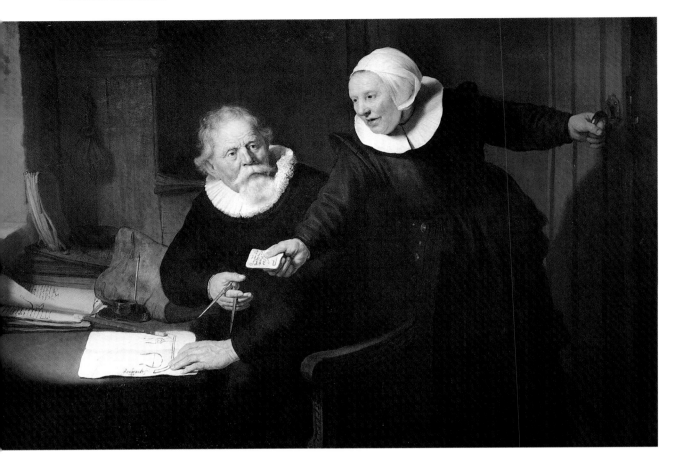

FIG. 18
Rembrandt van Rijn: *The Shipbuilder and his Wife*, 1633

diagonal on which the figures are placed, the concentration of light on the faces, the use of expansive gestures and the depiction of a single dramatic moment when Griet Jans delivers an important message to her husband while he is at work. Hogarth, on the other hand, extemporises on the theme by producing a playful, decorative composition, light in colour and replete with elegant details and balletic movements (Garrick's wife was a dancer). The composition is essentially a pyramid enlivened by diagonals that suggest further geometrical forms. The artist is here working within the French rococo manner. It was, however, not the stylistic differences between the two paintings that George IV appreciated but, rather, the high level of artistic skill that transcended such issues. As such, George IV's taste was essentially conservative.

The Shipbuilder and his Wife cost George IV 5,000 guineas at auction in London in 1811. It was the most expensive picture that he bought and, indeed, it was one of the most valuable items in his whole collection. The painting had once belonged to Jan Gildemeester, who lived in Amsterdam and formed a notable collection of Dutch paintings. This collection was sold in 1800, but George IV acquired several pictures from that source at

FIG. 19
William Hogarth: *David Garrick and his Wife*, c. 1757

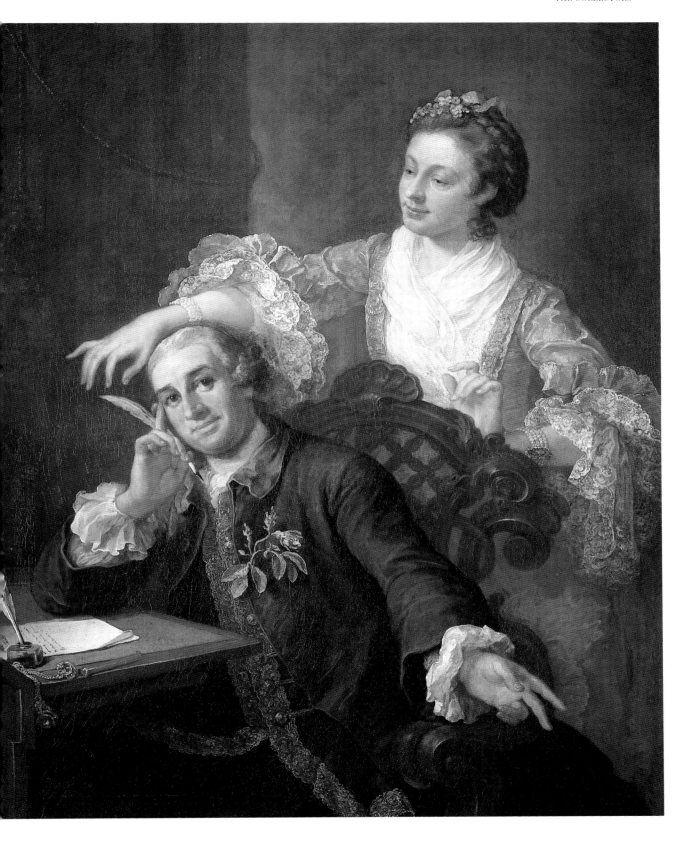

subsequent sales. *An Evening Landscape* by Cuyp (FIG. 73) had also been in the Gildemeester collection and before that it had belonged to Jan van der Linden van Slingeland in Dordrecht who had owned over twenty paintings of the highest quality by this artist.

It was Dutch collections of this standard, together with the sale of collections formed by French *émigrés* like Charles-Alexandre Calonne (FIG. 20), from which British collectors such as George IV were able to take rich pickings. The provenance of a painting was of increasing significance: it gave lustre to a picture like gilding to a piece of furniture. Middlemen such as Buchanan, Jean-Baptist-Pierre Lebrun, Pierre-Joseph Lafontaine and Michael Bryan played a vital role in the supply and distribution of such pictures.

Although the final decision always lay with George IV, he relied on friends to find pictures or to recommend purchases. Lord Yarmouth (later the third Marques of Hertford), Sir Charles Long (later Lord Farnborough), Walsh Porter and the painter Sir Thomas Lawrence, all of whom were influential connoisseurs and collectors in their own right, were active at various times as advisers.

The Marquess of Hertford played a leading part in the formation of his family collection, which was bequeathed to the nation as the Wallace Collection in 1897. He was a thoroughly disagreeable man, dissolute and autocratic, but with a wonderful eye for art. The marquess was a close friend of the king and they shared the same tastes. He represented George IV in the sale room for almost ten years (1810–19) purchasing over forty works mainly by Dutch painters, including *The Shipbuilder and his Wife*.

Their preference, however, was for small cabinet pictures depicting landscapes or genre scenes of exquisite quality and close detail. The king had so far bought Dutch pictures keenly but intermittently, and in 1814 the collection was greatly enhanced by the acquisition of eighty-six paintings from the heir of Sir Francis Baring, the founder of the family banking firm. They included major works by Cuyp, Hobbema, Terborch and Steen, and brought the total of Dutch and Flemish paintings in George IV's collection to over 200. This transaction enabled George IV to sell some items that he did not like from his own collection such as the still lifes. Seventy-seven of his paintings were sold anonymously at Christie's on 29 June 1814. He had by now acquired enough pictures to operate a system of exchanges, which was how he obtained *Landscape with St George* by Rubens (FIG. 15) and *Christ and St Mary Magdalen at the Tomb* by Rembrandt (FIG. 21), one of the artist's most beautiful religious pictures.

This enthusiasm for Dutch and Flemish art allied George IV more closely with his grandfather Frederick, Prince of Wales (1705–51), than

FIG. 20
Elizabeth-Louis,
Vigée-Lebrun:
Charles-Alexandre de Calonne,
1784

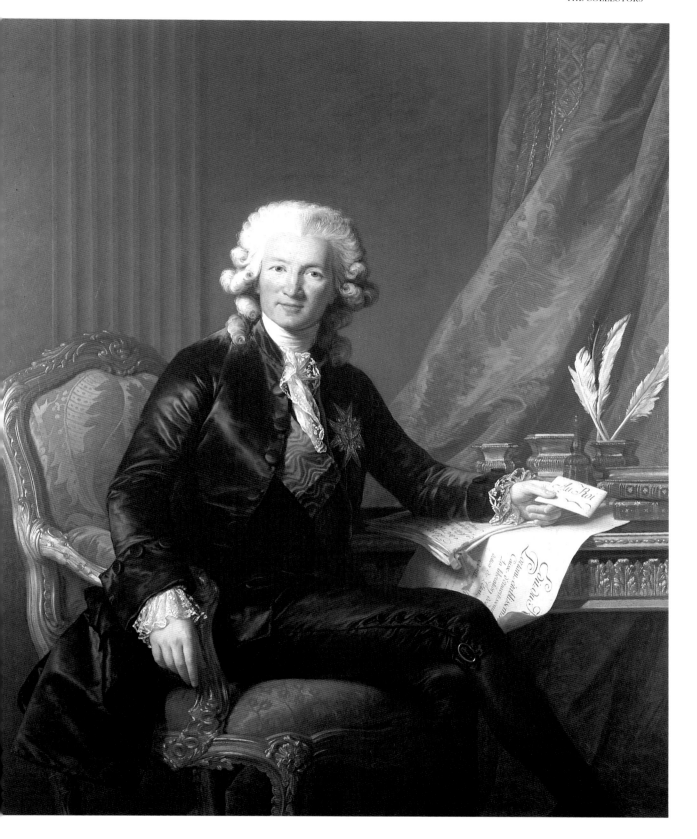

with his father. He shared with Frederick, for example, an admiration for Rubens and Teniers, as well as for British painting. The appreciation of Dutch and Flemish paintings had been widespread in pre-Revolutionary France. Quite apart from style, the subject matter appealed to the French aristocrats. Pure landscapes, genre scenes, domestic interiors, military, hunting or equestrian scenes had in the first instance an obvious attraction that could easily be diverted to the more fluid structure of early nineteenth-century British society. Paintings by Cuyp, Wouwermans (FIG. 22), van Ostade, Terborch, Ruisdael or Hobbema came to reflect in different ways the social and even the political sentiments and aspirations of British collectors during the early first half of the nineteenth century. Where today attempts are made to understand the social context of a work of art, early nineteenth-century connoisseurs tended to disengage themselves from any such detailed analyses and to interpret paintings more in accordance with

FIG. 22
Philips Wouwermans:
Cavalry at a Sutler's Booth,
1650–60

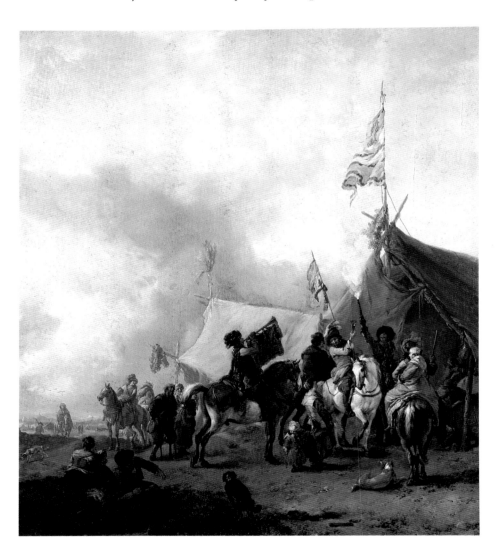

FIG. 21
Rembrandt van Rijn: *Christ and St Mary Magdalene at the Tomb*, 1638

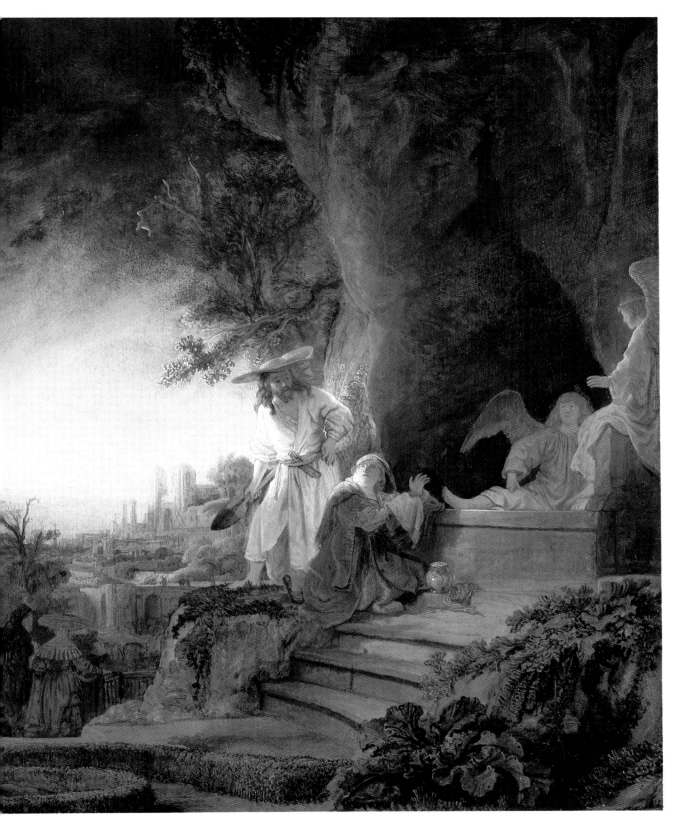

their own ideals. Pictures were appreciated more as a mirror of the times of the collector, or simply as aesthetic objects, rather than as the product of an earlier century with different social or political mores. There is, in short, a clear distinction between how George IV looked at a Dutch interior and the moral overtones sought by George Eliot, as described in a famous passage at the opening of Book Two of *Adam Bede* (1859) or, indeed, how a Dutch seventeenth-century painting is perceived today. George Eliot wrote:

> It is for this rare, precious quality of truthfulness that I delight in many Dutch paintings, which lofty-minded people despise. I find a source of delicious sympathy in these faithful pictures of a monotonous homely existence, which has been the fate of so many more among my fellow mortals than a life of absolute indigence, of tragic suffering or of world-stirring actions. I turn, without shrinking, from cloud-borne angels, from prophets, sibyls, and heroic warriors, to an old woman bending over her flower-pot, or eating her solitary dinner, while the noon-day light, softened perhaps by a screen of leaves, falls on her mob-cap, and just touches the rim of her spinning wheel, and her stone jug, and all those cheap common things which are the precious necessities of life to her.[18]

While George IV successfully added major works by Dutch and Flemish artists to the Royal Collection, there were areas that he neglected. He showed no great interest in Spanish, Italian or early Flemish painting. Indeed, he turned down the Arnolfini portrait by Jan van Eyck (now in the National Gallery in London) after it had been placed on deposit in Carlton House for his inspection for as long as two years (1816–18). British painting, however, was a genuine passion and in supporting British artists George IV combined the roles of monarch and collector.

The early years of the nineteenth century in Britain were of great significance in the history of the visual arts and George IV played a leading role in their promotion. At the annual dinner of 1811 at the Royal Academy he is reported to have told the guests:

> Others . . . might be more able to judge of the excellence of works of art [but they] could not exceed him in his love of the arts or in [his] wishes for their prosperity.[19]

In sum, George IV consciously supported contemporary art to an extent that few other monarchs have ever done, and in 1810 he declared openly to Benjamin West, the second President of the Royal Academy, that he wanted to collect British art as opposed to just old masters.

While his parents felt little sympathy for Sir Joshua Reynolds, George IV either commissioned or acquired a number of portraits by Reynolds of members of the royal family, famous military or political figures and leading personalities. The artist's late *Self-Portrait* (FIG. 23) was given to the king by Reynolds's niece, Lady Thomond, and from the same source came the narrative painting *Cymon and Iphigenia*, to which George IV later added *The Death of Dido*.

George III and Queen Charlotte respected the work of Thomas Gainsborough and so did their son. When still in his early twenties George IV commissioned whole-length portraits of his friend Colonel St Leger (FIG. 24)

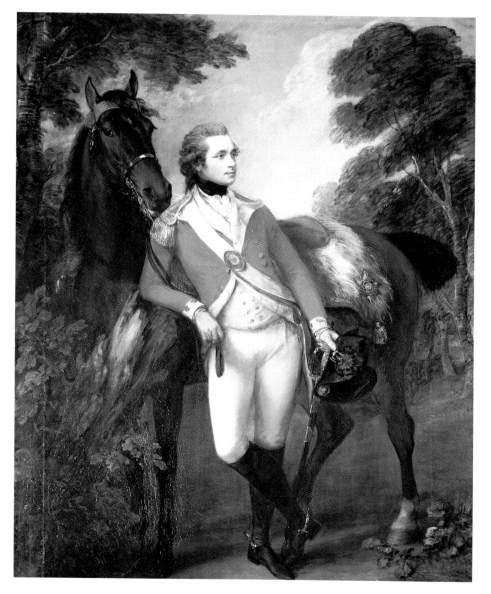

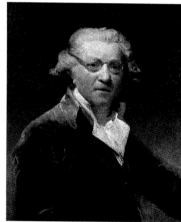

FIG. 23
Sir Joshua Reynolds:
Portrait of the Artist, 1788

FIG. 24
Thomas Gainsborough:
John Hayes St Leger, 1782

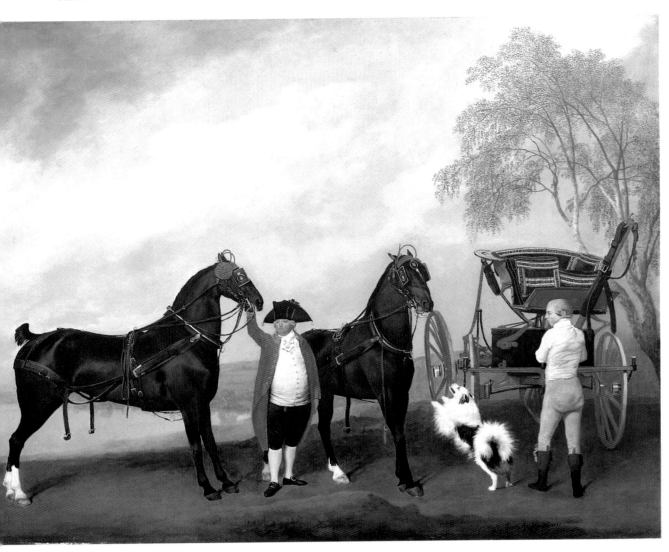

FIG. 25
George Stubbs: *The Prince of Wales' Phaeton*, 1793

and of his three eldest sisters, but even more interesting was the purchase of Gainsborough's only surviving mythological painting, the large-scale *Diana and Actaeon* (FIG. 61), at the sale in 1797 of the possessions of Gainsborough Dupont, the artist's nephew.

After the deaths of Gainsborough in 1788 and of Reynolds in 1792, George IV favoured William Beechey, John Hoppner and ultimately Sir Thomas Lawrence. George III and Queen Charlotte had found Lawrence's energetic style, vivid colouring and lush distribution of paint too modern, but he provided the perfect visual evocation of their son's reign, culminating not only in his portraits of George IV (FIG. 16), but also in those done for the Waterloo Chamber in Windsor Castle – a specially created pantheon of military heroes, diplomats and powerful heads of state responsible for overthrowing Napoleon.

Another British artist patronised by George IV from an early date was George Stubbs. Of the eighteen paintings by Stubbs in the Royal Collection all are associated with George IV, whose passion for animals, particularly horses, led him to commission works from other equine artists such as Sawrey Gilpin, George Garrard, Benjamin Marshall and James Ward. The canvases Stubbs painted for George IV, however, are often of more than usual personal significance, including *The Prince of Wales' Phaeton* (FIG. 25), *William Anderson with two Saddle Horses* (FIG. 79) and *Soldiers of the Tenth Light Dragoons* (FIG. 26).

An artist who also engaged George IV's attention was the Scottish painter Sir David Wilkie, whose early genre paintings, such as the *Penny Wedding* (FIG. 161), reminded his patron of his Dutch and Flemish pictures, even if the composition is also partly indebted to Watteau. Wilkie, however, soon abandoned this early style and subject matter. A period of travel in France, Italy and Spain during the mid-1820s enabled him to adopt a more heroic style better suited to history painting. While in Spain he began a series of pictures on the theme of local Spanish resistance to the French invasion. The most dramatic of these compositions is *The Defence of Saragossa*

FIG. 26
George Stubbs: *Soldiers of the Tenth Light Dragoons,* 1793

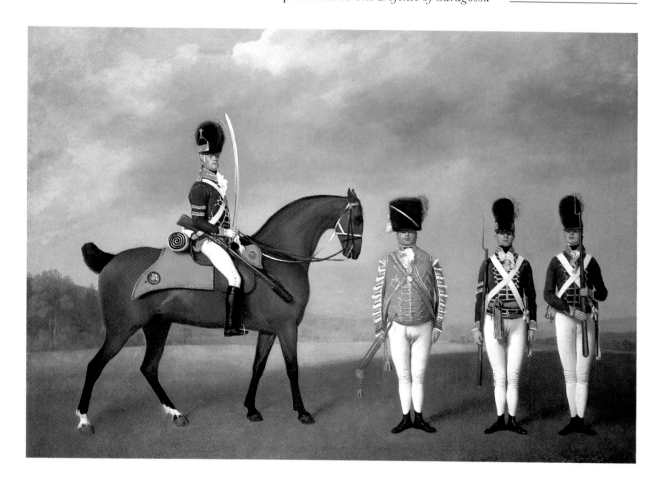

(FIG. 27), where the wife of the dead gunner seen in the lower right-hand corner takes charge of the gun which is aimed at the French forces by the guerrilla leader Don José Palafox – an incident that was also hymned by Byron in *Childe Harold's Pilgrimage* (Canto I, Stanza 54–59). George IV bought the three finished pictures from Wilkie and ordered a fourth to complete the series, in which he recognised the artist's debt to Murillo.

The king was aware of the continuing debate on the need to support a British school of history painting, principally to rival the French tradition. One of its most vigorous spokesmen, Benjamin Robert Haydon – a friend of Wilkie – frequently offered works to George IV, who bought only the large-scale *Mock Election* (FIG. 28), which presents a microcosm of contemporary British society as well as an insight into the turmoil of Haydon's own life. The king's later rejection of further works by Haydon no doubt heightened the artist's instability that led to his suicide seven years later in 1846.

The greatest contemporary painter from whom George IV commissioned a painting was certainly J. M. W. Turner. *The Battle of Trafalgar* (FIG. 125), begun in 1823, commemorated the famous naval victory of 1805. The painting was on a monumental scale (in fact it is the largest picture Turner undertook) and proved to be controversial, particularly with naval experts. Together with *The Glorious First of June* of 1795, by Philip James de Loutherbourg (FIG. 124), the picture was hung in the Entrée Room of St James's Palace flanking a portrait of George III, but in 1829, with characteristic generosity, George IV gave both paintings to the Royal Naval Institution at Greenwich.

It is easy to be misled by writers like Thackeray and to assume that George IV was vacuous and reckless. There is no evidence of this in his collecting activities: he undoubtedly spent heavily, but to very good effect. The leading collector of his age and a supporter of British artists, he also took a keen interest in promoting art. He lent items from the Royal Collection for exhibitions at the British Institution, regularly attended the annual dinner at the Royal Academy, and supported the creation of a National Gallery, which was founded, somewhat belatedly, during his reign – in 1824, at the house of John Julius Angerstein at 100 Pall Mall. When the building in Trafalgar Square, designed by William Wilkins, was opened in 1838, the columns from the portico of Carlton House were re-used for the flanking entrances on the main facade. Furthermore, an equestrian monument of George IV by Sir Francis Chantrey, originally (1829) set on top of Marble Arch when it stood before Buckingham Palace, stands today in Trafalgar Square in a position midway between Nelson's Column and the National Gallery. Such symbolism does full justice to George IV's contribution both as a monarch and as a lover of the arts.

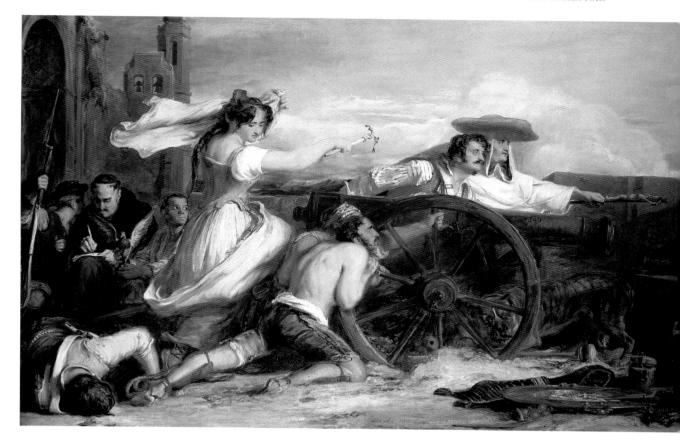

FIG. 27
Sir David Wilkie: *The Defence of Saragossa*, 1828

Princess Victoria, the daughter of the Duke and Duchess of Kent, and later to become Queen, visited Windsor Castle in 1826 to pay her respects to her uncle, George IV. Although she was only seven at the time, she was quite equal to the task. She departed saying:

> I am coming to bid you adieu sire, but as I know you do not like fine speeches I shall certainly not trouble you by attempting one.[20]

She enjoyed her visit, listening to the band, fishing, riding in the king's phaeton and going to his menagerie. She had to kiss the king, which she described later as

> . . . too disgusting because his face was covered in grease paint.[21]

It is unlikely that they discussed art, but Queen Victoria became as enthusiastic about painting as her uncle, visiting collections and exhibitions with equal relish.

She was born with the collecting instinct, but, not surprisingly, her outlook was different. First, she was a competent artist in her own right.

65

An early portrait by her first drawing master, Richard Westall, shows her with her drawing materials accompanied by a pet. Later she learnt from William Leitch and Edward Lear how to use watercolours and then from Edwin Landseer how to etch. Artists attached to the court such as George Hayter, Landseer and F. X. Winterhalter were often required to give lessons or advice. Secondly, she was more cautious, although not ungenerous, with money and, thirdly, she was opinionated. These opinions, recorded in her *Journal*, can at times seem childish, sometimes infuriating, sometimes humorous, but very often right. In October 1842, for example, the queen wrote that she had

> . . . sat to that tiresome Sir M. Shee, who had made a little sketch of the large picture, whom we all found a most distressing production and totally devoid of talent.[22]

Queen Victoria comes into the category of those who know exactly what they like in art. She frequently made sure that she got what she liked, either by going directly to the artist, or by bullying a dealer or even an owner. For example, she and Prince Albert saw and admired *Ramsgate Sands: 'Life at the Seaside'* by W. P. Frith (FIG. 29) at the Royal Academy exhibition in 1854. The painting was bought by the dealer Messrs Lloyds for £1,000 and was acquired by the queen later in the same year for an identical sum. The picture provides a marvellous cross-section of Victorian society parading itself on the beach of a famous seaside resort, which Queen Victoria had visited, and it is easy to understand why Frith's composition appealed so strongly to royal taste.

The art trade was well-established by the time Queen Victoria came to the throne and was thriving as new types of collector from a much wider spectrum of society came to the fore. It was an expanding business. Men such as Ernest Gambart handled several artists and made a great deal of money from selling their work, which, if popular, was engraved for further sale in a wider market. Although on occasions Queen Victoria could not bypass the dealers, she preferred a direct relationship with the artists, either, as with Landseer and Frith, visiting them in their studios, or, as in the case of David Roberts and Winterhalter, summoning them to Windsor Castle, Buckingham Palace, Osborne House or Balmoral Castle. Fortunately, what she liked was often very good and, since she was keen to support a wide range of contemporary British art, her acquisitions added a new dimension to the Royal Collection. She reacted quickly to what she saw and was prompt in her judgements, but her interest was genuine and her intentions were commendable. Queen Victoria generated a great deal of interest in the art of painting by directly encouraging artists in their

FIG. 28
Benjamin Robert Haydon:
The Mock Election, 1827

FIG. 29
William Powell Frith:
Ramsgate Sands: 'Life at the Seaside', 1852–3

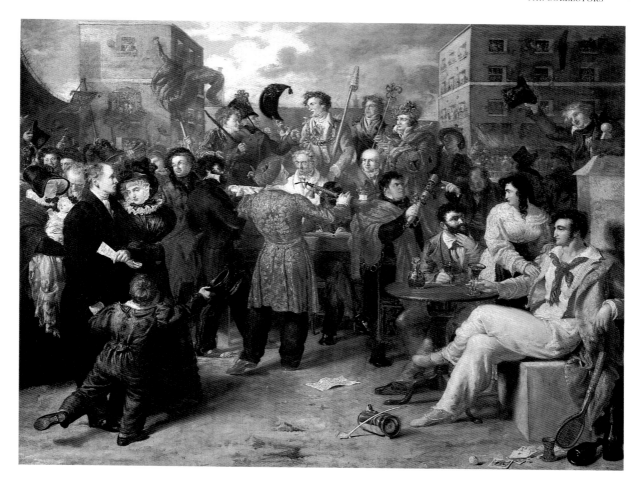

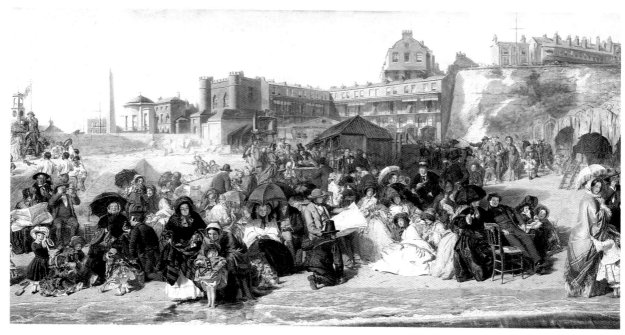

labours and by being attentive to their needs (she was deeply affected by the death in straitened circumstances of her first drawing master, Richard Westall), as well as being fascinated by their working processes, and in the history of art, generally.

A deeply significant influence on Queen Victoria was Prince Albert, whom she married in 1840 and whose advice she relied on until his death from typhoid fever in 1861. Not only was Prince Albert a man of varied interests, but he was also strongly motivated by the desire to turn theoretical concepts to practical advantage. Painting, for example, should be didactic or provide an accurate record of a particular person or event in a commemorative sense; alternatively, it should be morally uplifting or spiritually reassuring. It was difficult for artists to live up to these ideals all the time and David Wilkie and George Hayter failed to retain the queen's support in the field of portraiture. Wilkie, for example, was discredited for the inaccuracy in his painting *The First Council of Queen Victoria* (FIG. 30), and for the failure to secure a proper likeness in the State Portrait (Port Sunlight, Lady Lever Art Gallery). Of the first the queen records in February 1838 that Lord Melbourne

. . . spoke of Wilkie's picture of the First Council, which I saw this morning and which though a fine picture contains very few good

FIG. 30
Sir David Wilkie: *The First Council of Queen Victoria*, 1838

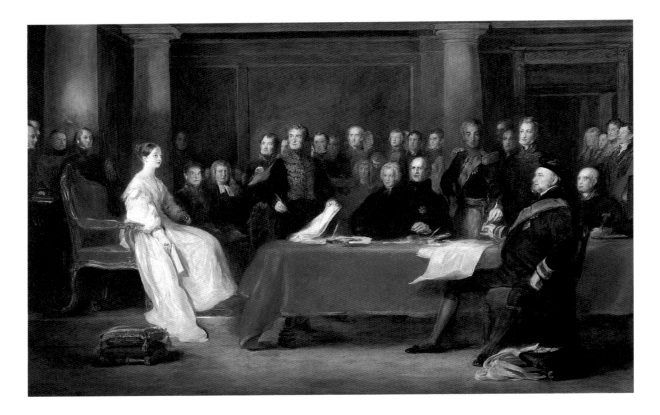

likenesses; Lord Melbourne's is quite detestable and really quite vexes me,[23]

but by November 1847 the painting had become

. . . one of the worst pictures I have ever seen, both as to painting & likenesses.[24]

Sittings for the State Portrait took place in October and November 1838, but it, too, failed to impress, and again Lord Melbourne's view was significant. In March 1839 the queen wrote:

Talked of the *too atrocious* full length picture which Wilkie has made of me, and which is put in the Gallery, and which Lord M. is quite shocked at; talked of the horror of sending it to Paris; of its being such a mistake to make him Portrait Painter.[25]

Hayter fared better than Wilkie, but in the end the portrait painters who gave most satisfaction were, from 1842, the German F. X. Winterhalter and, after Prince Albert's death, the German Heinrich von Angeli and the Dane Laurits Tuxen. Winterhalter painted over one hundred pictures for

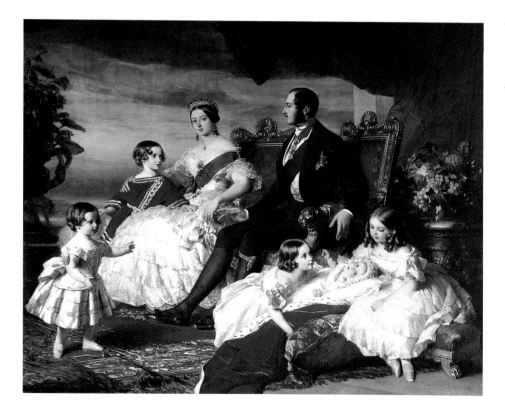

FIG. 31
Franz Xaver Winterhalter:
The Family of Queen Victoria,
1846

Queen Victoria. They are notable for their bravura passages in the handling of draperies and convincing likenesses, but Winterhalter remained a limited, somewhat superficial, although not unskilful, painter. Queen Victoria aptly likened his large picture of *The Family of Queen Victoria* painted in 1846 (FIG. 31) to the Venetian artist Paolo Veronese:

> We went over to see Winterhalter's picture, which is a 'chef d'oeuvre' – like a Paul Veronese, such beautiful, brilliant, fresh colouring – and we were enchanted.[26]

On being shown it the next day, Lord Palmerston apparently declared it to be 'the finest modern picture he ever saw'.[27] But, in reality, Winterhalter had little imagination and when asked in 1851 to paint a slightly more cryptic composition entitled *The First of May* (FIG. 32), he had to rely on Prince Albert's expertise.

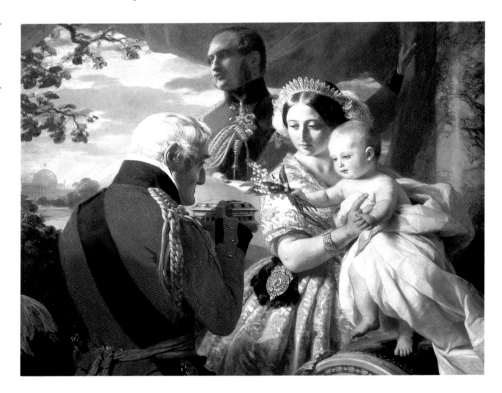

FIG. 32
Franz Xaver Winterhalter:
The First of May, 1851

Artists such as Winterhalter and Landseer, both of whom gained the queen's confidence, often produced pictures of a more personal nature to be given as presents at Christmas or on birthdays. This became an established form of present giving within the royal family, and an important aspect of their patronage. Two of Landseer's greatest pictures – *Eos* (FIG. 87) and *The Sanctuary* (FIG. 89) – were painted as gifts for Prince Albert, in 1841

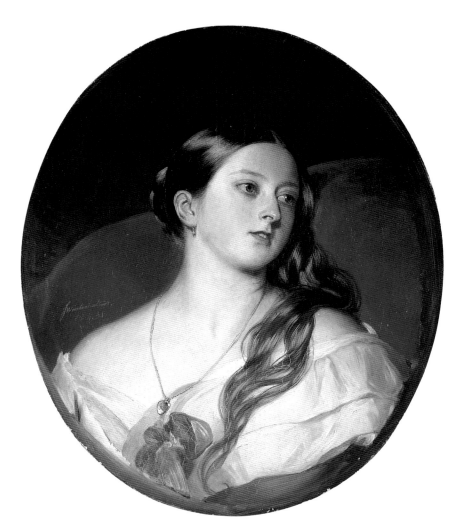

FIG. 33
Franz Xaver Winterhalter:
Queen Victoria, 1843

for Christmas and in 1842 for his birthday. An even more unusual commission was granted to Winterhalter for a picture that was to be given on
Prince Albert's birthday in 1843 (FIG. 33). Queen Victoria described this with
good reason as her '*secret* picture', which refers to the somewhat surprising
portrait of the young queen 'with my hair down, resting against a curtain'
– a surprisingly alluring pose.[28] She records in her *Journal*:

> I cannot say how delighted my beloved Albert was with the
> Winterhalter picture. The surprise was so great, and he thought it so
> like & so beautifully painted. I felt so happy & so proud to have
> found something that gave him so much pleasure.[29]

The gifts were not always limited to contemporary pictures and on several
occasions Prince Albert gave the queen old master paintings, including
works by Bernardo Daddi (FIG. 34) and Benozzo Gozzoli.

The pleasure that Queen Victoria and Prince Albert shared in art had

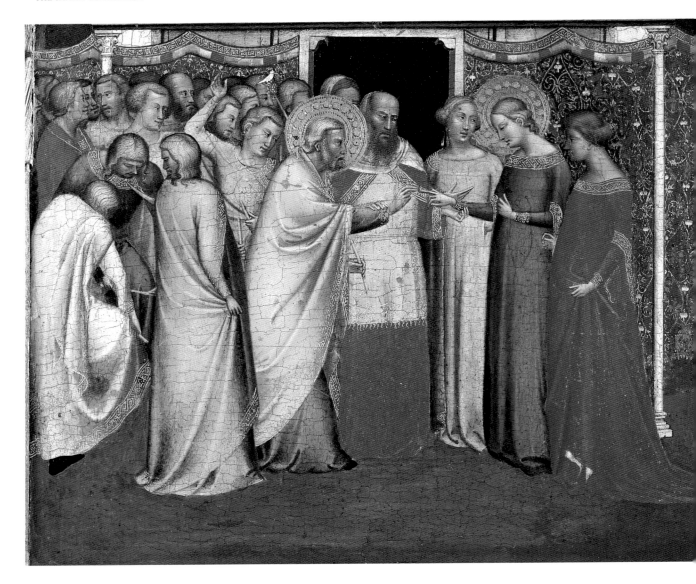

FIG. 34
Bernardo Daddi: *The
Marriage of the Virgin*, c. 1335

important consequences for the Royal Collection. Together, but usually at
Prince Albert's instigation, they reorganised whole sections, arranging, for
example, the prints and miniatures at Windsor Castle where Prince Albert
had also established an archive for the study of Raphael which is still of
great significance. The paintings caused greater anxieties. The queen wrote
in her *Journal* on 31 December 1843:

> Went to St George's Hall [Windsor Castle] to look at more old
> pictures, & the more I see them the more thunderstruck & shocked I
> am at the way in which the pictures, many fine ones amongst them,
> & of interesting value, have been thrown about & kept in lumber
> rooms at Hampton Court, whilst this Castle, and Buckingham Palace

are literally *without* pictures. George III took the greatest care of all
of them, George IV grew too ill to settle many things, except in the
Corridor at Windsor Castle, and William IV, who was not famed for
his good taste sent all the pictures away. My care, or rather more
my dearest Albert's, for he delights in these things, will be to have
them restored, to find places for them, and to prevent, as much as it
is in our power, pictures of the Family, and others of interest and value
from being thrown about again.[30]

This pledge was upheld and Queen Victoria rehung both the Corridor in
Windsor Castle and the Picture Gallery in Buckingham Palace. Indeed,
Prince Albert's interest in and knowledge of painting were exercised on a
wider, national basis on his appointment in 1841 as Chairman of the Royal
Commission on the Fine Arts responsible for redecorating the newly built
Houses of Parliament. Prince Albert chose to encourage the revival of fresco
painting for such an official public building and successfully organised a
competition of scenes from British history to be painted by British artists.
During the same period he commissioned fresco decorations based on John
Milton's *Comus* for the Garden Pavilion at Buckingham Palace, and an
allegorical subject of Britannia for a dominant position at the top of the
principal staircase at Osborne House. The prince's organisational skills
were tested even further by the staging of the Great Exhibition of 1851 in
London and the *Art Treasures Exhibition* held in Manchester in 1857 – this last
was the largest art exhibition ever held, and it was seen by nearly a
million and a half people in the space of four months.

Prince Albert's taste, nurtured by advisers such as Ludwig Grüner,
was essentially historicist. Grüner was an artist by training, but finished
his career as Director of the Print Room of the Dresden Museum. He
published numerous books, mainly on early Italian art, which in turn
inspired Queen Victoria and Prince Albert.

Mr Grüner, who directs the decoration in the Cottage [the Garden
Pavilion in Buckingham Palace], & is a man full of talent, showed us
some beautiful designs of interiors of Churches and Palaces in Italy,
etc.[31]

runs an entry in the queen's *Journal* for 1845. Grüner became a moving
force within the Arundel Society, established in 1849 by John Ruskin and
Lord Lindsay amongst others, for promoting the appreciation of early
Italian art.

Prince Albert was himself a pioneering collector of early Italian and
German paintings. He was one of the small group of collectors in Britain

who took an active interest in acquiring early paintings dating from the fourteenth and fifteenth centuries. The appeal of such paintings was partly the result of an acknowledgement of their place in the evolution of art, but it was also due to the aesthetic pleasure derived from simple outlines, clear colours and unelaborate compositions. William Roscoe, Edward Solly, François Cacault, Artaud de Montor, William Davenport-Bromley, William Young Ottley and the Hon. W. T. H. Fox-Strangways were buying primitive paintings that had become more readily available following the desequestration of ecclesiastical property in Italy after the invasion of the peninsula by Napoleon. Large altar-pieces were frequently divided up and sold piecemeal by dealers such as Johann and Ludwig Metzger in Florence. This was an area of collecting in which no previous royal collector had

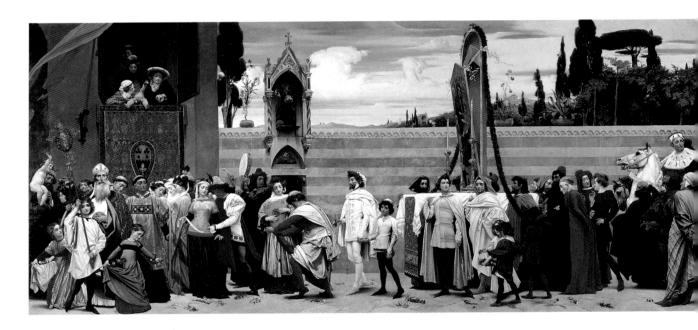

FIG. 35
Frederick, Lord Leighton:
Cimabue's Madonna being carried through the Streets of Florence, 1853–5

been a specialist. In the evolution of the Royal Collection Prince Albert was filling in a gap left by Charles I and George IV. Most of these early paintings were hung in Prince Albert's Dressing and Writing Room at Osborne House.

The largest group of early paintings owned by Prince Albert came to him almost by default. A German collector, Prince Ludwig Kraft Ernst Oettingen-Wallerstein, negotiated a private financial loan with Prince Albert in 1847 and deposited his collection of German, Netherlandish and Italian paintings in London as surety. The pictures were put on display in Kensington Palace in 1848, but since no buyer was found, they were ceded to Prince Albert. After his death in 1861, Queen Victoria presented twenty-two of them to the National Gallery in accordance with Prince Albert's wishes. These included some remarkably distinguished German paintings. The queen did not continue collecting in this area after Prince Albert's death.

The historicist approach to collecting conditioned Queen Victoria and Prince Albert to appreciate the work of the German Nazarene artists who first established themselves in Rome in 1812. The style of their paintings was based on early Italian and German art. Unfortunately, the royal couple's enthusiasm did not extend to the Pre-Raphaelites, whose style depended on the Nazarenes and whose pictures they saw at exhibitions during the 1850s, but did not feel compelled to buy. The queen inspected *Christ in the House of his Parents* by J. E. Millais in 1850, but it was only in 1898 that she received *The Beloved* by William Holman Hunt, which was a replica of the head of Christ from the artist's T*he Shadow of Death*.

Queen Victoria's and Prince Albert's interest in art was enlightened but ultimately limited. Their taste was somewhat predictable and their visual curiosity easily satisfied. Few surprises abound in their purchases or commissions. While on a State Visit to Paris in 1855 they did go with Napoleon III and the Empress Eugénie to see the Universal Exhibition of 1855. The queen noted in her *Journal* for 20 August:

> In the Exposition des Beaux-Arts are all the different schools, French, English, German, Italian, Spanish, Belgian, etc., and there were some very fine things – many of course not new works, for collections have been made of all the different masters . . . Winterhalter's large picture of the Empress and her ladies is very fine.[32]

There is no mention of Ingres or Delacroix, let alone of the ensuing momentous developments on the Paris art scene, just as in the context of British painting the achievements of J. M. W. Turner or John Constable seem to have eluded them. Dependable French artists such as Meissonier or Delaroche and reliable British artists such as Frith, Maclise, Phillip or Frost – all of whom were successful either at the Salon or at the Royal Academy – were acceptable, but more challenging or innovative works were eschewed. The avant-garde, if such a phrase may be allowed, was a whole dimension of collecting that was either ignored or held in abeyance.

The characteristics of Queen Victoria's and Prince Albert's collecting habits are revealed in their acquisition in 1855 of the large composition by Leighton, *Cimabue's Madonna being carried through the Streets of Florence* (FIG. 35), which illustrates a scene from Vasari's *Lives of the Artists* (1568) showing the S. Maria Novella altar-piece – then thought to be by Cimabue and now attributed to Duccio – as it passed through the streets on its way to being set up in the church in Florence. Cimabue and his young pupil,

Giotto, are in the centre; Dante stands on the far right where Charles of Anjou, King of Naples, is on horseback. Florentine citizens line the streets or peer down from windows while in the background there is a view of San Miniato al Monte. Subjects from the lives of early painters coincided with the revival of interest in early Italian and German art. Leighton, who spent a great deal of his early life in Germany and Italy, often depicted such subjects and here he quotes from several famous fresco cycles in Florence, Pisa and Siena. The immense scale of this picture makes it comparable with a fresco.

In spite of its size it is painted with a high degree of finish. Its chief fault is the lack of a sense of movement, partly due to the mathematical rigidity with which the composition has been mapped out on the canvas. There is also no penetration into depth so that the procession is like a frieze. The picture was, in fact, painted in Rome and, interestingly, the model used for the figure of Cimabue was also drawn by Degas, who was in Rome at the same time.

This enormous picture was exhibited at the Royal Academy in the summer of 1855, where it was a great success with the critics and the public. On the opening day Queen Victoria purchased the picture at a cost of £630. She wrote in her *Journal*:

There was a very big picture, by a young man, called Leighton, his 1st attempt at the age of 20 . . . It is a beautiful painting quite reminding one of a Paul Veronese, so bright, & full of light. Albert was enchanted with it, so much so that he made me buy it. The young man's father said, that his future career in life, would depend on the success of this picture.[33]

Subsequently, Leighton became President of the Royal Academy (1878) and was the first artist in this country (rather against the queen's better judgement) to be raised to a peerage.

CHAPTER 2

The Genius of Italy

The renowned Dr Samuel Johnson once pronounced at dinner that:

A man who has not been to Italy, is always conscious of an inferiority from his not having seen what it is expected a man should see. The grand object of travelling is to see the shores of the Mediterranean. On those shores were the four great Empires of the world; the Assyrian, the Persian, the Grecian and the Roman. All our religion, almost all our law, almost all our arts, almost all that sets us above savages, has come to us from the shores of the Mediterranean.[1]

Travellers from the north of Europe have always felt the lure of Italy, whether it be in the form of medieval pilgrimage, education at an Italian university, or exploratory cultural visit. The paintings in the Royal Collection illustrate several aspects of Britain's fascination with Italy.

For early monarchs the attractions of Italy were political and mercantile. Diplomatic alliances with individual city states reflected the shifting balance of power within Europe and promoted financial interests through trade and banking. Such connections also brought cultural advantages. During the fifteenth and sixteenth centuries English monarchs had close connections with several Italian city states which were then at the height of their power. These included Milan, Ferrara and Naples, but it was Urbino that had special significance. When ruled by Federigo da Montefeltro (1444–1482), Urbino was the classic example of the Renaissance city state. Federigo, who was created Duke of Urbino in 1474, was both an outstanding soldier and a supremely cultured man. His considerable wealth (approximately 50,000 ducats per annum from 1468 until his death[2]) was gained as a result of his activities as a *condottiere* (mercenary) – he was often paid simply not to fight at all. The annual income gained in this way was put to good use building the Palazzo Ducale in Urbino, which is arguably the most beautiful of all Renaissance palaces in Italy, and establishing a library of paramount importance. On both these projects large sums of money were lavished. According to one authority, 'no comparable sum was spent in so short a time by any other state or prince in Quattrocento Italy', including the Medici.[3] For Jacob Burckhardt in his famous account of the

Italian Renaissance, written in 1860, Urbino, under the rule of Federigo da Montefeltro and his son Guidobaldo (1472–1508), was the perfect example of the state as a work of art.[4]

It was hardly surprising that such an environment was the birthplace of Baldassare Castiglione, whose book *The Courtier* (1528) epitomises life at a Renaissance court and had a profound influence on Elizabeth I's court in England; of Raphael, whose paintings are one of the touchstones of Italian Renaissance art; and of Polydore Vergil, the historian whose vivid narrative style was one of Shakespeare's principal sources.

However, the overtures of the Yorkist king Edward IV and later of the Tudor king Henry VII to the court of Urbino were not inspired solely by its cultural assets. The motives were political and the instrument was the Order of the Garter, founded by Edward III in 1348, and England's oldest and foremost order of chivalry. Edward IV bestowed the Order of the Garter on Federigo da Montefeltro on 18 August 1474 in order to improve his relations with the papacy where the king as yet had no permanent representative. Federigo da Montefeltro's own standing with the pope was good, and his daughter Giovanna was in the same year betrothed to Pope Sixtus IV's nephew, Giovanni della Rovere. Through this tenuous connection England's interests at the papal court could be successfully advanced.

Federigo da Montefeltro was invested with the Order of the Garter at Grottoferrata, to the south of Rome, in September 1474 while in attendance at the papal court. Knights of the Order of the Garter were expected to attend the installation within eighteen months of their investiture, but Federigo da Montefeltro was installed by proxy, probably in the spring of 1475.

The nomination of Federigo da Montefeltro was a diplomatic coup for Edward IV and resulted in the institution of a 'cardinal protector' who represented the king's interests with the papacy on a permanent and thus more influential basis. For his part, Federigo da Montefeltro was clearly immensely proud of receiving the Order of the Garter. The motto and the emblem are carved in numerous places on the facade and on the inside of the Palazzo Ducale in Urbino. The *studiolo* (private study) in Urbino included an image by Justus of Ghent of Federigo da Montefeltro wearing the blue mantle of the Order of the Garter with the badge inscribed with the motto 'Honi soit qui mal y pense' ('Evil be unto him who evil thinks'). The *studiolo* of Federigo's other palace in Gubbio was decorated with panels illustrating the seven Liberal Arts, also painted by Justus of Ghent. An additional panel from the *studiolo* shows Federigo da Montefeltro listening to an oration by the humanist scholar Antonio Bonfini (FIG. 36). Federigo's small son Guidobaldo is seated with his father while his courtiers are

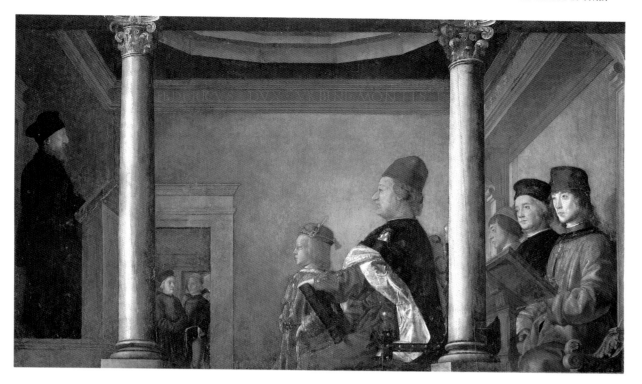

FIG. 36
Justus of Ghent: *Federico da Montefeltro, his son Guidobaldo and others, listening to a Discourse*, c. 1480

ranged behind him. When the duke was not on the field of battle, this was how he liked to spend his leisure hours.

Guidobaldo da Montefeltro was also bestowed with the Order of the Garter, at approximately the same age as his father, probably in 1504, by which time Henry VII had secured the English throne for the Tudor dynasty. Guidobaldo was invested in Rome in the presence of the pope in May 1504, but he delayed two years before securing a proxy for his installation. The person chosen to represent the young duke was Baldassare Castiglione, who on his return sent a written account commemorating the occasion, the *Epistola de Vita et Gestis Guidubaldi Urbini ducis ad Henricium Angliae regem*. More important than this work, however, was *The Courtier*, a dialogue set in the court of Guidobaldo da Montefeltro and inspired by Guidobaldo's wife, Elisabetta Gonzaga. It was an influential text about the conduct of Renaissance court society, and it also contains a passing reference to the author's visit to England in 1506 when Castiglione glimpsed the young Henry VIII, then Prince of Wales, 'who is growing up in all virtue under his great father, like a tender shoot beneath the shade of a noble and fruitful tree, to renew it when the time comes, with far greater beauty and fruitfulness'.[5]

The installation of the Order of the Garter was the occasion for the exchange of gifts. Federigo da Montefeltro had sent his proxy, Pietro degli Ubaldini, with horses and falcons, but Guidobaldo sent Castiglione with a painting by Raphael, *St George and the Dragon*, a most appropriate present in view of the fact that St George was the patron saint of the Order as well as of England. For some reason the picture is not described in the Tudor inventories, but it was given by the Earl of Pembroke to Charles I shortly after 1627 'in exchange of my Lord Chamberlaine for the booke of Holbein drawings'[6], meaning the famous series of portrait drawings by Hans Holbein the Younger which were themselves subsequently returned to the Royal Collection.

It is difficult to explain how the Earl of Pembroke came into possession of this important picture at such an early date, but presumably it was commissioned from Raphael either as a gift to the English king himself or, failing that, to a courtier. The antiquarian George Vertue, writing at the beginning of the eighteenth century, records that the Pembroke family claimed the picture was given directly to their ancestor by Castiglione himself – a claim that cannot now be substantiated.[7] Sadly, *St George and the Dragon* by Raphael is no longer in the Royal Collection, but in the National Gallery in Washington.

The Reformation led to the severing of relations with the papacy, undoing the careful diplomacy that Edward IV and Henry VII had so judiciously fostered. By the Act of Supremacy in 1534 Henry VIII became the spiritual head of the church in England as well as its secular protector. This important shift in loyalties was emphasised by the markedly propagandist paintings that Henry VIII acquired. Ironically, the one example

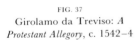

FIG. 37
Girolamo da Treviso: *A Protestant Allegory*, c. 1542–4

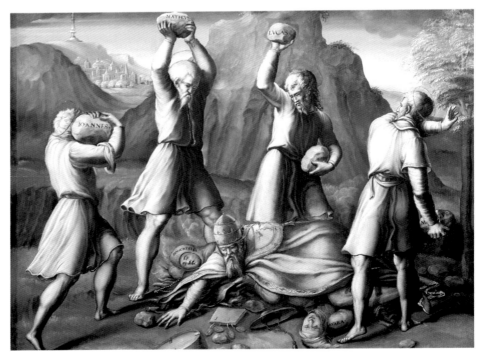

that survives in the Royal Collection is by an Italian, Girolamo da Treviso (FIG. 37). A pope sprawls on the ground with two female personifications of Avarice and Hypocrisy. These figures are being stoned by the four evangelists. In the foreground, cast aside as a result of the pope's fall, are a cardinal's hat and a document with four seals probably intended for a papal bull. Symbolically, also on the ground is an upturned candle which has been extinguished by a cooking pan. This contrasts with the burning candle in the top left-hand corner positioned over the city of Jerusalem. The artist here compares the true light of the new faith with the false doctrine of Rome.

Despite the break with the papacy, relations with Italy continued. The Stuart dynasty pursued the connection for two interconnected reasons: art and religion. Charles I's keen appreciation of Italian painting was certainly not disguised by religious scruples. His acquisition of the seven cartoons by Raphael for the tapestries commissioned by Pope Sixtus IV for use in the Sistine Chapel in Rome was possibly the single most important addition he ever made to the Royal Collection (FIG. 7). But Charles I was equally determined to employ Italian artists at his court. In this he was less successful than he was as a collector. Guercino refused an invitation to work in England on account of the bad weather and because he did not want to live among heretics. Negotiations with Francesco Albani also came to nothing. The king had to employ Orazio Gentileschi who, although capable of effectively dramatic compositions on a large scale (FIG. 38), was not a painter

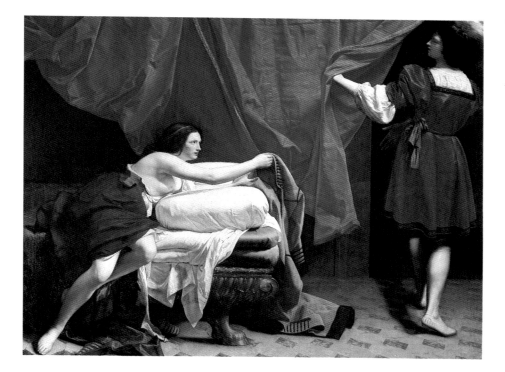

FIG. 38
Orazio Gentileschi: *Joseph and Potiphar's Wife*, c. 1632

of the first rank. Gentileschi was from Pisa, but later settled in Rome where his early mannered style was swept aside by the realism of Caravaggio. During the 1620s he travelled northwards, working in Genoa and Paris before arriving in London in 1626, where he worked first for the Duke of Buckingham and then for Charles I. As court artist Gentileschi painted the ceiling of the Great Hall in the Queen's House at Greenwich with an *Allegory of Peace and the Arts under the English Crown*. Despite efforts to return to Florence, he died in London in 1639, though during his last years he had been joined by his daughter Artemisia. She assisted her father in painting the ceiling in the Queen's House and one of her most important paintings was added to Charles I's collection. The *Self-Portrait as the Allegory of Painting* (FIG. 39) is not only an accurate indication of her tenebrist style and bold compositional sense, but also a revealing statement by a seventeenth-century female artist who, while living in Rome, had brought a charge of rape against the painter Agostino Tassi.[8]

Charles I's wife, the French-born Queen Henrietta Maria, continued to worship according to the Catholic rite, using for the purpose the Queen's Chapel at St James's Palace – one of the most beautiful of royal buildings – designed by Inigo Jones, and her chapel at Denmark House (later known as Somerset House). She was an important link with the papacy, who hoped by such alliances to counteract the growing influence of Protestantism. Papal agents kept a careful watch on developments in England, conducting secret correspondence, writing unofficial reports and supplying pictures. This last exercise served a dual purpose because it sustained Henrietta Maria in her faith and satisfied Charles I's interest in Italian art. The papacy could send gifts to Charles I using Henrietta Maria as cover. The correspondence between the pope's nephew, Cardinal Francesco Barberini, and the papal nuncio in London, Gregorio Panzani, demonstrates these links. Cardinal Barberini arranged for a batch of paintings to be sent to London early in 1636. The gift engendered a great deal of excitement when it arrived in Whitehall Palace.

> The pictures came in time, because just as Father Philip [the queen's confessor] brought the news to the Queen the King asked if the pictures were coming, and the Queen, to tease him, answered that they would not be coming any more. The King responded with great concern, why are they no longer coming; the Queen said, because they have already arrived; at which the King was very pleased. I then presented [the pictures] to the Queen, having them carried to her bed one by one, and she greatly appreciated them, and the room being full, all the principal ladies approved of the pictures. Especially pleasing to the Queen was that by Vinci, and that by Andrea del Sarto

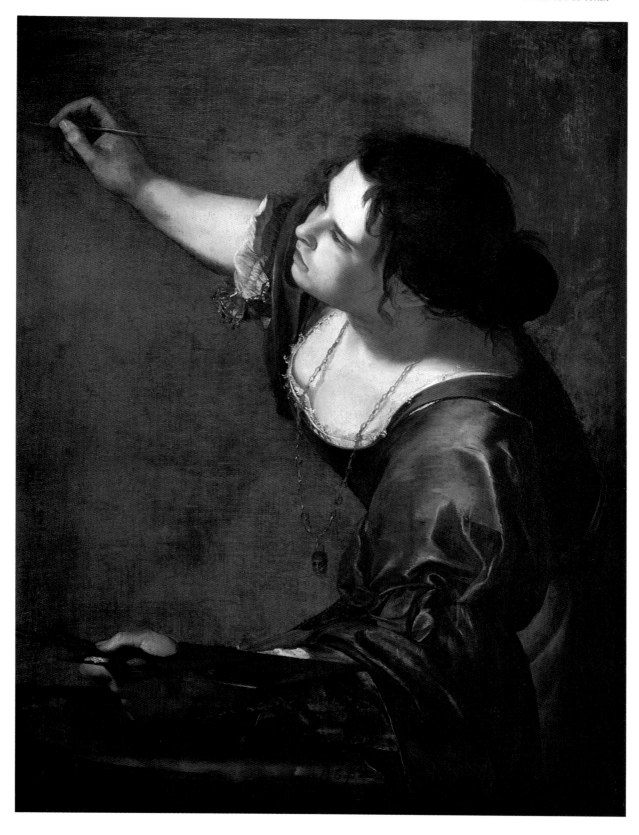

. . . I said that Your Eminence had done his best to seek out the said pictures to serve Her Majesty and that now Your Eminence would be pleased, when he heard that they pleased Her Majesty . . . She replied very courteously, thanking Your Eminence and repeating often that they pleased her very greatly, but that she would not be allowed to keep them, because the King would steal them from her . . .

The King came rushing to see the pictures the moment he was informed by the Queen that they had arrived and called Jones the architect, a great connoisseur of pictures, the Earl of Holland, and the Earl of Pembroke to be present. Immediately Jones saw them, he greatly approved of them, in order to study them better he threw down his riding cloak, put down his spectacles, and took hold of a candle and turned to inspect all of them minutely together with the King and accorded them extraordinary approval . . .[9]

The matter was still causing interest the following month when Panzani reported to Cardinal Barberini on the continuing enthusiasm for his gift.

Jones, the King's architect, believes that the picture by [da] Vinci is the portrait of a certain Ginerva Benci Venetiana, and he concludes this from the G, the B, inscribed on her breast. As he is very vain and boastful he repeats this idea often in order to show his great expertise of painting. He also boasts, that as the King had removed the note of the painters, which I had put on each picture, he guessed the names of almost all artists. He greatly exaggerates their beauty and says that they are pictures which should be kept in a special room with gilded and jewelled frames, and this he said publicly in the Queen's anti-chamber despite being a very stern puritan.[10]

The cardinal also realised that he could exploit Charles I's interest in contemporary Italian paintings. He had already ascertained from Orazio Gentileschi that 'the works of Lanfranco, of Spagnoletto [Ribera] and of Carracci, would not be displeasing to him as he had no works by these as he has by the other famous painters'.[11] An excuse was provided in 1637 by Henrietta Maria's desire for a large mythological painting by Guido Reni to decorate the ceiling of her bedroom in the Queen's House at Greenwich. The commission was negotiated by Cardinal Barberini who was given a free hand in choosing the subject. He selected a *Bacchus and Ariadne*, but regretted it. When he saw the painting in 1640 he began to realise that he might have made a mistake.

Both as regards the story and as regards the way in which the painter has chosen to depict it, the picture appears to me to be lascivious. I hesitate to send it for fear of further scandalising these Heretics, especially since the subject of the work was chosen here in Rome. I will have a sketch made and sent to you [the papal agent], and if these things bother neither the Queen nor Father Philip [the queen's confessor], we will have to let it appear that Her Majesty ordered everything and that I was solicitously carrying out her commands.[12]

The subject of the picture was clearly unsuitable for a country that had begun to be dominated by Puritanism, but even an awareness of the political implications of pursuing her contacts with Rome did not diminish Henrietta Maria's enthusiasm for Guido Reni's picture. The cardinal, however, was wiser and he retreated.

The figures are not as well draped as I should like, especially in these parliamentary times,[13]

he wrote in February 1641. The painting was never dispatched, and it is only known today through an engraving.

The pattern of these events was repeated later in the seventeenth century after the Restoration in 1660. Such developments were watched in disbelief by John Evelyn in December 1686:

I was to hear the Musique of the Italians in the new Chapel [at Whitehall Palace] . . . Nothing can be finer than the magnificent Marble work and Architecture at the End . . . The history or Altarpiece is the Salutation.[14]

Having witnessed 'the world of mysterious Ceremony', he records surprise that 'I should ever have lived to see such things in the King of England's palace'.[15] It was as though the Reformation had never taken place.

Cardinal Barberini continued to act as the go-between after the Restoration. His success, however, was limited: no major painting by a leading contemporary artist came to England during the seventeenth century, with the exception of the altar-piece of *St Agnes* by Domenichino (FIG. 40). The altar-piece is first recorded in 1663 in the apartments of the Duke and Duchess of York (the future James II and his first wife Anne Hyde, the daughter of the historian Edward Hyde, Earl of Clarendon). Their marriage had taken place in 1660 and it is possible that the altar-piece was a gift from someone such as Cardinal Barberini still desperately trying to maintain links between the English and papal courts.

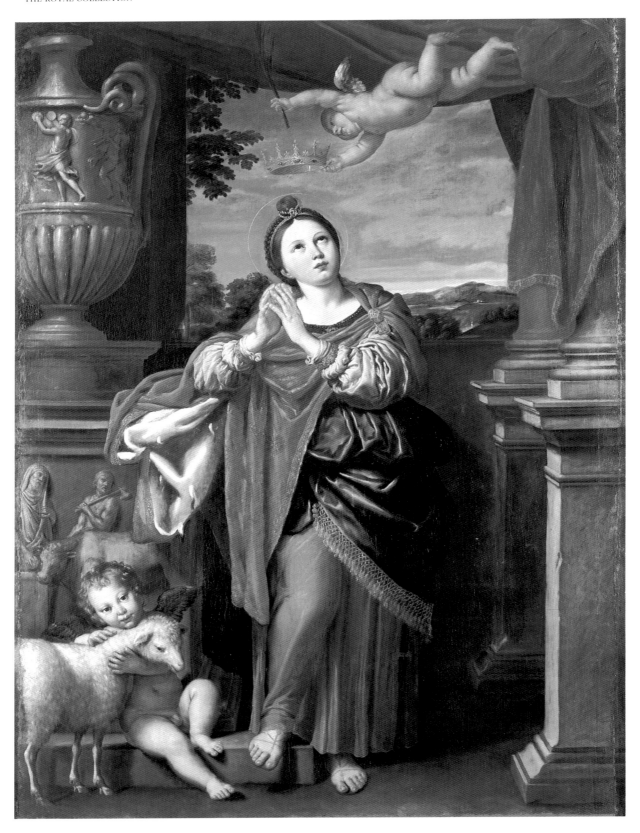

Yet, by the eighteenth century, Italy had become the focus of attention on a far wider basis and for different reasons.

The Grand Tour was one of the most important institutions of the time. The medieval pilgrimage and exploratory cultural tour of earlier centuries now gave way to a more formal visit that, in theory at least, provided the traveller with an opportunity for developing his taste, broadening his horizons and adding to his knowledge. It was almost exclusively the preserve of the aristocracy. Money and influence were needed because of the distances involved, the means of travel and the duration of the journey. The Grand Tour was an extension of the education system, serving either as a finishing school or as a supplement to university. It lasted one or two years and was undertaken in the company of a tutor or governor, often referred to as a 'bear leader'. Most travelled in extremely uncomfortable circumstances through France and Switzerland over the Alps to Italy and returned through Germany and the Netherlands. Italy was the ultimate destination.

It is difficult in the age of constant travel for either business or holidays to appreciate how much of an adventure a long-distance journey was in the eighteenth century. Discomfort was one form of challenge, but illness, danger, robbery and uncertainty were perpetual hazards. Yet, all these difficulties were offset by the experience of being in Rome, Florence or Venice. At least in theory, for there were many who undertook the Grand Tour simply to have a good time. Those who benefited most combined pleasure with learning. The result was that thousands of aristocrats flooded Italy, foreshadowing the coach parties and activities of tour companies of today. An exasperated Horace Walpole wrote:

> The English are numberless . . . 'tis dreadful, dealing with
> schoolboys just broke loose, or old fools that are come abroad at
> forty to see the world, like Sir Wilful Witwoud [of William Congreve's
> *The Way of the World*].[16]

Even in the eighteenth century there was a genuine fear that the ancient ruins and sites would not survive the onslaught.

By the Victorian and Edwardian periods the habit of travel had become more widespread and was undertaken by a wider cross-section of society. The spread of railways, the foundation of Thomas Cook's Tours, the publication of Baedeker's and Murray's detailed guides, the explosion in travel literature with such words as *Companion* and *Footsteps* in the titles, all encouraged people to venture into Europe and further afield, around the Mediterranean to Egypt and the Holy Land. The Victorians and the Edwardians found yet other reasons for travel. The Grand Tour for them

FIG. 40
Domenichino: *St Agnes*,
c. 1620

87

was intended to improve mind, body and soul all at the same time. The concept of the holiday was born. Those who considered themselves artists concentrated on local genre scenes as well as on topography. Queen Victoria often travelled in Europe for recreation. During the first quarter of the nineteenth century roughly 50,000 passengers left the country by the Channel ports every year and from then on the numbers increased dramatically so that before the outbreak of the First World War in 1914 the figure was roughly 660,000.[17]

Advice for those undertaking the Grand Tour in the eighteenth century was frequently given by those who remained at home or provided the money. English literature is full of anxious fathers repeating the words of wisdom spoken by Polonius to Laertes in *Hamlet*:

Give thy thoughts no tongue,
Nor any unproportion'd thought his act.
Be thou familiar, but by no means vulgar;
The friends thou hast, and their adoption tried,
Grapple them to thy soul with hoops of steel;
But do not dull thy palm with entertainment
Of each new-hatch'd, unfledg'd comrade. Beware
Of entrance to a quarrel, but, being in,
Bear't that th' opposed may beware of thee.
Give every man thine ear, but few thy voice;
Take each man's censure, but reserve thy judgment.
Costly thy habit as thy purse can buy,
But not express'd in fancy; rich, not gaudy;
For the apparel oft proclaims the man,
And they in France of the best rank and station
Are most select and generous, chief in that.
Neither a borrower, nor a lender be;
For loan oft loses both itself and friend,
And borrowing dulls the edge of husbandry.
This above all: to thine own self be true,
And it must follow, as the night the day,
Thou canst not then be false to any man.[18]

Lord Chesterfield warned his son in 1749 that he was 'not sent abroad to converse with your countrymen: among them, in general, you will get little knowledge, no languages, and, I am sure, no manners.'[19] Instead, 'the exercises of the Academy, and the manners of the court, must be attended to and acquired, and, at the same time, your other studies continued. I am sure you will not pass, nor desire, one single idle hour there . . . .'[20] A year later Lord Chesterfield reminds his son that 'a man of pleasure . . . refines at least his pleasures by taste, accompanies them with decency, and employs them with dignity.'[21]

Lord Chesterfield would not have approved of James Boswell, who travelled in Italy in 1765–6. The future biographer of Dr Johnson certainly confided in a letter to Jean-Jacques Rousseau:

> The study of antiquities, of pictures, of architecture, and of the other arts which are found in such great perfection at Rome occupied me in a wise and elegant manner.[22]

Yet Boswell was also keen to boast of his other exploits:

> I must admit that in the midst of my Roman studies I indulged in sensual relaxations. I sallied forth of an evening time an imperious lion . . . . I remembered the rakish deeds of Horace and other amorous Roman poets, and I thought that one might well allow one's self a little indulgence in a city where there are more prostitutes licensed by the Cardinal Vicar. I was however brought to a halt by an unpleasant occurrence which all libertines have to reckon with.[23]

Boswell suffered for the rest of his life from his sexual excesses indulged while on the Grand Tour. Meanwhile, Lord Auchinleck, his father, who was a Scottish judge, worried about the cost.

> . . . since you left Geneva in January last you have got no less than £460 sterling, which is much beyond what my income can afford, and much beyond what the sons of gentlemen near double my estate have spent on a tour: and that makes it quite necessary now to put an end to peregrination. You have had full opportunity to be satisfied that pageantry, civil and ecclesiastic, gives no entertainment to thinking men, and that there is no end nor use of strolling through the world to see sights before unseen, whether of men, beasts, birds or things and I hope . . . [you] will return with a proper taste and relish for your own country. For, if that were not to be your disposition, I should most heartily repent that ever I agreed to your going abroad, and shall consider the money spent in the Tour you have made as much worse than thrown away . . . . And hope to my infinite satisfaction to see you on your return a man of knowledge, of gravity and modesty intent on being useful in life.[24]

The only member of the royal family who went on the Grand Tour in the

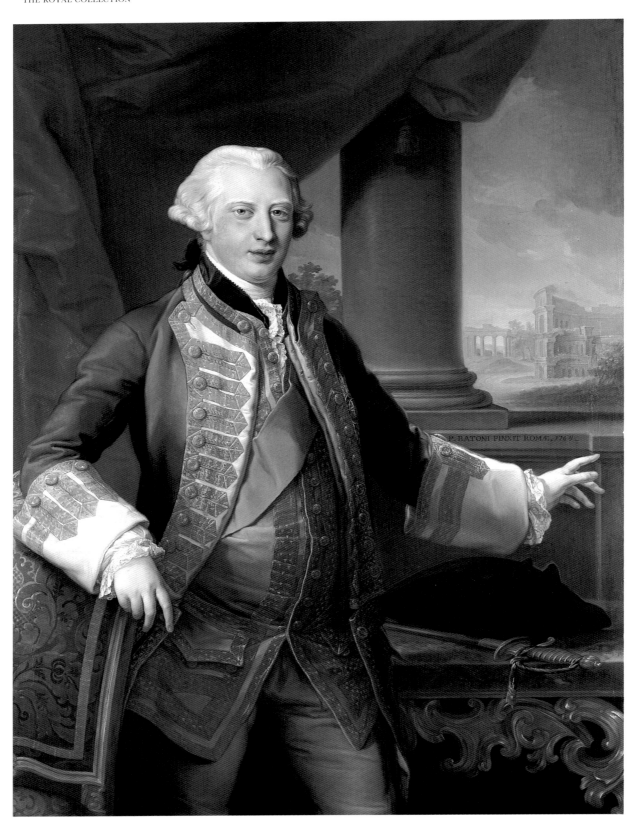

P. BATONI PINXIT ROMÆ, 1769.

proper sense during the eighteenth century was Edward Augustus, Duke of York (1739–67), the brother of George III, described by Horace Walpole as 'a very plain boy with strange loose eyes, but . . . much the favorite'[25], who was pursuing a career in the navy. He travelled in 1763–4 by ship to the Mediterranean via Portugal and Gibraltar, arriving at Genoa on 28 November 1763; he then visited Turin, Milan, Parma, Florence, Pisa, Lucca, Pistoia, Siena, Rome, Bologna, Mantua, Verona, Vicenza, Padua and finally Venice, before returning overland to Britain across France. Evidently he went to learn, for it is stated in the official account of the Duke of York's Grand Tour:

> His Royal Highness, after having first made himself perfectly acquainted with the religion, politics, arts, sciences, mechanics and natural genius of his own countrymen, thought proper to visit other nations.[26]

The Duke of York travelled incognito, as the Earl of Ulster, but his Grand Tour was almost a royal progress and thus anticipated the more formal State Visits of the next century. As it is expounded in the official account:

> The reception His Royal Highness met with in the different kingdoms and states through which he passed cannot but be pleasing to every true Briton, as it is a clear demonstration not only of the high opinion that part of Europe entertains of these happy isles, but at the same time shows how much the religious prejudices once so prevalent in those countries, have been overcome by a proper exertion of that reason which alone distinguishes true Christianity from Enthusiasm[27]

FIG. 41
Pompeo Batoni: *Edward Augustus, Duke of York*, 1764

When he reached Rome, the Duke of York was painted by Pompeo Batoni, who had a well-established studio in the city and specialised in this type of portrait intended to be taken home like a souvenir (FIG. 41). Wearing the undress uniform of an admiral and the Order of the Garter, the duke has laid his sword and cocked hat on a table and points towards the Colosseum in the background. This indicates the purpose of his visit, namely to see the sights of classical Rome. As a guide he had the services of Thomas Jenkins, an Englishman living in Rome, who acted as a banker for tourists but was basically a dealer in antique sculpture, and, for further instruction, the Duke of York had on hand the foremost authority on antique art, J. B. Winckelmann, a German who had settled in Rome as librarian to Cardinal Albani. Unfortunately, the duke does not seem to have taken full advantage of this situation, although on the instructions of the pope (Clement XIII) there was an exchange of gifts, including a set of prints of Rome specially bound for the Duke of York, which may possibly have been by Giovanni Battista Piranesi. In return the pope was given German porcelain.

One of the potential embarrassments for the Duke of York while in Rome would have been an accidental meeting with the exiled Stuarts, who lived in the Palazzo Muti-Papazzuri. The Stuart claim to the throne was expunged after the Glorious Revolution of 1688 forced James II to stand down so that the Protestant succession could be safeguarded. As the Hanoverian dynasty established itself during the early eighteenth century, so the Stuart cause diminished. Military and diplomatic attempts (usually in

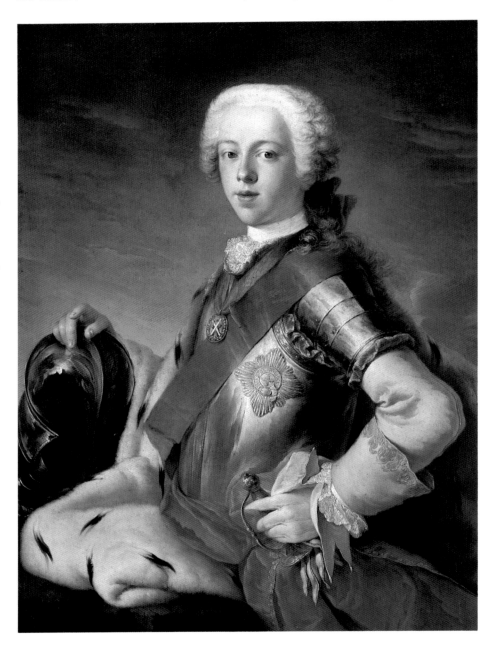

FIG. 42
Louis-Gabriel Blanchet:
Prince Charles Edward Stuart,
1737–8

the form of spying) made by the Old Pretender (James Stuart), and his son the Young Pretender (Charles Edward, FIG. 42), to overthrow the Hanoverian dynasty failed and they were forced to live out their days in Rome, assisted financially by the papacy and by the Hanoverians themselves. Charles Edward's brother Henry (FIG. 43) was elected a cardinal, and styled himself first as Cardinal York and then as Henry IX, but this was little more than an empty gesture. There is, however, a monument to the exiled Stuarts in St Peter's designed by Antonio Canova.

For most people on the Grand Tour, Rome was the climax. The eigh-

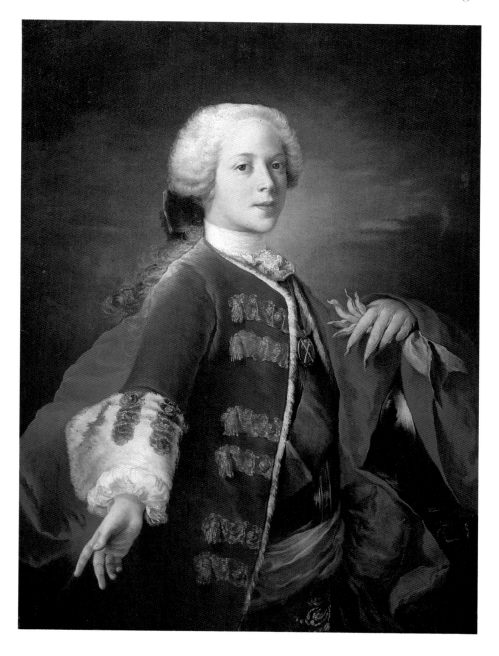

FIG. 43
Louis-Gabriel Blanchet:
Prince Henry Benedict Stuart,
1737–8

teenth century was keenly aware of the significance of the city. Rome was, of course, one of the spiritual centres of the world, but in the Age of Enlightenment, especially to a traveller from the north, it was its associations with the classics which made it so overpowering. Goethe, whose *Italian Journey* of 1786–8 is one of the most enjoyable and intelligent accounts, writes breathlessly of this moment:

> Now I have arrived, I have calmed down and feel as if I had found a peace that will last for my whole life. Because, if I may say so, as soon as one sees with one's eyes the whole which has been hitherto only known in fragments and chaotically, a new life begins.
>
> All the dreams of my youth have come to life; the first engravings I remember – my father hung views of Rome in the hall – I now see in reality, and everything that I have known for so long through paintings, drawings, etchings, plaster casts and cork models is now assembled before me. Wherever I walk, I come upon familiar objects in an unfamiliar world; everything is just as I imagined it, and yet everything is new.[28]

The Capitol was the centre of ancient and modern Rome. Like the important visitor depicted in a painting attributed to an anonymous Flemish painter (c. 1680–90), the sense of drama unfolds as the Piazza del Campidoglio, designed by Michelangelo, is approached up a flight of steps. At the top, straight ahead, is the Palazzo del Senatore flanked by the Palazzo del Museo Capitolino on the left and the Palazzo dei Conservatori on the right. On parapets at the top of the steps are the huge marbles of the Dioscuri and in the middle of the Campidoglio is the famous bronze equestrian statue of Marcus Aurelius dating from late antiquity. No wonder Lord Palmerston, who accompanied the Duke of York, naively remarked in a letter of 1763, 'I never had any idea till I came here what a good statue was, or what effect it was capable of producing . . . .'[29]

As you leave the Piazza del Campidoglio, past the Palazzo del Senatori in the centre, you come to the view of the Roman Forum that in 1764 inspired Edward Gibbon to write *The Decline and Fall of the Roman Empire*:

> After a sleepless night, I trod, with a lofty step, the ruins of the Forum; each memorable spot where Romulus stood, or Tully spoke, or Caesar fell, was at once present to my eye; and several days of intoxication were lost or enjoyed before I could descend to a cool and minute observation. . . . It was at Rome on the 15th of October 1764, as I sat musing amidst the ruins of the Capitol, while the barefoot

friars were singing vespers in the temple of Jupiter, that the idea of writing the decline and fall of the city first started into my mind.[30]

Canaletto, who spent several years at the start of his career working with his father painting stage scenery in Rome, obviously knew the city well, although he is more normally associated with Venice. He depicted the ancient ruins of Rome in a series of five paintings dating from 1742. In these, he shows the tourists with their guides earnestly making notes and absorbing information; he incorporates vignettes of daily life; and he includes an artist sketching. The large scale of the ruins impresses the tourists in the same way as the incisiveness of Canaletto's purely descriptive style impresses the viewer today. This style is characterised by crisp brush-work, firm outlines often drawn with a ruler or stylus, and crystal-clear light. Eighteenth-century tourists knew their classical history: each of these ruins would have been associated with a particular historical event or personality.

Today, the visitor to Rome can still walk about the Forum examining these same ruins, looking back first of all to the Palazzo del Senatore on the Capitol below which is the Temple of Saturn and the three remaining columns from the Temple of Castor and Pollux towering in the foreground (FIG. 44). Facing in the same direction, but to the right, is the Arch of Septimus Severus (FIG. 45). Behind this Canaletto has placed a ramp based on that approaching the Capitol from the other side. At the opposite end of the Forum is the Arch of Titus, with the three columns of the Temple of Castor and Pollux visible in the background and the wall and gateway to the Farnese gardens on the left seen through the arch (FIG. 46). Beyond the Forum is the Arch of Constantine, with the church of S. Pietro in Vinculo in the distance and a portion of the Colosseum visible at the edge (FIG. 47). Here the size and scale of the ruins of ancient Rome overpower the visitor. As Goethe wrote:

As I rush about Rome looking at the major monuments, the immensity of the place has a quietening effect. In other places, one has to search for the important places of interest; here they crowd in on one in profusion. Wherever you turn your eyes, every kind of vista, near and distant, confronts you – palaces, ruins, gardens, wildernesses, small houses, stables, triumphal arches, columns – all of them often so close together that they could be sketched on a single sheet of paper.[31]

Of the Colosseum, Goethe concluded, 'Once one has seen it, everything else seems small.'[32] People came to Rome to pay homage to the past.

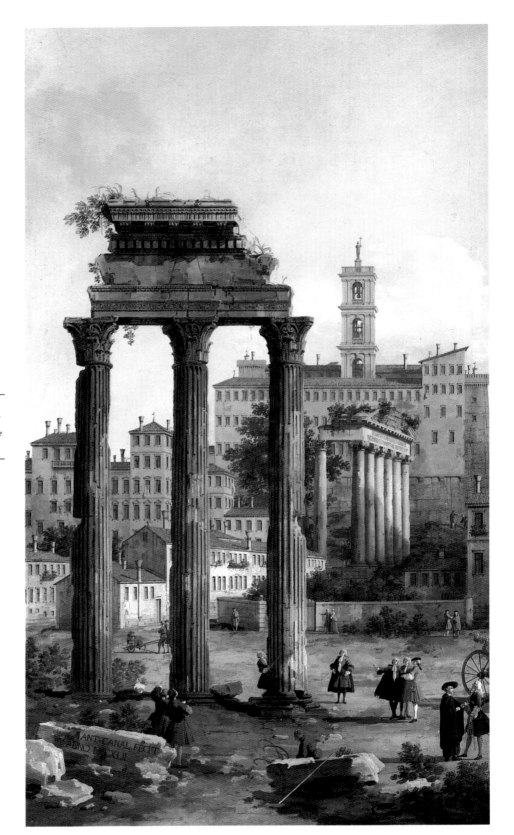

FIG. 44
Canaletto: *Rome: Ruins of the Forum looking towards the Capitol*, 1742

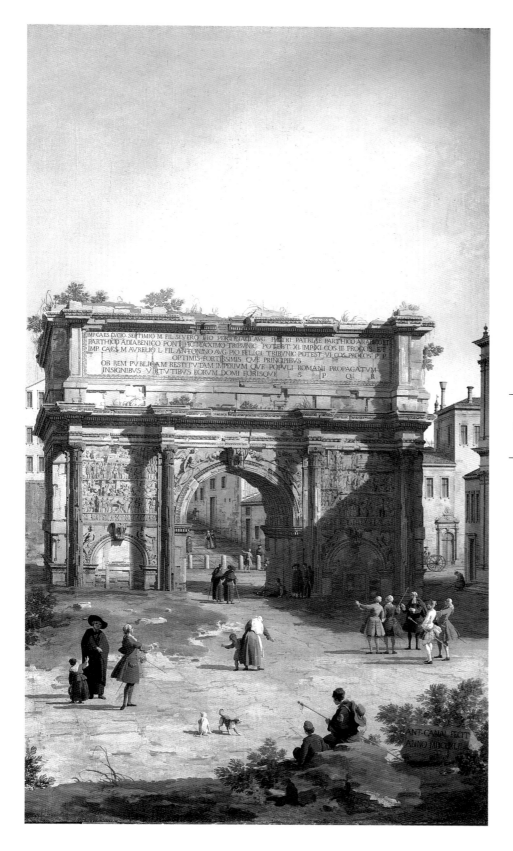

FIG. 45
Canaletto: *Rome: The Arch
of Septimius Severus*, 1742

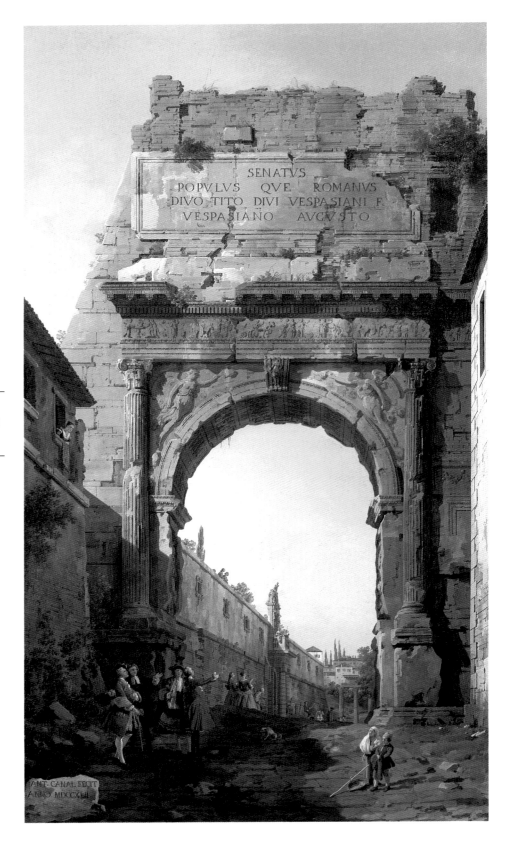

FIG. 46
Canaletto: *Rome: The Arch of Titus,* 1742

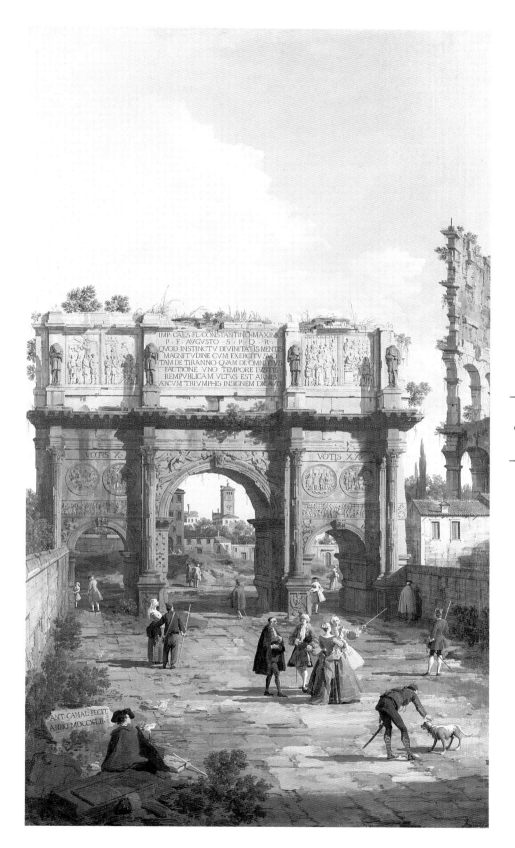

FIG. 47
Canaletto: *Rome: The Arch of Constantine*, 1742

Scholars came to study the ruins, artists to be inspired by them, general visitors to marvel at them. Goethe wrote:

> Here is an entity which has suffered so many drastic changes in the course of two thousand years, yet is still the same soil, the same hill, often even the same column or the same wall, and in its people one still finds traces of their ancient character.[33]

Yet there were disappointments, for Rome is essentially a palimpsest with the remains of different periods of history in close juxtaposition – the ancient world, the Renaissance, the Baroque and the nineteenth century, not to mention the excrescences of the twentieth. Several visitors from Petrarch onwards observed how the buildings of ancient Rome were half-buried, neglected or put to other uses. Those who knew Rome only through the texts of Suetonius, Tacitus, Livy or Caesar were shocked by the way the modern had displaced the old. Boswell, for example, was upset by the fact that the Colosseum was occupied by squatters and used as a refuse tip.

The visitor to Rome in whatever century is conscious of the passing of time, the transience of human existence and of the fragility of civilisation itself. This was the subject of a treatise by a fifteenth-century humanist, Poggio Bracciolini, entitled *On the Variety of Fortune*, quoted in the closing chapter of Gibbon's *Decline and Fall*:

> The hill of the Capitol, on which we sit, was formerly the head of the Roman empire, the citadel of the earth, the terror of Kings; illustrated by the footsteps of so many triumphs, enriched with the spoils and tributes of so many nations. This spectacle of the world, how it is fallen! how changed! how defaced! the path of victory is obliterated by the vines, and the benches of the senators are concealed by a dunghill. . . . The forum of the Roman people, where they assembled to enact their laws and elect their magistrates, is now enclosed for the cultivation of pot-herbs, or thrown open for the reception of swine and buffaloes. The public and private edifices, that were founded for eternity, lie prostrate, naked and broken, like the limbs of a mighty giant; and the ruin is the more visible, from the stupendous relics that have survived the injuries of time and fortune.[34]

By the nineteenth century and throughout our own, this problem has become exacerbated. In 1826 William Hazlitt wrote of Rome in a way that is not only reminiscent of Poggio Bracciolini, but still has a relevance for tourism in general:

It is not the contrast of pigstyes and palaces that I complain of, the distinction between old and new; what I object to is the want of any such striking contrast, but an almost uninterrupted succession of narrow, vulgar-looking streets, where the smell of garlick prevails over the odour of antiquity, with the dingy, melancholy flat fronts of modern-built houses, that seem in search of an owner. A dung-hill, an outhouse, the weeds growing under an imperial arch offended me not; but what has a greengrocer's stall, a stupid English china warehouse, a putrid trattoria, a barber's sign, an old clothes or old picture shops or a Gothic palace, with two or three lacqueys in modern liveries lounging at the gate, to do with modern Rome?[35]

Florence was a contrast (FIG. 48). It was smaller, less daunting, less of an intellectual challenge and altogether more sociable. If the first view of Rome stirred the mind, the first view of Florence aroused the senses. Hazlitt described it as 'a scene of enchantment, a city planted in a garden . . . . Everything was on the noblest scale, yet finished in the minutest part.'[36] It was these same attributes that inspired Henry James and E. M. Forster. The roads along the Arno provided opportunities for the display of fashion; a boat on the river could cool you off; and at night on certain festivals there were firework displays.

FIG. 48
Thomas Patch: *A distant View of Florence*, c. 1763

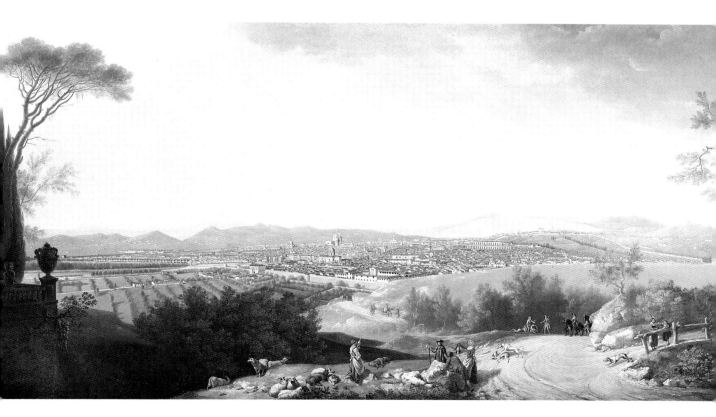

Florence appears to have been a friendly place with a sympathetic British minister, Sir Horace Mann, who for thirty years following his appointment in 1740 looked after British tourists and frequently invited them to his house in the Via S. Spirito near the Ponte Sta. Trinita. It was Mann who entertained the Duke of York when he was in Tuscany during the spring of 1764, and who conducted a long, fascinating correspondence with Sir Horace Walpole which is such an important source for the story of the Grand Tour.[37] Gibbon declared that Mann's 'most serious business was that of entertaining the English at his hospitable table'.[38]

An Englishman resident in Florence, Thomas Patch, painted the Duke of York leaving Sir Horace Mann's house in 1764 surrounded by all the leading personalities of the British colony in Florence, but, unfortunately, it is lost and known only through a description in a letter from Mann to Walpole. Patch, however, is an important figure: he had a keen interest in art, not only acting as a dealer, but also restoring pictures and publishing engravings of frescoes, as in his notable monograph on Masaccio (1770). He specialised in views of Florence and in caricatures of tourists.

Art was what attracted visitors to Florence and it was the collections of the Medici that they chiefly wanted to see. The German artist Johann Zoffany, who worked for George III and Queen Charlotte, was commissioned in 1772 by the queen to paint the Tribuna Gallery in the Uffizi (FIG. 49). This painting took seven years, being finished in 1777, but was not handed over to George III and Queen Charlotte until the 1780s. Members of the royal family had seen the Tribuna, but neither the king nor the queen ever went to Florence. Zoffany was therefore re-creating the effect and impact of the Grand Tour for people who had not experienced it.

The Tribuna was the epicentre of art for the eighteenth-century connoisseur. Designed by Bernardo Buontalenti in 1585–9 for Francesco de' Medici, it was intended as a shrine for the greatest works of art in the Medici collections. The contents were occasionally changed. A young aristocrat, Lord Winchelsea of Eton and Christ Church, whose visit coincided with the painting of Zoffany's masterpiece, wrote in 1772:

> The Tribune . . . is quite a Paradise, for the first time of going there
> one is really quite confused & amazed with the profusion of things,
> & I am sure that it would take a month to see compleatly that
> room only.[39]

The artist has lavished immense care on the architectural features of the room: the patterned floor, the rich cornice and the decorated cupola. The neat, careful handling of paint and fresh colouring extends throughout the picture. Zoffany has painstakingly assembled paintings, sculptures and bronzes, and grouped figures around them. In fact, the artist has cheated because he has not represented the Tribuna exactly as it was in 1772, but has introduced works of art from other parts of the Medici collection, such as the Palazzo Pitti, so that the visual effect is richer; there is also a certain licence in the scattering of objects on the floor. Zoffany's skill lies not just in the organisation of such a crowded composition, but also in the concern

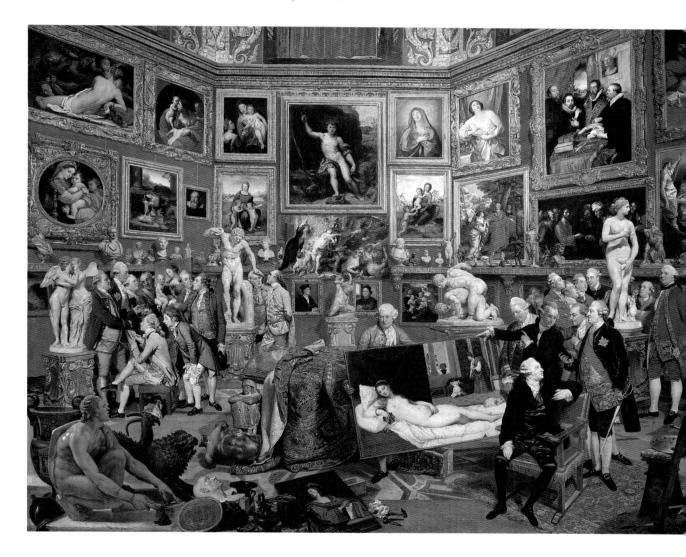

for texture. This is not limited to the distinction he makes between garments and the surfaces of objects such as marble, frames and fabrics, but extends to the various stylistic idioms of the paintings on the wall. Here are famous works by Rubens, Correggio, Titian, Guido Reni, Guercino, Pietro da Cortona, Hans Holbein the Younger, Annibale Carracci, and above all five works by Raphael – the apogee of art for the eighteenth-century connoisseur. In fact, the painting is really a homage to Raphael.

FIG. 49
Johann Zoffany: *The Tribuna of the Uffizi*, 1772–80

Apart from the works of art, Zoffany expended a great deal of effort on the figures. Standing grandly by the easel with the *Venus d'Urbino* by Titian is Sir Horace Mann; Thomas Patch has his hand on the top of the picture; Lord Winchelsea looks admiringly up at the *Venus de Medici* on the right. On the left, pointing at a canvas of the *Virgin and Child* by Raphael is Earl Cowper, a distinguished collector who lived at the Villa Palmieri near Fiesole and later actually owned the picture that is the subject of discussion. At the time when Zoffany's *Tribuna* was being painted, Earl Cowper was interested in buying *The Virgin and the Child* so that he could give it to George III, hoping thereby to be rewarded with the Order of the Garter. This ploy failed, however, and the picture of Raphael is now in the National Gallery of Art in Washington, where it is referred to as the Large Cowper Madonna. Interestingly, the figure holding the painting up is Zoffany himself, who seems to have abandoned his easel and stool (depicted in the lower right-hand corner) and moved round the back to include himself in the picture, like taking a photograph with a long-running exposure.

The evolution of Zoffany's painting was described by Sir Horace Mann with characteristic vigour and in his usual gossipy tone in a letter to Horace Walpole, who saw the work shortly after the artist's return to England:

> I am glad that you have seen Zoffany and his Portrait of the Tribune. . . . Your opinion of his laborious performance in all the parts you mention agrees with that of our best judges here; but they found great fault in the perspective which, they say, is all wrong. I know that he was sensible of it himself, and tried to get assistance to correct it, but it was found impossible, and he carried it away as it was. How or whether it has been done elsewhere, I know not. I told him often of the impropriety of sticking so many figures in it, and pointed out to him, the Great Duke and Duchess, one or two of their children, if he thought the variety were pictoresque, and Lord Cowper. He told me that the King had expressly ordered my portrait to be there, which I did not believe, but did not object to it, but he made the same merit with all the young travellers then at Florence, some of whom he afterwards rubbed out, as old Felton Harvey and one of the Queen's Chaplains with a broad, black ribbon across his forehead, and filled up their places elsewhere. If what he said is true, that the Queen sent him to Florence to do that picture, and gave him a large sum for his journey, the impropriety of crowding in so many unknown figures were still greater. But is it true that it is for the Queen's closet and that she is to give him £3,000 for it? This he asserted. It got him the name of Her Majesty's Painter, and in

that quality he had leave to have any Picture in the Gallery or Palace taken down, for you must have observed that he has transported some from the latter place into his Tribune. I should think too the naked Venus which is the principal figure will not please Her Majesty so much as it did the young men to whom it was showed. As to the question you make me of my own personage, I can only say that everybody thought it like me, but I suppose he took pains to lessen my pot-belly and the clumsiness of my figure, and to make me stand in a posture which I never kept to, but then I remember, for it was several years ago, that I was sadly tired when I was tortured by him to appear before their Majesties in my best shape and looks.[40]

Walpole had earlier had some fun at Mann's expense:

The first thing I looked for was *you*, and I could not find you. At last I said, 'Pray, who is *that* Knight of the Bath?' – 'Sir Horace Mann.' – 'Impossible!' said I. My dear sir, how you have left me in the lurch! – you are grown fat, jolly, young – while I am become the skeleton of Methusalem!

The idea I always thought an absurd one. It is rendered more so by being crowded by a flock of travelling boys, and one does not know nor care whom. You and Sir John Dick, as Envoy and Consul, are very proper. The Grand Ducal family would have been so too. Most of the rest are as impertinent as the names of churchwardens stuck up in parishes, whenever a country church is repaired and whitewashed. The execution is good; most of the styles of painters happily imitated, the labour and finishing infinite; and no confusion, though such a multiplicity of objects and colours. The Titian's Venus, as the principal object, is the worst finished; the absence of the Venus of Medici is surprising; but the greatest fault is in the statues. To distinguish them he has made them all of a colour; not imitating the different hues of their marbles, and thus they all look alike, like casts in plaster of Paris – however it is a great and curious work – though Zoffani might have been better employed. His talent is representing natural humour. I look upon him as a Dutch painter polished or civilised . . . .

P.S. I do allow Earl Cowper a place in the Tribuna; an English Earl, who has never seen his earldom, and taken root and bears fruit in Florence, and is proud of a pinchbeck principality in a third country, is as great a curiosity as any in the Tuscan collection.[41]

Zoffany continued to alter the painting after his return from Florence, but Mann and Walpole were correct in their predictions. Queen Charlotte disapproved of the introduction of figures into the composition and 'would not suffer the picture to be placed in any of Her apartments'.[42]

Today, however, as a record of one of the greatest galleries in the world at the height of its influence, the painting is an invaluable record. Few pictures delight both the mind and the eye as much as Zoffany's *Tribuna*. It makes the viewer want to linger, but it was necessary for those on the Grand Tour to move on: this time to Venice, where even greater joys lay in store.

Venice is an anachronism (FIG. 50). Edward Wright, in the early 1720s, recorded his reaction:

'Tis a pleasure, not without a mixture of surprise, to see so great a city as Venice may be truly called, as it were, floating on the surface of the sea; to see chimneys and towers, where you would expect nothing but ships and masts. It stands surrounded with waters, at least five miles distant from any land, and is thus defended by its third bulwark better than by walls and ramparts.[43]

FIG. 50
Canaletto: *Venice: The Bacino di S. Marco on Ascension Day*, c. 1734 (detail)

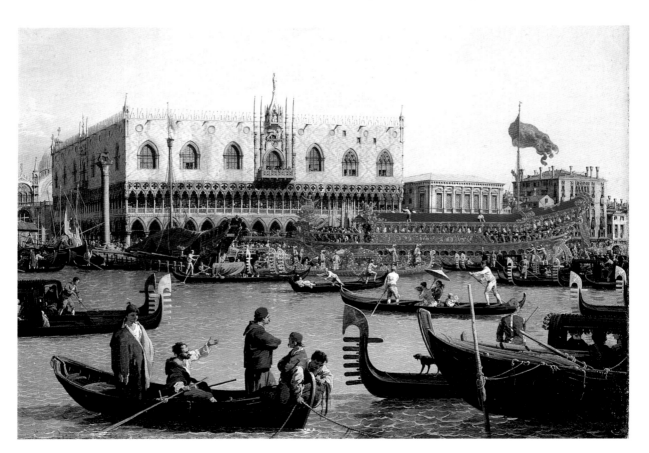

Venice was exotic. Apart from the architecture and the art the city offered other excitements. Boswell said that 'for the first week, I was charmed by the novelty and beauty of so singular a city, but I soon wearied of travelling continually by water, shut up in those lugubrious gondolas'.[44] By the eighteenth century, Venice was in decline, having lost its political and maritime influence, and it had now become the playground of Europe, famous for its carnival, festivals, high living and gambling. 'My fancy', Boswell records almost inevitably, 'was stirred by the brilliant stories I had heard of Venetian courtesans . . . . I went to see them . . . but the wounds of my Roman scars were scarcely healed before I received fresh ones at Venice.'[45]

The Venetian artist who depicts the most intimate scenes of the city's life is Pietro Longhi. The city did not have a good reputation: apart from the low moral tone, it was dirty, noisy and smelly. Yet none of this seems to have detracted from its beauties, which the Duke of York also experienced when he arrived in Venice on 25 May; he stayed for almost a month. He found Venice less cerebral than either Rome or Florence, and therefore far more congenial.

An artist called Richard Brompton was on hand to record this part of the Duke of York's tour in what amounts to a group portrait (FIG. 51). This

FIG. 51
Richard Brompton: *The Duke of York with his Entourage in the Veneto*, 1764

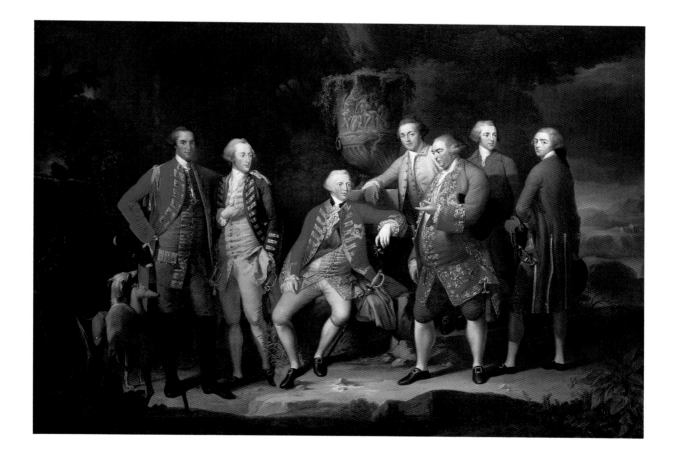

conversation piece was painted in Venice, although the setting is more likely to be the mainland. The vase carved in relief with the scene of Leda and the Swan behind the Duke of York perhaps suggests the context; but to his left are two members of his household who became unwell while in Rome and did not in fact travel to Venice. The large gentleman stepping forward to speak to the duke is John Murray, who held the post of British Resident in Venice and was responsible before the days of ambassadors for diplomatic and ceremonial matters. A compulsive womaniser, he was also a dealer, mainly in pictures, and described by Lady Mary Wortley Montagu as 'a scandalous fellow . . . not to [be] trusted to change a sequin, always surrounded with pimps and brokers'.[46] However, Murray's sister Elizabeth, described as 'a beauteous virgin of forty'[47], married Joseph Smith, who held the post of British Consul in Venice, responsible for promoting trade. This was Smith's second marriage: he was eighty-two. Smith formed an extensive and varied collection notable for its paintings by Canaletto, whose business affairs he handled. Smith had sold his collection of paintings, drawings, prints, books, cameos and gems to George III in 1762.

The figure leaning on the seat at the back is the second Viscount Palmerston, an enthusiastic collector and patron. Palmerston has left an account of the Duke of York's visit to Venice in a letter:

The Venetians were determined to treat him in no other light than as the King's brother, and for that reason put themselves to an immense expense. As to ceremonious dinners, suppers, balls, assemblies, with the long etc etc of princely amusements, they are all much the same in all countries, with the accidental difference of being, from particular circumstances, more or less disagreeable. All those to which I have the honour of attending his Royal Highness have been so, to so great a degree, that I will attempt no description of them, but by desiring you to imagine the greatest possible misery that a formal dinner or ball can bring with it, and you will then have some idea of what one may suffer when a state is determined to exert itself to the utmost. It is very fortunate that the Duke is not of the same opinion, as his whole time and thoughts seem employed on these objects. However, the Venetians gave one entertainment which is peculiar to Venice and which, for show, exceeds anything I ever saw. This is called regatta, which means no more than a boat race [FIG. 52]. The magnificence of it consists in the multitudes of the spectators and the magnificence of the vessels belonging to the noble Venetians, with which the canals are crowded, and which are so much beyond what can be seen in any other place that I can give no idea of them, but from the descriptions of Romance, or the account of Cleopatra's galley in Dryden. The Venetian state has a peculiar facility in entertaining princes beyond any other, because it is a constant maxim with them to impoverish their rich nobles; therefore, whenever anything is done, which in other countries would be a public expense, their government, though in a republican form, being one of the most arbitrary in Europe, they select out a certain number of nobility, who are obliged to do it out of their own private fortunes. This has been practiced now; four nobles were deputed to receive and attend upon the Duke of York, and in short to entertain him

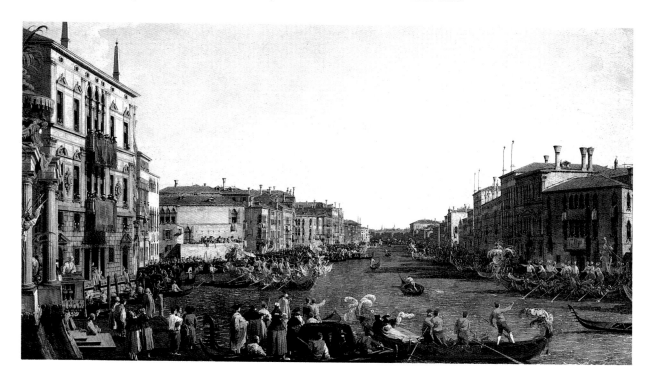

during his whole stay at their own expense. He was there three weeks, and in that time they must have spent three or four thousand pounds each. They were chosen probably more on account of their wealth than any other circumstance and, therefore, though their expense was very great, they did not, in their own persons, do the honours of it with dignity and the Duke did not take pains enough to show them civility, which he ought to have done, though I confess it required some command of temper, as they were ignorant and silly and their attendance was often very troublesome and oppressive.[48]

FIG. 52
Canaletto: *Venice: A Regatta on the Grand Canal*, c. 1734

Just as visitors in Rome were painted by Batoni, so in Venice they were drawn in pastel by Rosalba Carriera. A painting could remind one of the pleasures while excluding the more disagreeable aspects, and an image of Venice for display at home was an attractive souvenir. The artist whose style could best be adapted to supply such pictures was Canaletto, but the person who detected that there was a market to be exploited was the British Consul Joseph Smith, who lived in the Palazzo Mangilli-Valmarana on the Grand Canal. Strangely, no portrait of him has yet been identified, but Boswell visited him at his villa near Treviso. Smith appears to have met Canaletto in the mid 1720s and in order to promote his work he encouraged the artist to paint a series of twelve views of the Grand Canal (FIG. 53) which he then had engraved in 1735 for wider circulation.

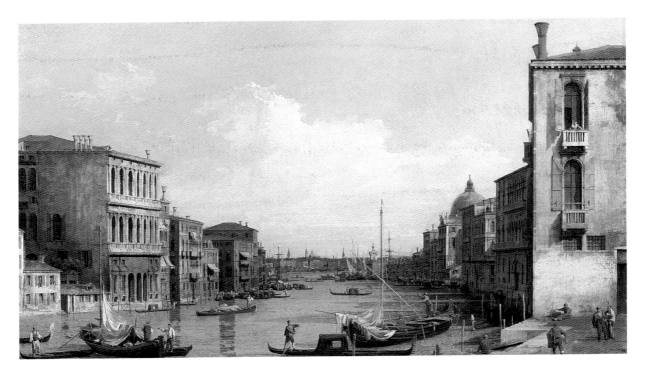

FIG. 53
Canaletto: *Venice: The Grand Canal from Campo S. Vio towards the Bacino*, c. 1730

FIG. 54
Canaletto: *Venice: The Piazzetta towards the Torre dell'Orologio*, c. 1725–30

Smith was the ideal patron because he had numerous aristocratic contacts such as the Duke of Bedford, the Duke of Leeds and Sir Robert Harvey, who duly bought Canaletto's work. Horace Walpole amusingly dubbed Smith 'the Merchant of Venice'.[49] However, the market did not last for long: at its height during the 1730s, it had already begun to decline by the beginning of the 1740s owing to war in Europe. Also the pressure of work affected Canaletto's style. His early representations of Venice dating from the 1720s are full of drama, with strong contrasts of colour and large-scale compositions populated by gesturing officials and scurrying figures (FIG. 54). The artist's theatrical training is evident here, but so too are the liberties he has taken with the topography of Venice. He prepared his paintings with drawings, but frequently these were revised so that

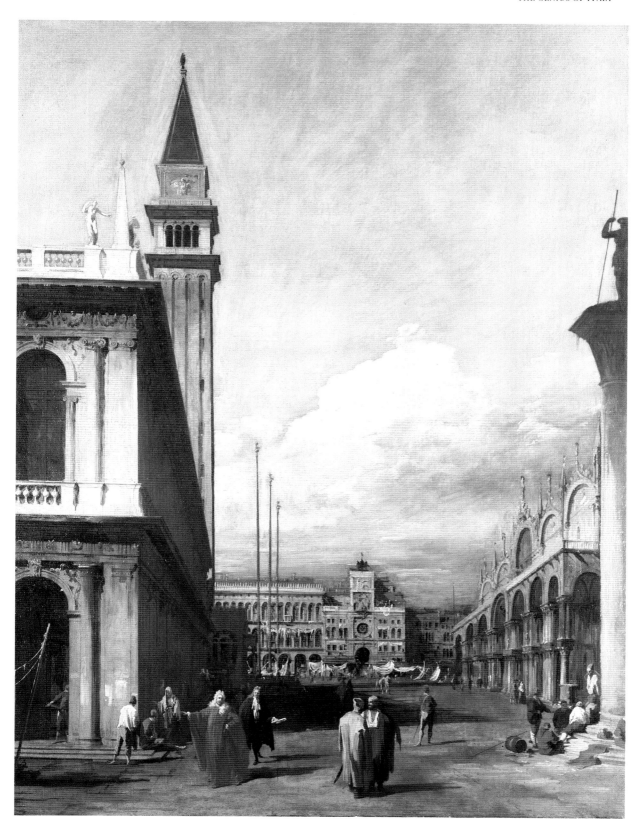

observations made from several viewpoints were amalgamated into a single composition that did not always coincide with reality. Canaletto, in short, was editing the topography of Venice and, although his sketchbooks reveal that he bobbed up and down the canal in a boat recording the changing roof-lines or the angles of chimney pots, these were then adjusted or refined in the final works.

The most radical examples of Canaletto taking liberties with the topography are his paintings of the Piazza San Marco dating from the 1740s (FIG. 55). Twenty years later the Reverend John Hinchcliffe, later Bishop of Durham, who was visiting Venice as tutor to John Crewe, afterwards first Baron Crewe, described how 'he chanced to see a little man making a sketch of the Campanile in St Mark's Place'.[50] The artist was Canaletto, still working towards the end of his life, and the finished painting was bought by John Crewe, to whom Canaletto also presented the preparatory drawing. The endless production of so many views of Venice done for Consul Smith brought about a change in Canaletto's style: it gradually lost its freedom and became routine or mechanical. Even so, Canaletto never fails to distil the magic of Venice in the crystalline light: the small waves on the water, the ceaseless movement of gondolas, the clouds passing far overhead, the hint of activity in the shadows and the reflections of the water on the buildings and against the hulls.

FIG. 55
Canaletto: *Venice: The Piazzetta towards the Torre del'Orologio*, 1743

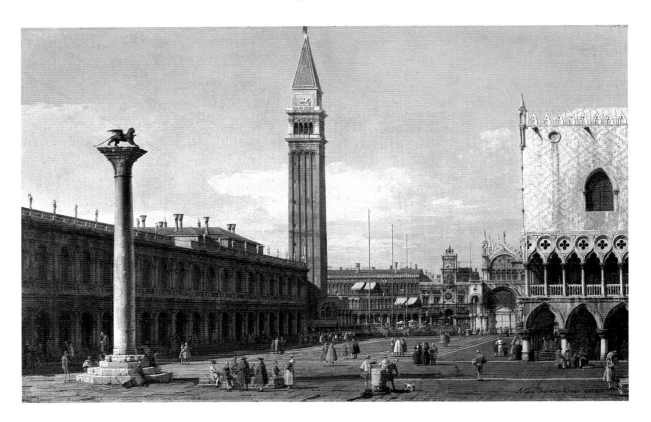

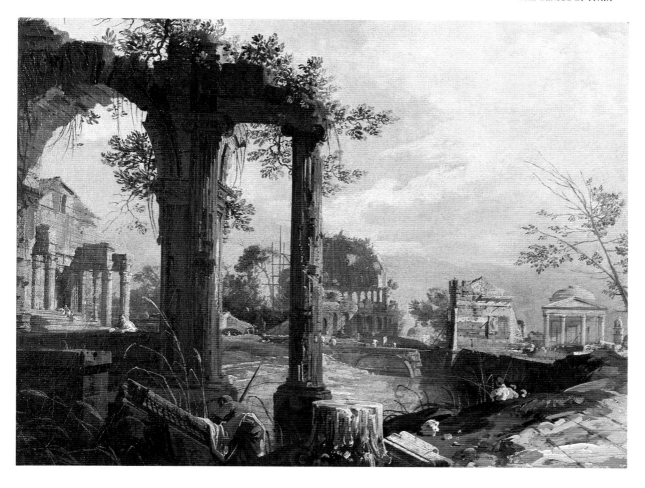

FIG. 56
Canaletto: *A Caprice View
with Ruins*, c. 1740

Canaletto's world may occasionally seem limited, but it was not. Just as he never really sanitised Venice, so he never failed to see the humorous side of life. Many of his paintings served as rather special picture postcards for those on the Grand Tour, but it would be a mistake to assume that this was the only aspect of Canaletto's art that contemporaries admired. It is unfair to expect Canaletto to anticipate the Venice of Ruskin, Proust, Baron Corvo or Thomas Mann, but there are hidden depths in his art. His caprices, or imaginative compositions, in which he combines ancient ruins of Rome with modern pastoral scenes based on the Venetian *terra firma* are perhaps more than just charming idylls in their dislocation of time and place (FIG. 56). But even within Venice Canaletto could find a sense of mystery, as in two very small pictures (FIG. 57) of the interior of the Basilica di San Marco, where the vast space sparkling with mosaics encloses shadowy forms and enfolds the worshippers. The definition found in San Marco by day becomes blurred at night in the darkness and the forms merge into one another as the eye moves upwards from the figures below to the grandeur of the architecture overhead.

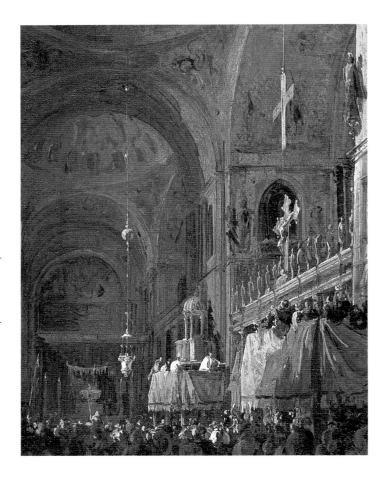

FIG. 57
Canaletto: *Interior of San
Marco*, c. 1735

The only writer who has captured this sense of space in San Marco is
Henry James:

> Still, it is almost a spiritual function – or, at the worst, an amorous
> one – to feed one's eyes on the molten colour that drops from the
> hollow vaults and thickens the air with its richness. It is all so quiet
> and sad and faded and yet so brilliant and living. The strange
> figures in the mosaic pictures, bending with the curve of niche and
> vault, stare down through the glowing dimness; the burnished gold
> that stands behind them catches the light on its little uneven cubes.
> St Mark's owes nothing of its character to the beauty of proportion or
> perspective; there is nothing grandly balanced or far-arching; there
> are no long lines nor triumphs of the perpendicular. The church
> arches, indeed, but arches like a dusky cavern. Beauty of surface, of
> tone, of detail, of things near enough to touch and kneel upon or lean
> against – it is from this that the effect proceeds. In this sort of beauty
> the place is incredibly rich, and you may go in there every day and
> find afresh some lurking pictorial nook.[51]

CHAPTER 3

The Kingdom of Nature

T he most perfect landscape must surely be the Garden of Eden, and perhaps no painter was better equipped to depict this paradise than Jan Breughel the Elder (FIG. 58). He was born in Brussels in 1568, the son of the famous Pieter Bruegel the Elder, and specialised in painting landscapes, animals and flowers.

Although appointed court painter to Archduke Albert and the Infanta Isabella in Brussels in 1609, Breughel preferred to live and work in Antwerp, where he held important administrative posts in the artistic hierarchy. His feeling for landscape and nature was heightened by exten-

FIG. 58
Jan Breughel the Elder:
Adam and Eve in the Garden of Eden, 1615

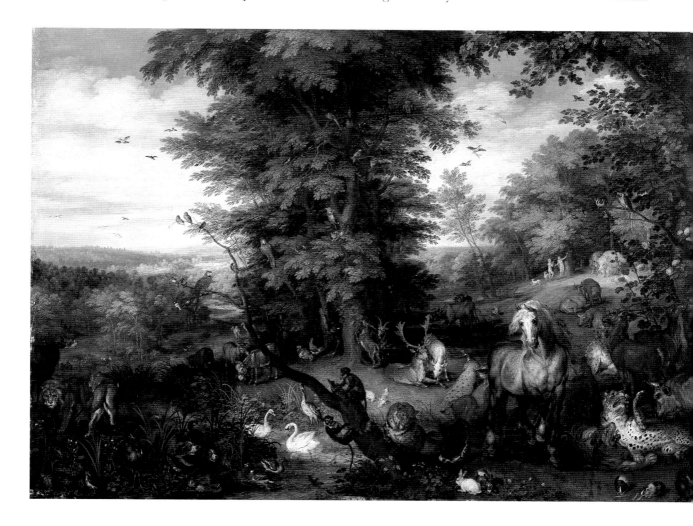

sive travel in Italy during the 1590s, visiting Naples, Rome and Milan, after which, during the first two decades of the seventeenth century, he went to Germany and to Prague.

Jan Breughel was a friend of Rubens and Van Dyck, but his style was markedly different owing to the small scale on which he preferred to work. His paintings are intensely concentrated with minute brush strokes and carefully finished surfaces incorporating a surprising amount of detail, which, like a miniature, is totally absorbing to the eye. The meticulous finish is partly due to the fact that these paintings are executed not on canvas or wood, but on thin sheets of beaten copper, which, like vellum, demands of the artist great intricacy and remarkable precision. Breughel painted *Adam and Eve in the Garden of Eden* in 1615 and his image of paradise recalls to mind the famous description in John Milton's *Paradise Lost*, which was published in 1667:

> Thus was this place
> A Happy rural seat of various view;
> Groves whose rich trees wept odorous gums and balm,
> Others whose fruit burnished with golden rind
> Hung amiable, Hesperian fables true,
> If true, here only, and of delicious taste:
> Betwixt them lawns, or level downs, and flocks
> Grazing the tender herb, were interposed,
> Or palmy hillock, or flow'ry lap
> Of some irriguous valley spread her store,
> Flow'rs of all hue, and without thorn the rose:
> Another side, umbrageous grots and caves
> Of cool recess, o'er which the mantling vine
> Lays forth her purple grape, and gently creeps
> Luxuriant; meanwhile, murmuring waters fall
> Down the slope hills, dispersed, or in a lake,
> That to the fringed bank with myrtle crowned
> Her crystal mirror holds, unite their streams.
> The birds their quire apply; airs, vernal airs,
> Breathing the smell of field and grove, attune
> The trembling leaves, while universal Pan,
> Knit with the Graces and the Hours in dance,
> Led on th'eternal spring.[1]

Both Breughel and Milton were forced to exercise their imagination in bringing the Garden of Eden before our eyes. The painter combines the careful depiction of a profusion of foliage and closely observed flowers

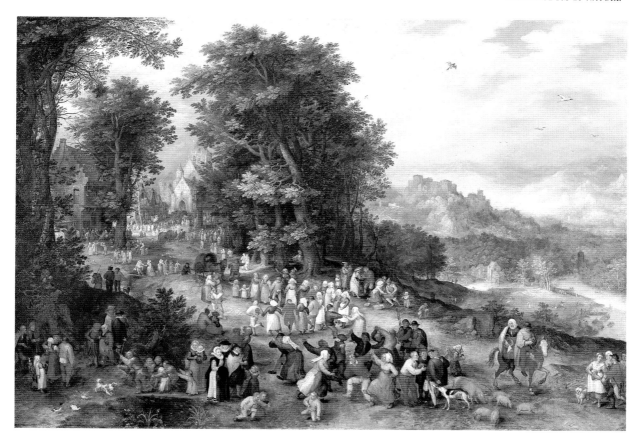

FIG. 59
Jan Breughel the Elder: *A Flemish Fair*, 1600

with more formal atmospheric passages for the sky and the far distance. Contained within this landscape is a veritable menagerie of exotic birds and wild beasts, together with more domesticated species such as dogs, horses, ducks and rabbits. Most of these animals Breughel could have drawn from life, or else purloined from other artists such as Rubens, from whom he borrowed the pose of the lions and the horses. Adam and Eve are not given a great deal of prominence within this paradise and they are indeed almost concealed by their surroundings in the middle distance. The moment shown is the Fall of Man when Eve takes the fruit of the Tree of Knowledge from the serpent and offers it to Adam.[2] The image of the Garden of Eden depicted by Jan Breughel is one of total harmony. It is a paradise lost that man has always longed to regain.

The artist's rendering of the Garden of Eden may have been the result of an act of imagination, but imagination, if it is to be at all potent, has to be based on experience. In this respect another painting by Jan Breughel, slightly earlier in date, needs to be considered. On the same scale and in the same style as *Adam and Eve in the Garden of Eden*, but painted in 1600, *A Flemish Fair* (FIG. 59) is totally different in subject and conception. Here, instead of the animals and birds populating paradise, are the inhabitants of a village enjoying themselves at a festival. The influence of the artist's father, Pieter Bruegel the Elder, is evident in the dancing peasants, whose activities not only provide anecdotal interest, but also lead the eye back into the distance towards the village itself, which is dominated by a church. The use of colour, drawing and shifts from light to dark enliven this area of the picture with pattern, rhythm and movement.

Contrasting this crowded area is the view on the right into the distance, past a neighbouring town perched on a hill towards the mountains. This part of the picture is dominated by a feeling of comparative calm and stillness. The beauties of nature are rendered with mellifluous tones of blue, silver and grey.

It was this kind of painting that made Jan Breughel the Elder one of the most popular artists of the day in Antwerp, where his fame was not far below that of Rubens and Van Dyck. However, *A Flemish Fair* is not, strictly speaking, pure landscape and the figures denote another dimension. There are, for example, social distinctions apparent between the well-dressed family in the foreground left of the centre and the dancing peasants. Yet other social distinctions are present in the picture, such as between those who have carts or ride horses and those who walk.

Landscape painting is not always as innocent as it seems and it often raises issues reflecting society as a whole. *The Garden of Eden* represents the yearning for paradise; what in the Renaissance was termed the Golden Age or during later centuries the Ideal. *A Flemish Fair*, on the other hand, demonstrates how hard it is to find paradise on earth. It might be found fleetingly in a few moments of celebration, but it is always subject to constraints (not all of them necessarily bad) imposed by society, forcing a closer definition of individual relationships or of man's relationship with the environment.

Fortunately, that environment has for the most part been an inspirational force, and it can be advocated that the finest landscape painting always combines imagination with observation. Claude Lorrain is an artist who created an arcadian world derived from close observation of nature and a knowledge of the classical past. Claude was born in France in 1600, but spent most of his long life in Italy, based in Rome, where he trained first as a pastry cook. The luxuriant countryside of the Campagna, characterised by lush greens and warm earth browns seen under a golden light, became the hallmark of his paintings and the touchstone of the ideal landscape so cherished by British collectors during the eighteenth century.

George IV, towards the end of his reign, bought a painting of great beauty by Claude – *Coast Scene with the Rape of Europa* dating from 1667 (FIG. 60). It is in the artist's most developed style and is one of the numerous mythological themes that he favoured. The literary source that he used for

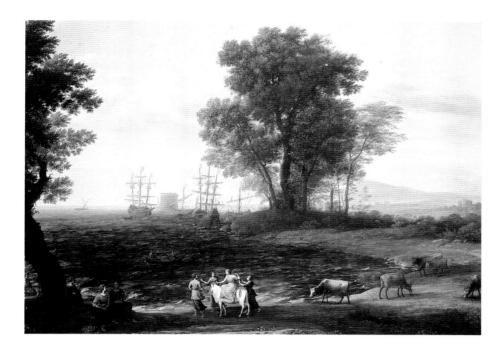

FIG. 60
Claude Lorrain: *Coast Scene
with the Rape of Europa*, 1667

such subjects is Ovid's *Metamorphoses*, which he resorted to as often as he
did to the *Aeneid* of Virgil for historical themes. Claude was painting for
patrons who were intellectuals and who undoubtedly had a working knowledge of such writers as Ovid and Virgil.

Ovid's poetic account of the Rape of Europa is highly charged. He
tells of Jupiter's love for Europa, the daughter of Agenor, and how, in order
to seduce her, the god disguises himself as a bull and joins her on the
seashore, where Europa is playing with her attendants:

> His hide was white as untrodden snow, snow not yet melted by the
> rainy south wind. The muscles stood out on his neck, and deep
> folds of skin hung along his flanks. His horns were very small, it is
> true, but so beautifully made that you could swear that they were the
> work of an artist, more polished and shining than any jewel. There
> was no menace in the set of his head or in his eyes; he looked
> completely placid.
>
> Agenor's daughter was filled with admiration for one so
> handsome and so friendly. But, gentle though he seemed, she was
> afraid at first to touch him; then she went close, and held out flowers
> to his shining lips. The lover was delighted and, until he could achieve
> his hoped for pleasure, kissed her hands. He could scarcely wait for
> the rest, only with great difficulty did he restrain himself.
>
> Now he frolicked and played on the green turf, now lay down,
> all snowy white on the yellow sand. Gradually the princess lost her

fear, and with her innocent hands she stroked his breast when he offered it for her caress, and hung fresh garlands on his horns; till finally she even ventured to mount the bull, little knowing on whose back she was resting.[3]

The story concludes with the bull carrying Europa out to sea.

The elements of Claude's composition are carefully ordered, but with shifts in scale that suggest a remote time and place. The trees on the left act as a piece of stage scenery from which the eye moves along the gentle curve of the cove until it reaches another group of trees that dominates the middle distance. On either side of these trees are the ships at anchor by a fortification with the horizon beyond, and to the right there is a view towards distant mountains. It is a spacious, simplified composition comprising languorous rhythms. There is a careful balance between the ideal and the real, so that the atmosphere is best described as ethereal. Claude has cleverly combined the tradition of marine painting with the pastoral,

FIG. 60A
Claude Lorrain: *Coast Scene with the Rape of Europa*, 1667 (detail)

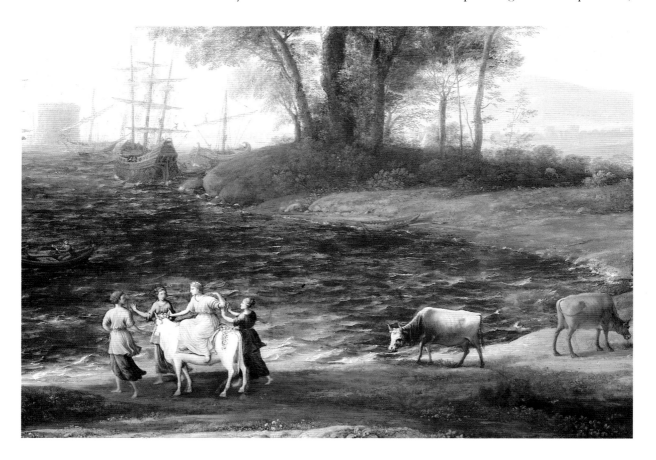

over both of which he has complete mastery. His skill lies in the use of tones. The sense of distance and the creation of atmosphere stem from the subtle play between the blues and the greens which give the painting an overall silvery shimmer.

Claude's technical ability is even more apparent in the attention to detail, extending from the foliage, the flowers in the foreground, the wave-lets lapping the shore which out at sea turn to spray when striking the hulls of the vessels, the garlands set out against the white bull, and even the bristles along the flanks of the grazing cattle (FIG. 60A). The effect of such detailing is of course cumulative. It all contributes towards the general effect, as evening approaches, of a cool breeze wafting off the sea, enjoyed by Europa and her servants, who pass the time refreshing themselves after a hot day. It is not difficult to appreciate why Claude Lorrain was a popular painter with those who made the Grand Tour. This is the landscape of association distilled in the imagination.

Another famous story found in Ovid's *Metamorphoses* is *Diana and Act-aeon*, a subject which is best represented in the Royal Collection by a painting that is by, perhaps somewhat surprisingly, Gainsborough (FIG. 61).

FIG. 61
Thomas Gainsborough:
Diana and Actaeon, c. 1785

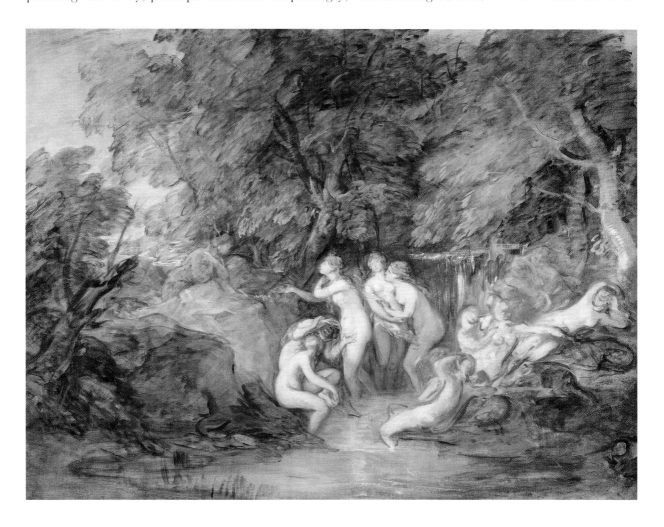

It is, in fact, the only subject from classical mythology that the artist ever attempted. The painting could be described as unfinished, but it might be more accurate to say that Gainsborough brought to it the degree of finish that he found to be the most appropriate. It is a late work dating from the 1780s and, interestingly, this large picture remained in the artist's studio until his death in 1788. It was subsequently bought for George IV at a price of two pounds three shillings.

The story of Diana and Actaeon involves sex, cruelty and violence. It is another highly poetic passage in the *Metamorphoses*:

There was a valley, thickly overgrown with pitchpine, and with sharp-needled cypress trees. It was called Gargaphie, and was sacred to Diana, the goddess of the hunt. Far in its depths lay a woodland cave, which no hand of man had wrought; but nature by her own devices had imitated art. She had carved a natural arch from the living stone and the soft tufa rocks. On the right hand was a murmuring spring of clear water, spreading out into a wide pool with grassy banks. Here the goddess, when she was tired with hunting in the woods, used to bathe her fastidious limbs in the pure water. When she entered the grotto she handed her javelin to one of the nymphs, who acted as her armour-bearer, along with her quiver and bow, unstrung . . . another attendant, more skilled than the rest . . . gathered up the tresses which lay scattered on the goddess's shoulders, and bound them into a knot, though her own hair hung loose . . . .

Now while Diana was bathing there in her stream, as usual, the grandson of Cadmus [Actaeon], who had for the present abandoned his hunting, came wandering with hesitant steps through this wood which he had never seen before. He reached the grove . . . and entered the cave, which was moist with spray. The nymphs, discovered in their nakedness, beat their breasts at the sight of a man, and filled all the grove with their sudden outcry. Crowding round Diana, they sheltered her with their own bodies, but the goddess was taller than they, head and shoulders above them all. When she was caught unclad, a blush mantled her cheeks, as bright as when clouds reflect the sun's rays, as bright as rosy dawn. . . . She wished she had her arrows ready to hand: instead, she caught up a handful of the water which she did have, and threw it in the young man's face. As she sprinkled his hair with the vengeful drops she also spoke these words . . . 'Now, if you can, you may tell how you saw me when I was undressed.' She uttered no more threats, but made the horns of a long-lived stag sprout where she had scattered the water on his brow. She lengthened his neck, brought the tips of his ears to a point, changed his hands to feet, his arms to long legs, and covered his body with a dappled skin. Then she put panic fear in his heart as well. The hero fled . . . . When he glimpsed his face and horns, reflected in the water . . . he groaned – that was all the voice he had – and tears ran down his changed cheeks. . . . What was he to do . . . ?

The pack . . . swarmed over the rocks and crags. . . . Actaeon fled where he had himself so often pursued his own quarry, fled, alas, before his own faithful hounds. . . . First Melanchaetes fastened his teeth in his master's back, then Theridamas and Oresitrophus. . . . While they held their master down, the rest of the pack gathered, and sank their teeth in his body, till there was no place left for tearing. . . . But his friends, not knowing what they did, urged on the ravening mob . . . and shouted for Actaeon, as if he were not there . . . . They lamented that their leader was absent, and that his slowness prevented him from seeing the booty that chance had offered. Actaeon turned his head at the sound of his name. Well might he wish to be absent, but he was all too surely present. . . . Only when he had been despatched by wounds innumerable, so men say, was the anger of Diana, the quiver-bearing goddess, appeased.[4]

Gainsborough's broad handling, undoubtedly influenced by the famous mythological paintings by Titian (FIG. 62), suggests something of the savagery and primitiveness of the story. The peculiar, almost tadpole shapes of the female forms help to create the feeling of a distant, alien world (FIG. 61A). Strangely, these forms seem to anticipate the figure types of Cézanne in the *Large Bathers* (Philadelphia, Museum of Art), Matisse in *Luxe, Calme et Volupté* (Paris, Private Collection), or even Picasso in *Demoiselles d'Avignon* (New York, Museum of Modern Art) – all painted within a few years of each other at the beginning of this century and marking one of the watersheds in the evolution of modern painting.

Gainsborough chooses the most dramatic moment of the story as Diana splashes Actaeon, who immediately begins to sprout antlers. The flurry of movement, the sense that animal forces are about to be unleashed, is hinted at by the agitated brush strokes and quickened rhythms. At first the painting looks almost monochromatic, but there is, in fact, a considerable amount of unified colour – rust reds, olive greens, pale yellows and ochres – against which Actaeon is camouflaged and the naked nymphs offset. Yet, Gainsborough was principally interested in tamed nature (FIG. 63). His passion for landscape was well-known:

I'm sick of Portraits and wish very much to take my Viol da Gamba

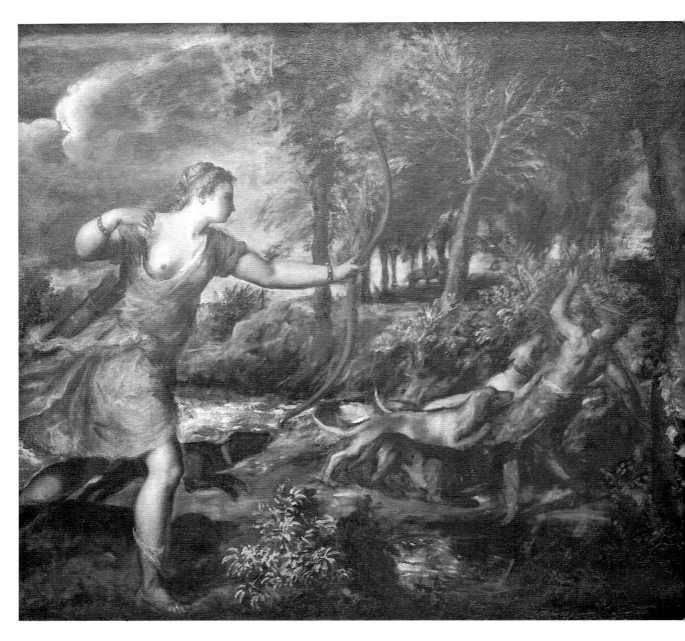

FIG. 62
Titian: *The Death of Actaeon,*
1570–75

FIG. 63
Thomas Gainsborough:
*Henry, Duke of Cumberland,
with the Duchess of
Cumberland and Lady
Elizabeth Luttrell,* 1783–5

and walk off to some sweet village where I can paint landscapes and enjoy the fag end of life in quietness and ease.[5]

Unlike Sir Joshua Reynolds, Gainsborough was a wholly spontaneous individual. He enjoyed music and had a lust for life, frequently celebrating the completion of a painting with a drinking bout.

His was undoubtedly a fresh and open response to nature, but he then transformed it in the studio into a well-ordered and picturesque landscape. The setting for Diana and Actaeon is recognisable as any English glade.

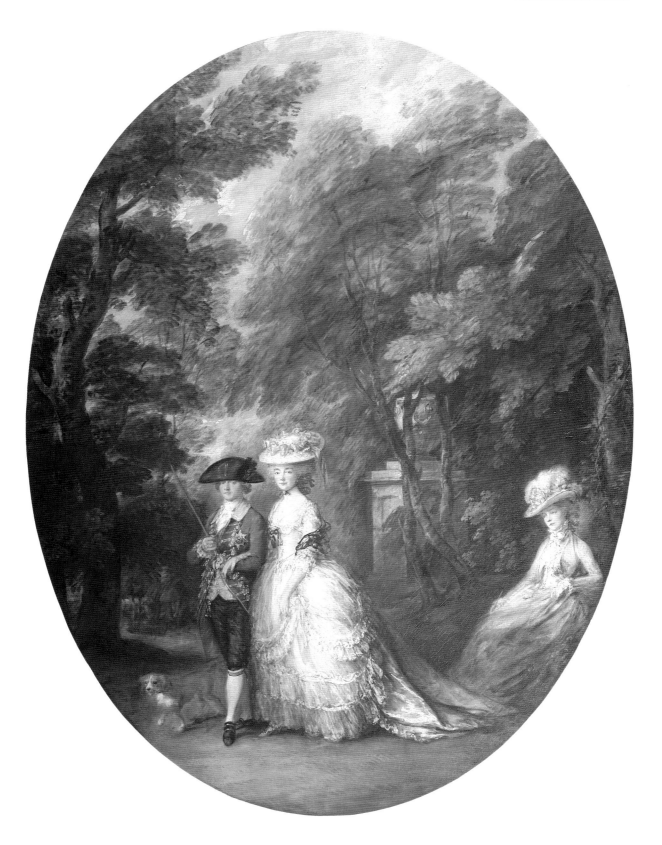

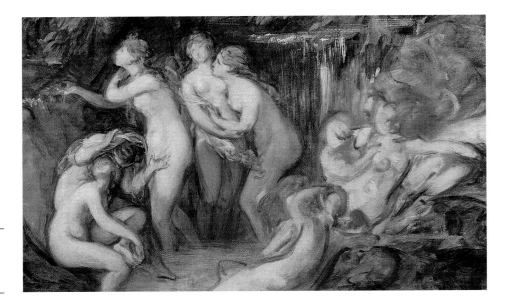

The trees have thick trunks and heavy branches with thick foliage. The pool in which the goddess bathes with her nymphs has clear and transparent water supplied by a stream that cascades in a small waterfall down a rock face – a marvellous passage of painting where the water resembles stretched silk (FIG. 61A). In a famous pronouncement on art made to one of his patrons who had asked for a painted view of his park, Gainsborough declared that landscape painting could not be like portraiture. In portraiture the artist sought for a close resemblance and some indication of character; in landscape painting, on the other hand, imitation or mere transcription was not sufficient in itself.

> Mr Gainsborough presents his humble respects to Lord Hardwicke, and shall always think it an honour to be employ'd in anything for His Lordship; but with regard to *real views* from Nature in this country, he has never seen any place that affords a subject equal to the poorest imitations of Gaspar [Poussin] or Claude. . . . Mr Gainsborough hopes Lord Hardwicke will not mistake his meaning, but if his Lordship wishes to have anything tollerable of the name of Gainsborough, the subject altogether as well as the figures, etc., must be of his own brain; otherwise Lord Hardwicke will only pay for encouraging a man out of his way, and had much better buy a picture of some of the good Old Masters.[6]

It is the application of imagination (possibly, if you like, merely locating the scene of Diana and Actaeon somewhere in Suffolk) that makes this late picture by Gainsborough so significant.

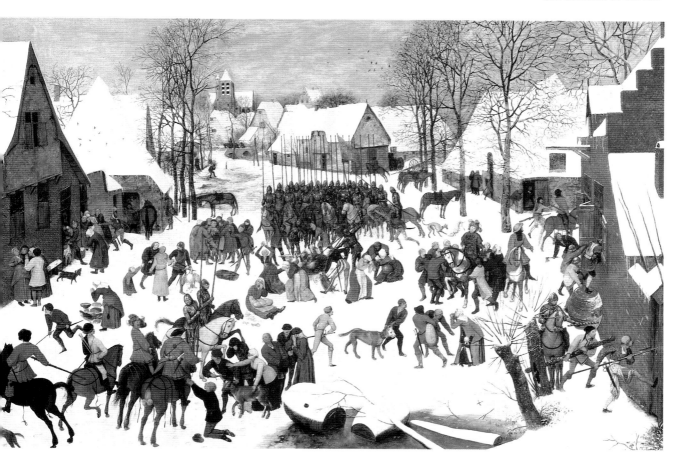

FIG. 64
Pieter Bruegel the Elder:
The Massacre of the Innocents,
c. 1565

Two other landscapes in the Royal Collection reveal the exercise of artistic imagination, but in totally different ways. The first is by Pieter Bruegel the Elder, the father of Jan Breughel, who worked in the Netherlands during the sixteenth century. His landscapes were painted in different circumstances. By the time of his maturity, they are set in a specific context that makes them topical and gives them a political significance. Or, as Kenneth Clark expressed it:

> He begins with proverbs and allegories, in which landscape is a
> setting and an accessory; he evolves to the great landscapes in which
> the accidents of human life are one with the weather and the seasons.[7]

The *Massacre of the Innocents* was painted in about 1565 (FIG. 64). Ostensibly, the subject is the slaughter of all the newly born children in the village of Bethlehem.[8] The Roman soldiers who carried out this brutal attack were acting under the orders of Herod, King of Judaea, who was also the representative of the Roman Empire. What is depicted, therefore, is the official political response to the news of Christ's birth.

It is a scene of naked aggression, symbolised by the column of mounted soldiers entering the village. Their arrival has been announced on the right by the mounted herald wearing a tabard and on the left by the two mounted civil servants in red, who have been sent to witness the brutal proceedings. Against such odds the villagers are helpless: pleading and remonstration are inadequate responses to weapons of steel brandished by professional killers.

Bruegel depicts a wide range of carefully observed figures that can be read as a pattern of movement and colour across the snow. The artist's skill as a draughtsman is everywhere apparent in the clear, springing out-lines, silhouetted forms, and vivid characterisation that runs the whole gamut of human emotion from fear, anguish, horror and pity to grim determination, outright brutality and sadism. So full of menace was this picture that early in its history (less than a hundred years after it was painted and possibly while it was still in the collection of Rudolf II of Prague), the subject was deliberately altered to become the sacking of a village, with animals substituted for the children. Recent restoration of the picture has revealed the forms of children beneath the animals, but for art historical reasons it was decided to retain the forms of both the animals and the children (FIG. 64A).

This is hardly Palestine. Bruegel has chosen to set the scene in a

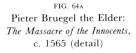

FIG. 64A
Pieter Bruegel the Elder:
The Massacre of the Innocents,
c. 1565 (detail)

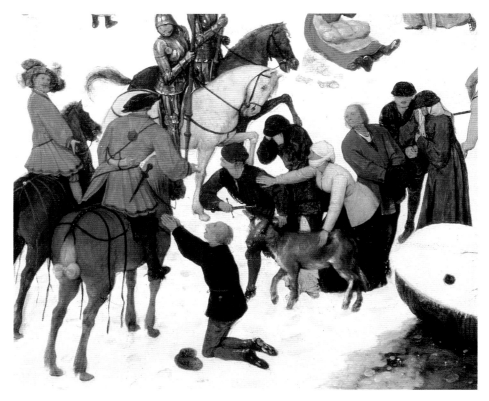

128

Netherlandish village in the grip of the severe winter of 1564–5, when it
was so cold that icebergs were seen in the North Sea and harbours were
frozen solid. All Bruegel's famous snow scenes, such as *The Hunters in the
Snow* (Vienna, Kunsthistorisches Museum), date from the late 1560s, and
few artists have depicted wintery conditions so convincingly – the way the
snow settles on roof-tops and trees, the imprint of footsteps, the slush of
melting snow, as well as the reflective qualities, even the muffled sounds.
A passage in the foreground showing barrels and planks frozen on the
surface of a pond has an oriental quality.

This picture was painted at the time when the Netherlands was under
Spanish domination. The atrocities committed by the representatives of
the Roman Empire can be equated with those of the Spanish occupying
forces under the command of the Duke of Alva. Scenes of oppression were
a common experience, just as in modern dictatorships there has been a
universal fear of the approach of footsteps and the knock on the door under
cover of darkness.

This Christmas scene, therefore, has an extra dimension and the
duality of the picture is vividly captured in the lower right-hand corner,
where soldiers break into the inn where Christ was born: they climb in
through windows and kick down doors, dislodging icicles as they do so
(FIG. 64B). With such details Bruegel heightens the drama, but at the same

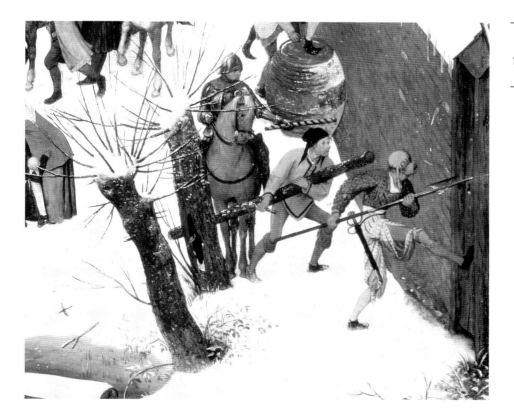

FIG. 64B
Pieter Bruegel the Elder:
The Massacre of the Innocents,
c. 1565 (detail)

time elsewhere in the painting he seems intent upon making an observation on man's place within the natural world. He shows us that this terrible crime has to be seen in a wider context, in which nature and individuals remain oblivious or unperturbed by such events: birds fly overhead, horses remain tethered to trees and on the left a man calmly dismounts and urinates against the side of a house. The principle of disassociation has been most effectively expressed in words in the poem by W. H. Auden, *Musée des Beaux Arts* (FIG. 65):

> About suffering they were never wrong,
> The Old Masters: how well they understood
> Its human position; how it takes place
> While someone else is eating or opening a window or just walking
>   dully along;
>   . . . In Bruegel's Icarus, for instance: how everything turns away
> Quite leisurely from the disaster; the ploughman may
> Have heard the splash, the forsaken cry,
> But for him it was not an important failure; the sun shone
> As it had to on the white legs disappearing into the green
> Water; and the expensive delicate ship that must have seen
> Something amazing, a boy falling out of the sky,
> Had somewhere to get to, and sailed calmly on.[9]

FIG. 65
Pieter Bruegel the Elder:
The Fall of Icarus, c. 1550

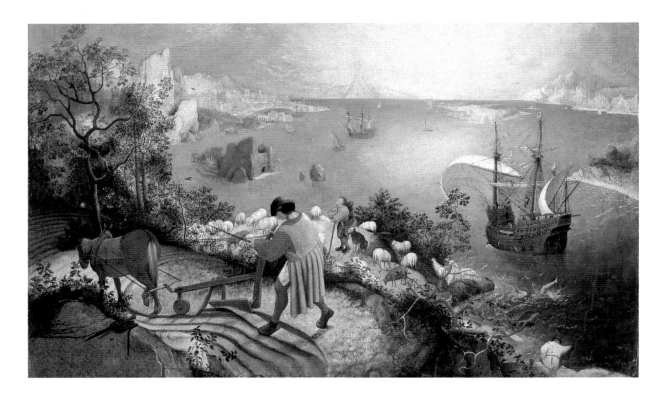

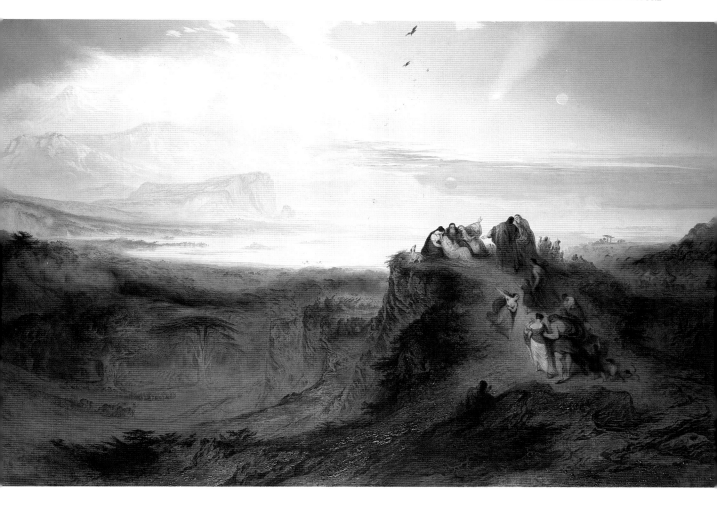

FIG. 66
John Martin: *The Eve of the Deluge*, 1840

Bruegel's landscapes are, in effect, a commentary on the human condition. While Bruegel sharpens the impact of *The Massacre of the Innocents* by reference to contemporary events, John Martin in *The Eve of the Deluge* (FIG. 66) resorts to science and theology to express his fears. Martin, like William Blake and J. M. W. Turner, was a visionary artist. Born in 1789, he painted cosmic themes on a suitably extravagant scale that both terrified and thrilled his contemporaries. He had humble beginnings in Newcastle-upon-Tyne as a herald painter to a coach builder and then, after he moved to London, as a painter on china and glass. His life was full of paradoxes. Financially, his paintings were successful, but academically they were rejected; he was practical and scientific in outlook, but lived in an imaginary world that can only be comprehended in terms of the cinema of D. W. Griffith, Cecil B. de Mille, William Wyler or Francis Ford Coppola; his paintings depict the unleashing of powerful forces dredged up from the depths of the mind, but at the same time these were buttressed by references to esoteric literary sources accompanied by his own explanations. As with many visionaries, there is often a great deal of sense buried within the marked eccentricity.

The Eve of the Deluge was acquired by Prince Albert in 1841 on the basis of a visit he had made to the artist's studio the year before when he saw *The Deluge* (Private Collection) and suggested that Martin paint related themes to form a sequence: *The Eve of the Deluge* and *The Assuaging of the Waters* (San Francisco, Museum of Art). The painter had previously depicted the *Coronation of Queen Victoria* and had hoped to become Historical Painter to the Queen.

The Eve of the Deluge illustrates a passage in the Book of Genesis where God despairs of the wickedness of man and determines that 'every thing that is on the earth shall die'.[10] The sins of man are equated with the revellers seen beneath the trees in the middle distance on the right. In the sky are the sun, the moon and the comet, a contiguity that foretells doom. On the peak of a distant mountain right of centre rising out of the ocean is the ark which will be the only means of escape from the deluge. In the foreground on the left is the dying Methuselah, confirming that the end is nigh. He is surrounded by Noah and his family, who alone will be spared. Methuselah instructs Noah to open the scroll written by his father Enoch so that he can compare the configurations in the sky of the sun, moon and comet foretelling Methuselah's death and the end of the world. It is likely

FIG. 67
Sir Peter Paul Rubens: *The Farm at Laeken*, c. 1617

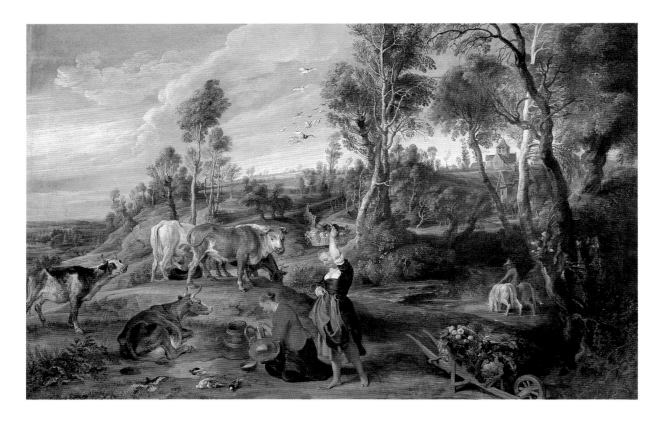

132

that Martin himself saw Napoleon's comet of 1811–12 and the return of Haley's comet in 1835, but otherwise he immersed himself in historical, religious and eschatological sources, which he discussed in the pamphlet he wrote to accompany the pictures in 1840. The result, however, is a landscape of the inner mind equated with nightmares and psychological disorders.

By contrast, there was another, more direct type of landscape which had come to prominence in northern Europe during the seventeenth century. Nature was first and foremost an inspirational force and its depiction alone, without a specific context, now gained a certain credibility. No artist has relished the fecundity of nature as much as the Flemish painter Rubens. The early landscape known as *The Farm at Laeken* (FIG. 67), dating from c. 1617 and acquired by George IV in 1821 towards the end of his life, has an enormous range of reference. Set on a hillside near a farm by a village church that can be seen through the trees, the foreground is filled with activity: cows are tended, horses drink at a stream, vegetables are stacked in a wheelbarrow, baskets of fruit are purveyed, milk is poured from an elegant jug, birds peck at the ground. The sheer abundance of nature, so carefully observed by Rubens in his drawings, is thus made apparent. This is equally true in the wind tossing the branches of the trees, the wide range of plant life, the richness of the foliage, and the birds soaring in the air. The clear light defines all these different forms and lends them greater variety. The result is a pantheistic celebration of nature which is matched by the sheer vitality of Rubens' brushwork, the vibrancy of his colour and the panache of his compositional power that allows him to contain so much energy within a painting of fairly limited dimensions. This is a baroque landscape full of kinetic energy matched only by the soaring, flowing, twisting rhythm of the artist's religious works.

Rubens painted only a small number of pure landscapes, but few painters have so successfully captured the essence of nature. This may be because, as the owner of the manorial estate of Het Steen near Malines, Rubens had a genuine interest in the countryside. He acquired the estate in 1635 and his ownership of it symbolises both his love of nature and his social status. The landscapes of *Winter* (FIG. 68) and *Summer* (FIG. 69) also reveal an artist who knows about the intensity of the cold and the sharpened senses of the early morning.

If, on looking at a landscape painting by Rubens, the viewer feels at one with nature to the extent of being part of the landscape, the viewer in Dutch seventeenth-century painting moves with the artist through the landscape. Jacob van Ruisdael, Meyndert Hobbema and Aelbert Cuyp, all Dutch seventeenth-century artists admired by George IV, chose not to exercise their imagination so much as to stress topographical fidelity and

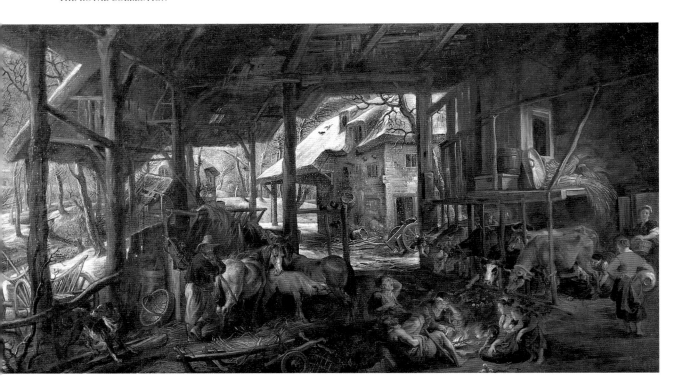

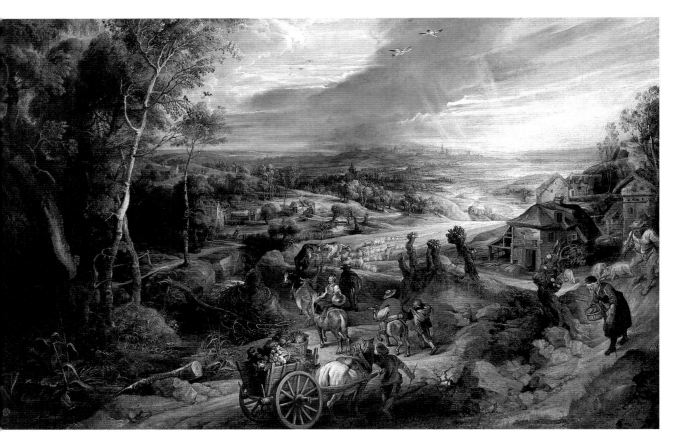

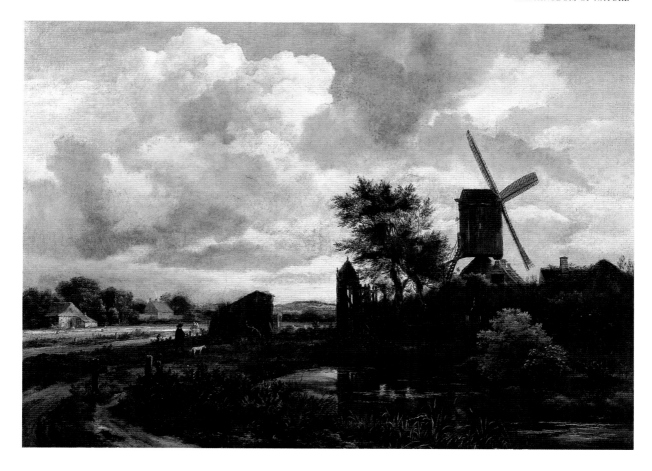

the realistic representation of nature. This was an approach that led ultimately to the development of Impressionism in the nineteenth century.

Windmill by a Stream (c. 1646, FIG. 70) is an early work by Ruisdael, who
was born in Haarlem, but later (c. 1656) moved to Amsterdam. This
picture impressed John Constable when it was shown at the Academy in
1821; he remarked that he 'could all but see the eels in the pools of water
– that there were acres of sky exposed'.[11] It appeals because of its accumulation of detail, specifically of trees, vegetation, clouds scudding across the
sky, reflections in the water and the sun momentarily bursting through to
accent a part of the landscape as though catching it in a spotlight. All is
movement and atmosphere: there is dampness in the air, moisture under
foot, smoke curling upwards; a breeze blows, rain clouds gather. Even
more significant, perhaps, is the fact that there is a great deal of evidence
of clearly defined human activity. This is a visual record of a thriving
mercantile republic. The windmill itself is a primary piece of evidence in
establishing the proper terms of reference for this painting, but so also is
the man walking his dog, the people working in the bleaching fields on the
left and the various forms of buildings. The windmill is flanked by a tall

FIG. 70
Jacob van Ruisdael:
Windmill by a Stream, c. 1646

FIG. 68
Sir Peter Paul Rubens:
Winter, c. 1620

FIG. 69
Sir Peter Paul Rubens:
Summer, c. 1620

135

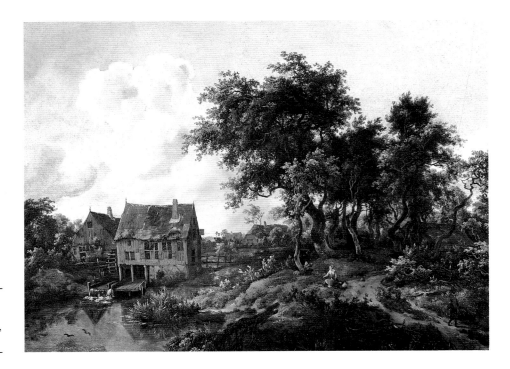

FIG. 71
Meyndert Hobbema:
Watermill beside a Woody Lane,
166(5 or 8)

tree balancing the achievements of man against those of nature itself.

Hobbema, a pupil of Jacob van Ruisdael, found a similar fascination in the landscape, but he had a sunnier disposition. Indeed, in 1668 he became a wine gauger of the Amsterdam octroi, which was a well-paid job, and he almost gave up painting altogether. His compositions are light, airy and luminous, gaining energy as much from the small feathery brush strokes as from the sunlight (FIG. 71). By contrast, *Wooded Landscape with Travellers*, which was painted in 1668, reveals tensions in rural society as the figures in the foreground are begging from the travellers moving through the countryside (FIG. 72).

Such tensions are rarely apparent in the work of Aelbert Cuyp, by whom there are several paintings in the Royal Collection, acquired by George IV. Dating from the late 1650s, *Evening Landscape* (FIG. 73) is a typical work with its gentle, languid rhythms, soft tones and even brush strokes. The artist never travelled to Italy, but he was influenced by those Dutch artists who had, just as the mountains on the right in this picture are inspired by his own journey up the Rhine to the German border. All is calm in this landscape. Nature is embalmed by a golden light: animals and people linger, enjoying the warm evening air.

Hazlitt wrote evocatively of Cuyp's paintings in his *Sketches of the Principal Galleries in England* after seeing *A River Landscape* in the Dulwich Picture Gallery. 'You may lay your finger on the canvas, but inches of dewy vapour and sunshine are between you and the objects you survey.'[12] The smoothness of the surface of *A River Landscape* reminded Hazlitt of the 'down of an unripe nectarine'.[13] The same description could be applied to *Evening Landscape*.

Cuyp shows man and nature in perfect harmony. His paintings reflect the happiness of his own life, spent in Dordrecht, where he was content to observe the numerous activities of river life from the banks of the Merwade and the Maas. His marriage in 1650 to a wealthy woman and his successful pursuit of a career in public life led to a decline in his artistic output. Something of Cuyp's social position is evident from the prominence in his paintings of fashionable dress, horses, servants, castles and country estates. It is not without significance that his works were being eagerly bought at the end of the eighteenth century by British collectors. In fact, at the sale in Dordrecht in 1785 of the collection of J. van der Linden van Slingeland, who owned over twenty paintings by the artist, it was the British who indirectly became the principal 'beneficiaries', thereby leaving comparatively few examples of Cuyp's work in Holland.[14] After the Linden van Slingeland sale, for example, *Evening Landscape* was in the collection of Jan Gildemeester and Sir Francis Baring before being acquired by George IV.

The attraction of Cuyp's pictures for British collectors of that date lay in his subject matter, in so far as their own way of life on country estates and their own social ideals were mirrored in these peaceful images. To those collectors, at least, it must have seemed as though the paradise lost in Jan Breughel's *Adam and Eve in the Garden of Eden* had been regained in such works as *Evening Landscape*.

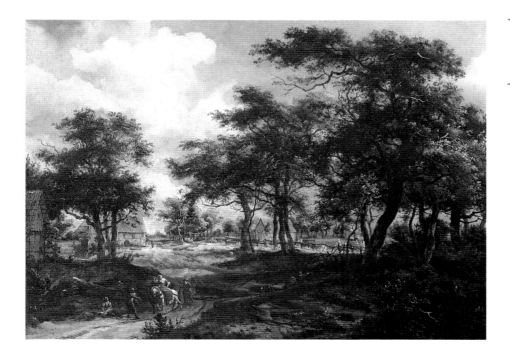

FIG. 72
Meyndert Hobbema:
Wooded Landscape with Travellers, 1668

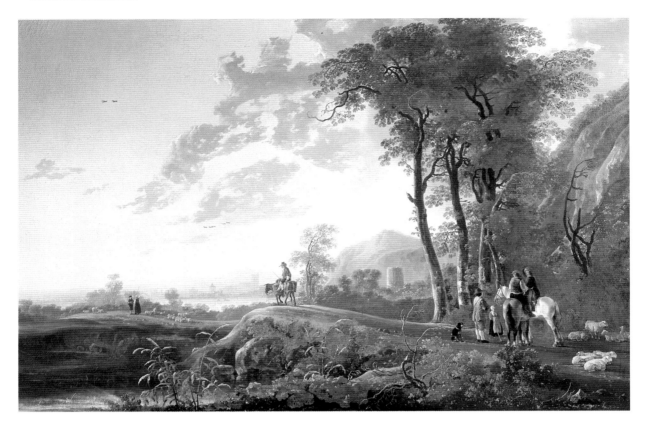

FIG. 73
Aelbert Cuyp: *An Evening Landscape*, 1655–60

FIG. 75
John Wootton: *A View of Henley-on-Thames*, c. 1742–3

FIG. 74
John Wootton: *A View of Park Place*, c. 1742–3

The impetus for the development of landscape painting in Britain during the eighteenth century came from artists such as Claude Lorrain and Dutch seventeenth-century painting in its various guises. Indeed, the earliest patrons of British landscape painters were those who liked the works of Jan Breughel, Claude, Poussin, Gaspar Dughet, Salvator Rosa, Rubens and Teniers early on in the century, and it was their counterparts only a few decades later who added to their walls works by Ruisdael, Hobbema and Cuyp.

Frederick, Prince of Wales, the father of George III, took a keen interest in British painters. In the early 1740s he commissioned John Wootton to paint views of his estate, Park Place, near Henley-on-Thames. Wootton was primarily known as a sporting artist and military painter and he was frequently employed in that capacity to provide decorative schemes for the hallways or dining rooms of great country houses such as Althorp, Longleat and Badminton. The views of Park Place, however, are outstanding early examples of landscape painting in Britain (FIGS. 74–75). Horace Walpole later described Park Place as 'one of the most charming places in England' where 'Pan and the Sylvan deities seem to have made it their favourite residence and Father Thames enobles it by his fair stream.'[15] Wootton provides a high degree of topographical accuracy in the rendering

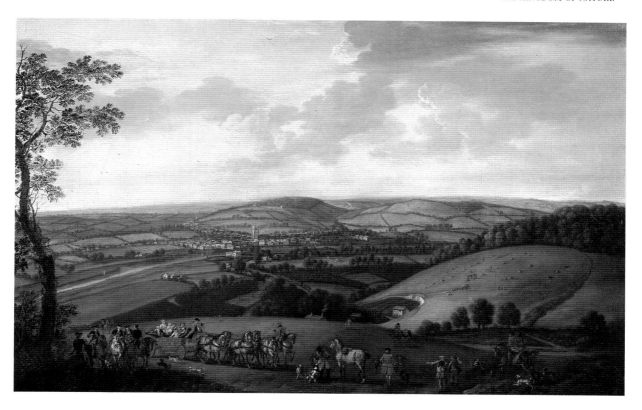

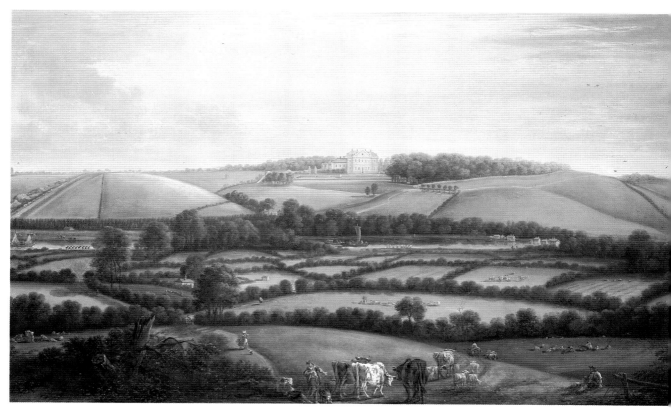

of the shapely hillsides, the town and the River Thames, but one is also aware to what extent this is an agrarian society with the patterned fields, gates, roads and barges. This is a landscape that not only evokes Walpole's poetic response, but also informs us about eighteenth-century economics. The principal figures – the family and friends of Frederick, Prince of Wales – are really subsidiary, lending only an anecdotal interest. It is evident, for instance, that Frederick, Prince of Wales, is about to go hunting, the traditional sport of kings, but these figures are by no means the subject of the picture.

The relationship between royalty and hunting has clear historical and social origins. To hunt successfully in the field was as important as commanding military forces. Both demanded courage and skill signifying powers of leadership. The purpose of hunting – to seek out and kill a quarry – has through the centuries also been linked to economic factors which are in turn connected with the laws of nature. Hunting scenes in the Royal Collection, therefore, span the centuries, beginning with Robert Peake's depiction of Henry, Prince of Wales, with the Earl of Essex, painted c. 1605. The prince is about to issue the *coup de grâce* to a stag (FIG. 5). The tradition can be traced through the eighteenth century (FIG. 79) to Queen Victoria and Prince Albert in Sir Edwin Landseer's *Royal Sports on Hill and Loch* and on to Edward VII either shooting pheasants at Sandringham or tigers in India.

The roots of British landscape painting lie in the topographical tradition, but they are also linked to patronage. The same may be said of animal painting. Both tradition and patronage can be found in such a painting as *The Duke of Cumberland visiting his Stud* by William Marlow and Sawrey Gilpin (FIG. 76). William Augustus, Duke of Cumberland, was the brother of Frederick, Prince of Wales, and therefore one of George III's uncles. He was an outstanding soldier, and also passionate about horses. After he was made Ranger of Windsor Forest and the Great Park in 1746, he established his stud. The painting shows Windsor Castle from the south looking up the Long Walk. The duke is inspecting his horses, which in this joint work were painted by Sawrey Gilpin.

As a horse painter Gilpin was surpassed by George Stubbs, from whom George IV commissioned several works during the 1790s. George IV was passionate about riding, hunting and horse racing. Some of his greatest debts were accumulated on horses, but his career on the turf ended in 1791 in a scandal at Newmarket. His extravagant lifestyle meant that he eventually grew too heavy to hunt or to ride at all. Before weight became a problem, however, Stubbs painted the Prince of Wales out riding by the Serpentine in Hyde Park (FIG. 77); he also portrayed some of the prince's friends, including Lady Lade – a woman of obscure origins, dubious morals

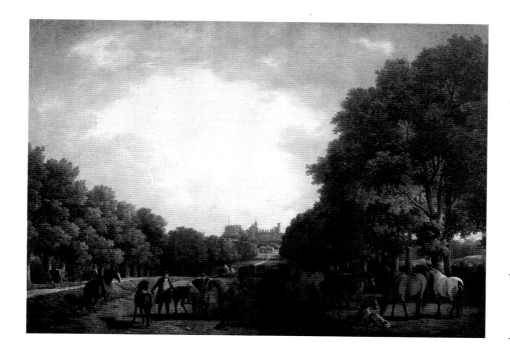

FIG. 76
William Marlow & Sawrey
Gilpin: *The Duke of
Cumberland visiting his Stud,*
c. 1764

FIG. 77
George Stubbs: *George IV
when Prince of Wales,* 1791

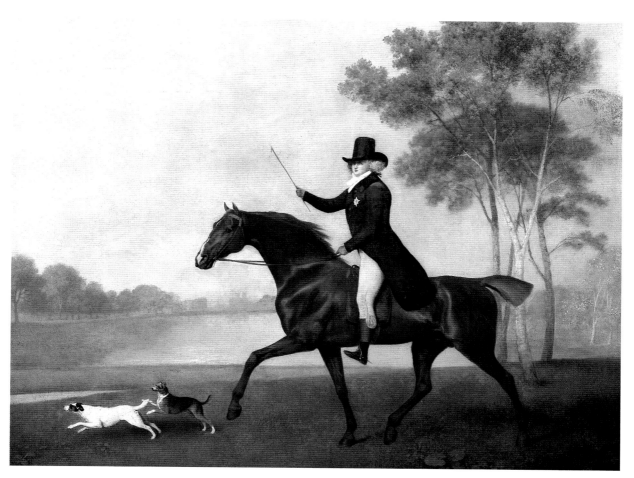

and foul language. Like her husband, Sir John Lade, she was a brilliant horsewoman. It was from the Lades that George IV bought his horses and with them he discussed equestrian matters. He was surprisingly loyal to them in the face of a great deal of adverse criticism and granted them an annual pension. The Lord Chancellor, Lord Thurlow, on being invited to dine with George IV in 1805 and discovering that Sir John Lade was to be a fellow guest, remarked, 'I have, Sir, no objection to Sir John Lade in his proper place, which I take to be your Royal Highness's coach-box, and not your table.'[16]

Stubbs, of course, buttresses his art with scientific investigation. His famous drawings on the *Anatomy of the Horse*, published in 1766 towards the end of his life, reveal the extent of his investigations (FIG. 78), but in his paintings this knowledge takes on a different dimension. *William Anderson*

FIG. 78
George Stubbs: *Finished Study for the Fifth Anatomical Table*, c. 1756–7

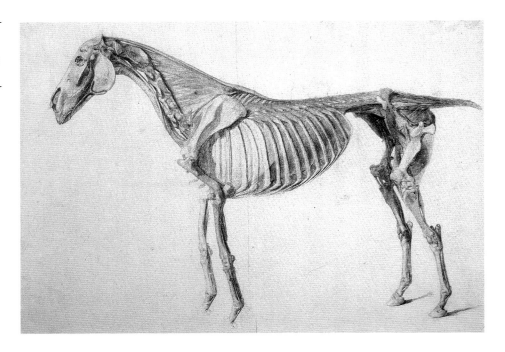

FIG. 78
George Stubbs: *Finished Study for the Fifth Anatomical Table*, c. 1756–7

with Two Saddle Horses of 1793 shows George IV's groom dressed in royal livery, leading a horse which has presumably been saddled up for the king to ride (FIG. 79). The scene is set on the Downs at Brighton. Such was George IV's horsemanship at this stage of his life that he is recorded on one occasion as having ridden from London to Brighton and back, a distance of 108 miles, in ten hours. Stubbs glories in the power and beauty of these animals silhouetted against a huge expanse of sky. The compositional emphasis is on the horizontal as the easy, fluid movement of the horses moving from left to right is emphasised by the gentle, undulating landscape. The only verticals are the figure of William Anderson and the trees seen in the middle distance. Otherwise, the eye is totally absorbed by the rhythm of the horses, the interlocking patterns of their flanks forming a unified design. This is a more subtle depiction than anything by Gilpin. It is, in fact, science translated into art, and the effect is one of poetic intensity.

Stubbs was not the only painter of horses who worked for George IV and it is interesting to compare how other artists treated the same subject. Ben Marshall (FIG. 80), for instance, stressed the sporting element and so his pictures are given a sharper, more closely defined context, whereas James Ward (FIG. 81) emphasised the musculature and compacted energy of the horse with Windsor Castle in the distance. Ward's animals positively quiver with tension. The muscles twitch in an expression of power rarely restrained and a wildness that is barely tamed.

By contrast, J. F. Herring, who worked for Queen Victoria and Prince

FIG. 79
George Stubbs: *William Anderson with Two Saddle Horses*, 1793

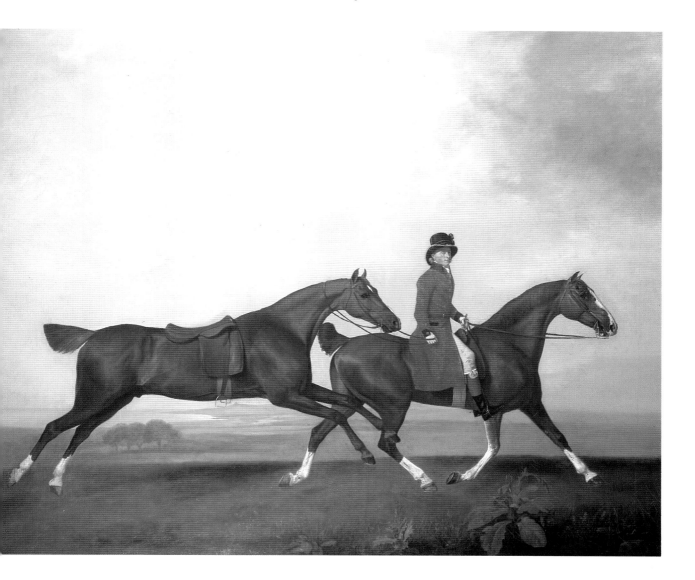

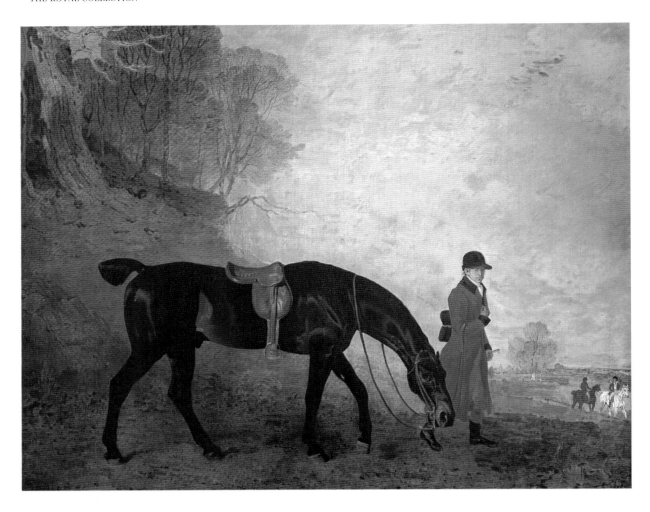

FIG. 80
Benjamin Marshall:
Curricle with a Huntsman,
c. 1794

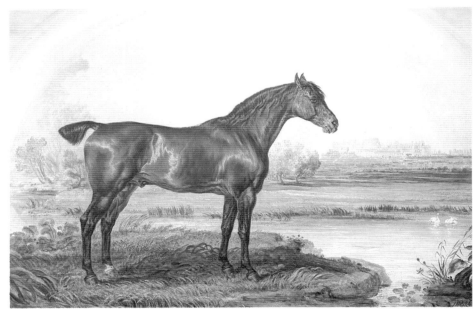

FIG. 81
James Ward: *Nonpareil*,
1824

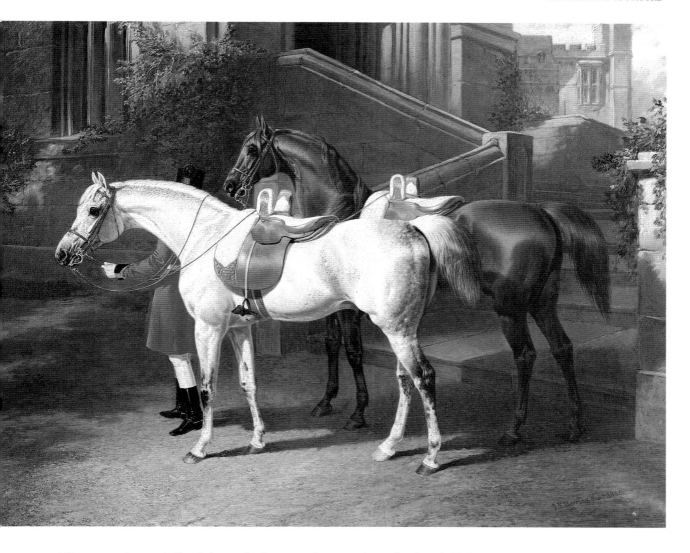

FIG. 82
John Frederick Herring:
Tajar and Hammon, 1845

Albert, and specialised in painting racehorses, has depicted Tajar and Hammon (FIG. 82) saddled up and patiently waiting for their riders in the precincts of Windsor Castle. It is a calm, almost reflective composition, though not without humour in the treatment of the groom hidden between the two horses.

George IV was not only interested in horses. Like many of his Tudor and Stuart forebears he was fascinated by exotic animals. Queen Anne had acquired a number of pictures by a Hungarian painter, Jakob Bogdani, who specialised in flower and bird paintings. Bogdani had settled in London in 1688 and first worked for William III. The birds he painted were kept in an aviary formed by Admiral George Churchill, younger brother of the first Duke of Marlborough, situated in what was then known as the Little Park at Windsor (near the present Dairy at Frogmore). George Churchill was a friend of Queen Anne's husband, Prince George of Denmark. He

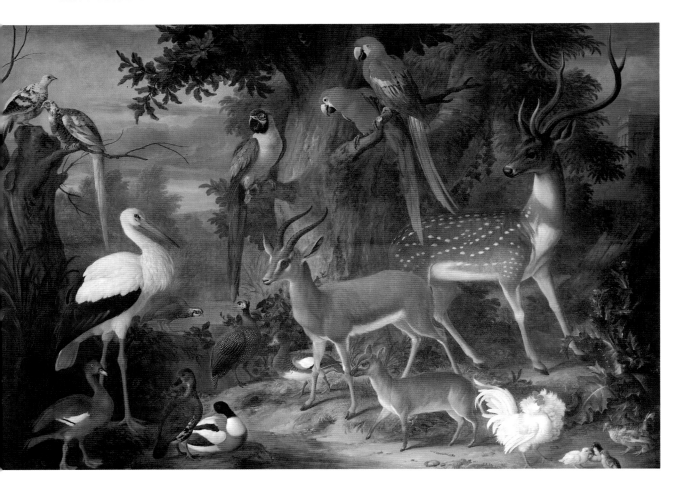

FIG. 83
Jakob Bogdani: *Birds and deer in a Garden*, 1708–10

was allowed to live in the Lodge in Windsor Great Park thanks to the kindness of Sarah, Duchess of Marlborough, who had been appointed Ranger to Queen Anne. The Lodge was apparently decorated with paintings by Bogdani which were acquired by Queen Anne after George Churchill's death in 1710. The Lodge was famous and is described by Daniel Defoe in *A Tour through the Whole Island of Great Britain* (1724–7):

The parks about Windsor are very agreeable, and suitable to the rest; the little park, which is so, only compared to the great park, is above three miles round, the great one fourteen, and the largest above thirty. This park is particular to the court, the other[s] are open for riding, hunting, and taking the air for any gentlemen that please.

The lodges in these parks are no mere lodges, though they retain the name, but palaces and might pass for such in other countries; but as they are all eclipsed by the palace itself, so it need only be added, that these lodges are principally beautified by the grandeur of the persons to whom the post of ranger has been assigned, who, having been enriched by other advancements, honours and profitable employments, thought nothing too much to lay out to beautify their apartments, in a place, which it was so much to their honour, as well as convenience, to reside; such is the lodge, which belongs to Admiral Churchill, the Duchess of Marlborough and others.[17]

There is an unusually large example of Bogdani's style, combining all his interests, in the Royal Collection (FIG. 83). It shows a chital, a gazelle and a small antelope with three macaws on the branch of a tree in the centre, and a stork, a guinea fowl, ducks, domestic poultry, geese and a red-legged partridge – all set in a landscape. There is a remarkable sensitivity in the drawing of the birds and the deer, as well as delicate brushwork, softness of touch and an engaging variety of colour. Not surprisingly, Bogdani's paintings were much prized and he became wealthy. This kind of special-ised painting was relatively rare in British art and Bogdani's work relates more closely to the Dutch and Flemish traditions as exemplified by Melchior de Hondecoeter (FIG. 84). The only British artist who could rival him was Francis Barlow.

During the reign of George IV even more exotic animals could be found in Windsor Great Park, where a Royal Menagerie had first been established in the mid-eighteenth century at Sandpit Gate, by William Augustus, Duke of Cumberland. By the early nineteenth century, this was administered by Edward Cross, an important dealer in foreign animals,

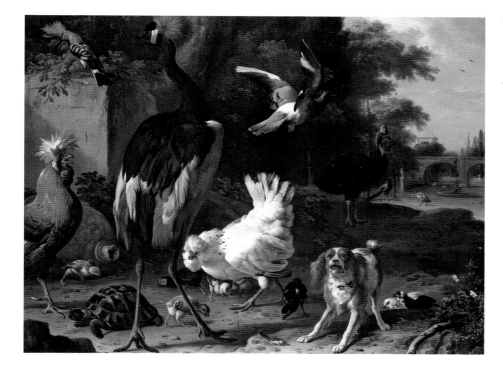

FIG. 84
Melchior de Hondecoeter:
Birds and a Spaniel in a Garden, c. 1680

who was also the proprietor of a menagerie in the Strand (Exeter 'Change) in London. One of the inhabitants of the Royal Menagerie was the Nubian giraffe (FIG. 85) which was given to George IV by Mehemet Ali, the Pasha of Egypt, in 1827. The giraffe arrived from Cairo at Waterloo Bridge on 11 August, but it was already in a weakened state, so much so that it could only be moved by a pulley and had to be given a steel support to prevent it from falling over. The giraffe was one of two calves captured on the plains of Senaar in the Sudan: the mother was shot; the larger calf was given to Charles X of France and the smaller one to George IV. The giraffe that came to England was accompanied by two Egyptian cows and two Arab keepers. By October the Swiss animal painter Jacques-Laurent Agasse had been commissioned to paint the giraffe with its keepers, and possibly Edward Cross, in the special paddock created within the menagerie. By the autumn of 1829 the giraffe, which had never really thrived, had died; it was duly stuffed by Gould and Tomkins and eventually given to the Zoological Society by William IV. George IV's interest in the giraffe was serious, but, unfortunately, political cartoonists took full advantage of the possibilities.

Edward Cross had earlier, in 1825, also imported two white-tailed gnus for George IV which were depicted, with a third added later, in the company of a herd of zebras in the grounds of Windsor Great Park by Agasse in 1828 (FIG. 86). These animals seem to have survived better in the conditions, along with monkeys, kangaroos, deer, elks, Mandarin horses, Brahmin bulls, a zebra, a leopard, a llama and several species of birds. All in all, Windsor Great Park could well have been a dangerous place.

Queen Victoria, who had been shown the Royal Menagerie personally by George IV in 1826, was also a great lover of animals and she had the added advantage of employing the greatest animal painter of the day – Sir Edwin Landseer. He combined masterly drawing with a great facility in the handling of paint, which was always brought to a high degree of finish. Like Stubbs, he had a profound knowledge of anatomy which was gained through dissection and also by studying at Cross's menagerie. Outwardly, Landseer had a totally successful career: the queen found him good-looking, he had perfect manners, he was a good mimic, but he was also touchy, unreliable with money and often difficult. Success came easily, leading to a knighthood in 1850, and in 1865 he refused the Presidency of the Royal Academy. Towards the end of his life his health broke down, he suffered from nervous depression and became unreliable as a result of alcoholism, leading to self-pity and bouts of madness. Through all of this Queen Victoria supported him, and the sheer quality of his paintings helps us to understand why. He is an artist whose work could easily be criticised for being sentimental, and some of it is, but he was, on the other hand,

FIG. 85
Jacques-Laurent Agasse:
The Nubian Giraffe, 1827

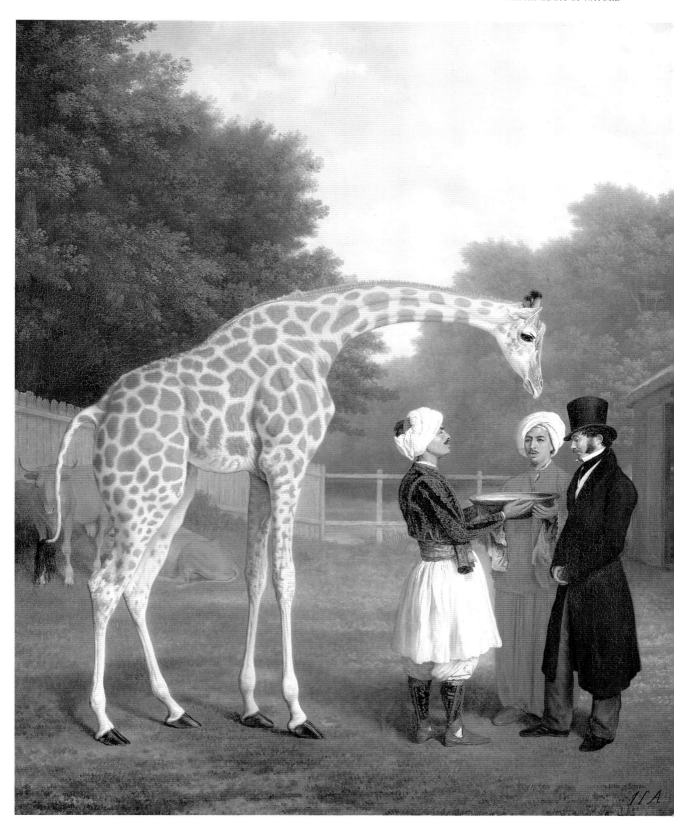

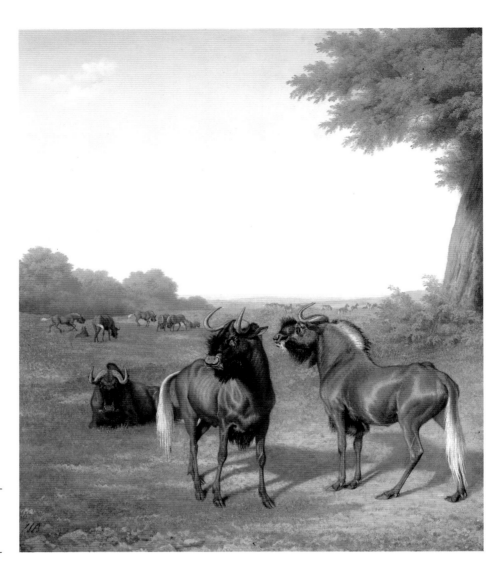

FIG. 86
Jacques-Laurent Agasse:
White-Tailed Gnus, 1828

supremely versatile, capturing not only the character of animals as pets, but also their behaviour in the wild. The beauty and the cruelty of nature preoccupied him. At his death in 1873 he left a huge fortune and was honoured with burial in St Paul's Cathedral.

Landseer's first visit to the Highlands in 1824 broadened his horizons, and many of his animal paintings combined landscapes and even historical narratives, often on a dramatic scale. Life in the Highlands fascinated him and several of his paintings depict the hardships of a poor rural society hidebound by tradition and surviving in a cruel climate. Not surprisingly, these paintings often have a moral dimension. Queen Victoria was not a demanding patron in this respect, however. The Queen and Prince Albert preferred to have their pets painted, beginning in 1836 with the queen's favourite spaniel, Dash.

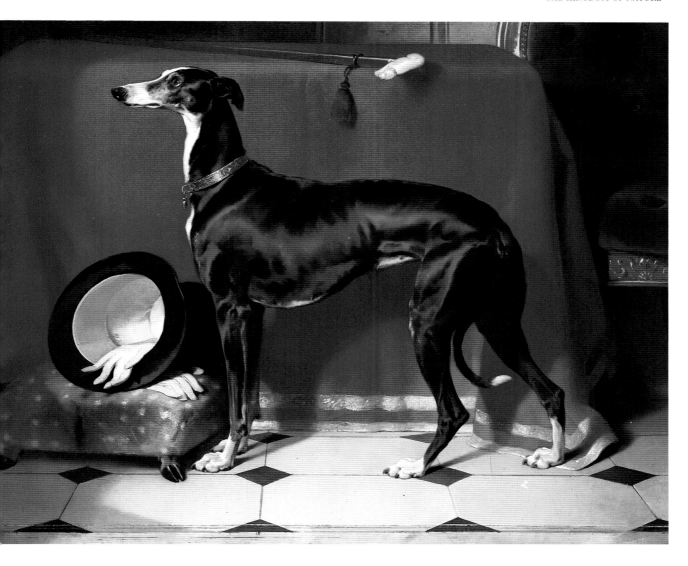

FIG. 87
Sir Edwin Landseer: *Eos*,
1841

One of Landseer's finest – indeed largest – works of this kind is the painting of *Eos* (FIG. 87), the favourite greyhound bitch of the Prince Consort, which he had brought with him from Germany. The dog is shown in Buckingham Palace surrounded by her master's top hat, gloves and cane. The presence of Prince Albert is only suggested, but the dog is unforgettable with the black sheen of her coat, posed against the red cloth, and the tensile strength of her body quivering with anticipation. The picture was painted as a surprise Christmas present for Prince Albert in 1841, but three years later the animal died and the queen wrote in her *Journal*:

> I could see by his look that there was bad news. . . . She had been his constant & faithful companion for 10 & ½ years and she was only 6 months old, when he first had her. She was connected with the

happiest years of his life & I cannot somehow imagine him without her. She was such a beautiful and sweet creature & used to play so much with the Children, & be so full of tricks. . . . As for poor dear Albert, he feels it so terribly, and I grieve so for him. It is quite like losing a friend.[18]

Another memorable painting by Landseer records one of Queen Victoria's own private enthusiasms. This was the performance of Isaac Van Amburgh, an American lion-tamer of Dutch extraction who put on displays at theatres such as Drury Lane and Astley's in London in 1839 (FIG. 88). The queen went five times and saw Van Amburgh lying in a cage with lions, tigers and leopards. Something of her excitement is evident in the entry in her *Journal*:

> . . . on the stage at the same time, a lion & lioness, a tiger & 2 chetas, or Kind of leopards. Van Amburgh remained about ¼ of an hour, showing them off & making them perform tricks. He has great power over the animals, & they seem to love him, though I think they are in great fear of him. He took them by their paws, throwing them down and making them roar, & he lay upon them after enraging them.[19]

FIG. 88
Sir Edwin Landseer: *Isaac Van Amburgh and his Animals*, 1839

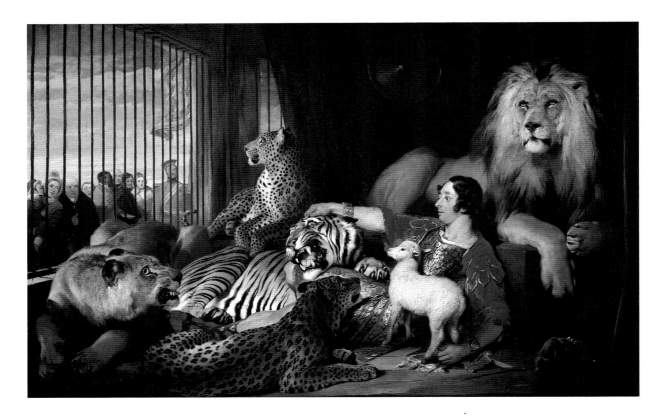

During the same year Queen Victoria was able to observe Landseer's progress on the painting. The compositional feature that most struck her was the location of the viewer inside the cage, with the visitors visible through the bars on the far side. Van Amburgh wore a coat of mail, presumably not as a form of protection, but, perhaps, judging from the footwear, as a costume, part Roman and part medieval. There are scratches on the skin of his right forearm and on his neck. The sheen on the coats of the animals reveals Landseer's superior technique, as in the laying on of glazes on the lion and lioness, or the way the spots emerge through the top layer of paint applied for the leopard. Immediately next to Van Amburgh is a lamb – a tacit Biblical reference – which not only heightens the drama of the occasion, but also no doubt in the Victorian mind pointed up the moral significance, bringing to mind Landseer's later, more literal work *The Lion and the Lamb* of 1871 (Johannesburg Art Gallery).

Landseer's paintings of deer were not always sporting pictures, but sometimes visionary, transcendental images. They date from the 1840s when the artist's own mental problems were emerging and they reflect a sense of fatalism not unrelated to Victorian philosophical preoccupations. *The Sanctuary* (FIG. 89), which was bought by Queen Victoria from the collector William Wells as a birthday present for Prince Albert in 1842[20], was the first picture by Landseer of a scene in the Highlands acquired by the

FIG. 89
Sir Edwin Landseer: *The Sanctuary*, 1842

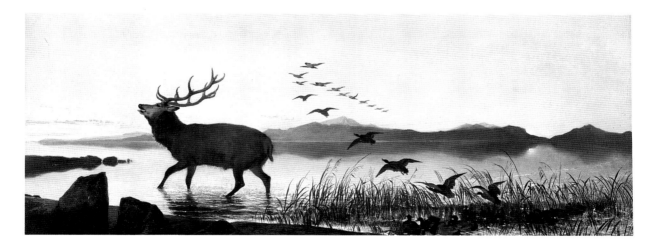

Royal Family, and it is the first of Landseer's deer paintings with symbolic overtones. It depicts a stag on the shore of Loch Maree, a twelve-mile-long loch in the county of Ross and Cromarty in the far north of Scotland. The animal has swum from the other side of the loch and the course the deer has taken can still be seen in the water. Frightened ducks fly off, forming a diagonal in the opposite direction. The scene takes place at sunset just as the sun slips down behind the distant mountains and the moon begins to rise. The colour contrasts between the blue-purple landscape and the pink-orange sky create a sombre note, but, nonetheless, serve to offset details such as the water dripping from the animal's body, luminous specks caught like pieces of molten glass in the dying light. The painting was inspired by a poem written by Landseer's friend, William Russell, called *The Stricken Deer*:

> See where the startled wild fowl screaming rise
> And seek in marshalled flight those golden skies.
> Yon wearied swimmer scarce can win the land,
> His limbs yet falter on the water strand.
> Poor hunted hart! The painful struggle o'er,
> How blest the shelter of the island shore!
> There, whilst he sobs, his panting heart to rest,
> Nor hound, nor hunter shall his lair molest – Loch Maree.

The stag has escaped death in the chase and seeks sanctuary on the other side of the loch. The sense of calm, the sublimity of the still landscape, the almost palpable silence and the ethereal light heighten the effect of the imagery. The stag is perhaps a symbol of man, noble but doomed amid the beautiful but overpowering forces of nature.

CHAPTER 4

The Sword and the Sceptre

A s head of state the British monarch plays an important part in the conduct of foreign policy. Until the seventeenth century when the sovereign held absolute power, foreign policy was not only conducted personally by monarchs, but it was also devised by them. The establishment of a constitutional monarchy during the second half of the seventeenth century under the later Stuarts meant, in effect, that responsibility for devising foreign policy passed to the government of the day. The monarch's role changed: although able to offer practical advice based on experience and personal knowledge, the sovereign became, to a certain degree, the instrument of policy, symbolically representing the country overseas and entertaining visiting Heads of State. This is most evident at the diplomatic level when ambassadors present their credentials to the sovereign on arrival at the Court of St James's and take their leave at a farewell audience when they return to their own countries. Each year in Buckingham Palace all the High Commissioners and ambassadors, together with selected members of their embassy staff, attend a formal gathering, known as the Diplomatic Reception, in order to be presented to members of the royal family. At the heart of such events is a formality that might now be regarded as outmoded, but, in fact, the emphasis on protocol remains a potent way of expressing outward and visible respect for another country and it is always within the parameters of good manners that the real business of foreign affairs is best conducted.

The finest expression of such pageantry in the context of foreign affairs is the State Visit. Twice a year a foreign Head of State visits Britain. In addition, the sovereign and other members of the royal family travel extensively overseas. Royal tours in the modern sense were established in formal terms by George V, who in 1901, when he was the Duke of York, visited Australia and New Zealand with the Duchess of York. The tour was undertaken on behalf of Queen Victoria in connection with the opening of the first Federal Parliament of the Commonwealth of Australia. It lasted eight months and, according to the Duke of York's own calculations, involved travelling 45,000 miles during 231 days, laying 21 foundation stones, presenting 4,329 medals, reviewing 62,000 troops and shaking hands officially with 24,855 people.[1]

If today pageantry and protocol are considered to be taken too seriously there can be no comparison with what happened in the sixteenth century. The most spectacular diplomatic event in Europe at that time was the meeting in 1520 of Francis I of France and Henry VIII at the Field of the Cloth of Gold. Henry VII, who had established the Tudor dynasty and striven to demonstrate its legitimacy, had carried through cautious and peaceful policies that led to the development of trade and important geographical discoveries; but his son had different priorities. Where his father was a realist, Henry VIII was an idealist. In addition, he was prodigiously gifted, being highly cultured and athletic. As a young man he was determined to make an impact on Renaissance Europe, where Francis I had just succeeded to the French throne at the age of twenty-one and where Charles V had just become Holy Roman Emperor aged nineteen. In the early years of his reign, therefore, Henry VIII resolved to gain success through military glory. This policy changed during the 1530s as ecclesiastical problems stemming from the divorce of his first wife, Catherine of Aragon, began to predominate. By the 1540s, as an old man, corpulent, arrogant and suspicious, he resumed an aggressive policy on the continent which ended in ignominy. It was during these years, however, that two large narrative paintings recounting the events surrounding the Field of the Cloth of Gold were undertaken jointly by artists of English, German and Netherlandish origins, possibly for display in Whitehall Palace. These paintings are early examples of history painting.

The meeting known as the Field of the Cloth of Gold was the ratification of the Treaty of London which had been negotiated by Cardinal Wolsey in 1518. Wolsey's achievement was considerable, since he obtained

FIG. 90
Anonymous: *The Embarkation of Henry VIII at Dover*, c. 1545

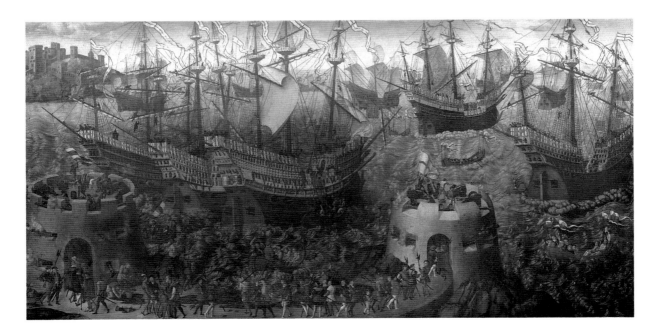

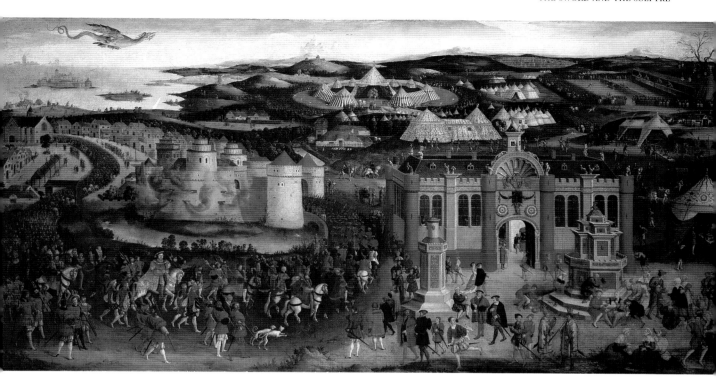

FIG. 91
Anonymous: *The Field of the Cloth of Gold*, c. 1545

agreement from all the major European powers as well as from more than twenty lesser powers. Yet, regardless of these efforts, the attempt to create a multilateral treaty of universal peace lasted only a year. When he set out from Dover (FIG. 90) on 31 May 1520, Henry VIII did not imagine that Wolsey's success would be so shortlived. *The Embarkation of Henry VIII at Dover* shows the harbour at Dover overlooked by the castle. In the foreground are two forts from which royal salutes are being fired. Five principal vessels have set sail for France and others can be seen through the rigging. The vessels are dressed overall with pennants decorated with the Cross of St George. The royal coat-of-arms flies from the bows, while the sides of the vessels are protected by shields, some emblazoned with Tudor colours. The king is aboard the *Henri-Grâce-de-Dieu*, the largest vessel in the Tudor navy, equipped with golden sails and golden pennants.

The meeting between Francis I and Henry VIII took place in June 1520 just to the south of Calais, at a place now dominated by industrial developments. The English were based at Guisnes and the French at Ardres. The valley designated for the meeting was between these two points and it was here that the two kings negotiated in a golden tent which is the scene depicted at the top centre of the anonymous painting entitled *The Field of the Cloth of Gold* (FIG. 91). Several events are shown in the picture. The left foreground is dominated by the king entering the town of Guisnes. The procession, which includes Wolsey and other members of the royal household riding alongside the king, snakes its way through the town while a royal salute is fired from the castle, frightening the swans in the moat. The king's entourage comprised 3,997 people (including nearly all the nobility) and 2,865 horses.

The right half of the painting reveals the scale of the proceedings, for what at first sight looks like a permanent structure is, in fact, a temporary one, being, in modern parlance, a hospitality tent. Six thousand men working three months in advance were required to erect this canvas palace. It was set on brick foundations, but the walls and the roof were solely of canvas on a timber framework. The canvas has been painted illusionistically to suggest blocks of masonry, patterned brickwork and a roof made of slates. The timber was specially imported from the Netherlands and in such quantities that it had to be floated along the coastal waters because the load would have sunk any vessel. Real glass was used for the windows and the facade was adorned with free-standing sculpture, presumably made of wood.

Henry VIII and Catherine of Aragon were housed in this tented palace. The inside was hung with sets of tapestries and included a gilded banqueting hall. Two fountains were located in front of the palace, each flowing with wine. Behind the palace was the king's golden dining tent with the kitchen arrangements, including a massive oven, off to the right.

Above the kitchen area is the tiltyard, 900 feet long and 320 feet wide, with Francis I, Henry VIII and their respective wives watching the jousts and the tourneys in which the king of England took part. The tiltyard was designated by a Tree of Honour (again artificial) hung with the shields of the participants. This entertainment was such an important aspect of the proceedings that the steel mill from Greenwich was temporarily transported to France for the occasion.

The meeting of the Field of the Cloth of Gold involved more than just formal discussions between monarchs. The feasting and the jousting were a symbolic part of the celebrations that lasted over two weeks (7–24 June). The dragon, top left of the composition, was a gigantic firework which was released on 23 June before the mass which closed the proceedings.

Protocol dictated every aspect and even the valley in which Francis I and Henry VIII met privately on three occasions had been levelled so that its natural features would not allow any form of advantage to be taken by the French or the English. The whole affair is well-documented, so that the quantity of food and drink consumed, and the standard of the jousting and tourneying, are recorded. At the same time it is known that the wind and the rain rather spoiled the enjoyment.[2] The Venetian ambassador wrote extensive reports on the proceedings and Shakespeare's imagination fed on the early historical accounts that resulted in one of the more poetic passages in his play *King Henry VIII*, spoken by the Duke of Norfolk:

> Today the French
> All clinquant, all in gold, like heathen gods,
> Shone down the English; and to-morrow they
> Made Britain India: every man that stood
> Show'd like a mine. Their dwarfish pages were
> As cherubins, all gilt: the madams, too,
> Not us'd to toil, did almost sweat to bear
> The pride upon them, that their very labour
> Was to them as a painting. Now this masque
> Was cried incomparable; and the ensuing night
> Made it a fool and a beggar. The two kings,
> Equal in lustre, were now best, now worst,
> As presence did present them; him in eye,
> Still him in praise; and, being present both,
> 'Twas said they saw but one; and no discerner
> Durst wag his tongue in censure. When these suns –
> For so they phrase 'em – by their heralds challeng'd
> The noble spirits to arms, they did perform
> Beyond thought's compass; . . .[3]

The whole affair now smacks slightly of Hollywood, but in historical terms it shows the world of medieval chivalry changing into Renaissance *realpolitik*.

What inspired Henry VIII's foreign policy was his desire as a young man to emulate the achievements of Edward III and Henry V, both of whom won notable victories against the French in previous centuries. Edward III was an important figure not just because of his success in the Hundred Years War, but also because he founded the Order of the Garter, which was instituted on St George's Day (23 April) 1348 and is associated above all with Windsor Castle. A jewelled collar with an elaborate ornament representing St George killing the dragon is part of the insignia worn by members of the Order. The first official history of the Order of the Garter was published by Elias Ashmole in 1672. Garter Day is still celebrated at Windsor Castle by a procession from the Castle to St George's Chapel, where a special service of dedication is held commemorating the Order. Including the sovereign, there are twenty-four Knights Companions of the Garter in all. The Order is open only to monarchs and princes and to people who have served the country with distinction. It is the highest chivalric honour that the sovereign can bestow and upholds many of the religious and historical associations of monarchy.

The American artist Benjamin West, who became Historical Painter to George III in 1772 and subsequently Surveyor, between 1786–9 painted a series of eight canvases illustrating events from the reign of Edward III for a room in Windsor Castle. This room was the Audience Chamber and it is only known now through an illustration in W. H. Pyne's *History of the Royal Residences* (1819) (FIG. 92), since it was dismantled when George IV redesigned the castle. Fortunately, the eight paintings were preserved, which is just as well, since they are amongst the earliest examples of a history cycle in this country.

As one might expect, two of the paintings refer to the Order of the Garter: the first, which was over the mantelpiece, is a depiction of St George killing the dragon and the second shows the inauguration of the Order. The emphasis, however, is on Edward III's campaign in the Hundred

FIG. 92
Charles Wild: *The King's Audience Chamber, Windsor Castle*, 1817

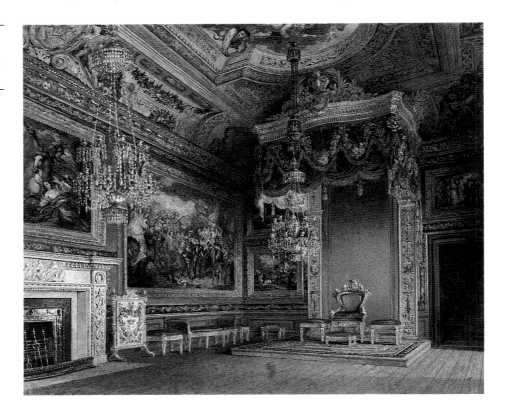

Years War against the French during the late 1340s – a campaign in which the king's wife, Queen Philippa, and the king's son, the Black Prince, played prominent parts. Scenes such as *Edward III Crossing the Somme* (FIG. 93) are visual interpretations of the accounts that West had read in Jean Froissart's contemporary *Chronicles* or David Hume's *History of England from the Invasion of Julius Caesar to the Revolution of 1688* (1761). Such paintings combine great imagination with antiquarian research. For where West suggests the fury of battle by the clash of arms, the billowing flags and the sun emerging from behind the clouds, other aspects of the composition, including the armour, coats-of-arms and weapons such as the long bow, are based on authentic examples published by antiquarian scholars such as Joseph Strutt[4] and Francis Grose[5].

Martial exploits were only part of medieval kingship and it is significant that in three of the scenes Edward III exercises magnanimity, as in *The Burghers of Calais* (FIG. 94), a subject made more famous in the nineteenth century by Rodin. The king entered Calais on 3 August 1347 after a siege lasting a year. It was agreed that the inhabitants of the town would be spared if the six chief citizens surrendered themselves 'bare-headed, bare-footed, and bare-legged, and in their shirts, with halters about their necks and the keys of the town and castle in their hands'.[6] This they duly did,

FIG. 93
Benjamin West: *Edward III Crossing the Somme*, 1788

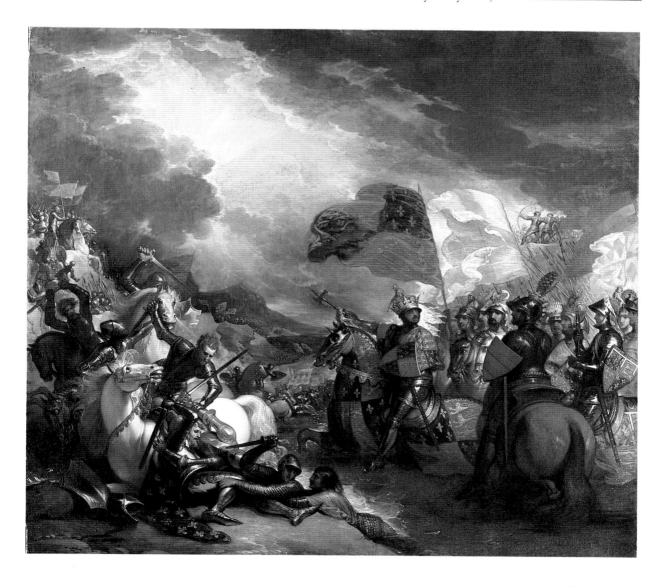

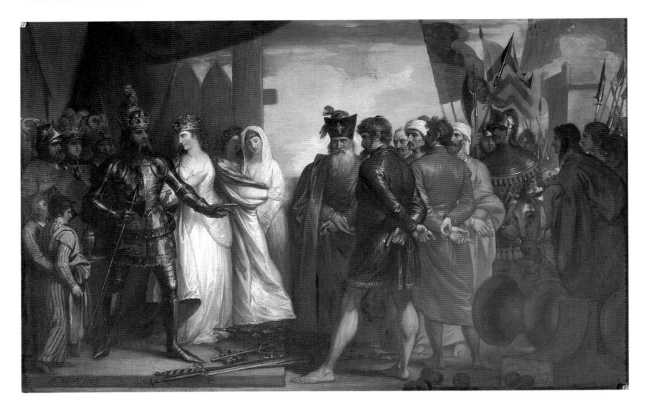

FIG. 94
Benjamin West: *The
Burghers of Calais*, 1789

though it was clear that the king had resolved to have them beheaded. The queen intervened and implored mercy, which was then exercised.

These history paintings tend to be derided nowadays: they resemble pageants and it is perhaps their serious mood that in the end might seem to render them ridiculous. Yet the recreation of the past is an act of imagination and West dramatises the concept of chivalry extremely successfully, even if it is too literal.[7]

A more immediate sense of history underpins another much later sortie by a British monarch into France. In 1855 Queen Victoria and Prince Albert were preoccupied by the Crimean War in which Britain and France were allied with Turkey against Russia. The mood of optimism of the year before had quickly evaporated, owing to lack of military success, great loss of life and appalling conditions. The French, ruled by Napoleon III and the Empress Eugénie, were equally concerned: the emperor himself decided to rush off to the Crimea and take over supreme command in order to defeat the Russians. This was a brazen attempt by Napoleon III to gain the prestige of winning the war for France, thereby belittling the British contribution and reviving memories of his uncle, the first Emperor Napoleon. Queen Victoria's sympathies lay with Louis Philippe, the previous ruler of France as king, who was deposed in the revolution of 1848 from which Napoleon emerged as victor, first as president and then from 1851 as emperor. Napoleon III, therefore, appeared at first to be an adventurer and an upstart not to be trusted. Instead of dashing off to the Crimea, he was persuaded to undertake a State Visit to England in the spring, which would be followed by a return visit to France by Queen Victoria and Prince Albert in the summer.

These visits came at an awkward moment in Anglo-French relations and a great deal depended on how the emperor and Queen Victoria reacted to one another. Both visits are a supreme example of how ceremonial occasions can be combined with diplomatic concerns. As it happened, political necessity was converted into firm friendship.

The emperor and empress arrived in London on 16 April 1855 and were entertained in lavish style at Windsor Castle. The imperial suite was dominated by the state bed, around which were elaborate embroidered bed-curtains with the initials of the imperial couple, LN and EI, intertwined. Napoleon III's Gallic charm, extravagantly good manners, mysterious air and exceedingly long waxed moustaches enchanted Queen Victoria and made up for his lack of stature and languorous air. The Empress Eugénie – of Spanish origin – was tall and elegant. She was nervous at first, but became more loquacious as she relaxed. Her complexion and sense of fashion (she introduced the crinoline to England in the course of this visit) complemented the emperor's personable airs. Among the events were visits to the Great Exhibition and the opera, a review in the Great Park at Windsor, a ball in St George's Hall and a musical reception in the Waterloo Chamber, both in the castle.

The emperor was also invested with the Order of the Garter, an event which was recorded later in a painting by E. M. Ward (FIG. 95). After it all,

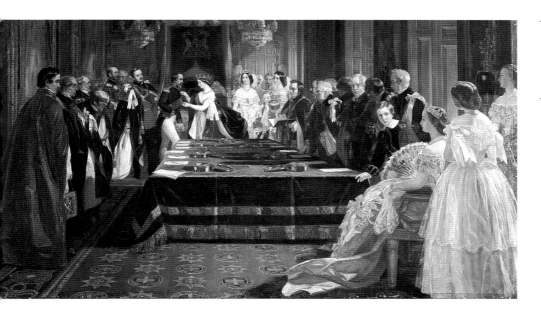

FIG. 95
Edward Matthew Ward:
The Investiture of Napoleon III with the Order of the Garter, 18 April 1855, 1860

a rather breathless Queen Victoria recorded of the emperor in her *Journal*:

> That he *is* a very *extraordinary* man with great qualities there can be
> no doubt – I might almost say a mysterious man. He is evidently
> possessed of *indomitable courage, unflinching firmness of purpose, self reliance,*
> *perseverance and great secrecy*: to which should be added a great reliance
> on what he calls his *star* and a belief in omens and incidents as
> connected with his future destiny. . . . At the same time he is
> endowed with a wonderful *self-control*, great calmness, even *gentleness*
> and with a power of *fascination*, the effect of which upon those who
> become more intimately acquainted with him is most sensibly felt.[8]

But the purpose of the visit was not forgotten:

> It is a dream, a brilliant, successful, pleasant dream, the recollection
> of which is firmly fixed in my mind. On all it has left a pleasant,
> satisfactory impression. It went off so well – not a hitch or *contretemps*
> – fine weather, everything smiling; the nation enthusiastic, and happy
> in the firm intimate alliance and union of two great countries, whose
> enmity would be fatal. We have war certainly, but war which does not
> threaten our shores, our homes, and internal prosperity, which war
> with France ever must do . . . .[9]

The return visit took place four months later, in August 1855, during the
siege of Sebastopol in the Crimea. When Queen Victoria and Prince Albert
landed at Boulogne with their two eldest children and proceeded to Paris,
she became the first British sovereign since the fifteenth century (Henry VI
in 1431) to enter the city. Paris was in the middle of the Universal Exhibition, one of the many events that marked the revival of French fortunes
during the middle decades of the nineteenth century. On his own territory
the emperor scored an even greater personal success with the queen. Paris
was beautiful and being modernised; the emperor was attentive and solici-
tous. Whilst viewing the paintings in the Universal Exhibition Prince
Albert expressed enthusiasm for one work in particular, *The Brawl*, by
Meissonier, whereupon Napoleon III gave it to him. With considerable
abandon Queen Victoria wrote:

> For the Emperor personally I have conceived a real affection and
> friendship . . . . I know *no* one who puts me more at ease, or to
> whom I feel more inclined to talk unreservedly, or in whom
> involuntarily I should be more inclined to confide than the Emperor.[10]

Later Queen Victoria described the visit in a letter to her uncle Leopold I, King of the Belgians, as 'the *pleasantest* and *most interesting* and triumphant ten days that I think I ever passed'.[11] The royal couple were based at St Cloud, to the south-west of the city, but they were also entertained at the palaces of Versailles and the Tuileries. After a ball at Versailles there was a grand firework display at which the final set-piece was an outline of Windsor Castle. There was also a review of the troops on the Champs de Mars. On that occasion, the queen and her two eldest children watched from the balcony of the Ecole Militaire, while Prince Albert, on horseback next to Napoleon III, took the salute from a regiment of Zouaves who swirled by in the dust.

The most important event from the historical point of view was the visit to the tomb of Napoleon I at Les Invalides.[12] This took place late at night on Friday 24th August. Arm in arm in the torch light, while the National Anthem was played and thunder rolled across the sky, Queen Victoria and Napoleon III gazed at the tomb of the principal enemy of her grandfather, George III. Queen Victoria knelt with her eldest son while French generals cried. This dramatic scene was later painted by E. M. Ward (FIG. 96) as a pendant for the composition of Napoleon III receiving the Order of the Garter during the visit to England (FIG. 95).

Symbolically, these two moments in 1855 sealed the Anglo-French alliance and the various paintings commemorating the two visits form part

FIG. 96
Edward Matthew Ward:
*Queen Victoria at the Tomb of
Napoleon, 24 August 1855,*
1860

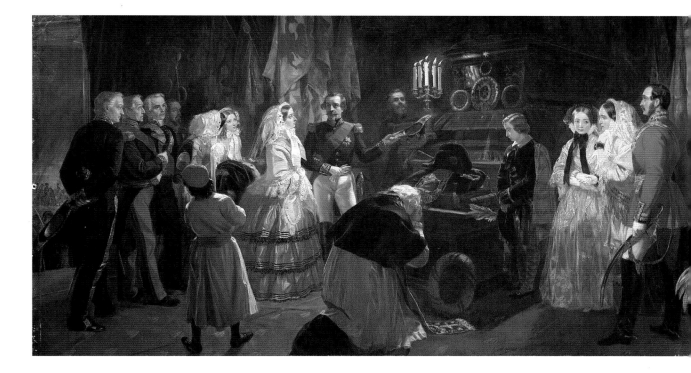

of the decorative scheme of a room in Buckingham Palace known as the 1855 Room. As Queen Victoria wrote to her uncle:

> In short, the *complete* Union of the two countries is stamped and sealed in the most satisfactory and solid manner, for it is not *only* a Union of the two Governments – the two sovereigns – it is that of the *two nations*![13]

It had, of course, not always been so. Only an alliance of other European powers had eventually brought about the defeat of Napoleon I on the battlefield of Waterloo in 1815. On one of the evenings during the State Visit of Napoleon III and the Empress Eugénie to Windsor Castle a musical reception had been given in the Waterloo Chamber, which, in order to save embarrassment, had been renamed the Music Room for the occasion (FIG. 97).

The Waterloo Chamber had been created by George IV to commemor-

FIG. 97
Joseph Nash: *The Waterloo Chamber, Windsor Castle,* 1848

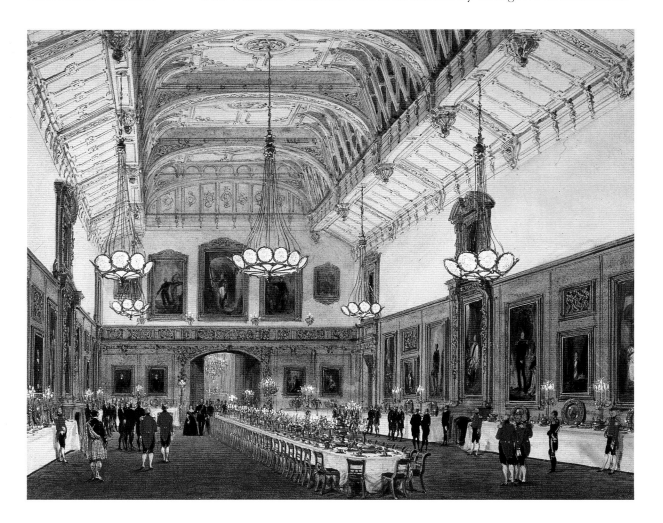

ate the downfall of Napoleon. It was, in fact, devised in the tradition of the Long Gallery in an aristocratic house. It is reminiscent of the Gallery in Stafford (now Lancaster) House and its proportions are not dissimilar to the Picture Gallery at Buckingham Palace. Also, it contains some of the finest portraits in nineteenth-century European art. These were specially commissioned from Thomas Lawrence by George IV and were to be of the Heads of State, military commanders and diplomats who had combined to defeat Napoleon. Originally, the suggestion had been to have two large narrative history paintings of the type produced by West for George III, but in the end, partly because Lawrence lacked confidence in that category of painting, a series of single portraits was preferred. The project can be related to the Renaissance tradition of *uomini famosi* fresco cycles of illustrious figures from history or literature (FIG. 98) that were, in turn, related to an earlier manuscript tradition. Significantly, at the end of his life Lawrence regarded himself

> as having been honor'd by a Mission of more importance, distinction and (perhaps) difficulty, than was ever assigned by their Patron Monarchs to the Hands of Vandyke, Rubens, or Titian, in which Mission, by the Monarchs of every court and their respective Governments, it has been acknowledg'd that without one exception, I have succeeded.[14]

Lawrence, born in 1769, was an infant prodigy. As a portrait painter he had already worked for George IV's parents and had succeeded Reynolds as Principal Painter by 1792, but his style was perhaps too advanced for George III and Queen Charlotte. The bravura of his brushwork, the intensity of his colours, the theatrical panache of the poses with figures placed before dramatic settings are the essence of portraiture as conceived during the romantic period. Yet, this dashing, sparkling style should not be mistaken for superficiality, for Lawrence, like Goya and Delacroix, frequently penetrated below the surface and plumbed the depths of character.

The portraits in the Waterloo Chamber are amongst the finest achievements in European art. They are not limited to those combatants including the Duke of Wellington (FIG. 99), Prince Blücher, Count Platov, Prince Schwarzenburg, General Uvarov, or Charles, Archduke of Austria, who fought Napoleon on his various campaigns and finally overcame him at Waterloo. Apart from the Duke of Wellington, who is shown holding the Sword of State in front of St Paul's Cathedral on the occasion of a special Thanksgiving Service, these portraits depict the figures on the field of battle with smoke-filled backgrounds (FIG. 100). There are also the Heads of State who are rather more sedate. Admittedly, George IV flutters like a butterfly

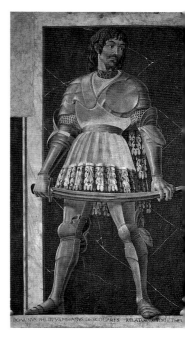

FIG. 98
Andrea del Castagno: *Pippo Spano*, c. 1450

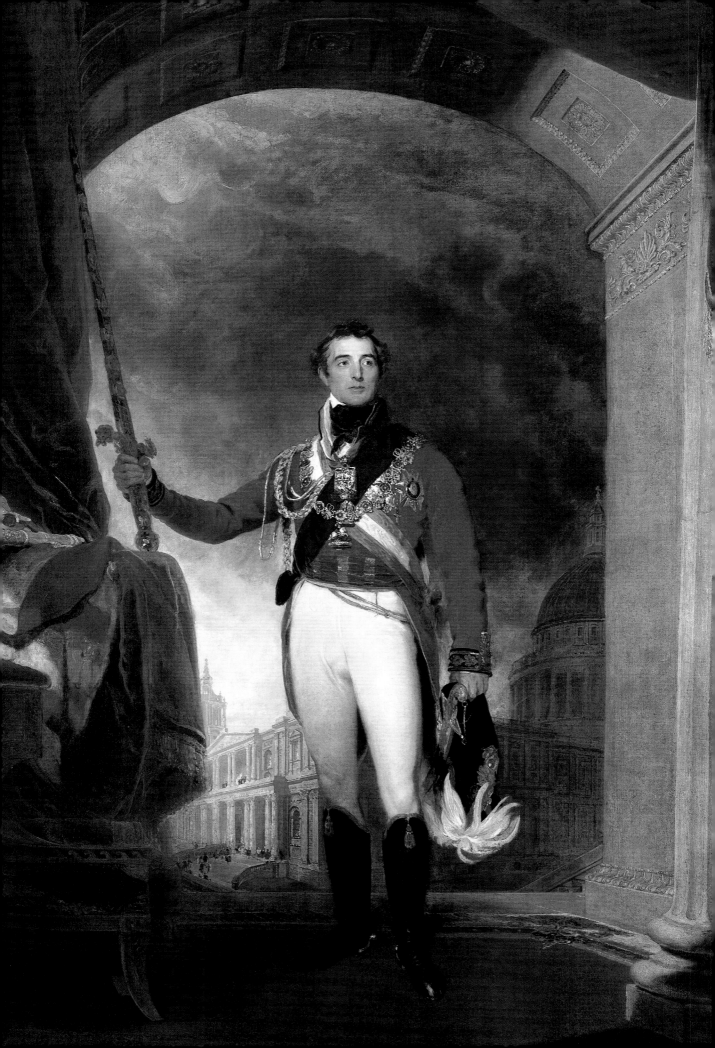

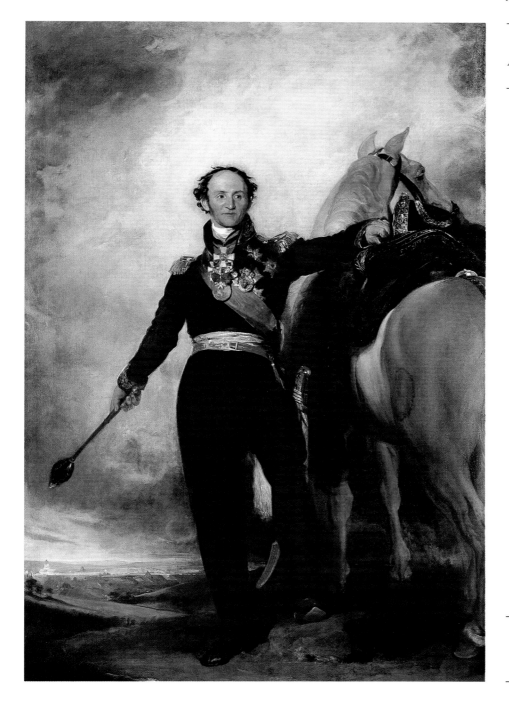

FIG. 99
Sir Thomas Lawrence:
*Arthur Wellesley, First Duke of
Wellington*, 1814–15

FIG. 100
Sir Thomas Lawrence:
*Matvei Ivanovitch, Count
Platov*, 1814

in his Garter robes, but Francis I of Austria, Frederick William III of
Prussia and Alexander I of Russia correctly seem more removed from the
proceedings and more formal.

The third category of portrait in the Waterloo Chamber includes the
diplomats and politicians, usually painted in three-quarters length and
often shown seated. The figures are dressed overall in their orders or hold-

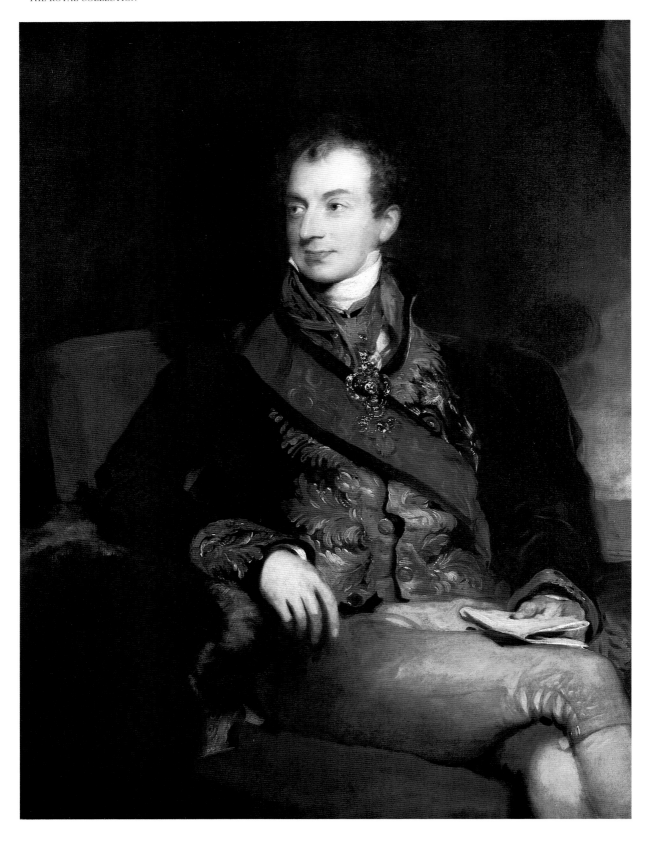

ing the memoranda that they spent so much of their time writing. These men clearly have agile minds and are armed with carefully reasoned arguments. Here are such figures as Cardinal Consalvi, Metternich (FIG. 101), Castlereagh, Liverpool, Humboldt, Hardenberg, Capo d'Istria, Nesselrode, Münster and the Duc de Richelieu – a veritable roll-call of influential people at one of the great turning points in European history. For it was at the Congress of Vienna, held in the autumn of 1814, that the boundaries on the map of Europe were redrawn and territory was reallocated in an attempt to establish a balance of power so that a long-lasting peace could be maintained. The Congress of Vienna has proved to be a point of reference for European diplomacy ever since. Napoleon was a prisoner on Elba, and this was a time for celebration as well as for work; they celebrated in style. As the aged Prince de Ligne commented, 'Le Congrès ne marche pas, mais il danse.'[15]

Lawrence began work on the portraits for the Waterloo Chamber in 1814 but in the spring of 1815 Napoleon I escaped from Elba and landed in France. The Congress of Vienna continued until June. The Battle of Waterloo was fought on 18 June 1815. Apart from the uncertainties and upheavals, the main problem for Lawrence was arranging sittings with such a cosmopolitan and peripatetic group of people. The task thus became long and drawn out as the artist moved from London to Aix-la-Chapelle, Vienna, Rome, Paris, and back to London. Two whole years were spent in Vienna alone (1818–20), where, thanks to the efforts of the ambassador, Lord Charles Stewart, Lawrence was involved in an endless round of dinners, theatres, fêtes and reviews. This lifestyle suited the painter and is reflected in the vibrant qualities of his portraits in the Waterloo Chamber. Most of the portraits were finished, or nearly so, by 1820, but they remained undelivered to the king. Ironically, both George IV and Lawrence died in 1830 before the project was completed and therefore neither saw the Waterloo Chamber as it was originally conceived. The international flavour of the undertaking encouraged one knowledgeable observer, the artist James Northcote, to remark that 'there has been nothing like it except in the instances of Rubens and Vandyck. . . . It wd. raise the credit of English art abroad and make it more respected at Home.'[16]

If any portrait in the Waterloo Chamber reinforced this statement, it was the image of Pope Pius VII (FIG. 102) painted in Rome in 1819. Luigi Barnaba Chiaramonti was one of the greatest popes in history and one of the outstanding figures of the nineteenth century. Having been elected pope in 1800, his chief task was to stand up to Napoleon I, who was now at the height of his power. This he did by a policy of peace (in the portrait the finials are inscribed with his personal motto, *Pax*). The Concordat of 1801 led to official recognition for the Catholics in France in return for

FIG. 101
Sir Thomas Lawrence:
Clemens Lothar Wenzel,
Prince Metternich,
1818–19

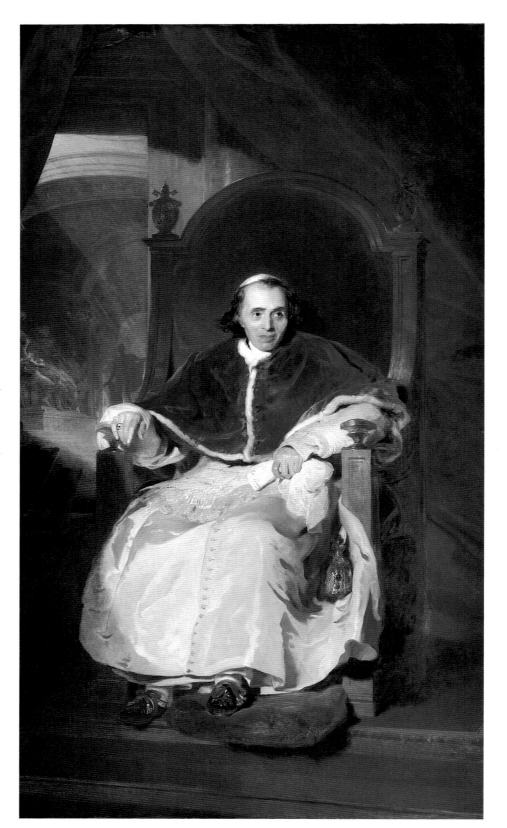

FIG. 102
Sir Thomas Lawrence: *Pope
Pius VII*, 1819

recognition of the Republic, but three years later Napoleon I was proclaimed emperor and Pius VII was summoned to Paris to attend the coronation, where his role was to anoint the emperor, although not to crown him. Pius VII's failure to condone all of Napoleon I's policies led the new emperor to invade the Papal States, for which he was excommunicated. At this point the pope was arrested under cover of darkness and imprisoned at Fontainebleau from 1809–14.

Restored after the downfall of Napoleon, Pius VII concentrated on making Rome the cultural and spiritual capital of Europe, while he himself became the focus for the Italian Risorgimento. Valuable works of art plundered by Napoleon and his agents and carried off to Paris for display in the Musée Napoleon were returned and suitably housed in the specially built Braccio Nuovo in the Vatican. Reference to this can be seen in the background of Lawrence's portrait where famous classical sculptures such as the Laöcoon, the Torso Belvedere and the Apollo Belvedere are shown. The document held in the pope's hand bears the name of the famous sculptor Antonio Canova, who was appointed Prefect of the Fine Arts in Rome by Pius VII and later created Marchese d'Ischia. Nothing can detract, however, from the impact of the stooped, elderly (aged seventy-five), tired figure seated on the *sedia gestatoria*. The pose echoes that used in the famous portraits of popes of former centuries by Raphael, Titian and Velazquez. Lawrence's characterisation does not suffer by comparison. He regarded this as one of his finest portraits and it won universal praise. The artist himself wrote:

> No picture that I have painted has been more popular with the friends of the subject, and the public . . . and, according to my scale of ability, I have exercised my intention: having given him that expression of unaffected benevolence and worth, which lights up his countenance with a freshness and spirit entirely free (except in the characteristic paleness of his complexion) from that appearance of illness and decay that he generally has while enduring the fatigue of his public functions.[17]

The worldly resignation in the face, the spiritual calm, the guile and the determination are all readily apparent. From May to December 1819 Lawrence stayed in the Palazzo del Quirinale in Rome, where the pope was then resident, so that while painting the portrait he was able to observe the sitter at fairly close quarters, in addition to having nine sittings. It is characteristic of Lawrence that he did not fail to observe the elegance of the papal slippers that emerge from below the pontifical robes with one foot nonchalantly raised on a cushion. The hands are equally eloquent and it was this feature that moved Sir Walter Scott to opine:

> There was a picture of the Pope . . . which struck me very much. I
> fancied if I had seen only the hand, I could have guessed it not
> only to be the hand of a gentleman and person of high rank, but of
> a man who had never been employed in war, or in the sports. . . . It
> was and could be only the hand of an old priest, which had no ruder
> employment than bestowing benedictions.[18]

Queen Victoria's hand, by contrast, was small and plump. When she was
painted at the age of eighty, in 1899 (FIG. 176), by the German artist Heinrich
von Angeli, Queen Victoria was the most powerful ruler in the world,
having been created Empress of India (FIG. 103) in 1877.

The British Empire can be clearly defined. Geographically, it
amounted to the largest area of the world ever to identify with a single
nation, comprising nearly a quarter of the land mass spread across several
continents (approximately 11 million square miles) and nearly a quarter
of the known world's population (approximately 372 million).[19] What had
begun during the seventeenth and eighteenth centuries as essentially a
commercial interest was gradually transformed into a political hegemony.
The end of the Empire was not signalled until 1947 with the independence
of India. The focus of the British Empire at its height was Queen Victoria
herself – a sad, somewhat reclusive figure with a common-sense attitude
to life and an indomitable spirit that inspired others to daunting levels of
self-sacrifice. As Rudyard Kipling wrote:

> Walk wide o' the Widow of Windsor,
> For 'alf o' Creation she owns,
> We've brought her the same with the sword an' the flame,
> An' we've salted it down with our bones.[20]

The Victorians felt that they had a messianic role to play in the world and
the Empire was the perfect outlet for this. Queen Victoria, like her successors Edward VII and George V, was immensely proud of the Empire.
She acquired portraits of its leading figures; she secured views of the Can-
adian and Australian landscape; and she added to the Royal Collection
pictures commemorating some of the main exploits carried out in her name.
These included *The Battle of Meanee* (or Meeanee) of 1843 by Edward
Armitage, a famous engagement won by Sir Charles Napier against considerable odds that completed the annexation of Scind in India; the *Guards
at Tel-el-Kebir* in Egypt by Richard Caton Woodville seen in battle in 1882
against Arabi Pasha, at which engagement Queen Victoria's third son,

FIG. 103
Heinrich von Angeli: *Queen
Victoria (Empress of India)*,
1885

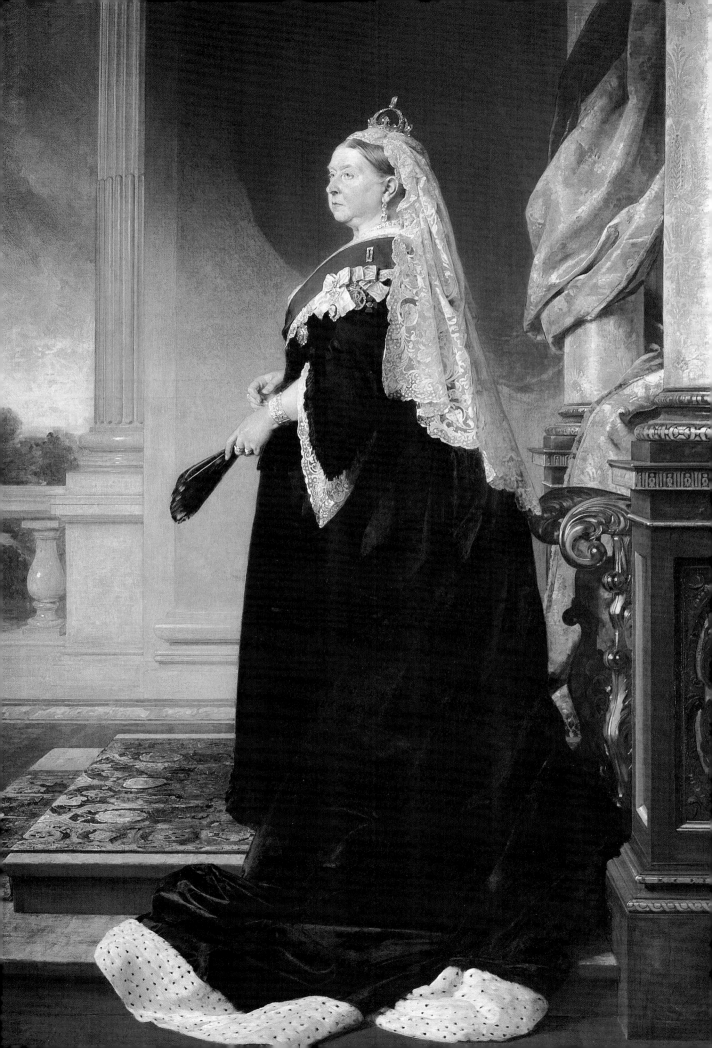

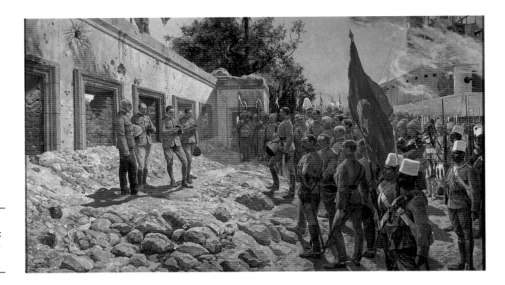

FIG. 104
Richard Caton Woodville:
*Khartoum: Memorial Service
for General Gordon*, 1899

the Duke of Connaught, commanded the Guards Brigade and, according to General Sir Garnet Wolseley, showed conspicuous bravery; and, again by Woodville, the paintings recording the Sudan campaign and the death of General Gordon at Khartoum in 1885 – *'Too Late': The Last March of General Sir Herbert Stewart* and *Khartoum: Memorial Service for General Gordon* (FIG. 104), which was conducted by Lord Kitchener while on a later campaign to recover the Sudan in 1898.

The defence of Rorke's Drift (FIG. 105) was one of the more praiseworthy engagements of the Zulu War of 1879, following the disaster of Isandhlwana. The queen had expressed an interest in having a painting by the country's foremost battle painter. This was Lady Butler, who had been born in Switzerland in 1846 and was brought up abroad before becoming one of the most celebrated painters of the Victorian period. She was asked by the queen to paint a 'subject to be taken from a war of her own reign'.[21] At first, the artist contemplated depicting a scene connected with the death of the son of Napoleon III, the Prince Imperial, who was killed while serving for the British army in the Zulu War, but she was persuaded not to do this and so chose the gallant defence of the mission station at Rorke's Drift. The mission station was garrisoned by 121 able men mostly of the 24th (Second Warwickshire Regiment) and 36 hospital cases. It was attacked on the afternoon of 22 January by 4,000 Zulu of King Cetawayo's impi warriors under the command of his half-brother Dabulamanzi. One sentry is reported as saying 'Here they come! black as hell and thick as grass!'[22] Although lacking adequate defences, the assault was held off for twelve hours and when the Zulus retired eighty British soldiers were still left. Eleven Victoria Crosses were awarded, the highest number for any single engagement. The Zulu losses were terrible.

Lady Butler did not find her painting of *Rorke's Drift* an easy commission. She had to show hand-to-hand fighting, which she did not normally depict, and it was an exactly contemporary scene. Furthermore, her husband, Sir William Butler, a distinguished soldier who was in South Africa at the time, had grave doubts about the rights and wrongs of the Zulu War. Butler served not only in the Zulu War, but in Egypt at Tel-el-Kebir, in the Sudan, being involved in the attempt to relieve General Gordon, and in South Africa. For two years (1896–8) he lived in Dover Castle where Lady Butler had a studio.

Regardless of the difficulties, the painting of Rorke's Drift was a success, mainly on account of accurate drawing and the skilful rendering of the action at night. For obvious reasons, Lady Butler concentrates on the British soldiers, and the Zulus have been merged into the darkness in the left foreground with the exception of a single figure who grabs the muzzle of a rifle. The composition is essentially circular and portraits of all but three of the recipients of the Victoria Cross are included. The defence was commanded by Lieutenant John Chard and supported by Lieutenant Gonville Bromhead. They are seen together prominently in the centre. The picture is bathed in a lurid light cast by the flames emanating from the roof of the mission station. It was, in fact, these lighting effects that the artist found particularly difficult to achieve. She had drawn the men's portraits from life, and many of those who participated in the action itself were asked to put on their uniforms and to re-enact the scene for the artist.

FIG. 105
Elizabeth Thompson, Lady Butler: *The Defence of Rorke's Drift*, 1880

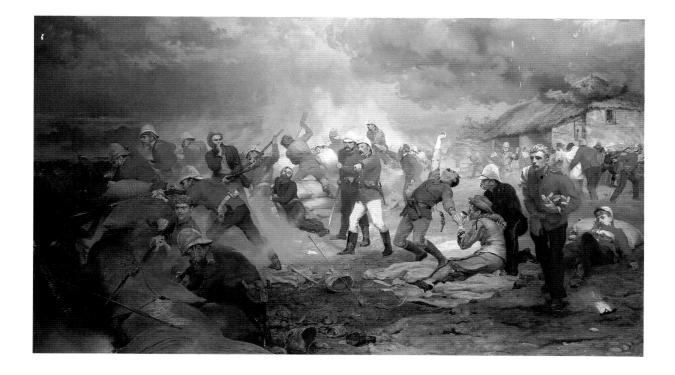

India was the part of the Empire that Queen Victoria felt most attached to, although she never went there. For many years towards the end of her life she was attended by Indian servants. Evidence of her fascination for India is found in the Durbar Room at Osborne House, built in 1890–1 and decorated under the supervision of Rudyard Kipling's father, Lockwood. Along the Durbar Corridor outside this room is a remarkable series of portraits by a Viennese painter, Rudolf Swoboda, some of which were painted in India in 1886–8 and others in London in 1888–93 and in 1893–7, when representatives came from India for the opening of the Imperial Institute and the Diamond Jubilee.

The close concern for India that the queen had shown from the beginning of her reign was put on a formal basis when, at the suggestion of Benjamin Disraeli, she assumed the title of Empress of India on May Day 1876. Henceforth, she signed herself 'Victoria Regina et Imperatrix'. In India a special durbar was held near Delhi on 1 January 1877, the preparations for which were almost as elaborate as those for Henry VIII's expedition to the Field of the Cloth of Gold. An enormous painting of the event was achieved by Val Prinsep, who knew India well, having been born in Calcutta into an Anglo-Indian family. He published his own personal account of the commission and his preparations for the painting in *Imperial India, an Artist's Journals* (1879). The Viceroy, Lord Lytton, is seated beneath an elaborate canopy, while the Chief Herald, Major Barnes, advances up the steps carrying the promulgation. Watching the scene intently, and no doubt nervously rehearsing the loyal addresses that took up so much of the ceremony, are the Indian princes identifiable by their banners. Lord Lytton sent a telegram describing this imperial assemblage:

> The Viceroy presents his humble duty to the Queen. Her Majesty's title as Empress of India was proclaimed at noon this day upon the Plain of Delhi, with the most impressive pomp and splendour in an assemblage attended by fifty ruling Chiefs with their followers: a vast concourse of native Princes and nobles from all parts of India; the Khan and Sirdars of Khelat, the Ambassadors of Nepaul, Yarkand, Siam, and Muscat; the Envoys of Chitral and Yassin; the Governor-General of Goa and Consular body, all the Governors, Lieutenant-Governors, and chief authorities, military, civil, and judicial, of British India, besides an immense gathering of her Majesty's unofficial subjects of all classes, European and native. The flower of her Majesty's Indian Army was drawn up on the Plain, and made a splendid appearance. . . . On this occasion all the ruling Chiefs have intimated their intention of sending, for presentation to the Queen, separate addresses of congratulations and loyal devotion.

Many of the native noblemen have also announced their intention of honouring the day by large subscriptions to British charities or the construction of important public works.

There can be no question of the complete success of this great Imperial ceremony. The weather has been most favourable. The Viceroy lays his humble congratulations at the feet of her Majesty, and earnestly prays that the Queen's loyal subjects, allies and feudatories of this country, may be to the Empress of India a New Year's gift of inestimable value in return for the honour which she has conferred to-day upon this great dependence of the Crown. The Viceroy trusts that it may please Providence to prolong for many years her Majesty's beneficent and prosperous reign.[23]

The greatest expression of imperial power, however, was delayed until Queen Victoria's Diamond Jubilee, held on 22 June 1897, when she was aged 78. *The Times* referred to the event as:

That great day of national and Imperial rejoicing upon which the hopes of all have been fixed for many weeks and months . . . . It may be summed up by saying that the Queen and Empress of a great kingdom and of a huge Empire, preceded first by a procession representing the political and military strength of dominions, colonies and dependencies, and then by a military and Royal procession of unparalleled grandeur has successfully made an unexampled progress through the greatest city of the world between enthusiastic crowds of her subjects, and before visitors from all quarters of the earth.[24]

An artist, John Charlton, who specialised in depicting ceremonial occasions and had successfully rendered the Golden Jubilee ten years previously, was on hand to record the event (FIG. 106). He positioned himself at St Paul's Cathedral where a short service of thanksgiving was to be held on the steps outside, since the queen was too infirm to go inside without difficulty. It was from this point that the artist thought the 50,000 participants in the ceremony would be seen to full advantage, with numerous carriages carefully ordered according to precedent. The queen was in an open state landau drawn by eight creams, which was, in fact, the seventeenth carriage in the procession. She had left Buckingham Palace at 11.15 a.m. accompanied by her daughter Helena, Princess Christian of Schleswig-Holstein, and the Princess of Wales. On the right of her carriage rode the Prince of Wales and the Duke of Connaught and on the left, the Duke of Cambridge, the queen's cousin and chief personal ADC.

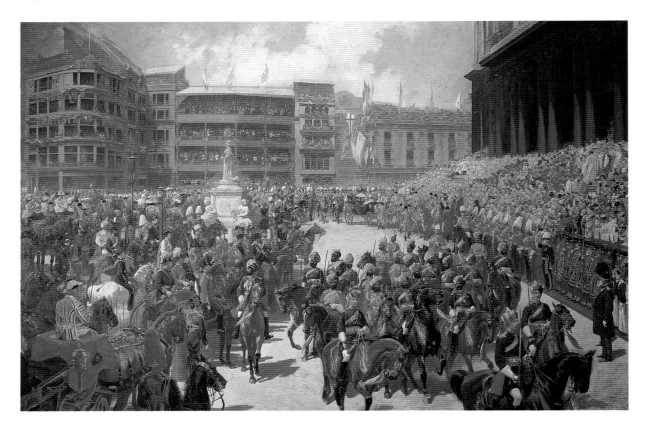

FIG. 106
John Charlton: 'God Save the
Queen': Queen Victoria arriving
on the occasion of the Diamond
Jubilee Thanksgiving Service,
22 June 1897, 1899

Charlton brought such a degree of accuracy to this painting that only
with the aid of an elaborate key can all the figures in the picture, which
includes those who preceded the queen in the procession and even the
artist himself, be identified. The emphasis throughout was on the British
Empire. There were, for example, escorts of cavalry and infantry from
all parts of the Empire. Prominent were the Indian cavalry, who rode
immediately in front of the queen with the newly appointed Field Marshal
Viscount Wolseley, Commander-in-Chief – the epitome of the British
Empire. During the procession the artist made thirty or so hurried sketches
on the spot and for the rest relied on his memory. He then made careful
portrait studies and sketches of the uniforms and horses. After that he
submitted a design of the whole picture to the queen and drew three large
cartoons. It took him fourteen months to complete the painting, which was
shown at the Royal Academy exhibition in 1899.

Queen Victoria described her Diamond Jubilee, as well she might, as
'a never-to-be-forgotten day. No-one ever, I believe, has met with such an
ovation as was given to me. . . . The crowds were quite indescribable, and
their enthusiasm truly marvellous and deeply touching.'[25] The weather was
good, the crowds were enormous and enthusiastic. The whole Empire
shared in the ovation given to this diminutive, but much respected, figure.

The correspondents of the leading newspapers produced endless purple passages. 'History may be searched,' boomed *The Times*, 'and searched in vain, to discover so wonderful an exhibition of allegiance and brotherhood amongst so many myriads of men . . . . The mightiest and most beneficial Empire ever known in the annals of mankind.'[26] London was assuredly at that moment the centre of the world. Before she set out Queen Victoria had sent via the Central Telegraph Office a message across the world to all parts of the Empire. 'From my heart I thank my beloved people. May God bless them.'[27] By the time she had returned to Buckingham Palace later in the day most of the colonies had replied to the message.

The people addressed by Queen Victoria included those who formed the subject of a painting by Swoboda entitled *Waiting for the Train* – a haunting image of Indians waiting patiently at a country level crossing (FIG. 107). Here is the heat and dust of India; a world of poverty contained within an immense landscape. The contrast between the celebrations in London in June 1897 and the reality of India so vividly captured by Swoboda is marked. It is a contrast that not only informs us eloquently about the British Empire, but also, in a different political context, remains a reflection on the state of the world today.

By the end of her life Queen Victoria had come to personify the British Empire. But she had never herself had to defend in person the extensive territories over which she ruled. It had not always been thus for British monarchs.

The last British monarch to command troops on a field of battle was George II at the Battle of Dettingen in 1743. He was sixty years old and showed considerable bravery against French forces disputing the succession to the Austrian throne. He began the battle on horseback, but finished fighting on foot.

George II was no lover of painting – he left that to his wife Caroline of Ansbach – but he loved, in the words of Horace Walpole, 'Germany, the army and women'.[28] This love of the army was shared by his son, William Augustus, Duke of Cumberland, who had also fought at Dettingen and had been wounded. After his appointment as Commander-in-Chief, the duke carried out significant administrative reforms in the army, involving discipline, training, the formation of regiments and the issuing of uniforms and colours. By the middle of the eighteenth century, the army was gradually becoming standardised, as well as more efficient. The result was the mounting supremacy of British land forces that the Duke of Marlborough had first inspired at the beginning of the eighteenth century and the Duke of Wellington was to maintain at the beginning of the nineteenth.

A mediocre Swiss artist, David Morier, depicted the new uniforms and arms drill associated with the Duke of Cumberland's reforms in a series

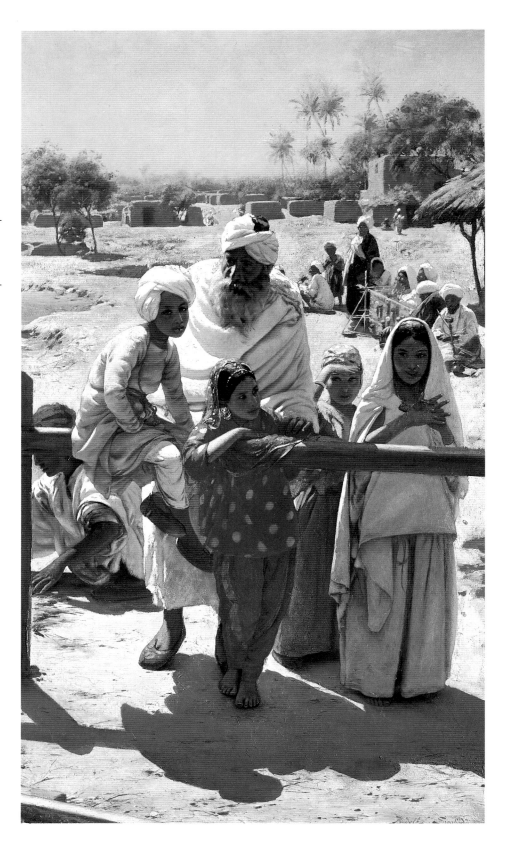

FIG. 107
Rudolf Swoboda: *Waiting for the Train*, 1892

of small pictures. These are not great paintings, but they are important documents for the development of the British army, comparable with the series produced at the beginning of the nineteenth century for William IV by the French artist Alexandre-Jean Dubois Drahonet (FIG. 108). This obsession with military uniforms was a hallmark of the Hanoverian dynasty and nobody had a greater sense of military sartorial elegance than George IV.

In 1793, when he was Prince of Wales, he was appointed Colonel Commandant of the Tenth Light Dragoons and immediately commissioned George Stubbs to depict a group of soldiers from the regiment (FIG. 26). This

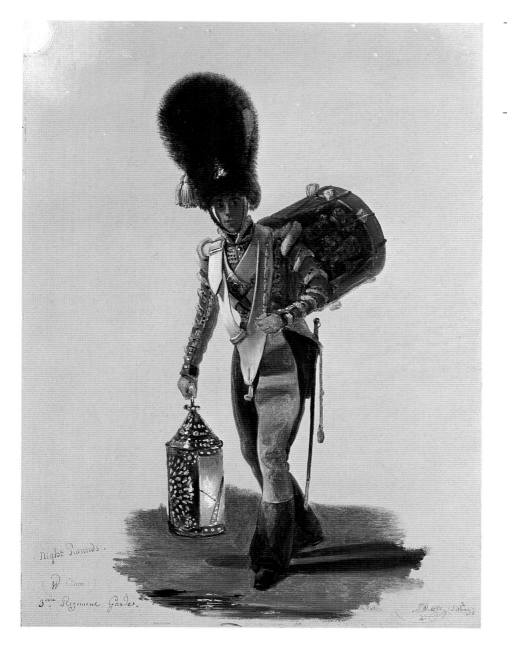

FIG. 108
Alexandre-Jean Dubois Drahonet: *British Infantry. Night Rounds. Drummer William Cann, Scots Fusilier Guards*, 1832

is a remarkably understated painting, being principally a precise record of newly designed uniforms, but the figures are clearly characterised and there are perhaps touches of humour in the splayed feet of the soldiers, quite apart from the geometrical precision that characterises so many paintings by Stubbs. The artist depicts a mounted sergeant, a trumpeter, a sergeant shouldering arms and a trooper presenting arms. The last two figures wear 'tarleton helmets' named after a famous hero of the American War of Independence, Colonel (later General) Sir Banastre Tarleton Bt., who is shown wearing this headgear in a famous portrait by Reynolds (London, National Gallery). The trumpeter wears a jacket with 'reversed colours' in order to make him more visible, since at this date it was musicians who transmitted orders on the field of battle. Aspects of the uniform – the braiding and the bearskin worn by the trumpeter – became popularly associated with the standard dress of the Hussars, as the Tenth Light Dragoons were officially designated in 1805.

George II's exploits on the distant battlefield of Dettingen were not to be repeated by a British sovereign. When George III and George IV were in turn Princes of Wales they pleaded with their fathers to be allowed to fight, but much to their chagrin permission was never granted. George IV was so frustrated that he fought the battles in his imagination and at times regarded himself as supreme commander of the alliance of European powers that brought about the downfall of Napoleon I.[29]

The fact that sovereigns did not themselves fight in the front line did not of course exclude the participation of other members of the royal family. Queen Victoria's son Prince Arthur, Duke of Connaught, fought in Egypt, and the present Duke of York served in the Falklands War. The sovereign's role as military leader remains highly symbolic and is at all times crucial for morale. This was especially the case during the First and Second World Wars when George V and Queen Mary, and George VI and Queen Elizabeth respectively played such supportive roles. However, experience is often gained by the heir to the throne in one or more of the armed forces and throughout history this has been regarded as part of the preparation for the duties that the sovereign has to perform.

Artists, therefore, portrayed the role of the sovereign in military affairs in several ways. George III's reign, for instance, was dominated by foreign wars – beginning with the Seven Years War, continuing with the War of American Independence and the annexation of India, and reaching a climax with the Napoleonic wars following the French Revolution. The American painter Benjamin West, who while serving as Historical Painter and Surveyor to the king also became President of the Royal Academy in succession to Reynolds, shows the military preparations of George III in a full-length portrait painted in 1779 (FIG. 109). The king is shown in uniform

FIG. 109
Benjamin West: *George III*, 1779

184

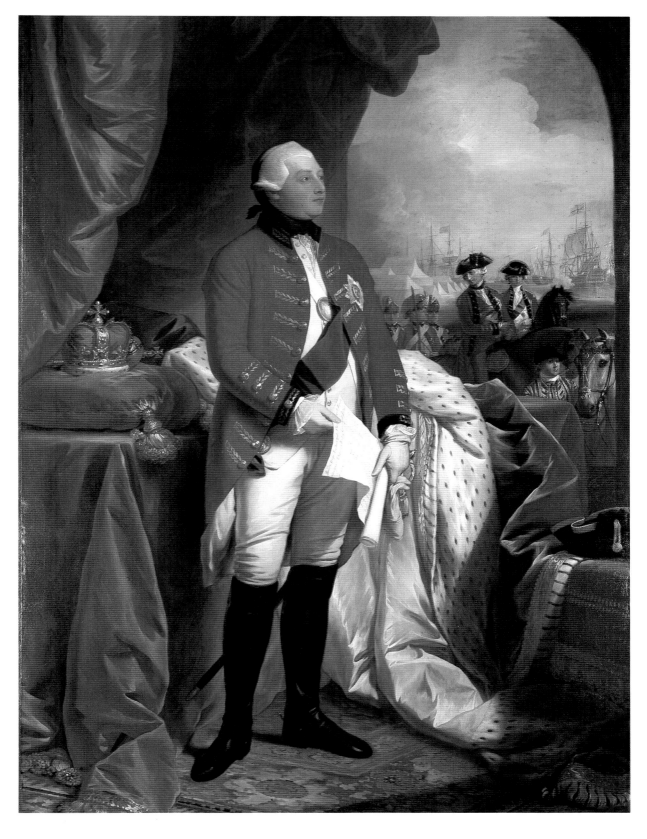

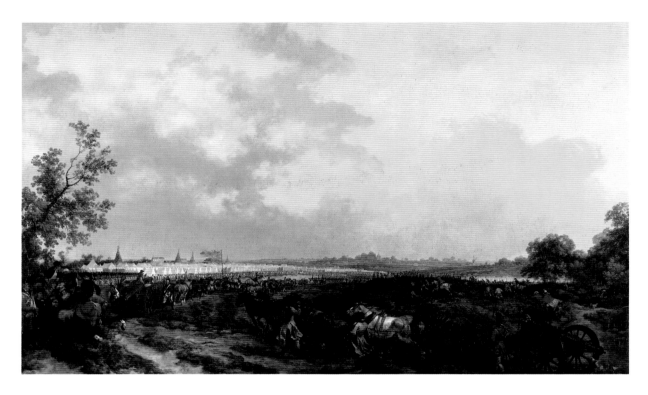

FIG. 110
Philip James de
Loutherbourg: *Warley
Camp: The Review*, 1780

wearing the Order of the Garter: the formal trappings of kingship, symbolised by the royal regalia and the ermine robe, have been set aside. He holds a paper on which troop dispositions are recorded, while in the background his charger is restrained by a groom wearing royal livery. Further back there is an encampment with a detachment of the Fifteenth Light Dragoons parading, and, beyond, the fleet is also assembling with the *Royal George*, a man-of-war on which Prince William, later William IV, was then serving, firing a salute. There is a sense of urgency in this portrait: the beat of the drum and the sound of the pipe are not far away as the country prepares for war.

George III was a patriot. Shortly after acceding to the throne he informed Parliament that having been 'born and educated in this country, I glory in the name of Briton'[30], and he began to take an active interest in the training of the militia. Two paintings by Philip James de Loutherbourg, an artist of Polish origins who worked in Germany and France before coming to London, show preparations at Warley Camp in Essex.

First there was a review of the troops which took place on the morning of 20 October 1778 (FIG. 110). The king is seen in front of the encampment with his staff. He is reviewing an artillery train which is moving into position to file past. The skyline includes landmarks in Essex, while in the foreground spectators run forward to obtain a better view of proceedings. The review was followed by manoeuvres culminating in a mock attack

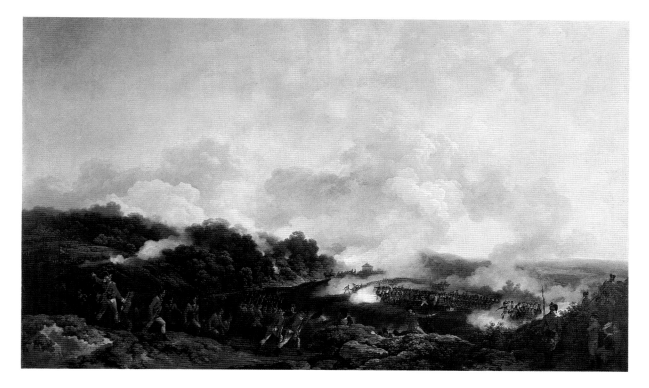

performed by the Light Infantry and Grenadiers who march accompanied by artillery through the wooded valley towards Little Warley (FIG. 111). The soldiers, under the command of General Pierson, performed manoeuvres of attack and defence, forming squares and columns while being fired upon by batteries concealed in the surrounding woods. The king is positioned with his staff by the observatory in the centre of the composition.

George III's interest in military affairs was not limited to land. The role of the navy throughout British history was of equal significance for the defence of the country. The seventeenth-century reforms of the navy in which Samuel Pepys played a memorable part proved to be immensely significant during the three Anglo-Dutch wars that are so vividly recorded in paintings by the two Willem van de Veldes, father and son. The marine paintings by these artists are notable not just because of the depiction of these vessels at the mercy of the elements and of firepower, but also because of the remarkable, almost poetic, sense of the spatial intervals in the placing of masts and the angle of the decks, quite apart from the details of rigging, flags and gunports.

By the reign of George III the chief naval threat came from France and the king was therefore duly attentive to maritime affairs. There was an official royal visit to the fleet between 22 and 26 June 1773 and this is recorded in four canvases by the king's Marine Painter, Dominic Serres. The fleet was assembled at Spithead and on the first day the king was received by the Board of Admiralty aboard the *Barfleur*, a vessel of ninety guns. The *Barfleur* is surrounded by the barges of the Board of Admiralty, the three flag officers and all the captains. At the mastheads are flying the Royal Standard, the flag of the Lord High Admiral and the Union flag. These were hoisted when the king came on board to the sound of a royal salute. This was followed by an extensive luncheon after which the king re-embarked in his barge. The other days were spent sailing about in the royal yacht, *Augusta*, inspecting the different squadrons.

Activities such as these have been continued by sovereigns up to the present day. Queen Victoria was particularly zealous in carrying out such duties and the painter especially favoured by her in these respects was George Thomas. He was principally a wood engraver, who made several illustrations for the *Illustrated London News* before specialising in painting formal events in watercolour or oil with care and precision. As has already been noted, Queen Victoria commissioned a number of paintings from him and she very much appreciated the emphasis he put on accuracy and fidelity to the various scenes. One such example shows a review staged during the State Visit of the King of Sardinia on 1 December 1855. It was a cold, foggy day and the inspection of the Royal Arsenal was followed by a review of the troops of Horse Artillery and a field battery on Woolwich Common. The king rides between Prince Albert and the Duke of Cambridge, in front of the lines. Queen Victoria recorded in her *Journal* that the king of Sardinia 'looks very wild on horseback'.[31]

A year later the queen and the Prince Consort, who had a particular interest in the reform of the army, attended a review at the new military barracks established at Aldershot (FIG. 112). The painting by Thomas was, in fact, made retrospectively in 1866 and includes General Knollys, who instructed Prince Albert in the art of soldiering. The queen wrote to her uncle Leopold, King of the Belgians:

> We had a delightful little *séjour* at Aldershot – much favoured by fine weather. The first day, Wednesday, the wind was too high for me to ride, but the second (Thursday) we had one of the prettiest and most interesting field days I ever remember. I rode about everywhere and enjoyed it so much. On Thursday and Friday morning we visited the Camp. The new Troops from the Crimea which we saw were the 34th, 41st, and 49th, particularly fine regiments; the 93rd Highlanders, the 2nd Rifle Battalion, and three Companies of splendid Sappers and Miners, all very fine; and the Scots Greys and Enniskillen Dragoons. The Prussians were *émerveillés* at the looks of our Troops on returning from the Crimea! We came here on the 18th and have really hot weather.[32]

Previously, in the spring of 1856, there had been a naval review at Spithead, also painted by Thomas, when the queen received the salute while sailing in the royal yacht *Victoria and Albert*. The vessels were lined up in double rows while the royal yacht passed down the lines. The queen recorded in her *Journal*:

> A more magnificent Fleet cannot be imagined, nor could any country boast of a similar show: 250 Pennants . . . and all steam! . . . Without undue boasting, I may claim to be Queen of the Seas and accept the crown Neptune offers to Britannia, as depicted in the fresco on the staircase at Osborne![33]

One further painting by Thomas records a more solemn occasion, *The Presentation of Crimean Medals by Queen Victoria on 18 May 1855* (FIG. 113). The presentation took place on Horse Guards Parade, more closely associated now with the Sovereign's Birthday Parade. The queen and Prince Albert, together with members of the household, stood on a dais while other members of the royal family looked down from the central window of Horse Guards. The Crimean War was still in progress and the ceremony was

FIG. 112
George Thomas: *Queen Victoria and the Prince Consort at Aldershot*, 1866

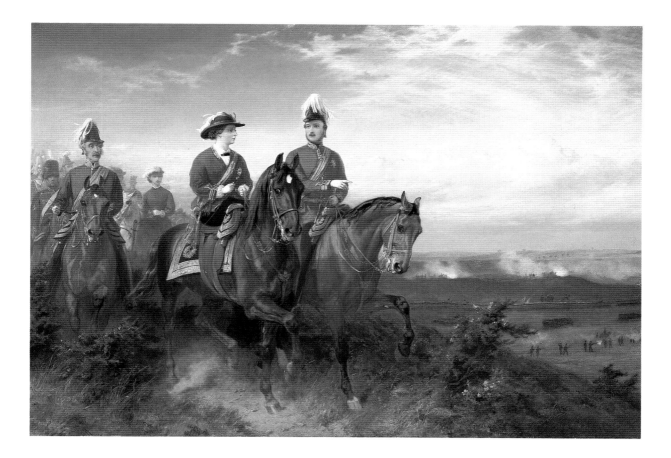

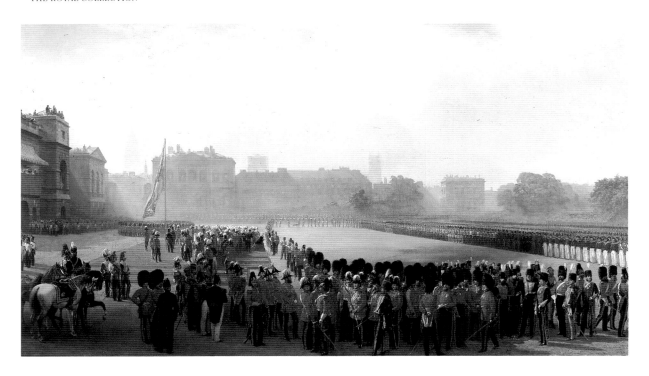

clearly intended to raise morale. The medals were presented to all ranks and to naval personnel. The parade was commanded by the Duke of Cambridge, who received his medal first and is seen amongst the senior officers in the foreground where others, such as the Earls of Lucan and Cardigan (of Battle of Balaclava fame), are also grouped. These figures all wear the Crimean medal; the presentation continues in the middle distance.

The parade was significant for another reason, which Queen Victoria notes in her *Journal.* For the occasion 'united high and low and brought *all* equally together as heroes . . . the first time that a simple Private has touched the hand of the Sovereign'.[34]

The Crimean War was a turning point in artists' depiction of warfare, but in order to appreciate why this was so it is necessary to see how battles had been painted previously. Ostensibly, military painting was closely related to topographical or landscape painting. Two large pictures by John Wootton, dated 1742 and commissioned by Frederick, Prince of Wales, represent incidents from the Duke of Marlborough's campaign during the War of the Spanish Succession: the Siege of Lille in 1708 (FIG. 114) and the Siege of Tournay in 1709. Because Wootton is undertaking these pictures thirty years or so after the events, he shows more concern for accuracy in the setting, situation and detail than for atmosphere or heroism. The paintings have a documentary air made even more apparent by the bird's-eye view that Wootton adopts so that he can reveal as much of the engagement as possible. This was the standard procedure for battle painting as it emerged from the seventeenth-century baroque tradition and it can be seen again in the series of pictures by Jan van Huchtenburg portraying the Duke of Marlborough's great victories against the French or in any of the numerous works by Adam Frans van der Meulen. It is, however, this documentary aspect that at first prevented the genre from being incorporated amongst the accepted ranks of great painting.

Landscape art, topography or genre were accorded a lowly status in such texts as Sir Joshua Reynolds' *Discourses on Art*. For Reynolds, history painting was of the greatest significance because it depicted and extolled moral as well as heroic virtues exemplified by the past. A perfect demonstration of this branch of history painting in the royal context was provided for George III by Benjamin West.

Between 1769 and 1773 West painted a series of pictures which were hung in the Warm Room on the ground floor of Buckingham House. The installation of these paintings is highly significant. At either end of the room were the two largest pictures, both taken from classical sources: *The Departure of Regulus* (FIG. 115) and *The Oath of Hannibal*. *The Departure of Regulus* is summarised by Livy in his *History of Rome*.[35] Apparently, the artist read the relevant passage aloud to the king.

The incident occurred in 250 BC, during the First Punic War between Rome and Carthage. The Roman Consul, Regulus, had been captured by

FIG. 114
John Wootton: *The Siege of Lille*, 1742

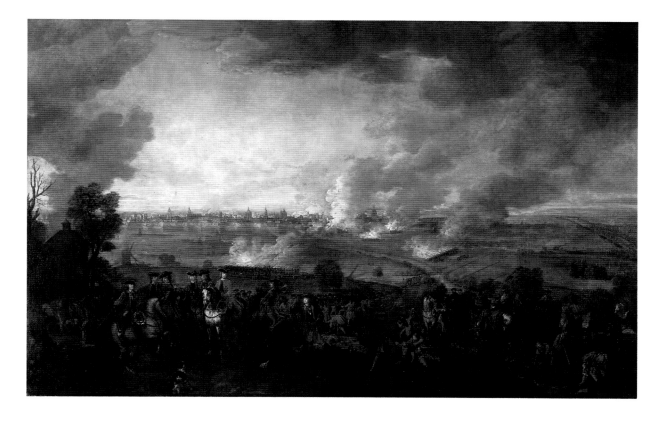

191

the Carthaginians. He was sent back to Rome to negotiate terms, but, since he regarded these as unfavourable, he advised the Roman Senate to reject them and so returned to Carthage knowing that he would face certain death. Regulus, in the centre of West's composition, takes his leave of the

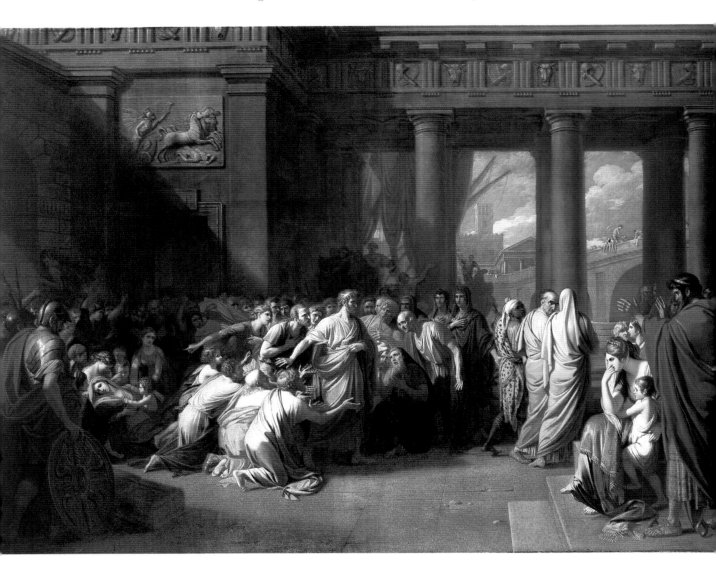

FIG. 115
Benjamin West: *The Departure of Regulus*, 1769

Senate, while on the right his wife and family mourn the outcome. The painting is stoical in mood and visually the inspirational sources are Raphael and Poussin.

The Warm Room also had two similar classical scenes serving as over-doors, illustrating the theme of magnanimity, but more important than either of these were the paintings on the main wall. On either side of the fireplace were two vertical compositions illustrating the deaths of two more heroes. The first shows the death of the Theban general Epaminondas from wounds received during the battle of Mantinea (362 BC) against the Spartans (FIG. 116). He was pierced in the chest with a spear, and it was obvious that when it was withdrawn he would die. He asks if his shield has been saved and his armour-bearer duly shows that it has been found

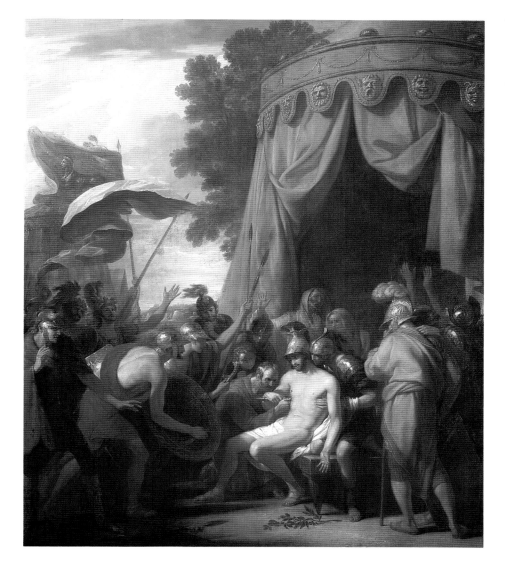

FIG. 116
Benjamin West: *The Death of Epaminondas*, 1773

on the field of battle. Safe in that knowledge, Epaminondas gives the order to withdraw the spear and so dies.[36]

Balancing this on the other side of the fireplace is *The Death of Chevalier Bayard* (FIG. 117). This scene is not inspired by the classical world, but by a hero of the Renaissance. Bayard was renowned for his soldiering abilities and he was known as the 'chevalier sans peur et sans reproche'.[37] His death emphasises the chivalrous nature of his character. He fell in 1524 during the Lombard wars, but it is the manner of his death that is important. He

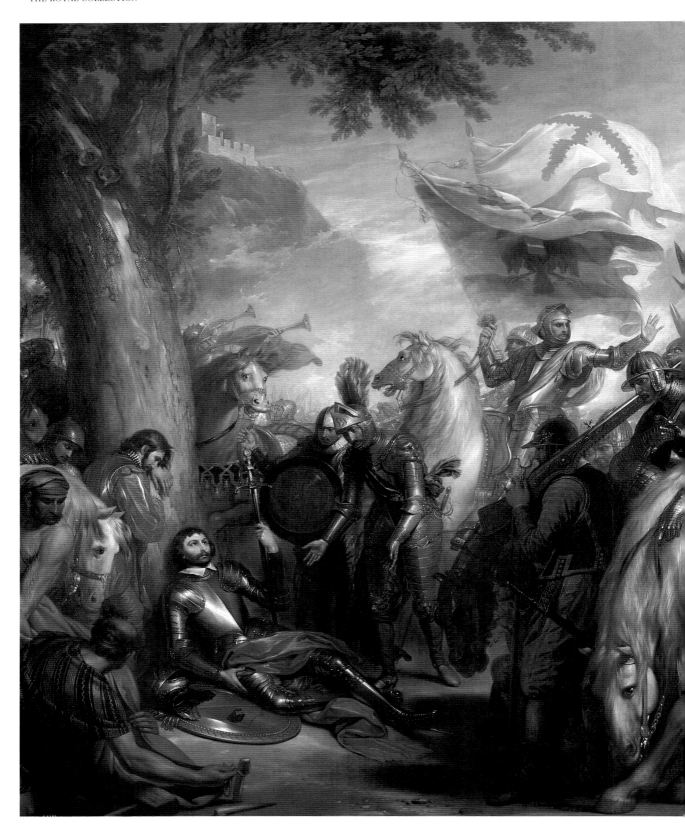

lies wounded, propped up against a tree: he recites the *Miserere* holding his sword by the hilt. As he does this his adversaries come to pay him homage. In both these paintings West refers to works by the Italian seventeenth-century painter Salvator Rosa, who was an important influence on British history painting.

Over the mantelpiece and separating these two paintings was *The Death of Wolfe* (FIG. 118). This picture celebrates the capture of Quebec by General James Wolfe in 1759 and marks the climax of the British campaign against the French in Canada during the Seven Years War. Wolfe had fought at the Battle of Dettingen aged seventeen and he was only thirty-two when he died. He captured Quebec by a brilliant manoeuvre, climbing a steep path leading up from the St Lawrence River. The French were taken by surprise and the final battle was fought on the Plains of Abraham. Both the French commander, General Marquis Louis de Montcalm, and Wolfe were killed. West creates a scene more closely associated with religious iconography – the *Lamentation over the Dead Christ* (FIG. 119). Wolfe lies on the ground attended by members of his staff. The boats on the St Lawrence River can be made out in the background at the right, while on the left a messenger runs up with news of the British victory. The group on the left comprised distinguished officers, including General Robert Monckton, one of Wolfe's principal commanders, while on the right a servant and a grena-

FIG. 117
Benjamin West: *The Death of Chevalier Bayard*, 1772

FIG. 118
Benjamin West: *The Death of Wolfe*, 1771

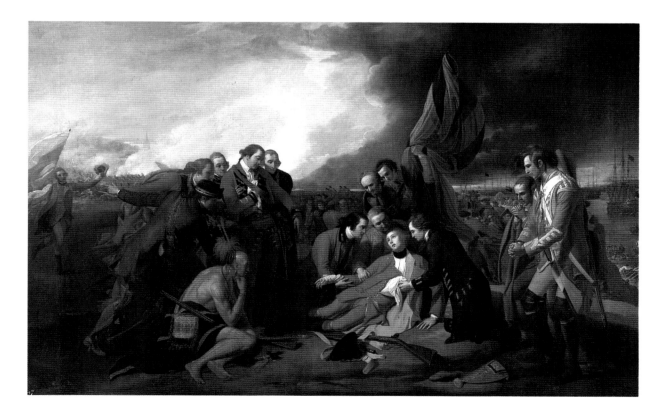

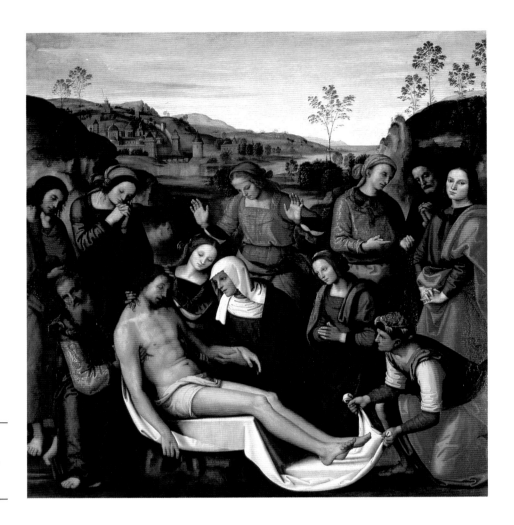

FIG. 119
Pietro Perugino:
*Lamentation over the Dead
Christ*, 1495

dier look on. The crouching Indian in the left foreground symbolises the New World.

Wolfe's death scene as painted by West is a key moment in the development of British painting. The original picture is now in the National Gallery of Canada at Ottawa: it was originally owned not by George III but by Lord Grosvenor. The king had heard about this picture, which had caused a sensation when first exhibited because West had chosen to show the figures in modern military dress. Reynolds had apparently urged West to 'adopt the classic costumes of antiquity'.[38] This was the issue: in history painting, if you divorce the subject you are treating from the context of antiquity or a clearly defined notion of the past, then you sacrifice the moral dimension associated with heroism. West argued that 'the same truth that guides the pen of the historian should govern the pencil of the artist'.[39]

Fortunately, George III did not wholly agree with Reynolds – he rarely did – and so commissioned West to paint a replica of *The Death of Wolfe* to form part of the decorative scheme for the Warm Room in Buckingham House. The treatment of *The Death of Wolfe* is innovatory and Reynolds himself later described the painting as revolutionary.[40] Only twenty years had elapsed between the event itself and West's painting. He was obviously aware of the difficulty of depicting such a recent episode in British history, because he makes such a clear reference to religious inconography, thus admitting that this is no ordinary death scene and so imposing upon it a sense of the universal. In doing this, however, West sacrifices historical accuracy by introducing figures who were not actually present at the scene (for example, the Indian or General Monckton) for the sake of compositional propriety. West was here trying to come to terms with a dilemma. How do you modernise history painting? How do you translate traditional virtues into a modern setting? Indeed, can a modern history subject be elevated to the level of the heroic and thus be held up as an exemplar in the same way as a scene from antiquity? This is why *The Death of Wolfe* was seen as a challenging painting.

At the centre of battle painting lay a paradox: if the work was to aspire to the status of art, this nearly always had to be achieved at the cost of historical accuracy, whereas fidelity to the truth meant only a banal transcription of events.

The dilemma raised by *The Death of Wolfe* was solved by the concept of nationalism that came to the fore at the beginning of the nineteenth century, prompted by the defeat of Napoleon I and the rise of the British Empire. History painting had already focused attention on the growth of a national school of painting and so ultimately it was military success that helped to lift battle painting on to a level of respectability. In France, encouraged by Napoleon, this shift had already occurred, and, indeed, military subjects had proved so successful there that English painters feared the comparison. Yet the defeat of Napoleon at Waterloo had changed people's attitudes, and battle painters began to be accepted, if not at the Royal Academy, then certainly at the rival exhibition space opened in 1805 in Pall Mall, known as the British Institution and founded specifically for the promotion of British art.

In addressing modern subjects, painters could now replace the stoical attitude to death stemming from antiquity with an image of heroism in which courage, compassion, but, above all, patriotism were exemplified. Such concepts are, of course, closely linked to the growth of biographies of military heroes and the erection of contemporary monuments recording great deeds. This represents an important shift in the appreciation of heroes and hero-worship: a shift from the universal to the particular. No longer was a hero the symbol of an abstract notion of truth or right, so much as the product of love of his or her country.

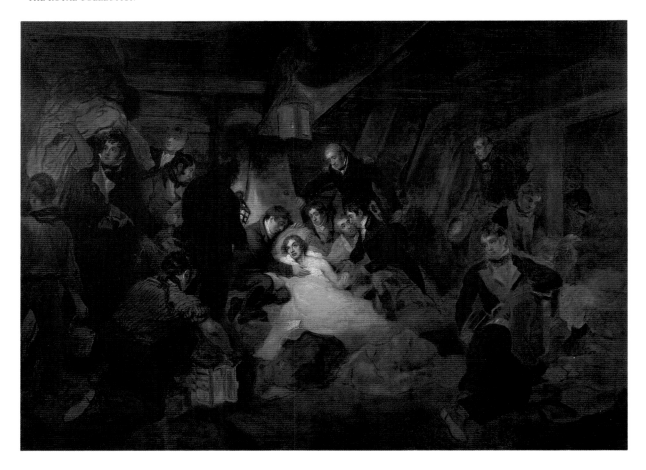

FIG. 120
Arthur William Devis: *The
Death of Nelson*, c. 1807

One painting that reveals a debt to West's *Death of Wolfe* is *The Death of Nelson* by Arthur William Devis (FIG. 120), which is in all probability a *modello* for the large painting of the same subject in the National Maritime Museum in Greenwich. Devis was granted privileges that were not open to West. He was allowed on board HMS *Victory* as the vessel returned with Nelson's body after the Battle of Trafalgar in 1805. A contemporary account describes how Devis was 'allowed to have all the attendants at the Admiral's death grouped in the Cockpit, *exactly as they were there* at the moment when he expired'.[41] The result was a faithful record of the death of a national hero.

Perhaps the finest evocation of this new, more realistic approach to history painting is epitomised by George IV's installation of pictures in St James's Palace. Central to the arrangement of the paintings in the State Apartments was the Throne Room. On either side of the king's own Coronation portrait by Sir Thomas Lawrence were two large battle scenes by George Jones: the *Battle of Vittoria* (FIG. 121) and the *Battle of Waterloo* (FIG. 122). Jones was born in 1786. He was a friend of J. M. W. Turner and lived until 1869. In terms of battle painting his career extends roughly from the Peninsular Campaign to the Indian Mutiny. His paintings were done with a certain amount of inside information, since he served with the army in Wellington's campaigns and had, in fact, formed part of the British force that occupied Paris in 1815. He had, therefore, an authoritative knowledge of modern military affairs, being a firm admirer – and indeed an acquaintance – of the Duke of Wellington, Sir John Moore and Sir Charles Napier.

Jones painted the *Battle of Vittoria* for George IV. Fought in June 1813, the battle took place at the foot of the Pyrenees. Wellington, in alliance with the Portuguese and the Spanish against the French, is seen in the left foreground mounted on a white charger. It is early evening and he is directing the final assault on the city, illuminated by shafts of sunlight piercing the clouds in the sky. It was an auspicious victory forming the climax of the Peninsular Campaign after which George IV appointed Wellington to the rank of fieldmarshal, and the king of Spain in gratitude presented Wellington with the paintings previously looted by Joseph Bona-

FIG. 121
George Jones: *The Battle of Vittoria*, 1822

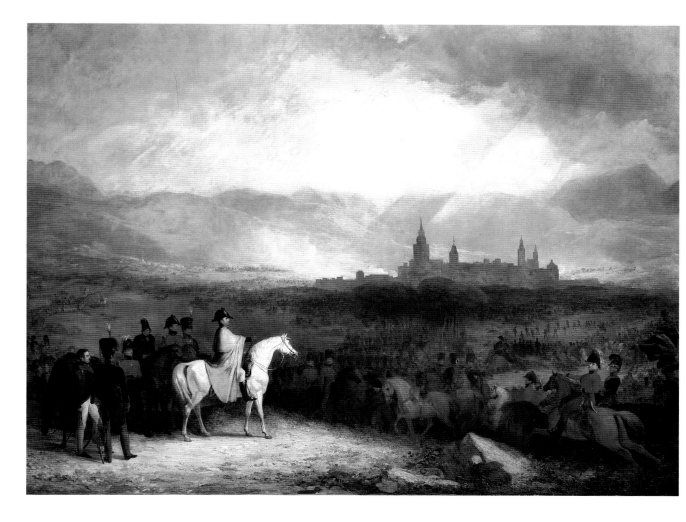

parte from the Spanish royal collection and now to be seen in Apsley House.

The companion picture shows the climax of *The Battle of Waterloo*. This time, in order to balance the other painting, Wellington is placed in the foreground at the right. The Hussars are seen charging on the right with the Union Brigade of Cavalry on the left. In the centre, down the slope, the Foot Guards advance towards the French, where, positioned in the sunken road, Napoleon can be seen trying to encourage the Imperial Guard in a last desperate effort.

What is most apparent in these two enormous paintings is the combination of a panoramic view of the battlefield with an accumulation of detail. Jones seeks accuracy in the disposition of regiments and the exact moment (usually the climax) in the engagement that he chooses to depict, but, at the same time, he does not fail to suggest the sweep of battle – the city set below the mountains or the rolling hills of the Belgian countryside – under an immense area of sky. The artist successfully unites a sense of design

FIG. 122
George Jones: *The Battle of Waterloo*, c. 1824

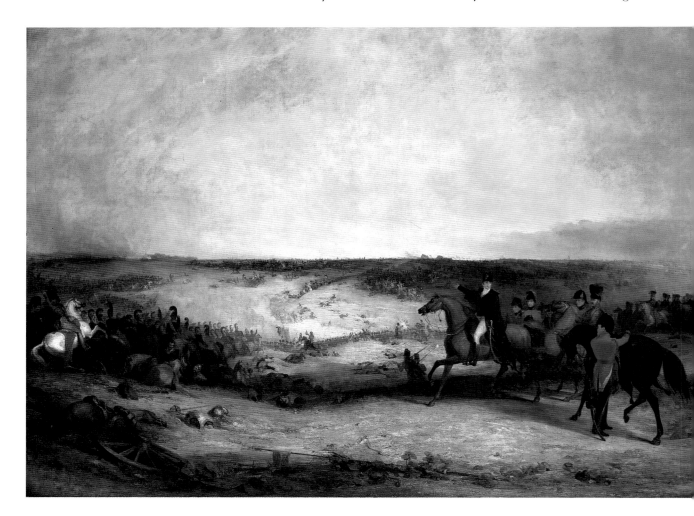

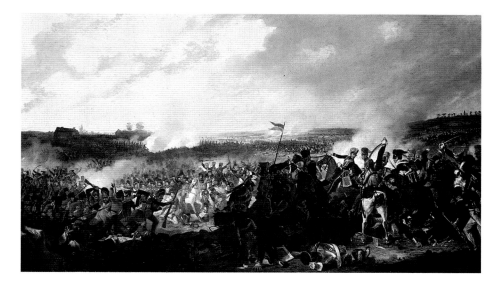

FIG. 123
Denis Dighton: *The Battle of
Waterloo: General advance of
the British lines*, 1816

and a sense of drama. He retains the pageantry of war, but does not neglect the details.

The Battle of Waterloo led, of course, to a surge of patriotism. Numerous painters depicted it and there was a large production of popular art in the form of illustrations and panoramas. The action also inspired a vast amount of prose and poetry – by Byron, Southey, Scott, Thackeray, Hugo, Chateaubriand, Stendhal, Michelet and others – usually following a visit to the battlefield itself. George IV's official military painter, Denis Dighton, went only a few days after the battle. An artist who had been commissioned in the army, but who had also been a pupil of the French history painter Paul Delacroche in Paris, his approach was not romantic.

Dighton made several depictions of the Battle of Waterloo for George IV, but one is of particular significance because it concentrates on the general advance of the British lines, an advance led by the Earl of Uxbridge, later the Marquess of Anglesey, who commanded thirty-one regiments (FIG. 123). The earl is on the right, pointing with his sword towards the French. He wears the uniform of a general officer of light cavalry and leads the Fifth and Sixth Hussar brigades. On the left are the First Foot Guards, also advancing towards the French. The composition is very dense and concentrated. The eye is transfixed by the gestures, actions and contortions of attack, defence and death. Most striking is the close proximity of the French lines, so that one is conscious not only of how physical this type of combat was, but also how personal. In fact, the battlefield of Waterloo was extremely constricted and the opposing lines were at no point more than a thousand yards apart. While Dighton indicated the setting with La Belle Alliance in the left background, before which Napoleon can be made out preparing to retreat, and the Observatory on the right, it is really the action in the foreground that is emphasised. It was during this final charge that the Earl of Uxbridge was struck by grapeshot on his right knee, occasioning the famous comment to Wellington: 'By God, I have lost my leg!' to which the duke replied, 'Have you, by God?' The leg was amputated on the field, but the earl's pulse did not change; his only complaint was that the knife was not very sharp.[42]

Dighton's painting illustrates an act of heroism. Indeed, George IV and the Marquess of Anglesey shared a passion for military painting. The Earl of Uxbridge's conduct on the field of battle was not only valiant (he had eight or nine horses shot from under him), it was also brilliant. His cavalry charges were ruthless in their efficiency and effectiveness, and won both the admiration of Napoleon and the eternal gratitude of George IV.

Before you enter the Throne Room in St James's Palace you pass through the Ante-Room. Two important and exceptionally large marine paintings once hung here on either side of a portrait of George III. These were the *Glorious First of June* by Philip James de Loutherbourg and the *Battle of Trafalgar* by J. M. W. Turner. Both paintings remained here for only a few years, because, with several portraits of naval interest, George IV gave them to the National Maritime Museum, where they are now displayed.

De Loutherbourg (FIG. 124) records the victory of the English fleet over the French revolutionary forces off Ushant on 1 June 1794, when eleven enemy ships were destroyed and ten more dismasted. Lord Howe's flag-ship, the *Queen Charlotte*, is seen with her fore-topmast broken, while two French ships on either side, the *Montagna* to the right and the *Jacobin* to the left, forge ahead. It is about 10 a.m. on the day of the sea battle. De Loutherbourg was an extremely versatile artist and, having been a fine romantic landscape painter, he concentrated during the last fifteen years of his life on history painting. Unlike the van de Veldes or Serres, de Loutherbourg placed little emphasis on documentary aspects. The facts of the battle are accurately recorded, but it is what is happening in the foreground that is most important. This, in human terms, is where the drama really lies and where the individual is confronted by fate. The artist emphasises the individual's personal sacrifice in battle. The contrast is between safety and danger or victory and loss. In the end, the plight of the individual is less important than the glory of the nation, just as in de Loutherbourg's earlier landscapes the individual is easily overcome by the forces of nature.

A similar equation can be found in Turner's *Battle of Trafalgar* (FIG. 125), the largest picture he ever painted. It dates from 1823–4 and was the artist's attempt to win several commissions from George IV. Early in 1806,

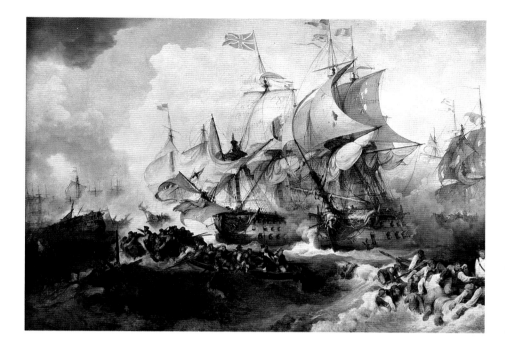

FIG. 124
Philip James de
Loutherbourg: *The Glorious
First of June, 1794*, 1795

Turner had seen HMS *Victory* return from the Battle of Trafalgar: she came up the Medway with Nelson's body still on board. But Turner failed to impress the experts. Courtiers, who no doubt meant well, but nevertheless trod recklessly on artistic sensibilities, pointed out that the rigging was not accurate, that HMS *Victory* was too far out of the water and that Turner had amalgamated five separate incidents of the battle into one picture. Turner continued to make alterations to the canvas in order to placate the critics, but to no avail. They were, of course, missing the point: nautical accuracy was not the subject of the picture. Turner telescopes events to create not just a compositional unity, but also a thematic unity, namely the defeat of the French by the English fleet.

HMS *Victory* is a symbol, sailing proudly on while both her foremast and her mizzen topmast fall. By contrast, off the port bow the French vessel *Redoubtable* sinks. Turner even hints at Nelson's own fate, because his personal flag flies from the top of the foremast which is shown falling, while Nelson's personal motto, *Palmam qui Meruit Ferat* ('Let him who best deserves it bear the palm'), is inscribed on a piece of wood in the foreground, thus revealing the true meaning of the picture. Turner emphasises the horrors of naval warfare. The scene of carnage in the foreground is worthy of Dante's *Purgatorio*. Yet possibly because of the purpose of the commission, Turner allows himself to overlay even these horrors with an aura of patriotism as the Union Flag flutters so prominently over the water.

Unfortunately for the Royal Collection, George IV decided against retaining both these masterpieces. Turner took this as a royal rebuff and

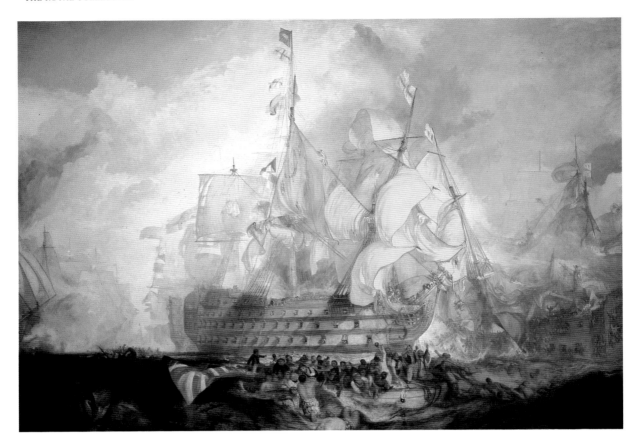

felt that the failure of the painting cost him a knighthood. John Ruskin, a passionate supporter of Turner, later defended the picture of *The Battle of Trafalgar* by saying that it was 'worth all the rest of the hospital [Greenwich] – grounds – walls – pictures and models put together'.[43]

Attitudes to war change and one of the turning points in British military history was assuredly the Crimean War of 1854–6. The Victoria Cross was instituted in 1856 (but with effect from 1854), and the war was widely reported. Magazines such as the *Illustrated London News* and newspapers such as *The Times* provided detailed accounts. Photographs by Roger Fenton and artists' illustrations were published. Although the Crimea was far away, people at home knew what was happening. The consequence was that death, pain, sickness, injury and incompetence could no longer be so easily overlooked, now that such unappealing aspects of war were open to public scrutiny.

Technology was also beginning to change the character of warfare: larger areas were fought over, greater distances were covered by trains and telegraph poles, more lethal long-range weapons were devised, more men and women were committed to the front lines. At the same time, war was becoming more democratic and, inevitably, more political. The Crimean

204

War brought to the surface social tensions within Victorian society: for the first time, the conduct and ability of high-ranking officers were challenged. Reform of the army was demanded by politicians and encouraged by Prince Albert.

Battle paintings dating from before the mid-nineteenth century had tended to idealise war. There are, admittedly, several bodies and open wounds, but no attempt is made to suggest or dwell upon blood and pain. Lady (Elizabeth) Butler belonged to a new school. As a painter, she was a phenomenal success. She became a celebrity and an establishment figure, with the army providing models and uniforms, and putting on special parades or displays for her to sketch and to study soldiers in action. Indeed, her achievement was such that for the first time battle painting outstripped history painting and thus at last became generally acceptable. Yet her pictures are ambiguous, even those full of action such as *Scotland for Ever!* inspired by the Battle of Waterloo (Leeds, City Art Gallery). Perhaps this was deliberate, for in her autobiography she wrote, 'My own reading of war – that mysteriously inevitable recurrence throughout the sorrowful history of our world – is that it calls forth the noblest and basest impulses of human nature.'[44]

These are the aspects of war that she captures in her famous painting *The Roll Call: Calling the Roll after an Engagement in the Crimean War*, which is signed and dated 1874 (FIG. 126). Like *The Death of Wolfe*, the painting dates from twenty years after the event, but there is here, by contrast, an element of tacit criticism. What we see are the remnants of a battalion of Grenadier Guards in a snow-covered landscape. The roll call is read out by a sergeant and witnessed by a mounted officer identified as Colonel Higginson. The setting is bleak, at the foot of a hill with birds of prey circling overhead. The snow suggests that the scene might be intended for the Battle of Inkerman, which was fought on 5 November 1854. What is remarkable about this picture is the way it combines obvious bravery with the dire consequences attendant upon it: terrible wounds, exhaustion, shock, fear and loss. An awesome stillness hangs over the scene and it is this sombre mood that stuns the viewer. There is nothing melodramatic about the composition and, if anything, it is understated: it avoids the ideal and stresses the human at all social levels, both officer class and ordinary ranks. The style is myopically realistic and the artist took immense care to be as accurate as possible with the uniforms and other such details. The mood is one of resignation, possibly inspired by the figures comprising the *Guard's Memorial in Waterloo Place* by John Bell (1860).

What singles out Lady Butler's paintings of the Crimean War (which also include *Balaclava* in Manchester City Art Galleries and *The Return from Inkerman* in the Ferens Art Gallery, Hull) is the actual moment that she

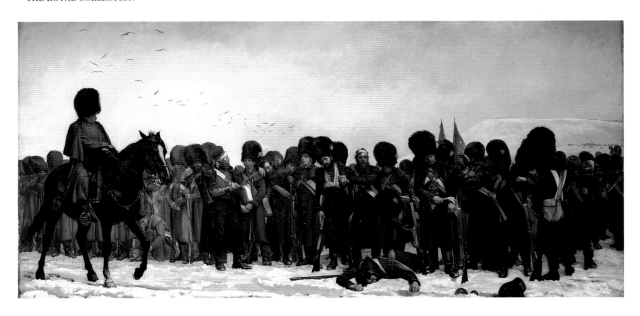

FIG. 126

Elizabeth Thompson, Lady Butler: *The Roll Call: Calling the Roll after an Engagement in the Crimean War*, 1874

chooses to depict. In all three cases it is the aftermath of battle, as opposed to the progress of battle, that is evoked. She sees bravery in adversity. It is not an unpatriotic subject because it extols the courage and self-sacrifice of the anonymous British soldier, but to modern eyes these come perilously close to being anti-war pictures. Yet at the same time *The Roll Call* was one of the most famous paintings of the nineteenth century in Britain. It was commissioned by the industrialist Charles Galloway and shown at the Royal Academy in the summer of 1874 – the date of the first Impressionist exhibition. It caused a sensation, attracting huge crowds which required a policeman to control them.

The painting went on tour to Newcastle, Leeds, Birmingham, Liverpool and Oxford. The Pre-Raphaelite artist Holman Hunt said that *The Roll Call* 'touched the nation's heart as few pictures have ever done'.[45] It also made Lady Butler's reputation. Unfortunately for Galloway, Queen Victoria liked the painting and he eventually ceded it to her on the basis that it was 'a *National* picture and one worthy of a place even in a Royal collection'.[46] The Prince of Wales referred to the painting in his speech to the Royal Academy of 1874 and the queen had it removed temporarily from public view so that it could be shown to the Tsar Alexander II. She sent the artist a bracelet as a token of her admiration. Even more symbolic is the fact that the picture was specially taken to be inspected by Florence Nightingale – who as the 'Lady of the Lamp' could so easily identify with the scene depicted in *The Roll Call*.

For the twentieth-century viewer, however, it is the ambiguity that fascinates. Here is a picture that shows both the bravery and the horrors of war that have become all too apparent in our own century.

CHAPTER 5

Private View

Amarked contrast runs through the paintings in the Royal Collection
between those works that belong in the public sphere and those
that are clearly of private significance. It is a commonplace of the
modern world that members of the British royal family have to pursue a
great part of their private lives in public. Indeed, the boundary between
public and private life in this context has become blurred, a situation
exacerbated by the activities of photographers, television reporters and
gossip columnists. In earlier centuries, only a very small proportion of the
population beyond the confines of the court would even have seen the
sovereign. The Tudors and Stuarts either went on royal progresses, or took
advantage of specific opportunities to show themselves to their people. The
Havoverians were more relaxed. Both George II and George III often
walked openly in public view, the former in St James's Park (FIG. 127) and
the latter at Windsor in the precincts of the castle. The levees in St James's
Palace, as depicted in the watercolour drawings of Thomas Rowlandson,
for example, tended to be crowded, disorderly and rowdy. George IV, when

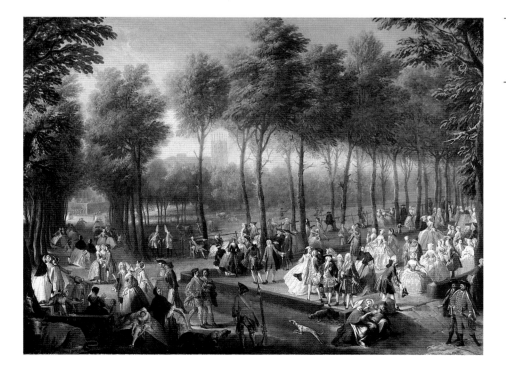

FIG. 127
Anonymous: *St. James's
Park and the Mall*, c. 1745

Prince of Wales and Prince Regent (from 1811), often paraded himself in public and his personal affairs became a target for caricaturists. During the reigns of both George III and George IV the development of the press and the circulation of prints made people more aware of the royal family's proclivities and indeed subjected them to criticism. *The Times* wrote at the time of George IV's funeral, 'There never was an individual less regretted by his fellow creatures than this deceased King. What eye has wept for him? What heart has heaved one throb of unmercenary sorrow?'[1] Few monarchs have been the object of as much vilification as George IV and

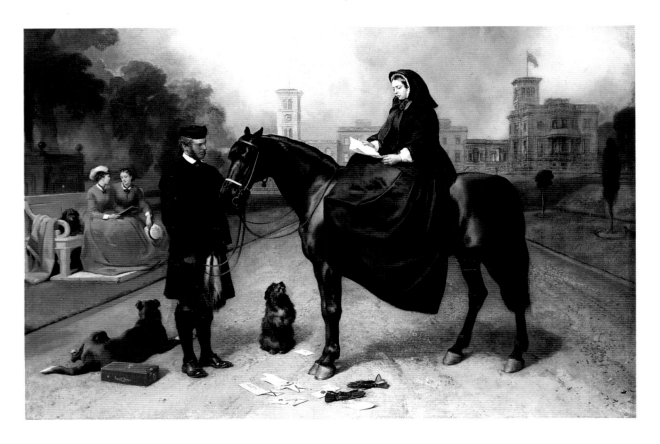

FIG. 128
Sir Edwin Landseer: *Queen Victoria at Osborne House*, 1865–7

today such ridicule seems to us, in the light of his unbounded love of life, his friendship with leading figures of the day, and his knowledge of the arts, somewhat surprising.

Queen Victoria served as a corrective to the excesses of George IV. Her happy marriage set an example of a very different kind, firmly based on family life and closely associated with places such as Osborne House and Balmoral Castle. Indeed, Queen Victoria's withdrawal from public life for twenty years or so after Prince Albert's death in 1861 caused some political concern for a time (FIG. 128). However, when she reappeared in public, as a small, rotund, formidable figure dressed in black, she had become a symbol at the head of a large Empire which was in itself likened to an extended family. An association was thus created between the royal family and the nation as a whole, and it is this that caused the public and private spheres to become overlaid. It resulted in an interpretation of monarchy less interested in wielding power than in setting a good example based on a sense of duty. Or, as one modern historian has described monarchy in the twentieth century, 'It came to be important that the institution should be seen to be the family of families, at once dynastic and domestic, remote and accessible, magical and mundane.'[2] This emphasis

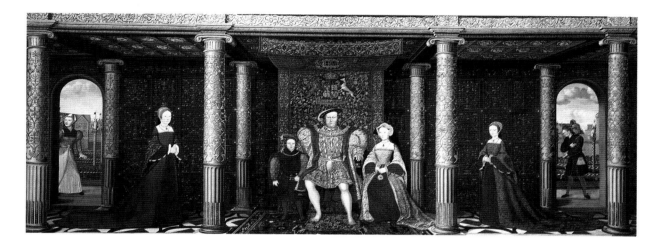

on the family has also proved a significant formula for monarchy in the twentieth century.

It is possible to trace this fascinating development from the public to the private role through certain portraits in the Royal Collection. The primary evidence exists in the type of portraiture now referred to as the royal conversation piece.

The conversation piece was not, of course, restricted to monarchy. A development of the greatest significance in British art, it evolved during the eighteenth century and comprised an insouciant, but artful, grouping of figures implying, although not necessarily denoting, informality.

The origins of the royal conversation piece can be found in a painting such as *The Family of Henry VIII* by an unknown English artist c. 1545 (FIG. 129). This shows the king seated in the centre of a wide horizontal composition. Flanking him are his third wife Jane Seymour, the mother of the young prince (later Edward VI) who is enfolded within Henry VIII's right arm, and the king's two daughters, the future Mary I on the left and Elizabeth I on the right. These figures are placed towards the outer edges of the painting, which in many respects resembles an altar-piece. The glimpses on either side of buildings and gardens where carved images of

FIG. 129
Anonymous: *The Family of Henry VIII*, c. 1545

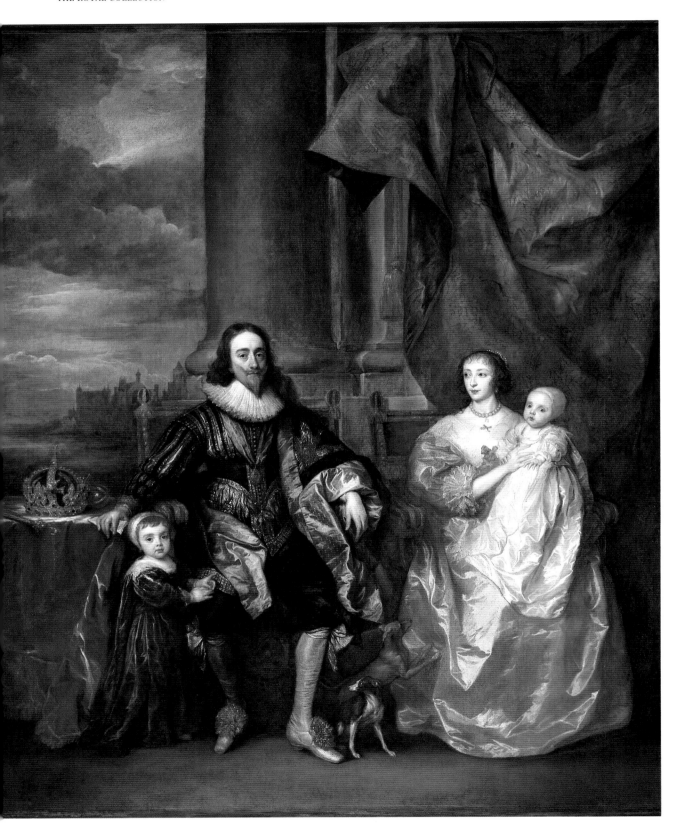

the king's beasts on columns can be seen help to identify Whitehall Palace. The purpose of this painting is purely dynastic, since it emphasises the continuation of the Tudor dynasty. It is an icon of Tudor monarchy reinforcing the status of an ageing king. The clue to its significance is that Jane Seymour had died in 1537, nearly ten years before the picture was begun, and the images of both Henry VIII and Jane Seymour can be related to well-established likenesses by Hans Holbein the Younger.

Soon after Van Dyck arrived in London in 1632 to work for Charles I, he painted a large canvas known as 'The Greate Peece', which was, in fact, his first commission as court painter (FIG. 130). This precedes the more formal, definitive images of Charles I he painted during the 1630s: *Charles I on Horseback with M. de Saint Antoine* (FIG. 11), still in the Royal Collection, *Charles I on Horseback* in the National Gallery, London, and *Charles I in Hunting Dress* in the Musée du Louvre, Paris. 'The Greate Peece' has a theme similar to that of *The Family of Henry VIII*, but it is handled in a rather more relaxed way. The official props are in place: the columns and looped curtains, the royal regalia on the table and a view of Westminster in the background. Yet the relationship of the two seated figures of Charles I and Queen Henrietta Maria to their children, the young Prince of Wales (the future Charles II) supporting himself against his father's knee and Princess Mary being held by the queen, together with the dog jumping up on the queen's dress, hint at domesticity. Van Dyck reveals his debt to Titian in this important portrait group, both in the warm colours and in the wonderfully varied textures of the garments, apart from the stormy sky gathering in the background on the left. The artist succeeds in moulding several disparate elements into a unified composition conceived on a grand scale that challenged Venetian painting of the High Renaissance.

FIG. 130
Sir Anthony Van Dyck:
'The Greate Peece', 1632

The reign in which the royal conversation piece fully emerges is that of George III. The German painter Johann Zoffany, who was much patronised by George III and Queen Charlotte, created one of the finest examples of this new type of composition, which had begun to be evolved in the work of painters like William Hogarth and Arthur Devis during the first half of the eighteenth century. *Queen Charlotte at her Dressing Table* (FIG. 17) was painted in 1765. The queen is seated in a room with her two eldest children, George, Prince of Wales, and Frederick, Duke of York. As Sir Sacheverell Sitwell has written, it is a painting of 'unclouded summer, and the warm stillness is only waiting for a clock to strike, for a chime to sound, and an exotic bird to sing'.[3]

Where French artists in the previous century had preferred to rely upon allegory or stiff formal poses maintained by the sitter even in the presence of impatient pets, Zoffany depicts Queen Charlotte and her two eldest children informally in a private room in a royal residence to which her subjects would not in the ordinary course of affairs have been admitted. A private, purely domestic moment is thus made public. This is especially true since, although privately commissioned, many such conversation pieces or informal royal portraits were exhibited publicly:

> The shift from a dynastic, pseudo-military, or courtly presentation of status to a more urban, patrician style of display was in keeping with an élite that cultivated its pleasures as much in town as in its Palladian parks and villas.[4]

FIG. 131
Sir Edwin Landseer:
Windsor Castle in Modern Times, 1841–5

Nearly a century later Sir Edwin Landseer echoed this type of composition – what has been termed 'the domestication of royal family portraiture'[5] – in a painting entitled *Windsor Castle in Modern Times*, dating from 1841–5 (FIG. 131). The Green Drawing Room, where Queen Victoria, holding a posy,

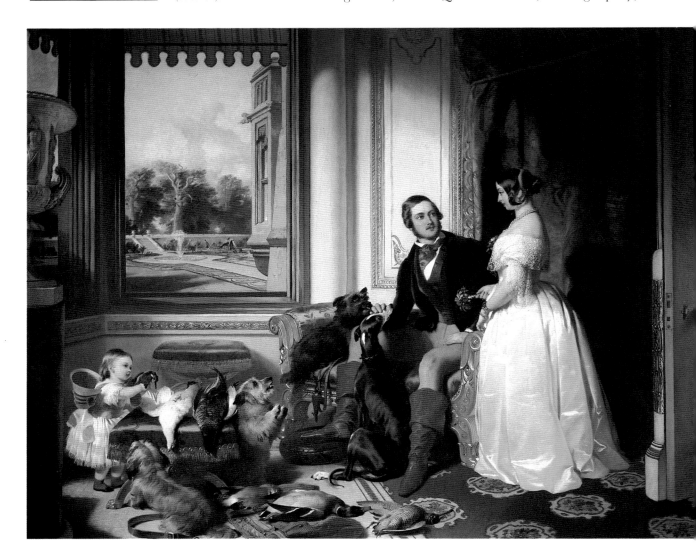

appears to have entered the room to welcome her husband back from a day's shooting, overlooks the East Terrace. The queen is shown in profile, while Prince Albert, still wearing his Freischutz boots, sits on the sofa pulling the ears of his greyhound Eos. Other royal dogs are included, together with several birds that have been shot. The young Victoria, Princess Royal, later Empress of Germany, plays with a dead kingfisher. Regardless of all this dead game, there seems to be no blood on the carpet. Outside, in the background on the terrace, there is a little vignette with a footman and two ladies-in-waiting pushing Queen Victoria's mother, the Duchess of Kent, in a wheelchair.

This is a crucial image, as it balances out a number of important factors. Examine, for example, the poses of Queen Victoria and Prince Albert. In the oil sketch made in preparation for this picture the two figures were shown standing side by side, with Prince Albert taller than the queen. Landseer changed this in the final composition so that Prince Albert is seated and the queen remains standing. The result is that Queen Victoria is shown combining her roles as monarch and dutiful wife. Further contrasts exist between manly sports and gentler female pursuits, also hinted at by the juxtaposition of hunting dogs with domestic pets. This painting, therefore, may at first sight appear to be a study of a Victorian marriage, but because of its emphasis on domestic virtues and family facilities, it is also a compelling example of the new image that monarchy was anxious to develop during Queen Victoria's reign. This image 'proclaimed simultaneously the status of dynasty and the virtues of marriage'.[6]

As an extension of this royal image-making, Franz Winterhalter devised a composition, *The Family of Queen Victoria* (FIG. 31), that happily combines the terms of reference of *The Family of Henry VIII* with '*The Greate Peece*'. Positioned obliquely to the picture plane, Queen Victoria and Prince Albert are surrounded by their children. The queen has her arm around the Prince of Wales (the future Edward VII). Prince Albert observes Prince Alfred taking a few tottering steps, while the two girls in the lower right corner, the Princess Royal and Princess Alice, tend to Princess Helena who looks up at the viewer from her cot. This portrait fuses the dynastic and domestic themes. So does a painting entitled *The Family of Queen Victoria* (FIG. 132) commissioned from the Danish artist Laurits Tuxen to mark the Golden Jubilee of 1887. As in the painting by Landseer, the figures are located in the Green Drawing Room in Windsor Castle, but it is a world far removed from *Windsor Castle in Modern Times*. In Tuxen's painting, the queen is surrounded by representatives from almost every royal family in Europe: her family connections had linked several dynasties. It is therefore not difficult to imagine how Queen Victoria regarded her own family as an example for all to see, or, indeed, as a visual metaphor for her reign.

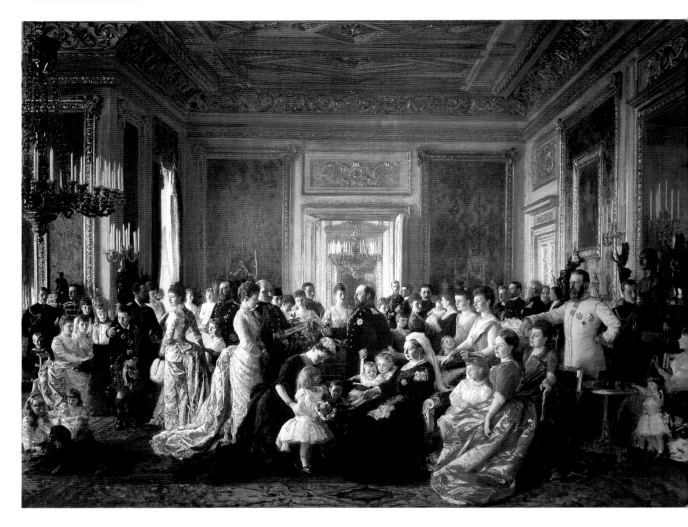

FIG. 132
Laurits Tuxen: *The Family
of Queen Victoria*, 1887

FIG. 133
Sir James Gunn: *Tea at
Royal Lodge*, 1950

Her identification with the nation and the Empire had become even more
pronounced.

Such ideas were cherished by Queen Victoria's successors and are
evident in Sir John Lavery's group portrait of George V and Queen Mary
with the Prince of Wales and the Princess Royal. Painted in the Blue Room
in Buckingham Palace in 1913, the finished portrait is in the National
Portrait Gallery in London, although the oil sketch is in the Royal Collection. There is a degree of informality in the grouping, but the uniforms
and the fact that both the male figures – one a king and the other to become
one for a short time – are standing, while the female figures are seated,
indicates a certain symbolic orchestration by the painter. It is a portrait
that suggests the artist has frozen time rather than distilled it.

The studied informality of such portraits is repeated in *Tea at Royal
Lodge* by Sir James Gunn, dating from 1950 and now in the National
Portrait Gallery (FIG. 133). King George VI and Queen Elizabeth are having

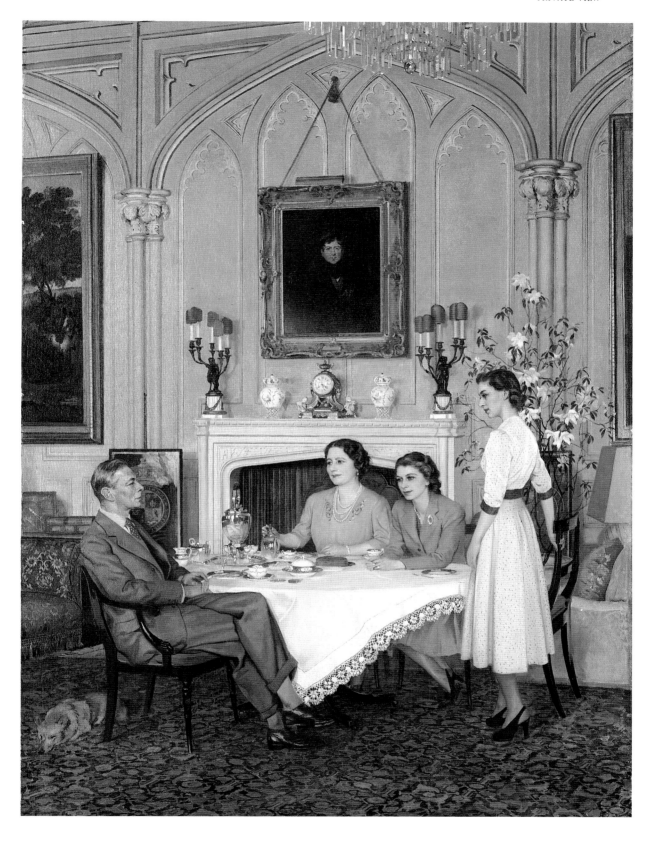

tea with their two daughters, Princess Elizabeth and Princess Margaret. This group is presided over by a portrait of George IV, who had rebuilt Royal Lodge, an extensive *cottage orné*, as a rural retreat in 1813–14. It is a worthy and totally convincing piece of painting by Gunn: good likenesses and accurate still life achieved with precise treatment of light and careful brushwork. Yet, like so much of royal portraiture of the twentieth century, it is a portrait that reveals the influence of photography.

These paintings seem at first sight to show monarchy off duty; but certainly from the mid-eighteenth century it was this private side of their lives that monarchs preferred to promote. It was how they wanted to be seen. The royal conversation piece was as potent an image of monarchy as the State Portrait, and it is this interchange between the formal and the informal that symbolises an aspect in the evolution of monarchy as an institution.

> Those monarchies that have survived into the late twentieth century have done so through a calculated combination of the ritual and the prosaic; of high ceremony and bourgeois demystification; garden parties along with the anointing oil.[7]

The same ambivalence can be charted in paintings of family events such as royal marriages and christenings, which, unlike Coronations or funerals, were private occasions taking place in locations such as St George's Chapel at Windsor Castle, the Chapel Royal at St James's Palace, or the private chapels in Buckingham Palace and Windsor Castle. It was in such settings that the shy young George III married Queen Charlotte in 1761; where George IV in a drunken stupor married Caroline of Brunswick in 1795; and where, soberly, Queen Victoria married Prince Albert in 1840. Today marriages take place in Westminster Abbey or St Paul's Cathedral, and reach a climax with balcony appearances and public displays of affection at Buckingham Palace. The ceremonial aspects of these private events in a public setting are emphasised, thus recalling more formal state occasions. Again, this pattern of grand display begins to emerge during the reign of Queen Victoria with the marriage of the Prince of Wales to Princess Alexandra of Denmark in St George's Chapel at Windsor Castle in March 1863, fifteen months after the death of the Prince Consort. The painting by W. P. Frith commemorating the wedding has no less than 140 identifiable figures (FIG. 134).

The marriage is seen from the south transept. The queen looks down from her private chapel overlooking the high altar. The Archbishop of Canterbury, Charles Langley, presides. The focus of attention is the royal couple. Behind Princess Alexandra tower her father, Prince Christian of

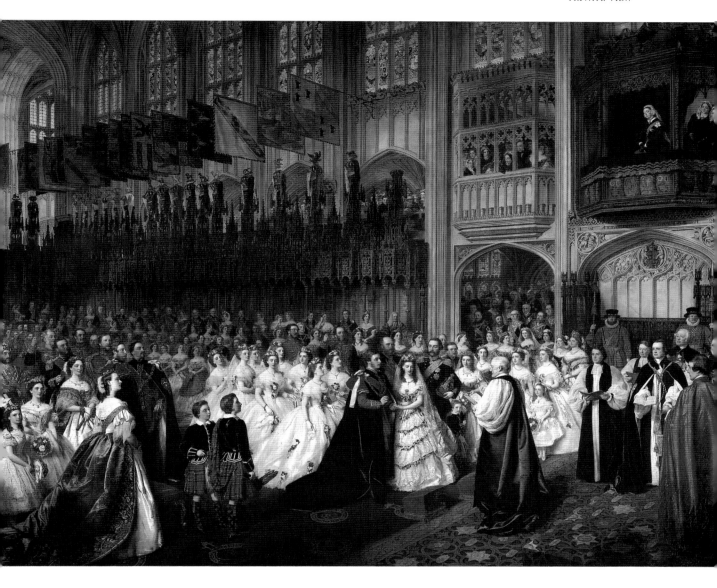

FIG. 134
William Powell Frith: *The
Marriage of The Prince of
Wales, 10 March 1863*,
1863–4

Denmark, and the Duke of Cambridge. Visible behind the Duchess of
Brabant and the Queen of Denmark with two small princesses is the
Maharaja Duleep Singh – the last Indian ruler of the Punjab. Although
he did attend the ceremony, Frith relied upon his memory for the composition and on photographs for the likenesses. It was a perpetual struggle
to arrange sittings with people at the height of the social season, but slowly
they trickled into his Bayswater studio, even members of the royal family,
such as the two royal princes, Leopold and Arthur, who are prominent in
the foreground wearing Highland dress. The brief sittings given to the
artist were supplemented by the use of a photograph of the two princes,
taken in March 1863, where the poses and dress match the finished picture.
Another difficulty was the need to record the numerous robes and dresses

worn at the wedding and these were sometimes sent to the artist for him to paint separately. Finally, in desperation, Frith moved into Windsor Castle to concentrate on the senior members of the royal family. He spent November and most of December 1863 there. As a result, he was able to proceed faster, but there was still a lot to do and he struggled on with the picture until early in 1865. It had taken over two years to complete. When

FIG. 135
Thomas Gainsborough:
George III, 1781

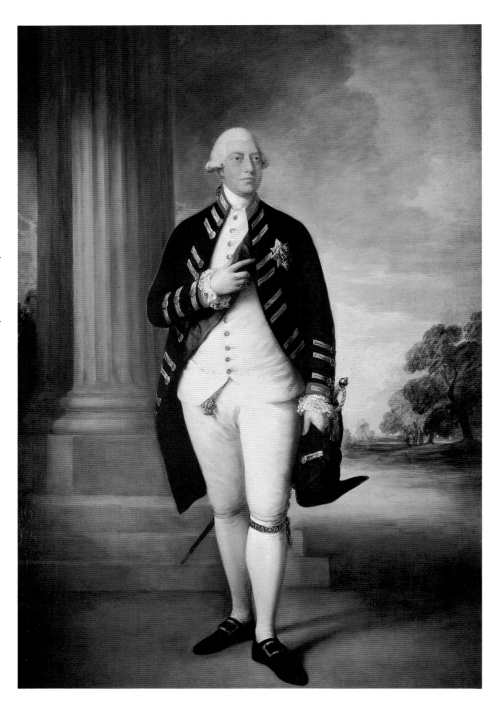

exhibited at the Royal Academy in 1865 it was another great success for the artist, but the anxieties of the commission and the sheer drudgery had drained him physically and exhausted his talent.

There was, of course, a more intimate side to marriage expressed through art. Those elegant full-length portraits by Thomas Gainsborough of George III (FIG. 135) and Queen Charlotte (FIG. 136) in middle age, dating

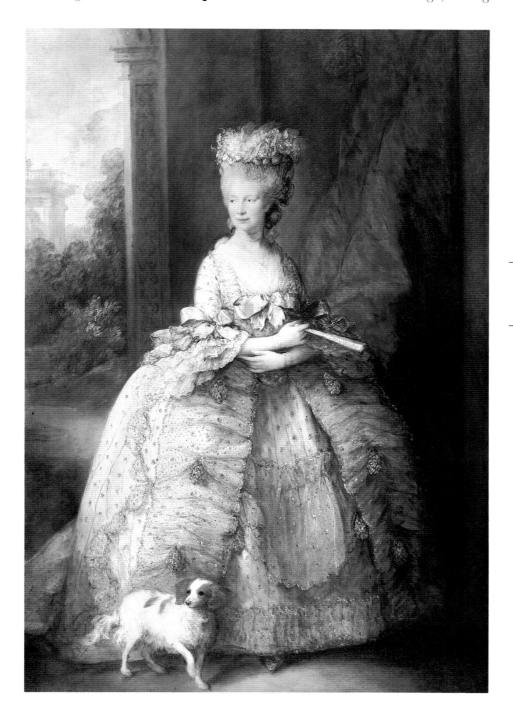

FIG. 136
Thomas Gainsborough:
Queen Charlotte, 1781

from 1781, are accurate testimony of their affection for one another. He remains somewhat shy and tentative, but still idealistic, while she is elegant and charming, swathed in chiffon and bedecked with pearls. For all their apparent formality, these portraits are for private delectation and they are painted with such sparkle – the king handsome and the queen comely – that they generate a feeling of matrimonial bliss. Sadly this was to be put to the test by the king's illness, which soon began to take its physical toll on the queen, too (FIG. 137).

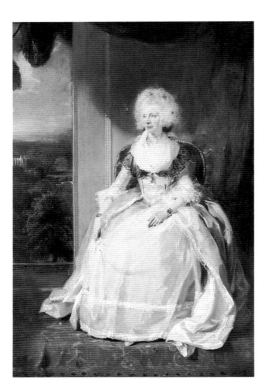

FIG. 137
Sir Thomas Lawrence:
Queen Charlotte, 1789

Charles Dickens described the Irish painter Daniel Maclise as an artist whose work was often found gift-wrapped for the occasion of the birthdays of Queen Victoria and Prince Albert.[8] Paintings such as Maclise's *A Scene from 'Undine'* could be found on the specially pre-pared tables of presents laid out on birthdays and at Christmas, but imagine Prince Albert's delight on his birthday on 26 August 1843 when he was presented with an unusually winning oval of Queen Victoria *en déshabillé* painted by Winterhalter (FIG. 33). The sensuality of the image comes as rather a surprise today and the viewer is left wondering how Prince Albert reacted across the breakfast table on that August morning of 1843. The queen herself referred to the painting as a 'surprise' and so it must have been.[9]

Not all love leads to the altar rail. Catherine of Braganza, the wife of Charles II, was much imposed upon in the sense that some of her Ladies of the Bed-chamber were mistresses of the king. The sexual mores of Charles II's court are best illustrated by the series of portraits known as *The Windsor Beauties* (FIG. 138). These were painted by Sir Peter Lely c. 1662–5 for Anne Hyde, Duchess of York, who wanted to have portraits of the most beautiful women in attendance at court. They were hung in the private apartments at Windsor Castle. Some of the Windsor beauties were the acknowledged mistresses of Charles II and of his brother, the Duke of York, the future James II, and so these portraits might in some respects be likened to modern-day 'pin-ups'.

Lely revels in the beauty of these women: the informal three-quarter length poses are alluring, the skin soft and pink, ringlets of hair frame the face, the garments are rich in texture and warm in colour. There is an air of dalliance and of coquetry. The disguise is thin, with hints of mythological antecedents or even of female martyrs. Lely is here taking his lead from Titian and the tradition of the Venetian courtesan. The critic William Hazlitt in the early nineteenth century described these portraits as

FIG. 138
Sir Peter Lely: *Elizabeth Hamilton, Countess of Gramont*, c. 1663

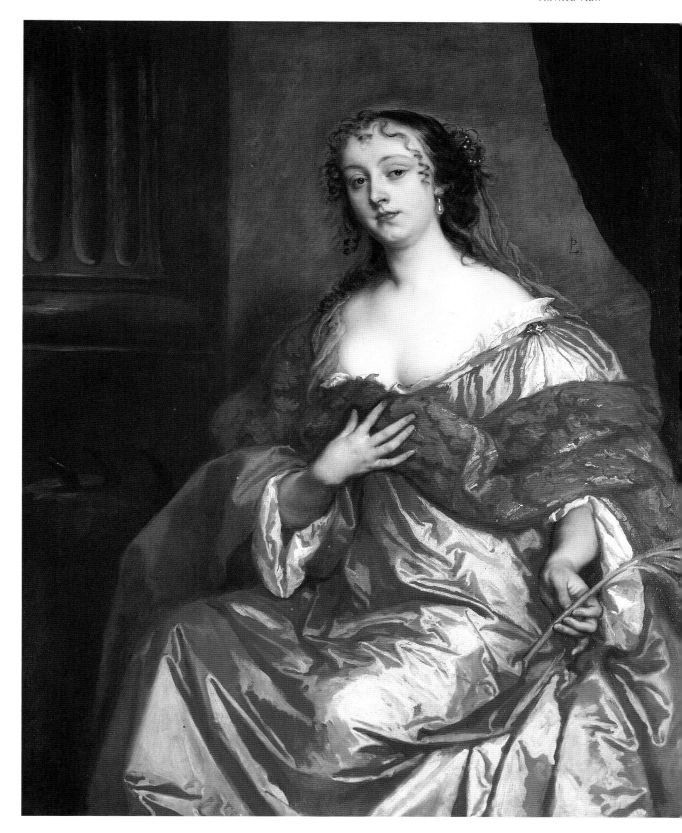

a set of kept-mistresses, painted, tawdry, showing off their theatrical or meretricious airs and graces, without one touch of real elegance or refinement, or one spark of sentiment to touch the heart.[10]

Hazlitt was surely missing the point. For here are Barbara Villiers, Duchess of Cleveland, one of Charles II's more rapacious mistresses who was beautiful and ambitious, and Francis Stuart, Duchess of Richmond, one of the greatest beauties of the Restoration period, who, adored by Charles II, finally annoyed the king by secretly marrying the Duke of Richmond in 1667, becoming his third wife. Apart from her striking looks, Francis Stuart often dressed in men's clothes as was the fashion (FIG. 139). Sets of these portraits by Lely and others were known to Samuel Pepys, who was also able to admire the sitters at first hand. He recorded in his *Diary* that on 15 July 1664 he had seen the Duchess of Richmond at Whitehall Palace 'in a most lovely form, with her hair all about her eares, having her picture taking there'. He adds, almost with direct reference to the Duchess of Richmond:

> Walking here in the galleries, I find the Ladies of Honour dressed in their riding garbs, with coats and doublets with deep skirts, just for all the world like men, and buttoned their doublets up to the breast, with perriwigs and with hats; so that, only for a long petticoat dragging under their men's coats, nobody could take them for women in any point whatever – which was an odde sight, and a sight did not please me.[11]

Another set of female portraits, known as the *Hampton Court Beauties*, creates a wholly different impression. Indeed, they denote a different moral climate. These are the women who were in attendance upon Mary II, the wife of William III, or, in the words of Daniel Defoe, they are:

> the principal Ladies, attending upon her Majesty, or who were frequently in her Retinue; and this was the more beautiful sight because the original were all in being and often to be compared with their pictures.[12]

They were painted specially for the queen in about 1690 by the court painter Sir Godfrey Kneller and have always hung at Hampton Court Palace. Celia Fiennes first saw these portraits in the Water Gallery (c. 1696) and again for the second time (c. 1701–3) in the Eating Room below stairs.[13]

These figures are painted full-length and are, therefore, rather more formal than Lely's. They are tall, elegant, refined and dignified. Intellect and beauty coalesce as virtue, and the varied backgrounds of landscape, fountains, woods and sculpture have an arcadian flavour tinged with melancholy.

Mrs Pitt was one of the most beautiful women of her day, but, unlike Lely, Kneller does not show her as a voluptuary. The Countess of Ranelagh (FIG. 140) was used by Henry Fielding as the model for his virtuous heroine Sophia Western in his novel *Tom Jones*, published in 1749:

> Sophia then, the only daughter of Mr Western, was a middle-sized woman; but rather inclining to tall. Her shape was not only exact but extremely delicate; and the nice proportion of her arms promised the truest symmetry in her limbs. Her hair, which was black, was so luxuriant, that it reached her middle, before she cut it, to comply

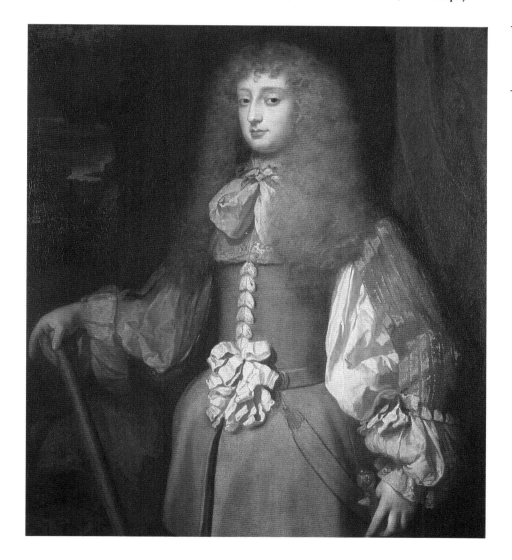

FIG. 139
Jacob Huysmans: *Francis Stuart, Duchess of Richmond*, 1664

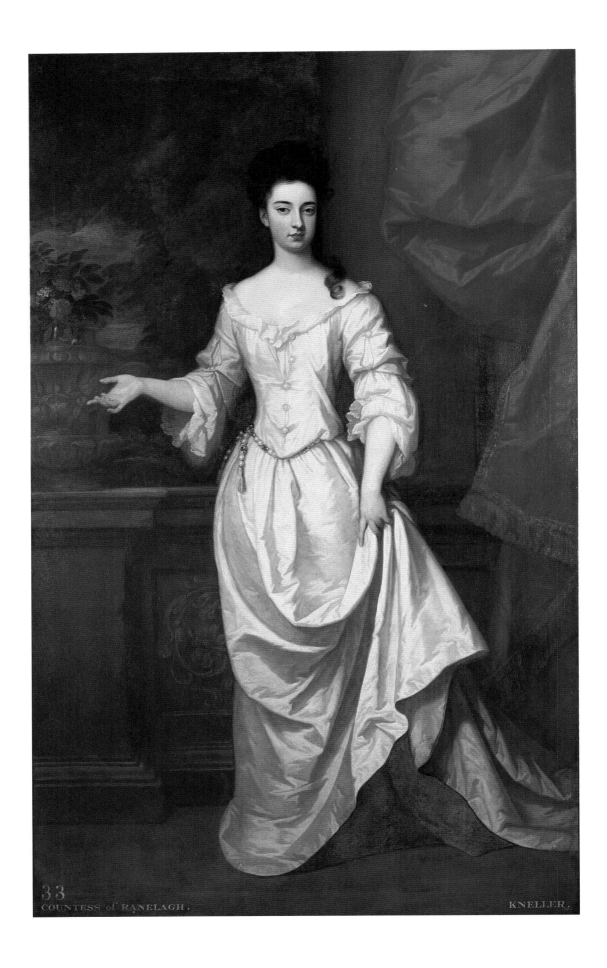

33
COUNTESS of RANELAGH.   KNELLER.

with the modern fashion; and it was now curled so gracefully in her neck, that few would believe it to be her own. If envy could find any part of her face which demanded less commendation than the rest, it might possibly think her forehead might have been higher without prejudice to her. Her eye-brows were full, even, and arched beyond the power of art to imitate. Her black eyes had a lustre in them, which all her softness could not extinguish. Her nose was exactly regular . . .

Her cheeks were of the oval kind; and in her right she had a dimple which the least smile discovered. Her chin had certainly its share in forming the beauty of her face; but it was difficult to say it was either large or small, tho' perhaps it was rather of the former kind. Her complexion had rather more of a lilly than the rose; but when exercise, or modesty, encreased her natural colour, no vermilion could equal it. . . . Her neck was long and finely turned; and here, if I was not afraid of offending her delicacy, I might justly say, the highest beauties of the famous Venus de Medicis were outdone. Here was whiteness which no lillies, ivory, nor alabaster could match. . . .

Such was the outside of Sophia; nor was this beautiful frame disgraced by an inhabitant unworthy of it. Her mind was every way equal to her person; nay, the latter borrowed some charms from the former; for when she smiled, the sweetness of her temper diffused that glory over her countenance, which no regularity of features can give . . . .[14]

FIG. 140
Sir Godfrey Kneller:
Margaret Cecil, Countess of Ranelagh, c. 1690

What is witnessed here in Kneller's portraits is the transition from Van Dyck to Sir Joshua Reynolds. Deportment and gesture imply exalted thoughts and noble passions. The viewer is left teetering on the verge of eighteenth-century sensibility.

Perhaps the most absorbing symbols of private life are the miniatures, which are tokens of allegiance or of affection. They were either worn attached to clothes, as in the Tudor and Stuart periods, or, as later, mounted with clusters of pearls to form bracelets or pendants. Queen Charlotte is frequently depicted by Zoffany and Gainsborough festooned with pearls and jewels, often with a miniature of George III serving as a clasp (FIG. 141). In Gainsborough's oil sketch of Mrs Robinson we can observe a greater air of dalliance (FIG. 142). Mrs Robinson holds an image of George IV when Prince of Wales, who first saw her playing Perdita in Shakespeare's *The Winter's Tale* on 3 December 1779 at Drury Lane. There followed a short love affair that proved rather costly for the royal family as George III had to pay £5,000 for the return of his son's letters, and the Prince of Wales paid her an annual pension of £500. Later she became the mistress of Colonel (later General) Sir Banastre Tarleton Bt., who was trained as a soldier and represented Liverpool in Parliament. Mrs Robinson was paralysed in 1783 from the waist down as the result of a miscarriage and subsequently devoted herself to literature, writing poems, novels, plays and faintly polemical works on the status of women in society. With characteristic generosity George IV gave the finished portrait of Mrs Robinson by Gainsborough to his friend the third Marquess of Hertford, who also admired the actress.

FIG. 141
Johann Zoffany: *Queen Charlotte*, 1771

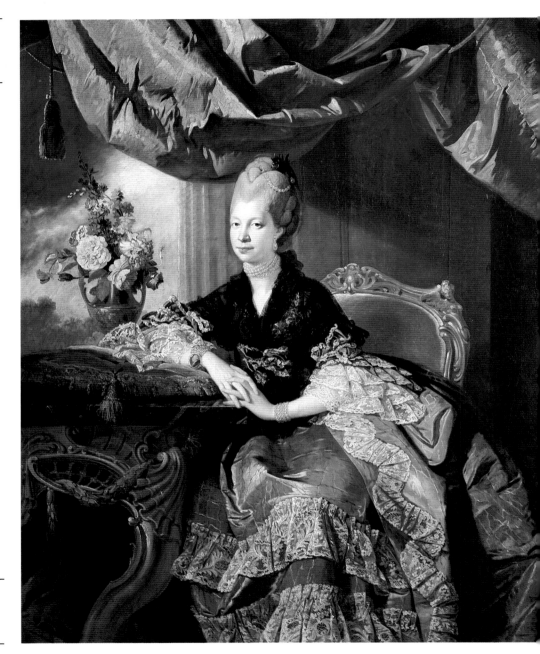

FIG. 142
Thomas Gainsborough:
Mrs Mary Robinson, 1781

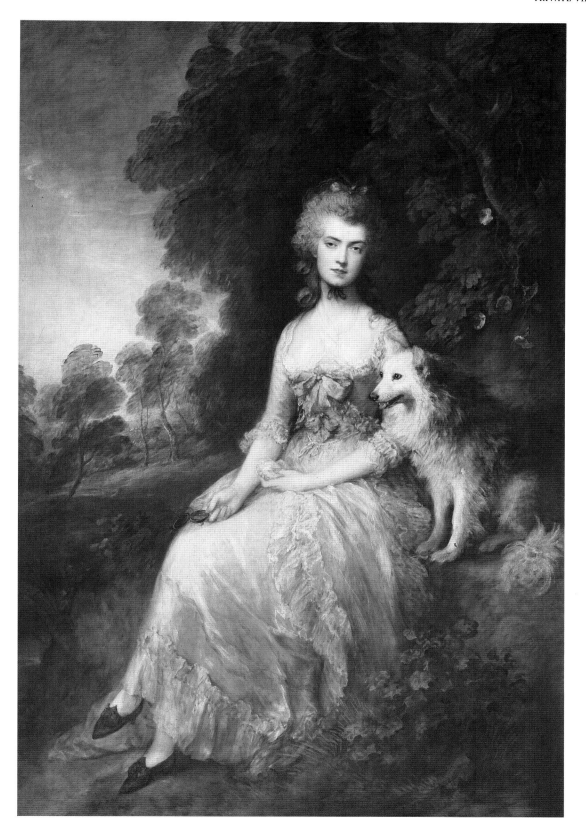

George IV's love life can best be illustrated with other miniatures. The most important sustained relationship during his early years was with Mrs Fitzherbert, whom he married secretly and illegally in 1785. Later, he enjoyed the company of more sedate women with rather matronly figures such as the Marchioness of Hertford, the mother of his friend the third Marquess, and Lady Conyngham. Many of these relationships were viciously pilloried by cartoonists of the day, but the miniatures are tokens of genuine affections that burnt ardently for a time. Miniatures retain secrets that somehow seem all the more precious because they were held in the hand or worn close to the heart.

Edward VII's private life was also expansive (FIG. 143). He, like George IV, enjoyed the company of actresses and society ladies, such as Lillie Langtry and Mrs Keppel. His name is associated with country-house parties, opulence and dreams of Empire. He spent much of his time in

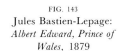

FIG. 143
Jules Bastien-Lepage:
Albert Edward, Prince of Wales, 1879

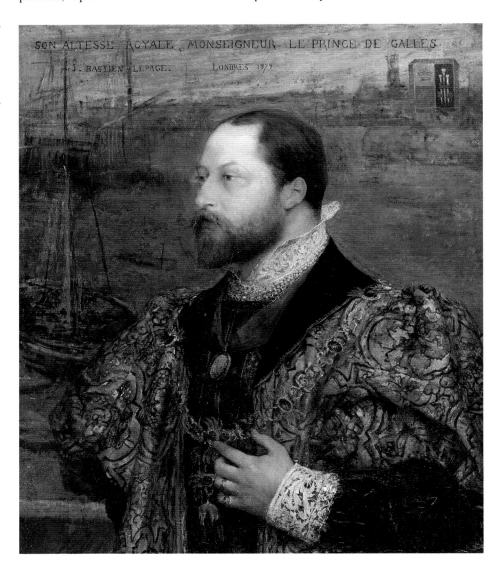

London, Paris, Biarritz, Baden-Baden, Homburg and Berlin in a lifestyle that was to be swept away in the Great War of 1914–18. In 1862, he acquired Sandringham House, which he subsequently rebuilt on a larger scale as a grand country mansion. Here there are sporting pictures showing Edward VII when Prince of Wales in India and shooting on the Sandringham estate. Also represented are his interests in sailing and horse racing, but offsetting these pursuits is a picture of *A Nymph by a Woodland Pool* by the French artist Gustave Doré, who is perhaps better remembered for his illustrations for the Bible, Dante, Shakespeare and Ariosto, as well as for his vivid drawings of London published in 1872. Doré belonged to the social set that formed around Edward VII when he was Prince of Wales, and it is not difficult to appreciate why a sensual image of a wood nymph appealed to the artist's patron.

Edward VII's likeness as a child can be found among a set of portrait roundels of Queen Victoria's children by Franz Winterhalter. These were painted between 1849 and 1859, and form a wonderful comparison with the set executed by Gainsborough of George III and Queen Charlotte with thirteen of their fifteen children. The earlier set was undertaken during the late summer and early autumn of 1782. As examples of Gainsborough's skills as a portrait painter, revealing a breathtaking technical prowess in the sheer liquidity of paint on a small scale, they are supreme (FIG. 144). Frederick, Duke of York, was absent in Hanover and so his portrait is not included in the set. Some of the images were poignant: Prince Alfred had died in August 1782 and Prince Octavius died soon afterwards, in May 1783. Queen Charlotte and her daughters were reduced to tears when they saw the image of Prince Octavius in the Royal Academy, which they visited in the summer of 1783.

The tradition of painting royal children was, and remains, extremely potent. Van Dyck depicted the children of Charles I on more than one occasion. In 1635 he painted the three eldest children, showing the Prince of Wales (the future Charles II) leaning nonchalantly against the base of a column with his legs crossed – relaxed, but every inch a future king (FIG. 145). He holds the hand of his younger brother James, Duke of York (later James II), who is in the middle of the composition. To the right of the Prince of Wales is Princess Mary, who later married the Prince of Orange and became the mother of William III. Although small, these figures have a certain stature, achieved by emphasising the vertical, by aligning the children with the paned curtains behind to offset the patterned carpet, and by providing a sense of scale in comparison with the dogs in the foreground. The domestic pets enhance the feeling of informality and the impression of youthful innocence.

This painting appears in the background of Johann Zoffany's picture

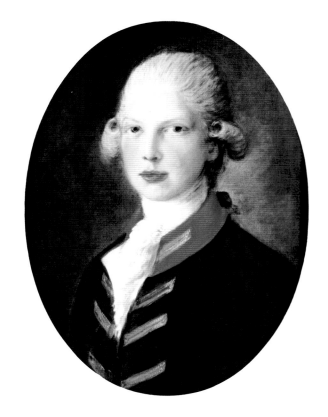

FIG. 144
Thomas Gainsborough:
Prince Edward, later Duke of Kent, 1782

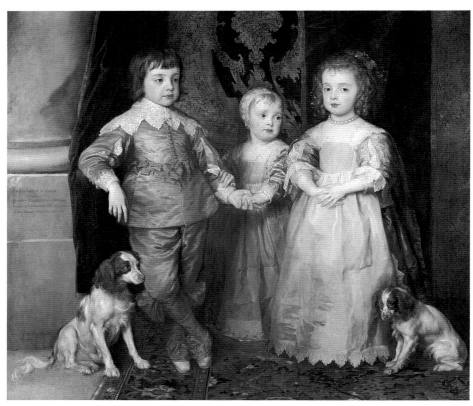

FIG. 145
Sir Anthony Van Dyck: *The Three Eldest Children of Charles I*, 1635

230

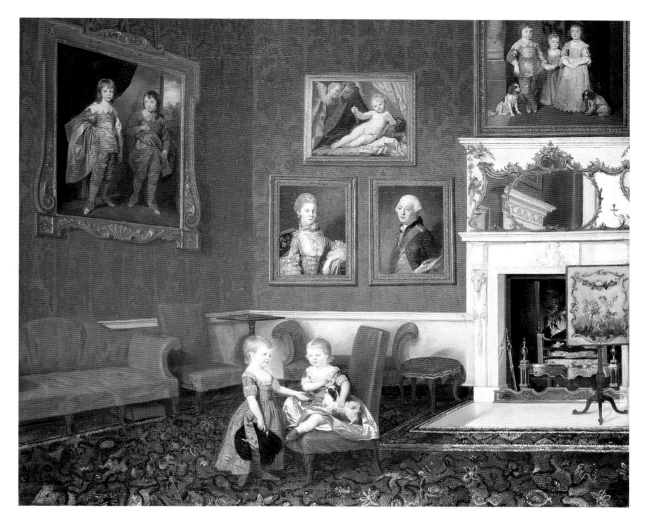

FIG. 146
Johann Zoffany: *George,
Prince of Wales, and Frederick,
later Duke of York*, c. 1765

of Queen Charlotte's two elder children, the future George IV and his brother Frederick, Duke of York, playing by the fire in a room in Buckingham House (FIG. 146). The juxtaposition makes a fascinating contrast: Zoffany treats his young sitters very much within the accepted terms of childhood, but Van Dyck invests his children with a feeling of monumentality in their forms and poses. Zoffany almost belittles the children by their surroundings, and, indeed, by drawing attention to Van Dyck's painting, does not help his own cause. Interestingly, a slightly earlier portrait of the three eldest children of Charles I by Van Dyck (Turin, Galleria Sabauda) was disliked by the king because the children were dressed in infants' clothes, as opposed to more grown-up attire. Thus, the children were dressed in more suitable clothes in the portrait of 1635 (FIG. 145). Two years later an enlarged composition (FIG. 147) includes as additional figures Princess Elizabeth holding Princess Anne on the right. The success of the picture, apart from the charm

FIG. 148
Franz Xaver Winterhalter:
*Albert Edward, Prince of
Wales*, 1846

of its subject and its technical brilliance, depends as much on the visual
ambiguity created by the Prince of Wales resting his arms on the head of
the mastiff as on the fact that it also reveals Van Dyck's abilities as a
painter of still life and landscape. As an evocation of innocence *The Five
Eldest Children of Charles I* remains unsurpassed, even by Gainsborough,
who often resorted to 'Van Dyck costume' to sharpen the viewer's response
when posing a child for a portrait.

Van Dyck and Zoffany were not the only court artists to face the
difficulty of depicting children in an adult world. Winterhalter painted
Edward VII as a child of five in 1846 (FIG. 148). This is a most winning
portrait. The sailor suit has an ambiguity that avoids defining the figure
as a child or a grown-up. The uniform was specially made for the Prince
of Wales by the tailor on the royal yacht and he wore it for a cruise taken
in September 1846 off the Channel Islands. The suit itself is now in the
National Maritime Museum and its use in the context of portraiture, following the example of French artists, started a fashion in Britain. The
portrait was described by the former Prime Minister, Sir Robert Peel, a

FIG. 147
Sir Anthony Van Dyck: *The
Five Eldest Children of Charles
I*, 1637

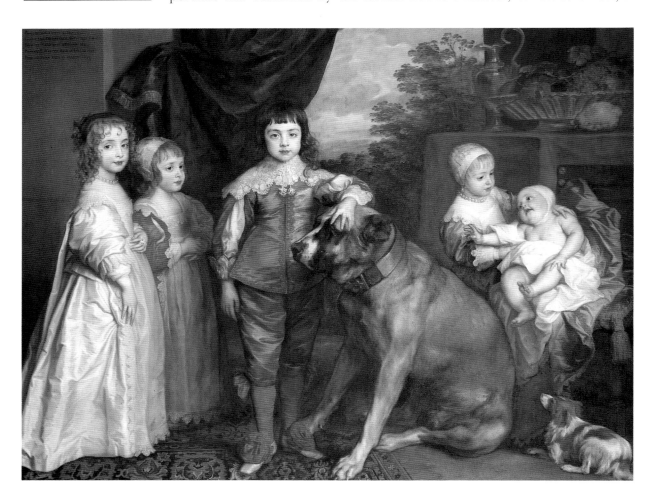

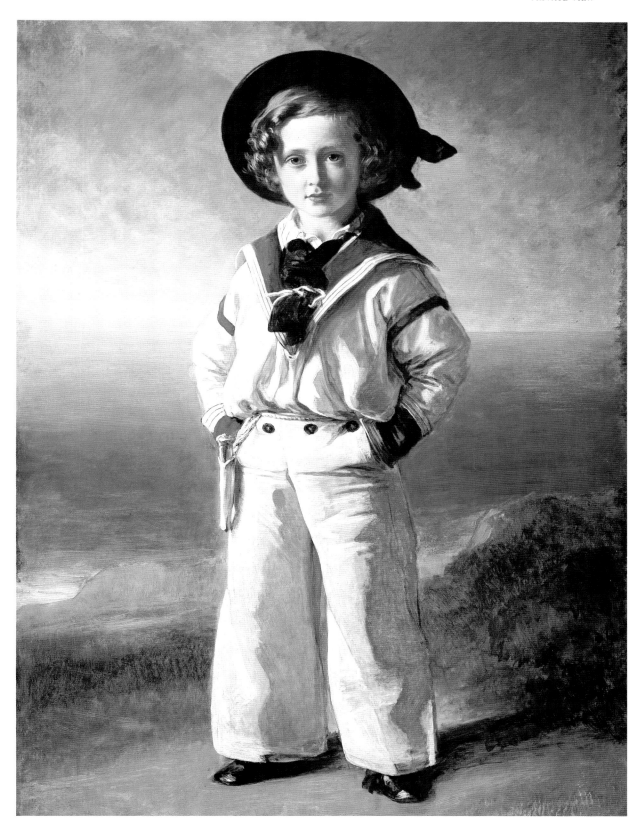

connoisseur of Dutch painting, as 'the prettiest picture he had ever seen'[15] and the queen regarded it as 'a perfect likeness and such a perfect composition'.[16] It is only challenged by the same artist's depiction of Prince Arthur in the uniform of the Scots Fusilier Guards.

By the time Edward Brock in 1931 and Philip de Laszlo in 1933 came to paint the present queen, then Princess Elizabeth and a little girl, their main rivals were no longer Van Dyck, Zoffany and Gainsborough, but photographers. The angled, hovering viewpoints denote the influence of photography, while the attributes of childhood – a dog or a posy of flowers

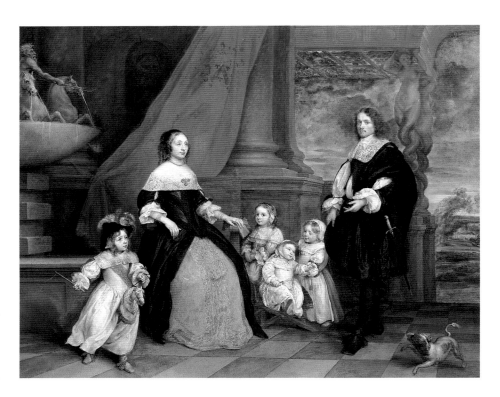

FIG. 149
Gonzales Coques: *The Family of Jan Baptista Anthonie*, 1661

– are points of reference in a well-established tradition. Childhood has traditionally been a metaphor for innocence, but in the case of royal children there is always a dilemma and the artist has to balance that innocence against future responsibilities.

No such tensions exist in depictions of ordinary children where artists are less hidebound by convention. The children of bourgeois families – the young boy riding his hobby horse in *The Family of Jan Baptista Anthonie* by Gonzales Coques (FIG. 149), or the children of Sir Balthazar Gerbier who were such an inspirational force for Rubens – possess an undeniable charm. They inhabit a different world from that of their royal counterparts in so far as the responsibilities they will assume are bound to be less burdensome and less intrusive. The innocence of childhood was a favourite theme of

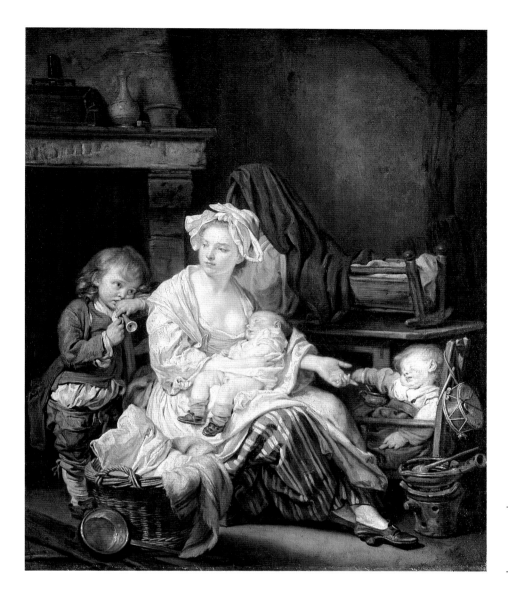

FIG. 150
Jean-Baptiste Greuze:
Silence!, 1759

French eighteenth-century and early nineteenth-century artists, who culti-
vated refined emotions amounting to feelings of *sensibilité*. Jean-Baptiste
Greuze was such an artist and his painting *Silence!* (FIG. 150) shows a young
mother exhorting her small son not to continue blowing his trumpet lest
the noise wakens the other two sleeping children. It is a painting of simple
manners and everyday emotions verging on sentimentality.

Of course, not all children were so fortunate. In the previous century
Mathieu Le Nain depicted a group of young card players in a style derived
from the tenebrism and realism of Caravaggio (FIG. 151). These boys are old
before their time. Innocence has been lost in preparation for the real world
where deviousness, brazenness and chicanery will be needed if they are
simply to survive.

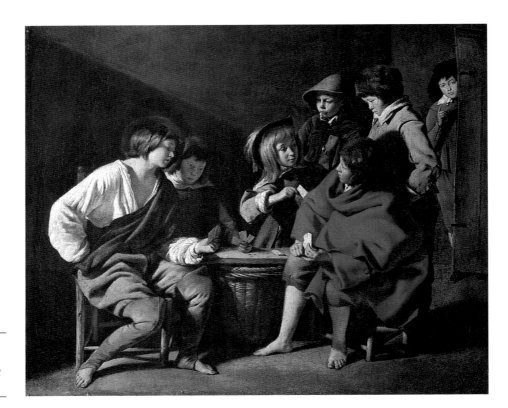

FIG. 151
Mathieu Le Nain
(attributed to): *The Young
Card-Players*, c. 1650

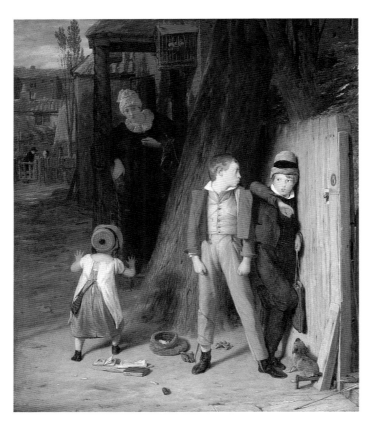

FIG. 152
William Mulready: *The
Wolf and the Lamb*, 1820

236

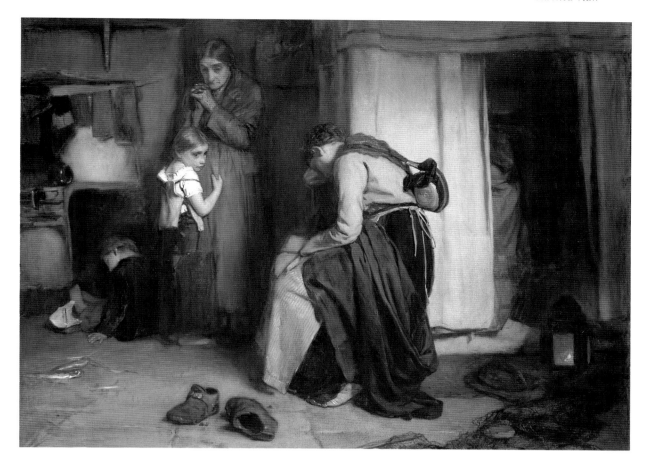

FIG. 153
Frank Holl: *No Tidings from the Sea*, 1870

A painting by William Mulready entitled *The Wolf and the Lamb* (FIG. 152) reveals how a later nineteenth-century painter dealt with a wicked world veiled by the moral overtones of the title. A boy on his way to school is set upon by a bully. His small sister turns to alert their mother, who seems to be dressed as a widow. The social realism of Victorian artists such as Frank Holl also stresses the hardships of childhood. *No Tidings from the Sea* (1870) (FIG. 153) shows the interior of a fisherman's cottage in the early morning after a storm. The seated woman has been out all night looking for her husband, who is presumed dead at sea. There are two small children: a little boy asleep on the floor with a toy boat beside him and a daughter who clings to the skirts of an elderly woman. It is a tragic scene that was observed by the artist himself in Northumberland.

Recent historians have argued that the reign of Queen Victoria witnessed a change in the role of the monarchy. This has been defined as 'the evolution from dynastic life to domestic ethos' and it has also been asserted that as 'imperial power atrophied, so the family fetish loomed ever larger as part of the royal mystique'. It is for this reason that, in terms of painting, 'ordinariness could be translated into relevance'.[17] Such shifts in perception have continued – indeed quickened – during the twentieth century. Queen Victoria and Prince Albert had nine children and were no doubt aware that the distinctions between private life and public life could become blurred. They therefore sought to redefine the concept of royal privacy. This took the form of escape to newly acquired residences where, although affairs of state could not be neglected, they could at least be conducted in a congenial, informal atmosphere.

Osborne House on the Isle of Wight was purchased in 1845 and almost immediately redesigned by Thomas Cubitt in conjunction with Prince Albert for the purpose of combining pleasure with business in an idyllic setting (reminiscent of fine days in the Bay of Naples) and providing ample opportunity for the education of children in the broadest sense. The design was inspired by Italianate villas, but the location with verdant grounds of a thousand acres, a private beach, and views of the Solent gave the place its singular charm. It was in the rooms of Osborne House that Queen Victoria and Prince Albert hung some of their more intimate paintings, not just of their family and places associated with their personal history, but also the work of contemporary and earlier artists that they particularly admired. The portrait of the Prince of Wales in a sailor suit by Winterhalter (FIG. 148) was an obvious candidate for display:

> Bertie's picture in sailor dress has at last come back to us, and is more beautiful than I can describe; such an excellent likeness, and as a picture such a 'chef d'oeuvre', and so wonderfully painted. It is a great delight to me, and I keep it here until we go to Osborne, where it is to be hung up.[18]

Family visits to Osborne took place about four times a year: spring, early summer when the queen celebrated her birthday (24 May), July, and just before Christmas. It was here, too, that Queen Victoria died on 23 January 1901.

Balmoral Castle was even further removed from the metropolis than Osborne House. Leased from the Earl of Aberdeen in 1848, Balmoral was purchased outright in 1852 (FIG. 154). Queen Victoria loved the place at first sight:

> We arrived at Balmoral at a quarter to three. It is a pretty little castle in the old Scottish style. There is a picturesque tower and gardens in front with a high wooded hill; at the back there is a wood down to the Dee; and the hills rise all around.[19]

A new, larger castle was built in what is known as Scottish Baronial style,

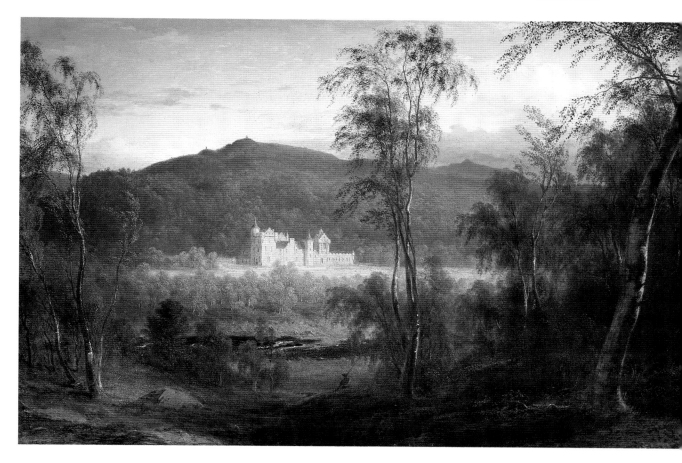

FIG. 154
James Giles: *A View of Balmoral*, 1848

having been designed by William Smith of Aberdeen under the direction of Prince Albert. Work started in 1853 and was finished by 1856.

If Osborne House stood comparison with the Riviera, Balmoral Castle evoked memories of Germany (especially Thüringia) and Switzerland. Both places, however, provided the royal family with a freedom that allowed them to pursue their lives away from the public gaze. Dickens wrote of

> the getting away from London, from dining-rooms and levees, and to a great extent from state cares and state conferences . . . . The getting away from all these things to be simply a lady living with her husband and children in a highland château, must have been a new and delightful feeling.[20]

Recreation in Scotland, which Queen Victoria and Prince Albert first visited in 1842, took different forms. The queen walked, rode and sketched while her husband stalked and shot. One painting more than any other sums up life at Balmoral: Edwin Landseer's *Royal Sports on Hill and Loch*

(FIG. 155), which the artist worked on from 1850 to 1870. It was a painting of which a great deal was expected.

The inspiration was a boat trip to Loch Muich on the Balmoral estate, which the queen had made in 1848.

> . . . we found a large boat, into which we got, and Macdonald, Duncan, Grant, and Coutts rowed. . . . We had various scrambles in and out of the boat and along the shore, and saw three hawks and caught seventy trout. I wish an artist could have been there to sketch the scene; it was so picturesque – the boat, the net, and the people in their kilts in the water, and on the shore.[21]

Landseer was duly summoned and shown Loch Muich in 1850.

> The Lake was like a mirror, & the extreme calmness, with the bright sunshine, hazy blue tints on the fine bold outline of hills coming down into our sweet Loch, quite enchanted Landseer.[22]

The artist then devised a composition, which the queen described in detail in her *Journal*, at the same time acknowledging the iconographical novelty of the subject matter:

FIG. 155
Sir Edwin Landseer: *Royal Sports on Hill and Loch*, 1850

> We went to look at Landseer's sketch. Albert was enchanted with it. It is to be thus: I, stepping out of the boat at Loch Muich, Albert, in

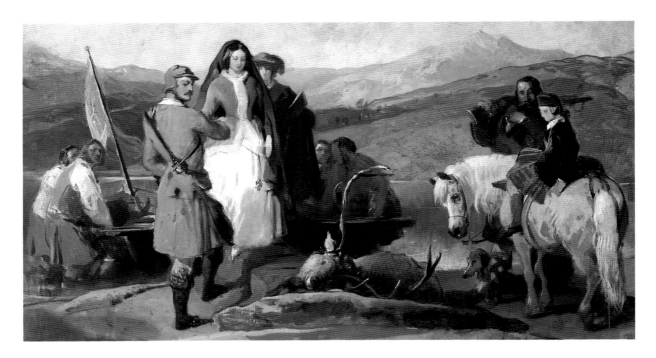

his Highland dress, assisting me out, & I am looking at a stag which
he is supposed to have just killed. Bertie is on the deer pony with
McDonald (whom Landseer much admires) standing behind, with
rifles & plaids on his shoulder. In the water, holding the boat, are
several of the men in their kilts, salmon are also lying on the ground.
The picture is intended to represent me as meeting Albert, who has
been stalking, whilst I have been fishing, & the whole is quite
consonant with the truth. The solitude, the sport, the Highlanders in
the water, &c. will be, as Landseer says, a beautiful historical
exemplification of peaceful times, & of the independent life we lead in
the dear Highlands. It is quite a new conception, & I think the
manner in which he has composed it will be singularly dignified,
poetical & totally novel, for no other Queen has ever enjoyed, what
I am fortunate to enjoy in our peaceful happy life here. It will tell a
great deal, & it is beautiful. Albert suggested a female figure, behind
mine, which is going to be added.[23]

Landseer began energetically with an oil sketch and a series of studies in
pastel, but he failed to complete the painting even after it had been displayed in an unfinished state at the Royal Academy in 1854 and received
mixed reviews. His compositional and stylistic dilemma is well expressed
by Sir Oliver Millar, who has written that

> the ghillies were made to look like the Apostles (Landseer himself
> likened Macdonald to a Giorgione); the agony in the faces of the
> dead stags is reminiscent of heads of Saints being torn apart in the
> more violent altar-pieces of the Counter-Reformation.[24]

Queen Victoria and Prince Albert were perhaps overkeen to see *Royal Sports
on Hill and Loch* brought to a conclusion. Landseer was closely observed
while at work and his progress (or lack of it) constantly assessed. The
artist's confidence soon evaporated. His assistant, George Dunlop Leslie,
remarked that:

> He used to scrape out with bits of glass, which were broken to a
> curved scimitar shape, and the floor in front of his picture was
> frequently covered with paint scrapings.[25]

In the end, Landseer grew tired and resentful of the queen's preoccupation
with the picture and he wrote, in April 1870, 'I have made up my mind
never to accept another commission and not to go to Osborne.'[26] The
project that was to have culminated in a picture 'illustrative of our life

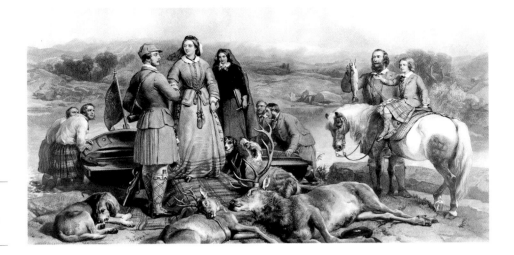

FIG. 156
W. H. Simmons after
Landseer: *Royal Sports on
Hill and Loch*, 1874

& pursuit in these *dear*, beautiful Highlands'[27] foundered, and the queen expressed the desire to take possession of the oil sketch, observing that it must be very 'valuable to her as a remembrance of happy times'.[28]

Although Landseer continued to work on the picture, the anxieties it induced undermined his health and when it was exhibited for the second time it was still unfinished. The painting finally entered the Royal Collection in about 1873. It was engraved in 1874 (FIG. 156); this was just as well, since its condition subsequently deteriorated and the canvas was destroyed during the reign of George V.

As a reasonably accomplished watercolourist herself, Queen Victoria encouraged her children to pursue their own artistic instincts. Osborne House and Balmoral Castle were inspirations in the quest for self-expression. The daughters of George III and Queen Charlotte had been able practitioners and, indeed, the tradition of royal artists continues today with the activities of the Duke of Edinburgh and the Prince of Wales, who have both depicted the same landscape at Balmoral that inspired Queen Victoria and Prince Albert.

Living surrounded by the natural beauty of Osborne House and Balmoral Castle is one form of inspiration; the Royal Collection itself could well be another. The paintings might foster an appreciation of art, and also provide insight into other people's lives. Although paintings in the Royal Collection illustrate the workings of monarchy, they also reflect society at large. A view *into* the palace is counterbalanced by the view *out* of the palace window. In 1954 when Pietro Annigoni was painting the portrait commissioned by the Worshipful Company of Fishmongers, the queen remarked to the artist during the first sitting, 'When I was a little child it always delighted me to look out of the window and see the people and the traffic going by.'[29] The Royal Collection is rich in everyday scenes in the lives of ordinary people. These paintings offer unselfconscious and intimate vignettes, windows on to a world that might otherwise have remained beyond the direct personal experience of royal collectors themselves.

Genre painting came of age in Holland during the seventeenth century: the occupations and recreations of ordinary people became for the first time the principal subjects within painting. This important development in European art was allied to the ethos of republican ideals and protestant beliefs, a powerful force in seventeenth-century Holland. Such pictures were also often of superlative quality in terms of technique and invention. The origins of Dutch genre painting lie in Flemish art in pictures such as *The Flemish Fair* by Jan Breughel the Elder (FIG. 59).

Adriaen van Ostade, an artist in this particular tradition, was as highly esteemed during the eighteenth and early nineteenth centuries as Rembrandt. *Interior of a Peasant's Cottage* (FIG. 157), dating from 1668, shows a

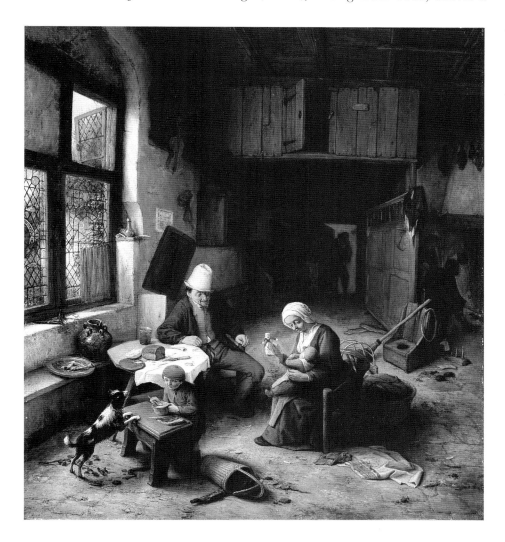

FIG. 157
Adriaen van Ostade:
Interior of a Peasant's Cottage,
1668

243

family scene. The mother entertains the baby with the doll; another child, seated on a stool, eats his meal, carefully observed by the dog. The father, at his ease, watches over the proceedings, which are beautifully lit by the sunlight entering the dark interior through the windows on the left. There is enough light by which to make out the debris of the meal and the trappings of domesticity rendered in the crispest detail. Such details tell us a great deal about peasant domestic life in seventeenth-century Holland, but, more than that, the scene provides a glimpse of the joys and cares of ordinary family life.

The influence of Dutch seventeenth-century artists can be found in British nineteenth-century painting. William Mulready's *Interior of an English Cottage* (1828) depicts a young mother with two small children, both asleep (FIG. 158). She is waiting for her husband to return and looks out at the visitor, unaware that her husband is approaching on horseback in the

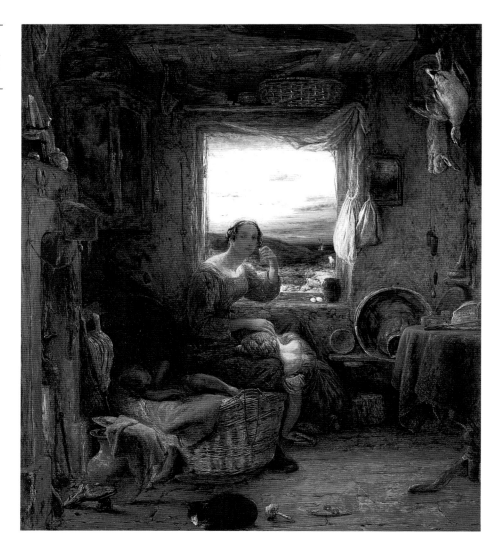

FIG. 158
William Mulready: *Interior of an English Cottage*, 1828

distance. The family is soon to be reunited in a genuinely private moment of joy.

Genre painting gave rise to a whole range of fresh subjects for artists. Everyday scenes denote a variety of activities, including moments of leisure. Pieter de Hooch's *Cardplayers in a Sunlit Room* (FIG. 159) depicts figures playing cards while two others, one drinking and the other smoking, observe the game. This is a painting in de Hooch's mature style, dating from 1658.

FIG. 159
Pieter de Hooch:
Cardplayers in a Sunlit Room,
1658

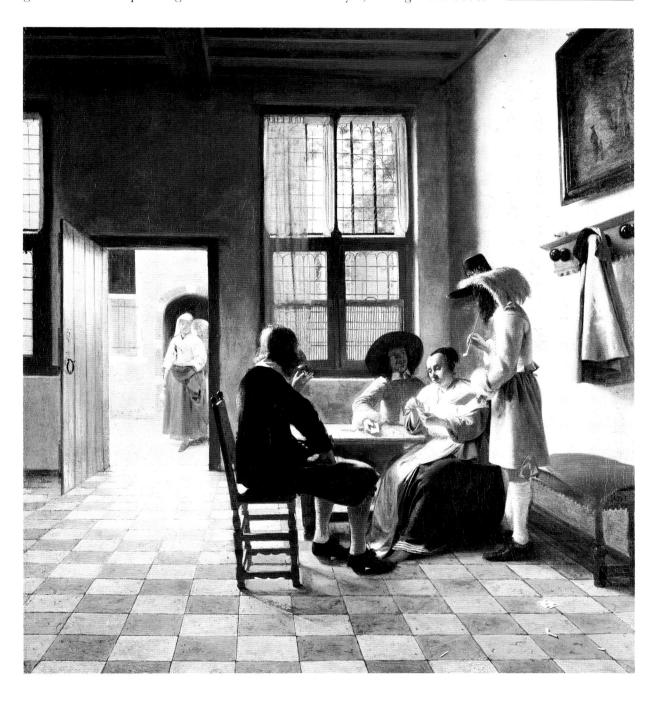

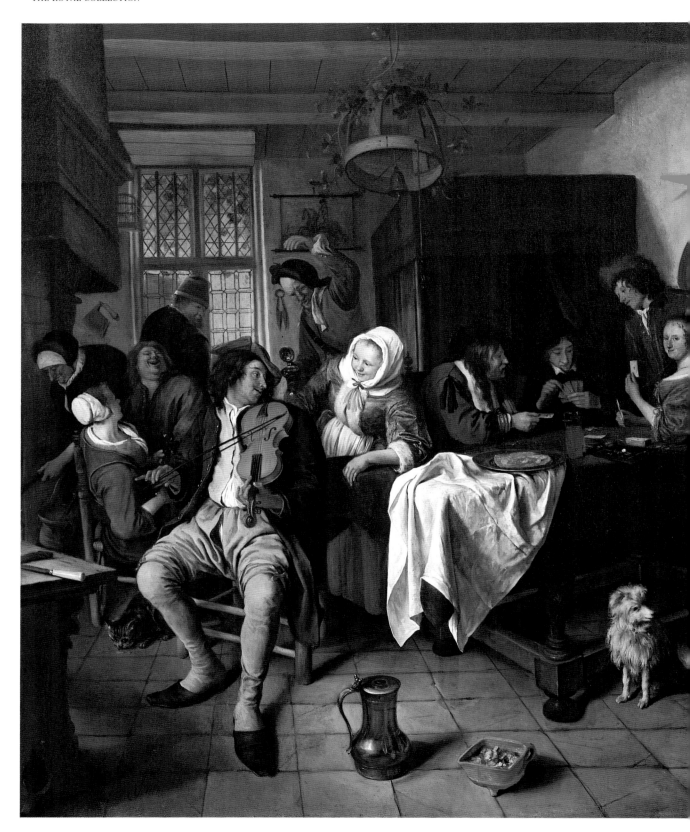

The carefully plotted pattern of the floor indicates his mastery of perspective, which allows the artist to provide an accurate rendering of the interior with a precise positioning of the figures within the room. The treatment of light is another major aspect of de Hooch's style. Here it is so refined that there is a distinction between the external and the internal light. The passage of light through the open door leading to the courtyard, or through the glass of the window and the cloth of the curtain, defines the figures around the table, prescribing outlines and giving substance to forms. Some features of this painting are not clear, however, such as the broken pipe and the card on the ground, but often in Dutch seventeenth-century paint-

FIG. 160
Jan Steen: *Interior of a Tavern*, 1665–8

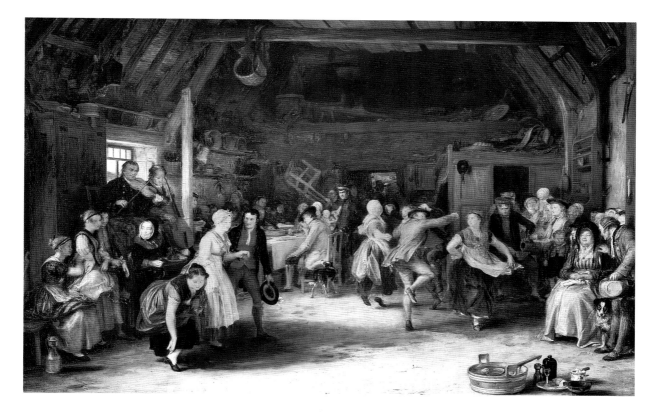

ings there is a subtle meaning in such accessories. For example, in Jan Steen's *Interior of a Tavern* (FIG. 160) another game of cards is being played. The woman on the far right turns to the viewer, holding up the ace of diamonds. This action, the way she is dressed and the coiffured dog suggest that she is a prostitute. Steen, who was the son of a brewer and at a later stage of his life owned an inn, is present in this picture on the left, but more prominent still is the violin player. Musicians also feature in David Wilkie's *Penny Wedding* (FIG. 161), a painting which dates from almost two centuries later (1818), but is much influenced by earlier pictures such as Steen's. The rhythms of the music are picked up by the dancers in the

FIG. 161
Sir David Wilkie: *The Penny Wedding*, 1818

FIG. 163
Godfried Schalcken: *A Family Concert*, c. 1665–70

centre, while towards the edges couples sit out, or eat and drink in the background. The circular distribution of the dancers gives a sense of kinetic energy to the whole scene. The fiddler on the left, silhouetted against the window, has been identified as Niel Gow, a composer for whose music Robert Burns often supplied the words.

The influence of the Flemish painter David Teniers the Younger is also apparent in Wilkie's work. Teniers frequently painted scenes of peasants dancing (FIG. 162). Here, a lone piper supplies the music, while dancers cavort wildly with arms and legs flying. This painting has everything – landscape and still life, as well as superbly individual studies, such as the bourgeois couple with wife, child and dog, the peasant helping the woman to her feet, the elderly figure bowed over his stick, the seated girl fending off the advances of the aged male peasant, the man being sick against the fence. All of life pulsates in this picture.

Music was not always such a public affair. The French artist Philippe Mercier depicts Frederick, Prince of Wales (c. 1740), playing his cello in the presence of his elder sisters and a dog which looks as though it is about to howl. This is a private, intimate moment, not dissimilar in mood from Godfried Schalcken's *Family Concert* (late 1660s), where the artist represents his own family enjoying the delights of music (FIG. 163). The curtains have been looped back to allow the viewer to glimpse this moment of private delectation, while the dog lies curled up on the floor asleep.

FIG. 162
David Teniers the Younger: *Peasants dancing outside an Inn*, c. 1645

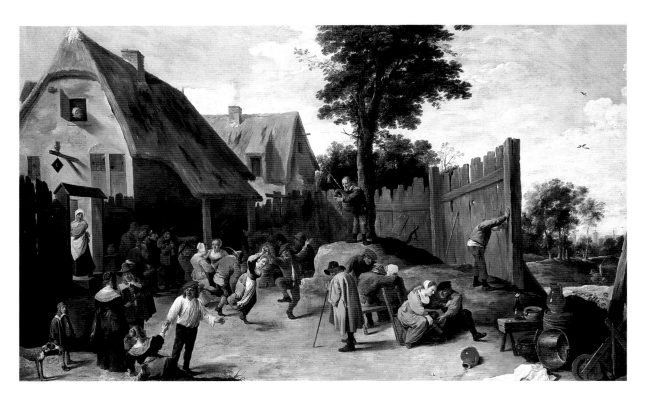

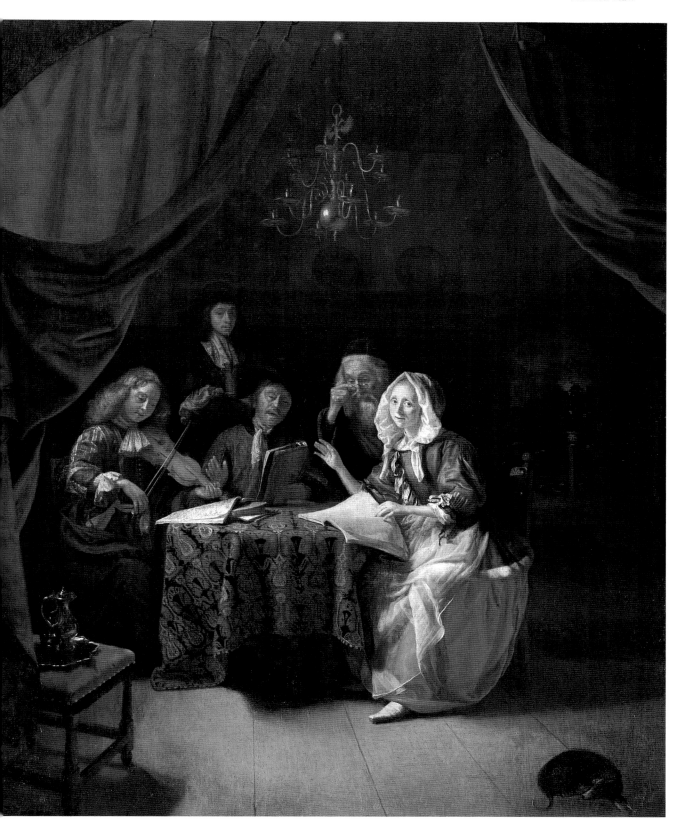

Music has other connotations, particularly in the context of love. There is a sense of dalliance between the woman descending the staircase holding a letter and the man playing the cello in a work by Metsu dating from c. 1665 (FIG. 164). The man looking down from the arch has been given the traditional pose of melancholy and is clearly excluded by the other two figures. Yet it is difficult to provide a proper explanation of the moment Metsu has depicted and the enigma, which may have been intentional, remains.

That is not the case in *The Listening Housewife* of 1655 by Nicholas Maes (FIG. 165). The housewife raises her index finger to her lips and stares directly out at the viewer. She shares the discovery of the embracing couple in the cellar on the left. Her pose is an admonition and suggests that the

FIG. 165
Nicholas Maes: *The Listening Housewife*, 1655

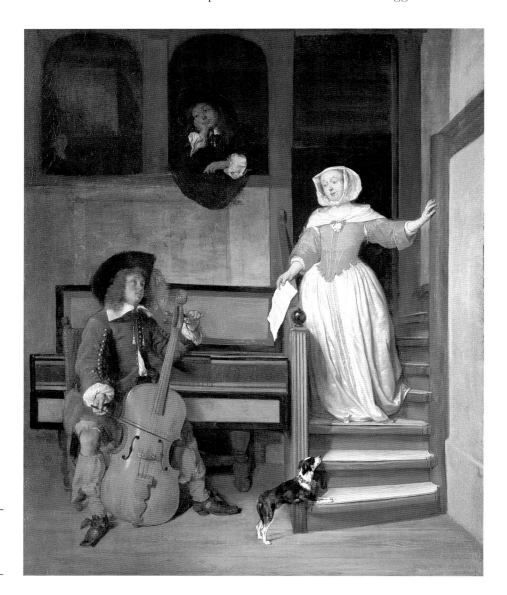

FIG. 164
Gabriel Metsu: *The Cello Player*, c. 1665

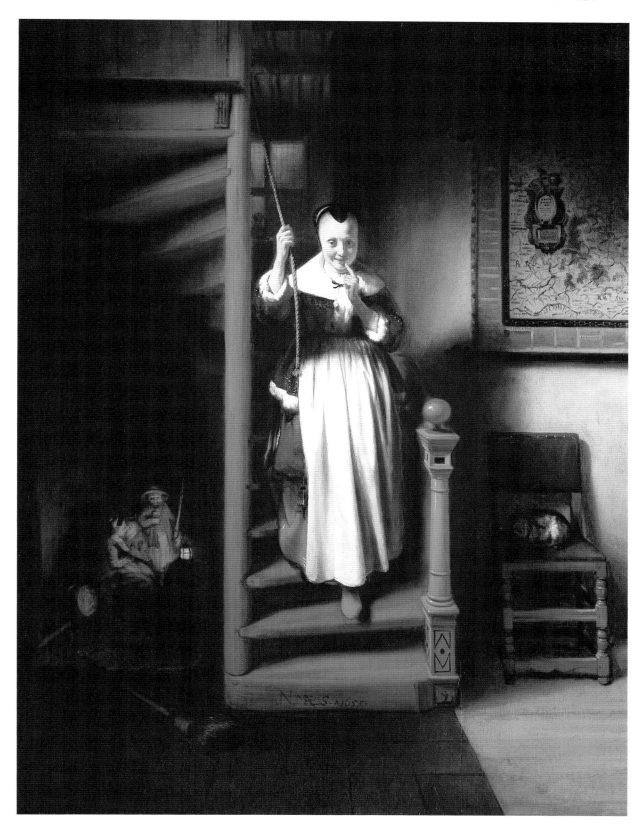

relationship between the amorous couple is in some way illicit or unaccept-able. This feeling is emphasised by the presence of a cat, which is a symbol of erotic desire, and the map, which possibly hints at worldliness. The real meaning of the painting, however, is not necessarily censorious. It is rather one of moral ambiguity expressed compositionally by placing the main figure on the turn of the stairs, and symbolically by the domestic setting, in that temptation often exists in places where you least expect to find it.

Moral ambiguity is a central concern of Dutch seventeenth-century artists and various degrees of subtlety are evident in a picture such as *A Woman at her Toilet*, painted by Jan Steen in 1663 (FIG. 166). Few of Steen's paintings are as contemplative in mood or as highly charged in meaning. The figure is seen through an elaborate archway flanked by Corinthian capitals at the top emerging from columns standing on bases decorated with escutcheons. The archway is, in essence, a framing device, comparable in treatment with the still-life objects in the foreground. Beyond the arch is a door leading into the bedroom. The woman is *en déshabillé* and is provocatively putting on one of her stockings. She is, in fact, a prostitute. This can be discerned not so much from her pose or dress, but from the symbols scattered about the room: the dishevelled bedclothes, the dog, the extinguished candle and the open jewellery box festooned with pearls spill-ing on to the table. Attention should also be concentrated on the still-life objects: the lute, the skull, the sheet music and the vine tendril stress the transitoriness of love, instead of love itself. The broken lute string symbol-ises the loss of chastity to which the tendril of vine meaning fertility or pregnancy is also related. The subject of this painting could be described as base love – but it is most elegantly expressed.

Painting could also be an expression of other, more elevated forms of love. Van Dyck's *Cupid and Psyche* (FIG. 12) is one of the most beautiful compositions undertaken by the artist and was owned for a time by Lely after Charles I's execution. It is, in fact, the only surviving painting of a mythological subject undertaken by Van Dyck during his time of full employment at the English court. The story of Cupid and Psyche was well-known in court circles. Based on *The Golden Ass* by Apuleius, it was adapted on numerous occasions for performance as a masque. Here Cupid is seen discovering Psyche asleep having disobeyed Venus by opening the casket she had collected from Proserpine in Hades. The sense of movement in Cupid's body at the moment of arrival is contrasted with Psyche's stillness. The two figures are set on opposing diagonals that are echoed by the trees above, but it is the tension between them that is the essence of the composition. The balance is between Beauty, represented by Psyche, and Desire, represented by Cupid. The story of Cupid and Psyche had, during the Renaissance, been given a neo-Platonic interpretation contrast-

FIG. 166
Jan Steen: *A Woman at her Toilet*, 1663

252

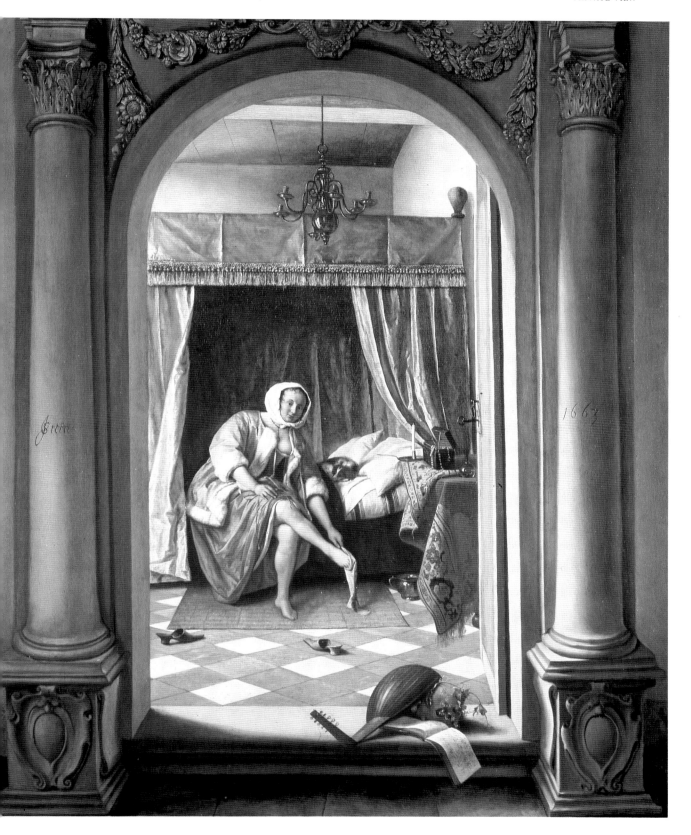

FIG. 167
Gerard Terborch: *The Letter*, c. 1660

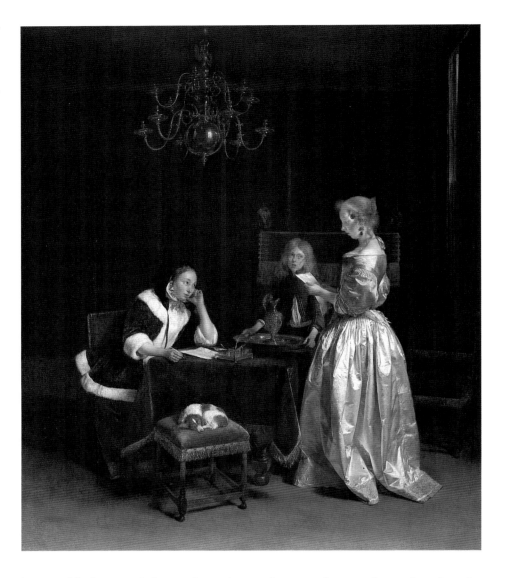

FIG. 168
Jan Vermeer: *A Lady at the Virginals with a Gentleman,* c. 1665

ing earthly love and the soul – a theme that was frequently explored at the court of Charles I and Henrietta Maria. The quality of Van Dyck's painting lies in the supreme delicacy with which the artist suggests the nature of ethereal love, particularly by the use of Cupid's gesture, which in the religious context is usually found in scenes of the Annunciation.

In Dutch seventeenth-century painting the treatment of love in its purest sense is often understated. In *The Letter* by Gerard Terborch (FIG. 167), the contents of the paper clearly refer to love, but the sharp profile of the girl, the anxious glances of the other figures and the deportment of the girl herself denote innocence. The restraint and tenderness of this picture are almost overwhelming, equalled only by the clearly defined interior and the immaculate rendering of the clothes.

The supreme exponent of this kind of painting in seventeenth-century

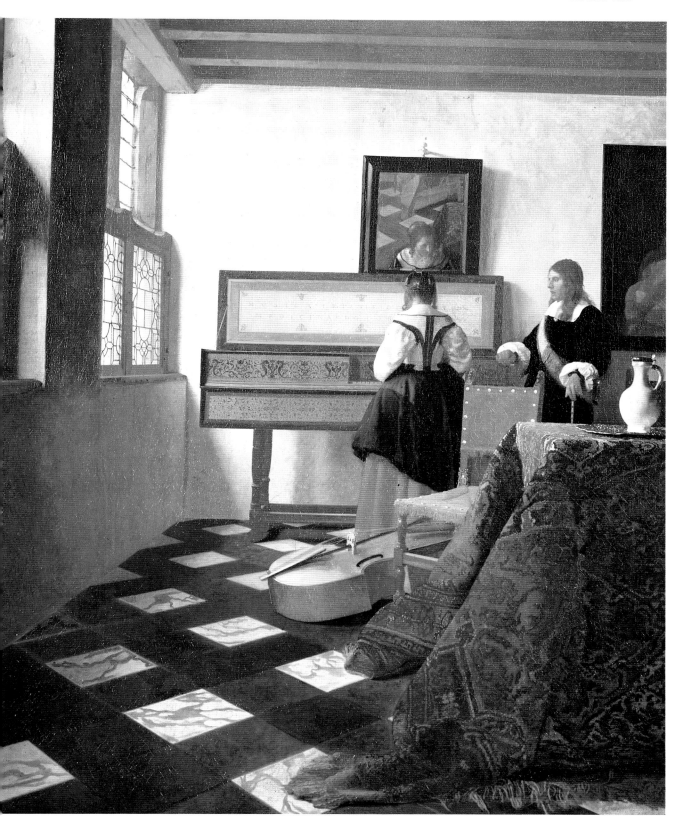

Holland was Jan Vermeer of Delft, who, although only rediscovered late in the last century, has become one of the most popular artists today. Vermeer's compositions are extremely disciplined both in terms of design and observation (FIG. 168). The beauty of the light, the varied rendering of the few carefully selected objects, the deep, warm resonance of colours combine scientific analysis with sheer poetry. The eye passes the table, the cello, and the chair before espying the two figures engaged in conversation by the virginals. The man is in profile and the woman is seen from the back, although her face is reflected in the mirror above. The mood and the association of music suggest that love – its discovery or its absence – is the unstated subject of this picture. One writer refers to this as Vermeer's 'studied obliquity of theme'.[30] The mood of the picture stems from the artist's sense of form and design, as well as from the controlled technique itself. Vermeer transmutes the beauty from his surroundings. The firm compositional control belies the depth of the feeling experienced by the figures, whose emotions are counterbalanced and offset by the inanimate objects in the room. The inscription on the virginals alludes to the ambivalence of emotion – 'Music is a companion in pleasure, a remedy in sorrow.' In this utterly absorbing picture, 'there rests, as gentle as the air itself, an allegory of liberty and bondage, an allegory, as the inscription informs us, of the pleasure and the melancholy of love'.[31]

CHAPTER 6

The Regal Image

We live in an age dominated by images and perhaps no iconography has become as debased as that associated with the British royal family. This situation has come about as a result of the commercialisation that pervades any royal event or any royal place. The debasement of royal imagery is part of the tremendous expansion of opportunities for travel and the development of tourism, a trend which began during the reign of Queen Victoria and has exploded during our own century. Every souvenir shop in a town like Windsor abounds in royal images on plates, mugs, key rings, sculptures, toys, jigsaws, tablemats, teatowels, even Spitting Image latex figures – a veritable landslide of goods of dubious quality. Such items are available all over the world. Photography and television have replaced more traditional items of royal iconography – and souvenirs even more so.

Yet royal image-making can be traced back to the Middle Ages. Before even the painted portrait, miniatures, medals, seals and coins had achieved a level of sophistication by the fifteenth century. Originally, the sovereign's image was circulated for the purposes of recognition, together with an assertion of rank, prestige and power. Embedded within such a simple, visual statement, therefore, is an immense potential for propaganda which attached itself almost by definition to any official image. This chapter traces the evolution of official royal portraiture from the Tudors to the present day, and examines the context in which royal iconography has operated over the centuries.

The Tudor dynasty towards the end of the fifteenth century showed an unusual concern for royal image-making. The intention was to demonstrate its hold on power, to underline its claim to the throne and to illustrate the continuation of its line of succession. Tudor royal portraiture was unashamedly creative and expansive. Henry VIII in the 1540s commissioned a series of portraits of earlier monarchs – Henry V (FIG. 169) and Richard III among them. The style was mostly based on traditional depictions of monarchs found on medals, coinage and seals. Such images were limited in scope, and it was during the reign of Henry VIII that there was a sudden advance in the representation of monarchs, combining the old forms with recent developments, in Renaissance art.

The arrival of Hans Holbein the Younger, from Germany by way of

FIG. 169
Anonymous: *Henry V*,
c. 1520

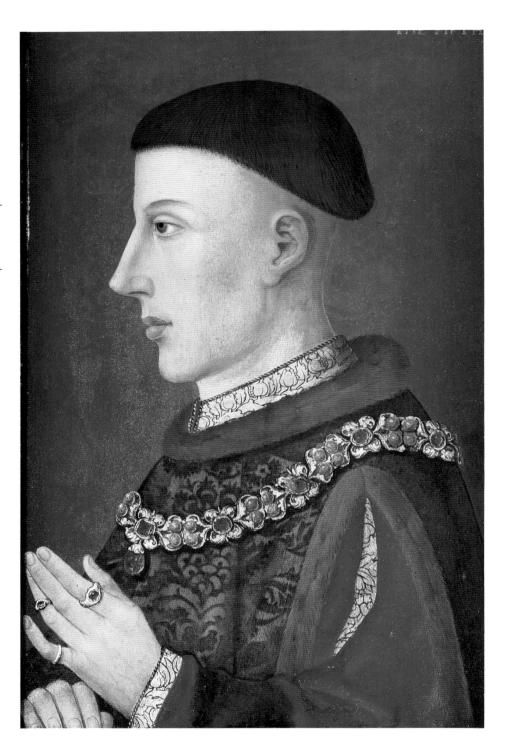

Switzerland, and the Reformation, when Henry VIII broke all ties with the papacy in Rome, hastened these changes. The presence in England of a major European artist, well-versed in Renaissance ideas of religious iconography for use in the secular sphere, immediately widened the terms of reference for royal iconography. The key image in this transformation was the Whitehall Mural painted by Holbein in Whitehall Palace in 1537. The mural was destroyed when Whitehall Palace was burnt down in 1698, but the composition was recorded for Charles II by the artist Remigius van Leemput (FIG. 170).

There are four figures in the painting, three of whom were already dead by the time it was started. Behind are Henry VII and his wife, Elizabeth of York, and in front are Henry VIII and his third wife, Jane Seymour, who had died the year before, shortly after giving birth to Henry VIII's sole male heir, the future Edward VI. Both women have their hands clasped and look towards their husbands. Of the male figures Henry VII at the back looks towards the viewer, but his expression is that of an elder statesman. He was pragmatic in outlook, paternalistic and

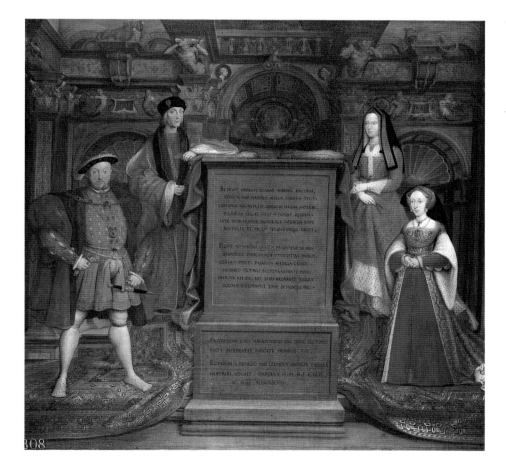

FIG. 170
Remigius van Leemput (after Hans Holbein the Younger): *Henry VII and Elizabeth of York, Henry VIII and Jane Seymour*, 1667

beneficent during his reign. By contrast, his son is a different kind of ruler, a man of unmistakable power and authority. Henry VIII dominates the composition, although he is not raised above the other figures or placed on a central axis. The preparatory cartoon for this figure is in the National

Portrait Gallery and, interestingly, in it Henry VIII is seen in three-quarters profile. Holbein has changed this for the final design, in which he stands almost face on with massive shoulders and huge bulging calves. The viewer is aware of the sheer bulk of his figure, its broad frame emphasised by the arms that encircle the upper half of the body. Standing with feet apart, the figure is resolute, immovable and all-powerful. His status is as undeniable as his stature; indeed, the two are closely related.

The inscription refers to the achievements of both Henry VII and Henry VIII, but it dwells upon the latter's success in forestalling the influence of the papacy and instituting Protestantism. The mural was essentially a display of magnificence, evident in the carpet in the foreground and the rich decoration in the Renaissance style of the background, creating an atmosphere of splendour and opulence as a backdrop to the king's physical presence in his private apartments. Contemporaries who saw it were reported to have felt overcome by it,[1] but what, in effect, happened was that they saw the king in terms of the mural. The actual presence of the monarch was enhanced by the image and this, in turn, became the standard way of representing the king. Holbein had created the definitive image of Henry VIII, which was widely disseminated and is today still easily recognised. Significantly, when Edward VI acceded to the throne aged only ten, the pose established for Henry VIII by Hans Holbein was repeated (in reverse) in order to bolster the young king's impact and importance.

FIG. 171
Michael Wright: *Charles II*, 1661

The only monarch to rival Henry VIII in the creation of a portrait that functioned almost as an icon was Charles II. The circumstances, however, were different. The portrait by Michael Wright (FIG. 171) was painted shortly after the Restoration in 1660. Here the artist has been careful to emphasise Charles II's newly restored regal status following his Coronation on 23 April 1661. The king is shown enthroned and wearing full regalia – an almost entirely new set devised at considerable expense (£31,978 9s. 11d.) for the occasion. Behind the canopy is a tapestry, but it is so arranged that it seems to extend the composition at each side like a triptych with folding shutters. This visual effect may have been deliberate because invested in every British monarch since the reign of Henry VIII are temporal and ecclesiastical responsibilities. Wright's portrait of Charles II has power. It is uncompromising and its purpose is unmistakable, but it is impossible to imagine that it could have been painted without the example of the portraits of Henry VIII by Hans Holbein the Younger.

Henry VIII's daughter by his second wife, Anne Boleyn, Queen Elizabeth I, paid particular attention to portraiture. In fact, more than one hundred images of her survive. These can be divided into various types, some being straightforward likenesses, while most have allegorical mean-

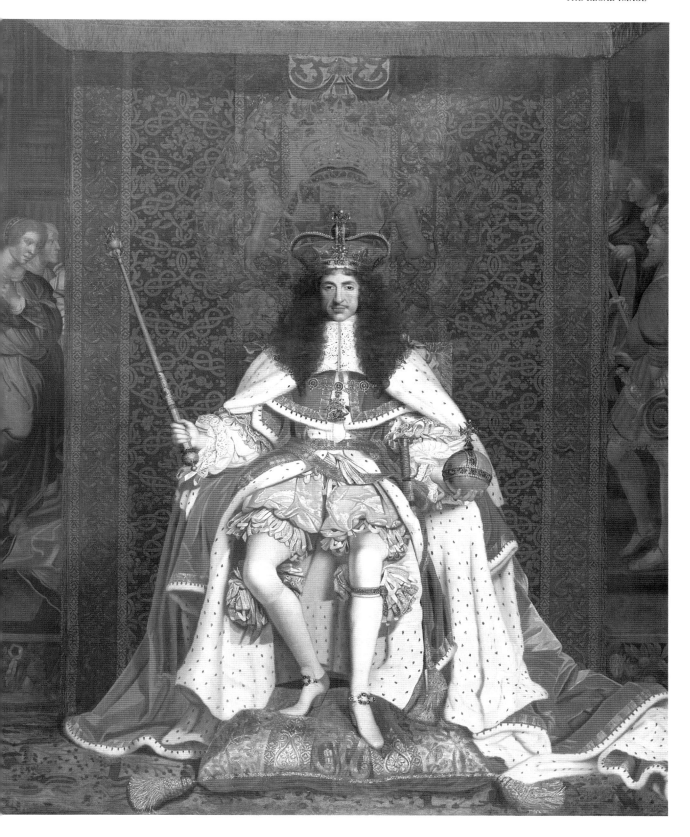

ings reflecting the nature of Queen Elizabeth's rule and the character of her court. These reveal the intellectual atmosphere of Elizabethan court circles – the world of Shakespeare, Marlowe, Sidney and Spenser – as many of these images are remarkably contrived. Elizabeth I was a superb propagandist. While the portraits often concentrate on her red hair, elegant fingers, love of jewellery and passion for learning, with the clear purpose of being nothing more than simple representations, others, such as *Elizabeth I and the three Goddesses* (FIG. 172), demand explication. This small

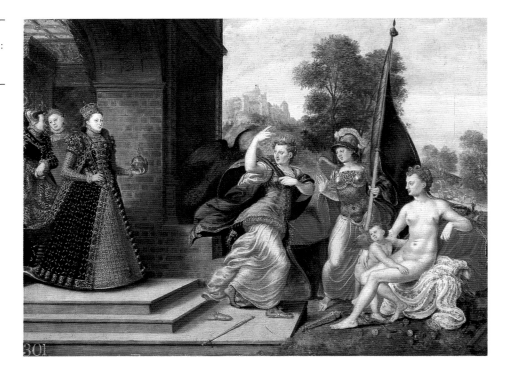

FIG. 172
The Monogrammist H. E.:
Elizabeth I and the three
Goddesses, 1569

panel shows Elizabeth I on the left carrying sceptre and orb and wearing a crown, emerging with her ladies-in-waiting from an interior. Her dress is decorated with Tudor roses and the interior is carefully observed and painted with considerable precision. As the queen advances, she puts to flight three goddesses – Juno with a peacock, Minerva with spear and shield, and Venus naked accompanied by Cupid with her chariot pulled by swans evident in the distance on the right. These three figures retreat in some disorder. The flattery stems from the fact that the artist is here exploiting the traditional iconography of the Judgement of Paris, when Paris was called upon to decide which of the three goddesses was the most beautiful. The implication is that Elizabeth I herself is more beautiful than all the goddesses and that she combines all their attributes. This leads to their discomfiture, which reinforces her status as queen. The landscape incorporates a view of Windsor Castle – one of the earliest representations

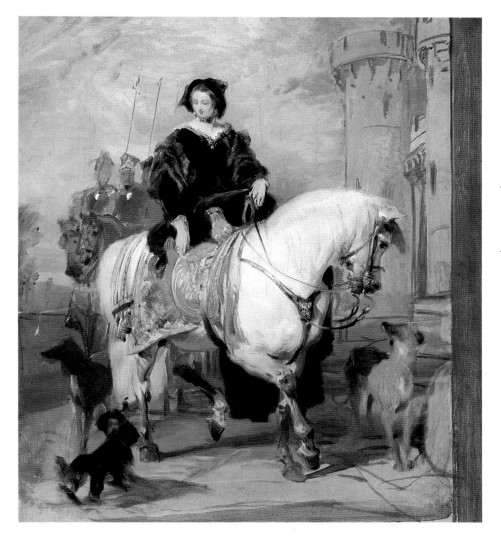

FIG. 173
Sir Edwin Landseer: *Queen Victoria on Horseback*, c. 1840

of this royal residence – which again draws attention to the queen's status.

A similar visual progression, but one with different emphases, can be traced in the context of Queen Victoria. Wilkie depicted the growing Princess Victoria (aged about twelve) in 1831, probably on the occasion of her birthday when a children's ball was given in her honour by William IV and Queen Adelaide. Childhood was soon to be left behind when Princess Victoria acceded to the throne in 1837 aged eighteen. At this stage, Sir George Hayter painted an official Coronation portrait in which the queen – shown unconventionally seated and looking upwards – appears to be weighed down by all the royal regalia (FIG. 200), but it was Wilkie who painted the State Portrait, which failed to impress the young queen. It was sad also that during the early years of the reign Landseer failed to complete his equestrian portrait, which never progressed beyond a series of preliminary oil studies (FIG. 173).

After Queen Victoria's marriage to Prince Albert in 1840, preference was soon given to German painters such as Franz Xaver Winterhalter, who in 1843 was commissioned to paint the royal couple in the robes of the Order of the Garter and in 1859 depicted the queen in the robes of state (FIG. 174) and Prince Albert in the uniform of a colonel of the Rifle Brigade (FIG. 175). These four images were regarded as official portraits and it was only towards the end of the reign that they were replaced by Heinrich

FIG. 174
Franx Xaver Winterhalter:
Queen Victoria, 1859

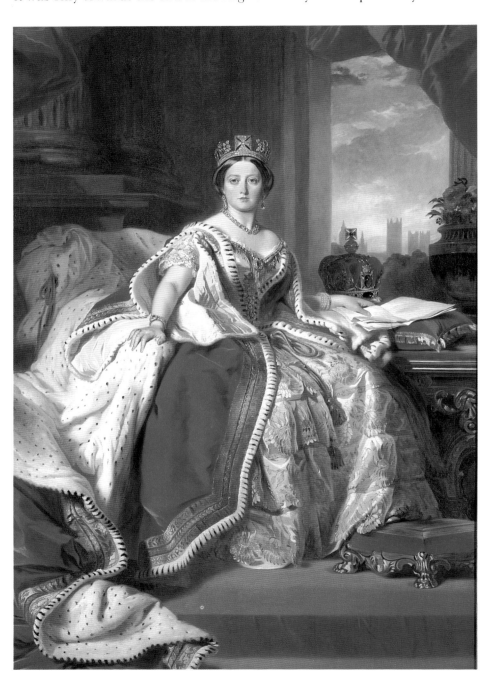

FIG. 175
Franz Xaver Winterhalter:
Prince Albert, 1859

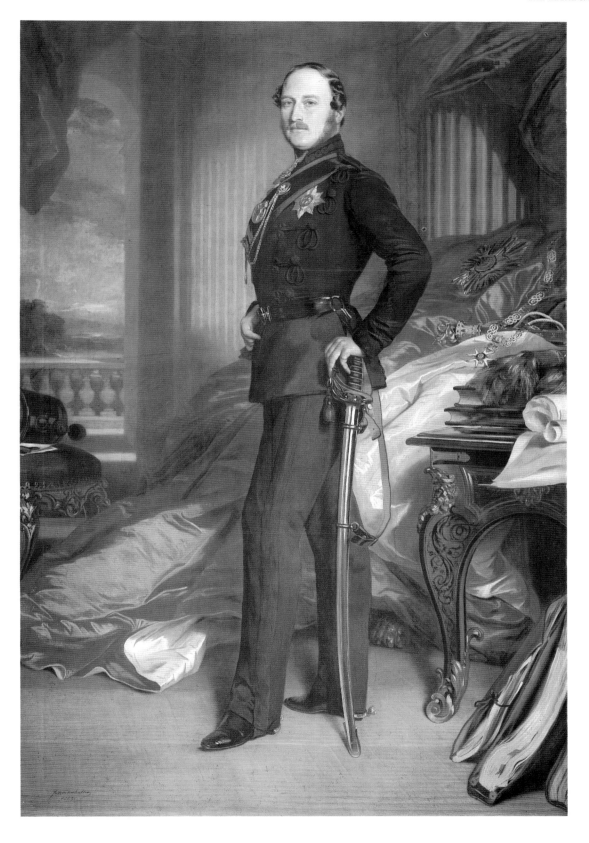

von Angeli's depictions of the ageing queen, who in one instance is shown full length as Empress of India. The final phase in Queen Victoria's personal iconography is represented by von Angeli's portrait of her in mourning, which dates from 1899 (FIG. 176). In three-quarters length, the figure is again characteristically dressed in black and supports her head with the left hand. The pose is traditionally associated with grief, as indeed are the faded roses on the table. Nearly forty years after the death of Prince Albert this portrait reveals the lingering poignancy of his death.

It is because of the deliberate way in which they chose to be painted that most people today can instantly recognise likenesses of Henry VIII, Elizabeth I and Queen Victoria. These images stand as testimony to the potency of royal portraiture.

The Royal Collection also offers a spectacular display of the evolution of the State Portrait from the seventeenth century to the present day. State Portraits, usually commissioned on the occasion of the Coronation as standard likenesses intended for replication and circulation, were the forerunners of the photographs, films and television images that are now *de rigueur*. They were the means by which the sovereign and the consort became known to people. State Portraits had an immense significance, which during the twentieth century has been somewhat eroded, although the tradition is still maintained. As one recent critic has expressed it, the decline of the State Portrait is, in fact, symptomatic of a wider dilemma that afflicts portraiture as a whole:

> The more images there are in the world, it seems, the less we respect each one. The decline of the portrait is yet another sign of our declining faith in the single image to reflect or adequately represent truth. It also suggests that the *kinds* of truth we expect painting to deliver are incompatible with the demands of formal portraiture.[2]

Formal portraiture presents a paradox, because

> . . . according to modernist dogma, it is the paramount duty of the artist to question or contradict or otherwise revolt against 'official versions' of the truth – which, of course, are precisely those versions of the truth which it has been the traditional function of the formal portrait to respect.[3]

In short:

> Modernist portraiture . . . regards the self not as something to be mythologised but interrogated, to be mercilessly laid bare. . . . Patrons

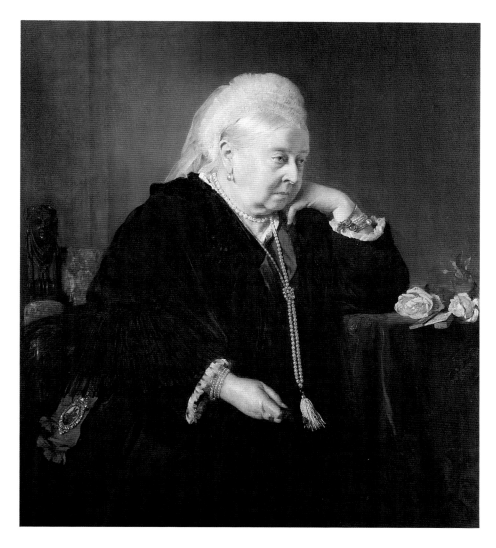

FIG. 176
Heinrich von Angeli: *Queen
Victoria in Mourning*, 1899

have not flocked to the great modernists, as they did to Leonardo,
or Titian or Reynolds: who wants to pay good money, after all, to
be publicly lacerated?[4]

The purpose of the State Portrait is primarily to record a likeness. Following the Tudors, the immediate forerunners of the tradition were Paul van
Somer and Daniel Mytens, who worked at the beginning of the seventeenth
century. The portraits of James I (FIG. 4) and Anne of Denmark (FIG. 3) by Paul
van Somer show figures uncertainly and stiffly posed: James I, who had thin
legs and weak knees, looks slightly tottery, while Anne of Denmark appears
to be almost too rooted to the ground, as if fastened to it, even though the
dogs might be trying to pull her over. Mytens offers a suave but formulaic
likeness of Charles I shortly after his accession (FIG. 177): it is amost facile and
unconvincing as a portrait, even though it is remarkably competent.

By contrast, Van Dyck reveals the essence of his sitter's character. His portraits have psychological insights which his immediate predecessors, van Somer and Mytens, lacked. Van Dyck was the artist who, during the reign of Charles I, established the parameters of modern state portraiture (FIG. 178). In this portrait dating from 1636, the king is shown wearing the

FIG. 177
Daniel Mytens: *Charles I when Prince of Wales*, 1623

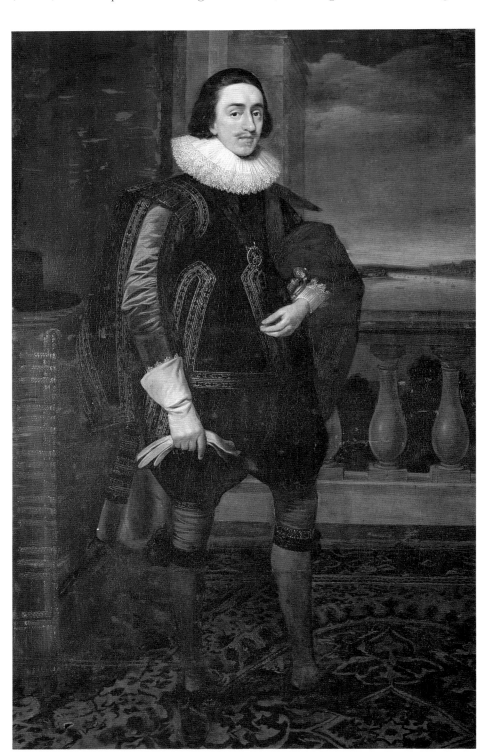

FIG. 178
Sir Anthony Van Dyck: *Charles I*, 1636

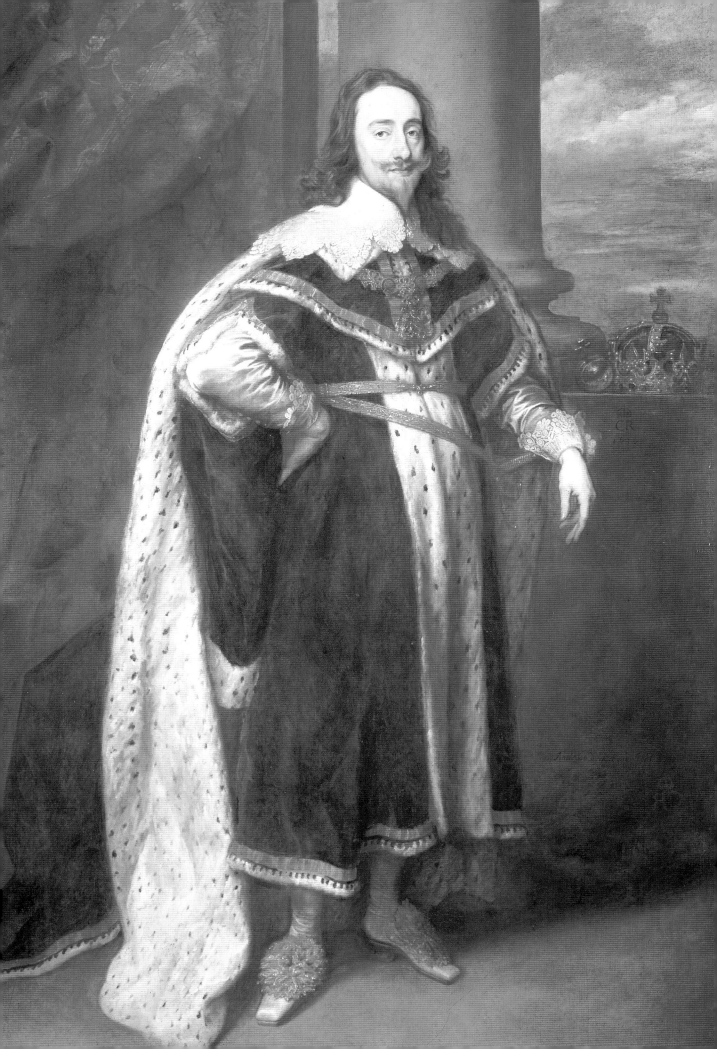

robes of state, but with the collar of the Order of the Garter. The royal regalia has been set aside on a ledge, while the column reinforces the vertical (the king was a short man) and the curtain to the left closes off the composition in contrast with the open sky on the right. The portrait formed a pair with one of the queen, Henrietta Maria, where there is a matching curtain and column, while a bowl of roses complements the royal regalia (Postdam, Sanssouci). The king's pose with one hand on hip has a certain nonchalance, but the figure still looks impressively regal, if not a little vain. The shoes are particularly elegant. Yet here, in 1636, before the outbreak of the Civil War, there is already stamped upon the image of the king all that brittle elegance, languid romance and prescient aura of martyrdom that are associated with his character and reign. With this portrait Van Dyck established a formula – column, looped curtain and varied disposition of the royal regalia – that was to be developed in later centuries.

The Scottish painter Allan Ramsay was appointed Principal Painter during the 1760s, early in the reign of George III. Ramsay had worked in Italy and his portraiture shows evidence of French influence. He had intellectual interests and corresponded with philosophers such as Hume, Rousseau and Voltaire, as well as being a friend of Samuel Johnson. Such instincts would have appealed to the serious-minded young king. The portraits Ramsay painted of George III (FIG. 179) and Queen Charlotte (FIG. 180) reveal the shyness and quiet dignity that characterised this idealistic, rather retiring couple who had numerous children and lived in close harmony. The formula here has become more expansive, almost like an elegant stage setting. The rococo style allows for more grace, with the sweeping curtains tied back to columns and positively acres of ermine robes, thick carpets and heavily gilded furniture, all depicted with a wider range of pale, suffused colours. Queen Charlotte, whom George III married without having seen her previously, was not a particularly elegant woman, and herself admitted after being thrown from a carriage that she had been much improved by a broken nose.[5] Yet (like Van Dyck with Henrietta Maria) Ramsay does not so much indulge in flattery as reveal the inner character that is then translated into a personal, undeniable, external form of beauty. The portraits have the trappings of absolute power, as found in the standard images of Louis XIV which Ramsay would have known, but, in the final analysis, they are not absolutist images.

Sir Thomas Lawrence used his brilliant bravura technique to capture the charm and ebullience of George IV at the time of his Coronation in 1820 (FIG. 16). The portrait is a dazzling display of pyrotechnics, a dashing, glittering evocation of robes and chains symbolising the florid, restless, overweight creature beneath all the heavy cloth. Painting with unflagging panache and a memorable sense of colour, Lawrence relates George IV

FIG. 179
Allan Ramsay: *George III*,
1760–61

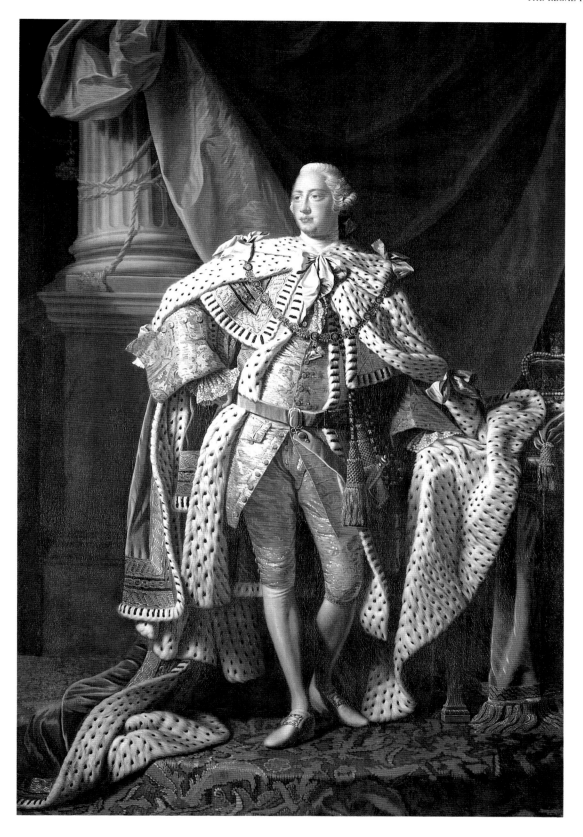

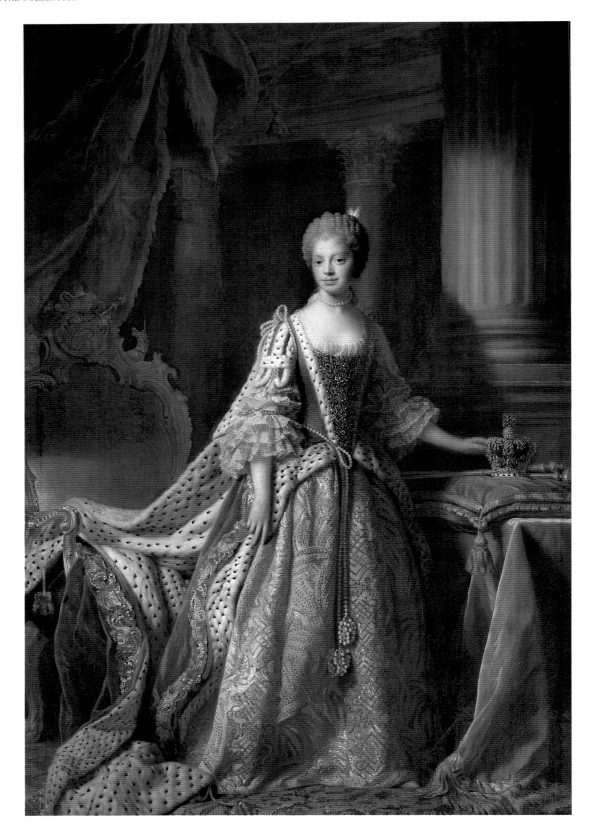

perfectly to that paradise of ormolu that he created around himself at Brighton Pavilion, Carlton House, Windsor Castle and Buckingham Palace.

The State Portraits by Van Dyck, Ramsay and Lawrence are memorable images, but the tradition has been difficult to sustain. Wilkie, for example, who painted William IV as well as Queen Victoria, had to measure himself against standards set by Holbein and brought to perfection by Van Dyck, Ramsay and Lawrence. Winterhalter and von Angeli suffered from the same comparisons, and by 1901, when Queen Victoria died, the impact of photography and the potential of film were beginning to be felt. Those painters commissioned to paint State Portraits during the twentieth century, therefore, strove not only to emulate the freshness of touch and the powerful sense of design of their predecessors, but also to overcome the challenge of modern technology. Perhaps not surprisingly, the artists have all too often proved unequal to the task. As one critic has expressed it:

> You can tell that a tradition has had its day when influence no longer results in development but in pastiche

and:

> Portraitists seem intimidated rather than spurred on by the past.[6]

FIG. 180
Allan Ramsay: *Queen Charlotte*, 1761–2

The first State Portraits painted during the twentieth century were undertaken by Sir Luke Fildes. He had earned a reputation as a notable illustrator and painter of heartrending representations of the Victorian poor. He came to portraiture late in life, during the 1880s, but nevertheless scored a notable success with the State Portraits of Edward VII and Queen Alexandra (FIG. 181). The sittings took place in the artist's house and the finished picture shows the king in field-marshal's uniform – a formidable military figure. On the basis of this portrait, the artist was commissioned ten years later to paint George V (FIG. 182).[7] As so often on these occasions, the preparatory oil studies are more effective than the finished portrait. The king is shown wearing naval uniform with the collar of the Order of the Garter and the insignia of the Royal Victorian Order. During the sittings, George V – as down-to-earth as ever in matters of art – had the newspaper read to him.

The responsibility for painting king George VI and Queen Elizabeth according to the established formula (FIGS. 183 & 184) fell to Gerald Kelly, who was described by Kenneth Clark as 'the most reliable portrait painter of his time'.[8] Kelly declared that 'a State Portrait should be romantically

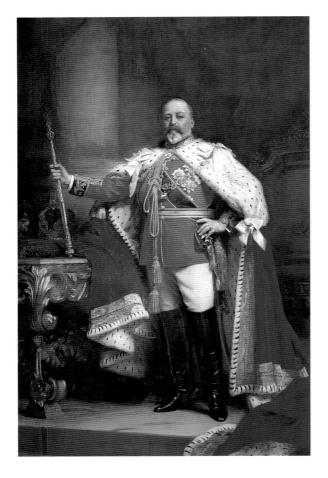

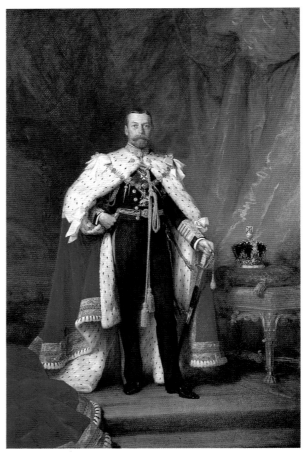

FIG. 181
Sir Luke Fildes: *Edward VII*, 1901–2

FIG. 182
Sir Luke Fildes: *George V*, 1912

FIG. 183
Sir Gerald Kelly: *King George VI*, 1938–45

decorative'[9], but he found this difficult to achieve partly because of the king's modest and retiring nature.

> The King was infinitely patient. He didn't like posing and he didn't pose for long, but he did pose frequently.

The problem was that

> . . . the king didn't like wearing his coronation robes . . . . He put these on, but he was self-conscious and uncomfortable.[10]

Kelly asked the architect Sir Edwin Lutyens to devise a suitable background and Lutyens obliged by providing the artist with models based on the style of the Viceroy's House at Delhi. Kelly's assistants helped by posing in the Coronation robes when they were not working on the complicated perspective of the floors. Progress on these portraits was interrupted by the outbreak of the Second World War, and they are notable for the

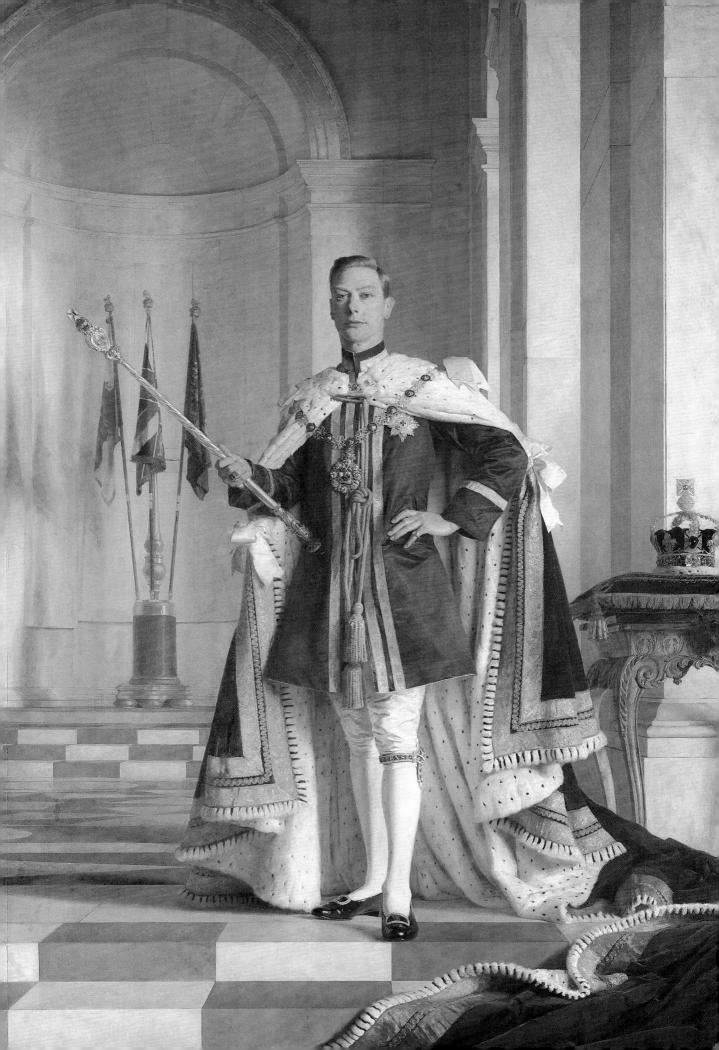

time they took to paint. Numerous oil sketches of the figures and the regalia survive and the completed images are imposing. Indeed, the statuesque forms, sharp treatment of light, mathematical precision and eye for detail echo the works of Piero della Francesca or Ingres. Kelly lived for the duration of the war in Windsor Castle, where he found the atmosphere and the company rather congenial. A temporary studio was established for him in the Grand Reception Room. The portraits were shown in the Royal

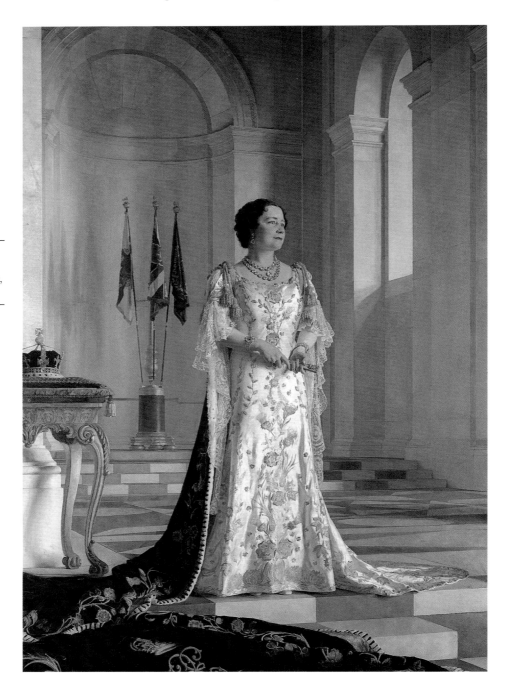

FIG. 184
Sir Gerald Kelly: *Queen Elizabeth, The Queen Mother*, 1938–45

Academy in 1945 and it seems that the artist was reluctant to finish them sooner. It has been claimed – only partly in jest – 'that Gerald, like Penelope, got up at night to undo the work he had done during the day'.[11]

The State Portrait for the present reign was undertaken by Sir James Gunn (FIG. 185) and it invites comparison with the depictions of Elizabeth I and Queen Victoria. Gunn was an unusually efficient and accurate portrait painter. He created a fine likeness, but one which also betrays the influence

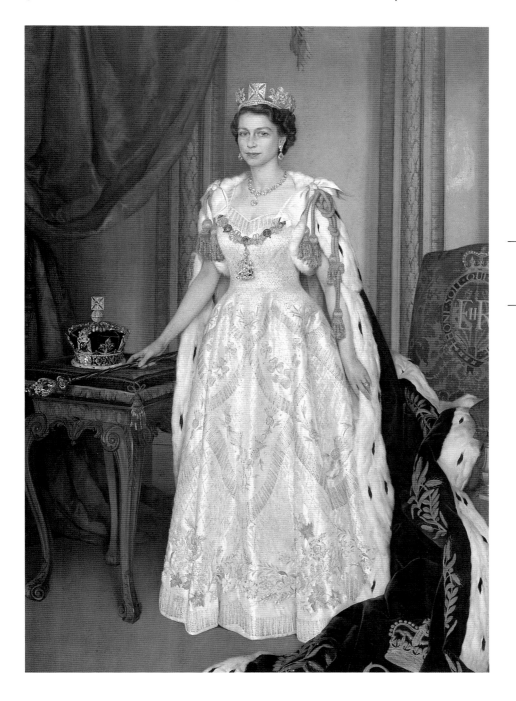

FIG. 185
Sir James Gunn: *Queen Elizabeth II*, 1954–6

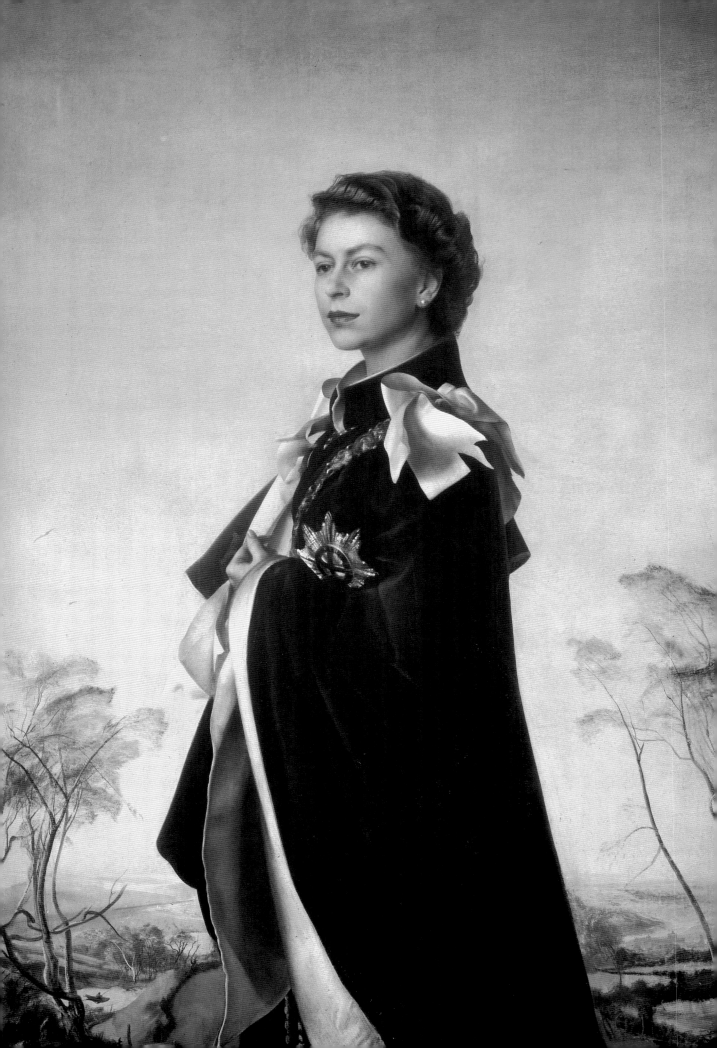

of photography. The difference between Gunn's painting and a photograph by Dorothy Wilding or Cecil Beaton is perhaps marginal.

A telling aspect of the present situation regarding the State Portrait is that the best-known image of the present queen is that by Pietro Annigoni, commissioned in 1954 for the Worshipful Company of Fishmongers (FIG. 186). The success of this portrait stems from its timeless quality, influenced by Italian Renaissance prototypes. It was inspired by the present, but anticipates the future. Silhouetted against the sky and seen in profile, the three-quarter length figure looms up from below, wrapped in the dark blue robe of the Order of the Garter. It is romantic and mysterious without losing any of the mystique, and it is interesting that Cecil Beaton made use of the same device in one of his photographs of the queen. Annigoni succeeded in creating an image that has become more durable than Gunn's State Portrait. In short, a commissioned painting with much of the resonance of a photograph has been invested with greater potency than the official portrait. In purely pictorial terms, the State Portrait would seem to have been usurped and only time will tell if as portraiture it can recapture the centre ground, or whether the tradition has been completely exhausted.

As a recent critic wrote:

Formal portraiture will almost certainly never be again what it once was because our resistance to it has become so engrained. The portraits of a Holbein, a Van Dyck, or a Reynolds tend to leave us cold, because they seem to offer images that would have been too wholeheartedly approved of by their sitters for modern tastes. The truth about people, Freud trained us to believe, is always hidden; it is something that they will only reveal involuntarily.[12]

The same critic cites Goya as the single exception in the history of royal portraiture, because he offers 'the kind of awkward disclosure we value'.[13]

There is, however, another tradition of royal image-making that helps to broaden our understanding of the role that art has played in presenting monarchy as an institution. This is narrative painting allied to commemorating great events, and what such pictures reveal is the conjunction of the public and private spheres in the life of a monarch. During earlier centuries such paintings were haphazard and inconsistent. Artists were on hand to record for posterity not only such events as births and deaths, but also more frivolous occasions, and in so doing to demonstrate the function – both political and social – of monarchy. Such paintings, therefore, served a dual purpose. For example, a painting by Gerrit Houckgeest dating from 1635 depicts Charles I and Henrietta Maria dining in public with the

FIG. 186
Pietro Annigoni: *Queen Elizabeth II*, 1954–5

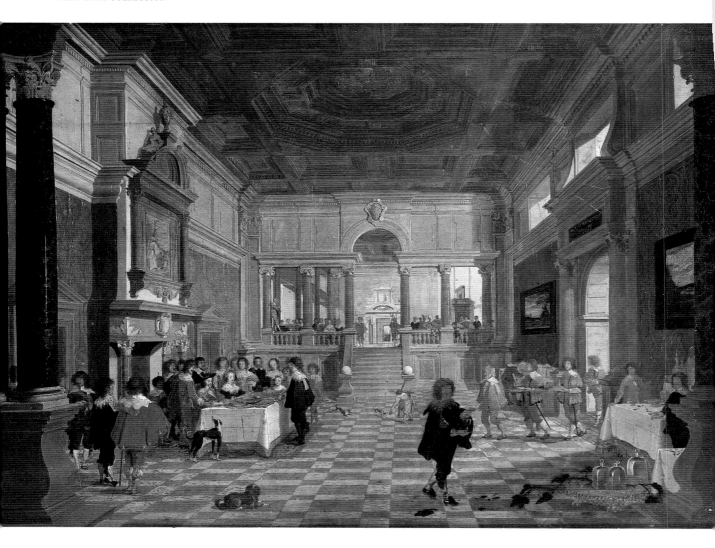

FIG. 187
Gerrit Houckgeest: *Charles I, Queen Henrietta Maria, and Charles, Prince of Wales, Dining in Public*, 1635

Prince of Wales (FIG. 187). This was a practice that symbolised the status of the king and queen. The courtiers as members of the royal household carried out specific tasks as the meal progressed, while elsewhere and at different intervals servants hurried in and out replenishing the table. This was a public event which people were intended to witness.

Entertainments were another aspect of public life. The huge canvas by Gerrit van Honthorst, discussed in Chapter 1, in which Charles I and Henrietta Maria, depicted as Apollo and Diana, are about to receive the homage of the arts and in doing so overcome vices such as Ignorance, Envy and Lust (FIG. 10) is somewhat impenetrable today; indeed, however well this sort of picture has been painted, the subject may seem ludicrous. But such obvious personifications and dry intellectual allusions were standard practice in court life of the seventeenth century. In fact, this painting directly emulates the masques devised by Ben Jonson and Inigo Jones frequently enacted by members of the early Stuart court, including the monarch, with elaborate costumes and scenery. The fun was somewhat cerebral and narrowly focused, but the symbolism was all-important.

The rarefied atmosphere of the court of Charles I was not emulated by his son, who is shown by the Flemish painter Hieronymus Janssens, dancing – as well he might have felt inclined to do – with his sister Mary of Orange at The Hague on the eve of his restoration in 1660 (FIG. 188).

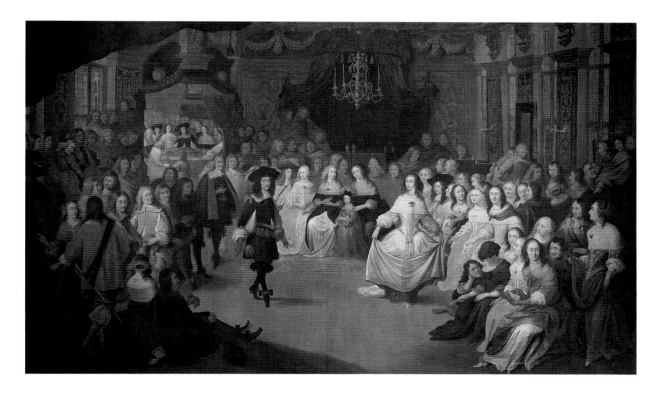

FIG. 188
Hieronymus Janssens:
Charles II Dancing at a Ball at Court, c. 1660

Shortly after the queen's accession to the throne in 1837, Sir Francis Grant was commissioned to paint *Queen Victoria Riding Out* (FIG. 189), which shows the queen in the company of her Prime Minister, Lord Melbourne, members of the royal household and her pet dogs riding in the grounds of Windsor Castle. The queen relied heavily at the beginning of her reign on the advice of Lord Melbourne and so, even if for her 'it is such a happiness for me to have that dear kind friend's face, which I do like and admire so'[14], there is a certain dualism inherent within the picture. This is also the case with the *bal costumé* held by Queen Victoria and Prince Albert in Buckingham Palace on 12 May 1842 – the first of three such balls dressed in the style of different periods.

At the ball of 1842 Queen Victoria was dressed as Queen Philippa and Prince Albert as Edward III (FIG. 190), who had founded the Order of the Garter and was held in the highest respect by his successors. Members

FIG. 190
Sir Edwin Landseer: *Queen Victoria and Prince Albert at the Bal Costumé of 12 May 1842*, 1842–6

of the royal household were expected to wear dress in the same style, but other guests were allowed to appear in costumes of any period or country. The setting for the ball and the design of the costumes were entrusted to J. R. Planché, who was an authority on the history of dress, a dramatist and a herald in the College of Arms. The *bal costumé* of 1842 marked an important moment in the revival of interest in medieval history and customs, but, like charity balls held today, there was also a philanthropic purpose in so far as the production of so many different costumes helped to sustain the declining weaving industry based at Spitalfields. So concerned was Planché for historical accuracy that he overlooked the difficulty of dancing quadrilles in medieval footwear. The ball was reported in *The Illustrated News* and there were also several official accounts. *The Times* commented that

> . . . Her Majesty's fancy dress ball on Thursday night was a scene
> of such brilliance and magnificence, that since the days of
> Charles II with the solitary exception of one fête given in the reign
> of George IV, there has been nothing at all comparable to it in all
> the entertainments given at the British court.[15]

Queen Victoria was zealous in commissioning paintings recording important events in which she participated, and none was of such profound personal significance as the inauguration in 1851 of the Great Exhibition, held in the Crystal Palace in Hyde Park. The Crystal Palace (the appella-

FIG. 189
Sir Francis Grant: *Queen Victoria Riding Out*, 1839–40

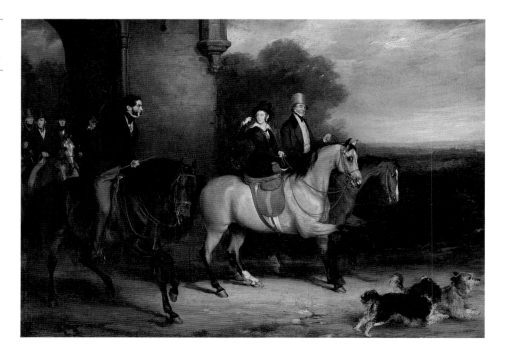

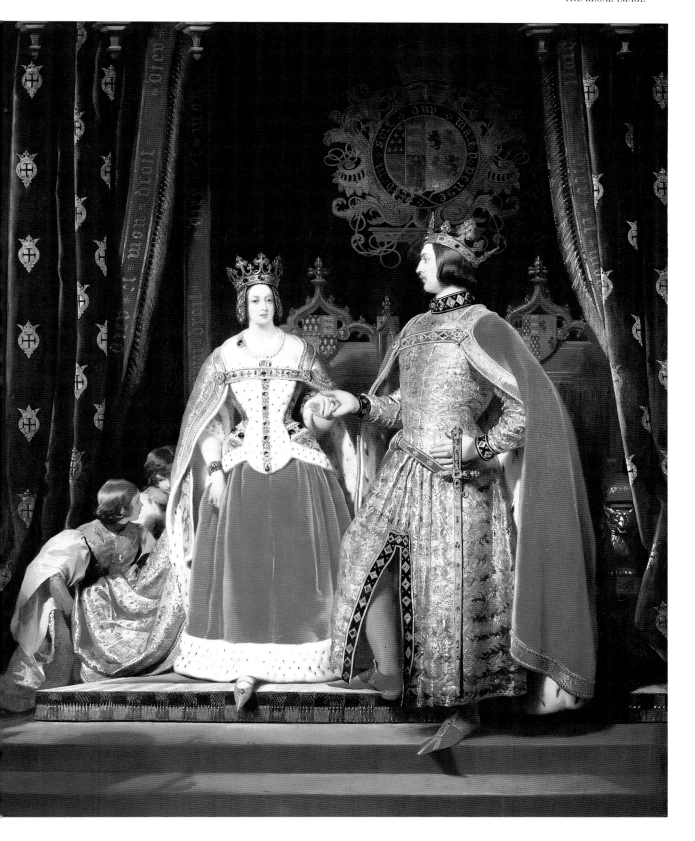

tion is due to *Punch* magazine) was designed by Joseph Paxton. It was a massive structure made of glass and iron and served as the principal focus of this elaborate exhibition, or trade fair, which celebrated new inventions, discoveries and all aspects of modernity. There were 14,000 exhibits from all over the world divided into four sections: raw materials, machinery and mechanical inventions, manufactures, sculpture and plastic arts. Britain, as the most advanced industrial nation at that date, gained immense

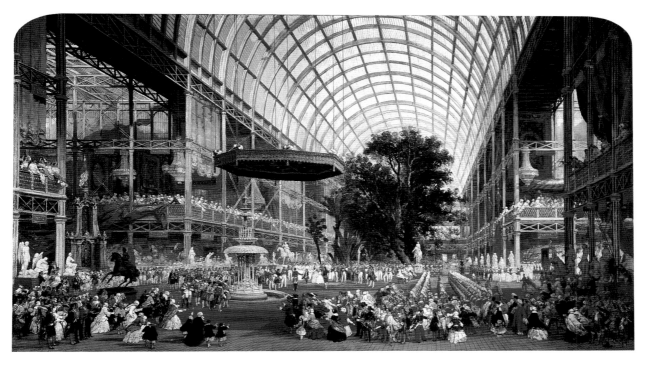

FIG. 191
David Roberts: *The Inauguration of the Great Exhibition, 1 May 1851,* 1852–4

national pride from the occasion. The opening took place on 1 May 1851 and Queen Victoria wrote enthusiastically, and at length, in her *Journal*:

> This day is one of the greatest and most glorious days of our lives, with which to my pride and joy the name of my dearly beloved Albert is forever associated! It is a day which makes my heart swell with thankfulness. The Park presented a wonderful spectacle, crowds streaming through it – carriages and troops passing quite like the Coronation Day, and for *me* the same anxiety.[16]

She describes the royal family's entry into the building with even greater relish:

> In a few seconds we proceeded, Albert leading me having Vicky at his hand, & Bertie holding mine. The sight as we came to the centre where the steps & chair (on which I did not sit) was placed, facing

the beautiful crystal fountain was magic and impressive. The tremendous cheering, the joy expressed in every face, the vastness of the building, with all its decorations and exhibits, the sound of the organ (with 200 instruments & 600 voices, which seemed nothing) & my beloved Husband the creator of this great 'Peace Festival', uniting the industry and art of *all* nations of the earth, *all* this was indeed moving, & a day to live forever.[17]

The artist David Roberts was summoned to Windsor Castle and asked if he would undertake a painting commemorating the occasion (FIG. 191). Detailed discussions took place between the queen, Prince Albert and Roberts. Ideas were exchanged, preliminary sketches were made on the spot, and the artist was shown the painting entitled *The First of May* by F. X. Winterhalter (FIG. 32), which included a view of the Crystal Palace. Roberts then had to report at intervals to Windsor Castle, Buckingham Palace and Osborne House in order to show what progress he was making. He was frequently asked to make changes for the sake of accuracy in details of dress and decoration. Writing to his daughter in April 1853, he reported:

I have just returned from the Palace where we had a thorough overhauling of the Picture . . . found it placed on an easel in the Great Gallery, a wretched light & the morning dismal. Whilst moving it about to get it in a decent light His R Highness was with me & The Queen close upon his heels. After looking at [it] for some time we had it moved into a room where there was a side light & here we entered into a close examination upon the whole I may say more than ever satisfactory & with the exception of certain improvements suggested by the Prince as to his own Dress & that of the Prince of Russia & The petty coat of the Princess Royal made Shorter which the Queen drew for me. I may say upon the whole I came off well. Nothing could exceed the kindness of which I was treated by both particularly the Queen.[18]

But a year later Roberts no longer considered the work so congenial. The royal critics found further fault with the picture and at this late stage Prince Albert suddenly observed that the perspective was wrong, thus involving some fairly extensive alterations, which were overseen by the queen. The artist records these moments as follows:

He [Prince Albert] also pointed out where the perspective was at fault – and he was right, in fact I had dozed [?] so long over the Picture – that with the multitude of figures the [illeg] absence of all that goes to make a picture architecturally – that try what I would – it was a most thankless effort – and in Strayning for effect the point of Vision in one place, had got out – I saw it at once – and begged, he would Speak freely what he thought would emprove it, as I had been so long on it I could scarse tell myself – I must say he went – Radicaly to work for by his proposed amendment, it took the heads off all the leading figures, including his own and her blessed majesty – I without hesitation with my palate knife decapitated the whole, and I must say, before doing so he expressed his regret at the necessity – But here I had cut myself out some Three or Four days work – never mind to it I went & worked till late – came in to town the same day, and early the following morning was again at Windsor; whilst painting Her Majesty in the most gracious manner, begged I would allow her to sit by me and see me painting – and would insist on my remaining to sit, which, I as a courtier did as ordered – although I confess to a sort of tremor, whilst being overlooked by the highest lady in the land, several of the children also came in – and had their remarks to make on the subject.[19]

Little wonder that the painting was not finished until 1854.

Queen Victoria also recognised the significance of annual social events that had become such a feature of her reign. The Danish artist Laurits Tuxen, who worked for Queen Victoria, Edward VII and George V, painted *The Queen's Garden Party at Buckingham Palace*, held on 28 June 1897 (FIG. 192). Since it was the year of the Diamond Jubilee, the cream of London society was present as well as representatives from the British Empire who had connections with the Court of St James's. This picture took three years to paint and Tuxen was paid £1,000. He laboured away arranging sittings and taking photographs. The garden party began at a quarter past five, but in the picture it is apparent that the queen is leaving the proceedings. In the background is the lake, and the royal tent is situated on the right. The queen is accompanied by the Princess of Wales and members of the royal household are in attendance. All the figures are identifiable. The Prince of Wales is seen in the lane beyond talking to a guest.

The paintings we have been discussing, extending from Gerrit Houckgeest in the seventeenth century to Laurits Tuxen at the end of the nineteenth, are concerned with the appearance of the sovereign in public. In each case there are modern parallels, for as Walter Bagehot wrote of the monarch in 1874:

To be invisible is to be forgotten . . . . But to be a symbol, and an effective symbol, you must be vividly and often seen.[20]

The performance of public duties by members of the royal family, especially the queen, is today marked by a great deal of planning, culminating in the major ceremonial events of the reign, but this has not always been the case. As one historian has pointed out, during the whole of the eighteenth and for much of the nineteenth century monarchy lacked

> . . . a coherent ceremonial language, as had been the case in Tudor and Stuart times, and as was to happen again towards the end of the nineteenth century.[21]

Before the reassertion of the primacy of royal ceremonial,

> . . . monarchs who were politically energetic but personally unpopular, trundling through the miserable streets of London by

FIG. 192
Laurits Tuxen: *The Queen's Garden Party at Buckingham Palace, 28 June 1897*, 1897–1900

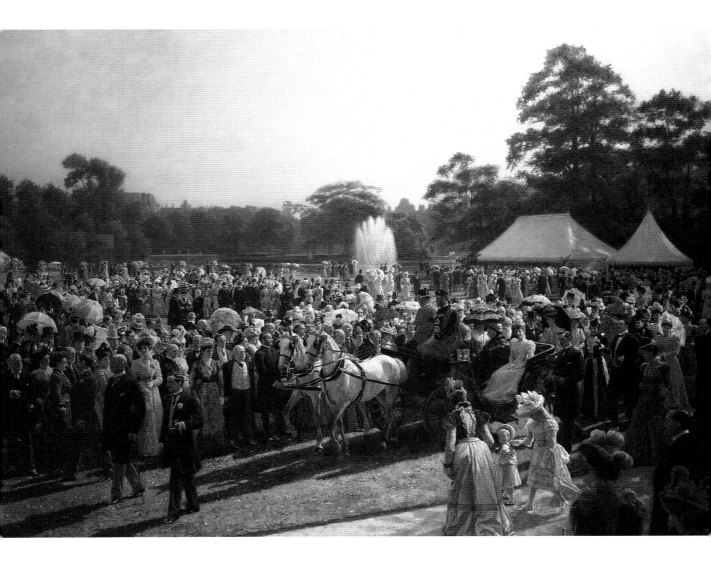

the conventional mode of transport, were more the head of society than the head of the nation.[22]

The deaths of national heroes such as Nelson or Wellington were marked by a greater display of public splendour than the deaths of George III, George IV, William IV or Prince Albert. This, however, changed during the reign of Queen Victoria, particularly after she became Empress of India in 1876, and her own funeral was a far grander event than that afforded to Gladstone, the four-times Prime Minister who had died three years earlier.

Religious and military ceremonial was revived, or reactivated, or specially created for the most important state occasions, on which Edward VII and George V also placed proper emphasis. As a result, nearly every aspect – processing, parading, carriages, music, uniforms, vestments and liturgy – underwent analysis and, if necessary, revision. So skilful were these changes and innovations that it seemed they had existed throughout history. The paradox is that the revival of royal ceremonial coincided with the years that Queen Victoria distanced herself from public life to such an extent that between 1861, when Prince Albert died, and 1886 she only opened Parliament six times. On the other hand, events such as the Golden Jubilee of 1887 and the Diamond Jubilee of 1897 gave rise to great outpourings of popular emotion focused on the queen and experienced throughout the Empire. Thus, subsequently,

> George V contrived to be both grand and domestic, a father-figure to the whole empire, yet also in his own right the head of a family with which all could identify.[23]

He combined 'private probity' with 'public grandeur', creating a 'synthesis which both his long-serving successors have emulated'.[24] To account for these developments, when 'the public image of the British monarchy, or its ritual, hitherto inept, private and of limited appeal, became splendid, public and popular'[25] has been the province of the historian. The development of pomp and display from the 1870s to 1914 coincided with the 'gradual retirement of the monarch from active politics'[26] in the sense that, although remaining the pivot of the constitutional process, monarchy was for the first time careful to rise above everyday politics.

Between 1914 and 1953, royal ceremonial has been seen to be 'a unique expression of continuity in a period of unprecedented change'.[27] This change has, of course, been further acknowledged by the coverage of royal events on radio or television, and has been further promoted by tourism. In sum:

. . . just as in previous periods of international change, the ritual of monarchy was of importance in legitimising the novelty of formal empire and in giving an impression of stability at a time of international bewilderment, so in the post-war world it has provided a comfortable palliative to the loss of world-power status.[28]

Whatever the reasons for this diapason in royal ceremonial, its principal stage and finest enactments have taken place in London. The scene is set as early as the mid-eighteenth century when the Venetian painter Cana-letto came to London in 1746 for a visit that lasted some ten years. He painted two panoramic views of the city from the terrace of Somerset House, which was still then a royal residence built in the Palladian style, possibly by Inigo Jones (FIGS. 193 & 194). For a short time the home of the Royal Academy after its foundation by George III, Somerset House was soon to be pulled down. These two paintings were made for Canaletto's principal patron in Venice, Consul Joseph Smith. Perhaps Smith wanted the paintings for sentimental reasons, since he himself did not return to England before his death in 1770.

Canaletto looks up the Thames towards Westminster Bridge, recently constructed in 1739–48, where the Banqueting House built by Inigo Jones,

FIG. 193
Canaletto: *View of London: the Thames from Somerset House towards Westminster,* 1750–1

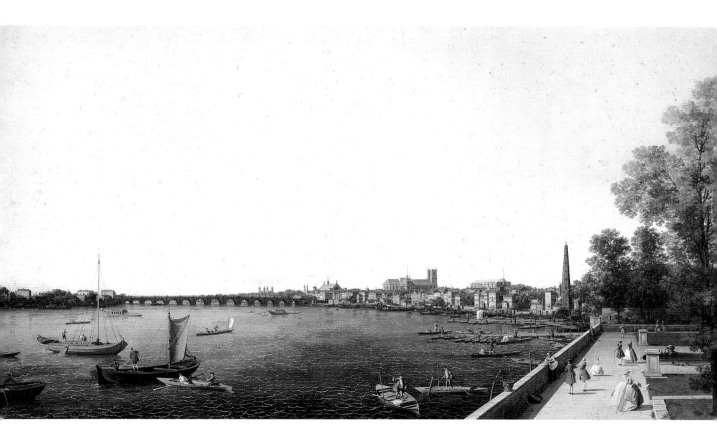

Westminster Abbey with its twin 'Gothick' towers designed by Nicholas Hawksmoor, Westminster Hall and the four towers of the church of St John Smith's Square can all be made out. Nearer to the spectator is the tower of the York Buildings Waterworks, a late seventeenth-century wooden structure used to supply the neighbouring streets with water. The view

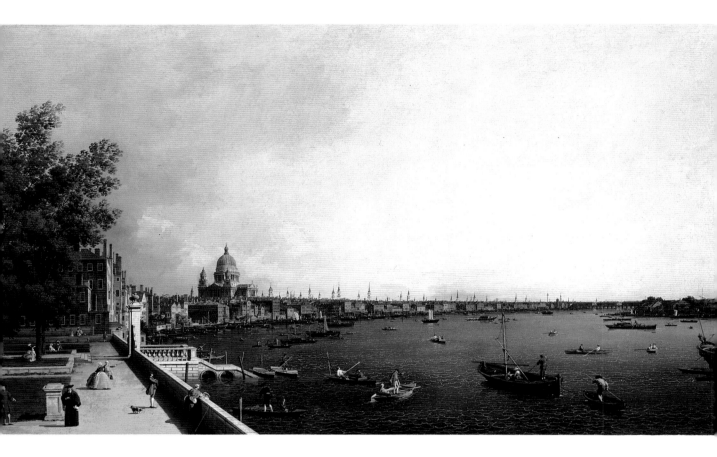

FIG. 194
Canaletto: *View of London: the Thames from Somerset House towards the City*, 1750–1

down the river is towards the City of London with Old London Bridge, on which there are houses, visible in the distance. The skyline is dominated on the left by St Paul's Cathedral and then, as the eye moves to the right, by a veritable forest of spires and steeples of the City churches built by Wren after the Great Fire of London in 1666. The Monument erected in 1671–7 to the Great Fire is visible on the right. Consul Smith would no doubt have noted to what extent London had been transformed since he had left England in 1700. What Canaletto depicts for us is a thriving mercantile city, resplendent in its architectural glories and, judging by the observers on the embankment and by the rivercraft, a city of increasing prosperity with a skyline that was soon to become as deeply etched in public consciousness as that of Athens or Rome. It is fascinating to reflect that Canaletto is here painting a growing, expanding city when he spent so much of his life catching the quintessence of the beauty of Venice in decline.

Even London on occasion resembled Venice; as for example during the Lord Mayor's water procession, staged in 1683. The barge of the City of London with the Lord Mayor aboard and accompanied by the barges of the City Livery Companies row past Whitehall Palace with the buildings of Westminster, including the Banqueting House, in the background. The king (Charles II) is visible as a spectator on Whitehall Palace Stairs. These ceremonial barges are comparable with those used in Venice and in both cities such barges continued in use during the eighteenth century. This painting serves as a reminder of the potential of the River Thames as a means of transport and communication.

At the same time that Canaletto was arriving in London, another artist, probably Joseph Nickolls, was painting in St James's Park (FIG. 127). He has positioned himself at the east end of the Mall with Westminster Abbey visible through the trees and a glimpse of Horse Guards on the left. In the eighteenth century London was already famous for its parks, areas of *rus in urbe*. Here royalty, aristocracy and all other ranks of society take the air or go about their business. This is the world depicted in the plays of Congreve, Vanburgh, Farquhar or Sheridan. The figure on the left in the red, wearing a hat and the ribbon of the Order of the Garter, is probably George II, while right of centre in the foreground is his son Frederick, Prince of Wales, accompanied possibly by the first Duke of Newcastle. For the rest, there are off-duty soldiers and sailors, milkmaids, nursemaids, clergymen, foreigners and *le beau monde*.

During the second half of the eighteenth century and at the start of the nineteenth, London, like many other cities in Europe, was modernised. A new layout of streets was devised. One such example was John Nash's urban plan for Regent Street which linked Regent's Park to the north with the area around St James's Park where Carlton House and Buckingham House (soon to be converted into a palace by Nash) were situated. This plan has been described as the 'stucco sceptre of the metropolis of George IV'.[29] Similar, more industrially orientated developments were taking place in the business community to the east. London Bridge was medieval in origin and before the building of Westminster Bridge it was the only link across the Thames. The original bridge, like the Rialto in Venice or the Pont-Neuf in Paris, was familiar because of the houses built upon it, so that the new design became a major landmark. The opening of the new bridge on 1 August 1831 was widely celebrated (FIG. 195). *The Times* described it as 'the most splendid spectacle that has been witnessed on the Thames for many years'.[30] Clarkson Stanfield's large painting, with its low viewpoint and broad range of characterisation, gives a good idea not only of the excitement prompted at the time by the presence of William IV and Queen Adelaide, who are seen arriving in the State Barge, but also of the sense of optimism that London's expansion during the opening decades of the nineteenth century generated. In terms of architecture and planning, this optimism did not really reveal itself until the late nineteenth and early twentieth centuries. London, unlike Paris or Berlin, was not a planned city:

> It is the city raised by private, not by public, wealth, the least authoritarian city in Europe.[31]

As such it was not designed for ceremonial:

> The basis of its building history is the trade cycle rather than the changing ambitions and policies of rulers and administrators.[32]

FIG. 195
Clarkson Stanfield: *The Opening of London Bridge, 1 August 1831*, 1832

Indeed, the only triumphal, ceremonial progress in the city is The Mall joining Buckingham Palace and Trafalgar Square, with the Victoria Monument at one end and Admiralty Arch at the other. Yet this ensemble was

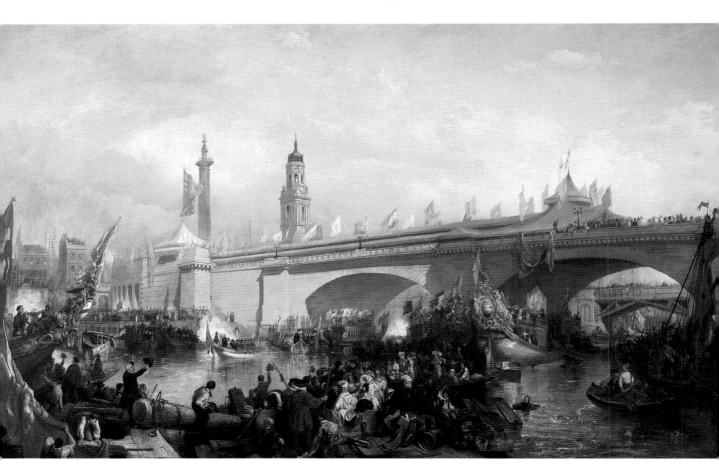

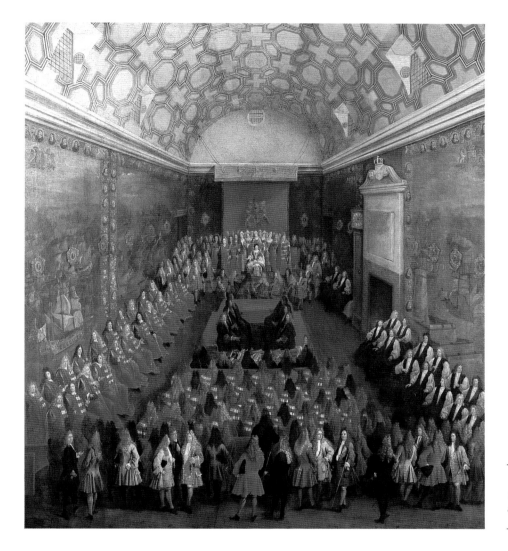

FIG. 196
Peter Tillemans: *Queen Anne
at the House of Lords*, c. 1710

not created until 1906–13, at which time the facade of Buckingham Palace
was also renewed by Sir Aston Webb. All of this was achieved under the
aegis of Viscount Esher, the most influential courtier of his generation and
'the *eminence grise* in British governing circles at the turn of the century'.[33]

The lack of a formal plan for the layout of the streets of London was
to a certain extent responsible for the delayed start in the process of per-
fecting royal ceremonies. The two great state occasions when ceremonial
is most in evidence are traditionally the Opening of Parliament and the
Coronation. The Opening of Parliament by Queen Anne at the very beginning of the eighteenth century is depicted in a painting attributed to Peter
Tillemans (FIG. 196). This shows the queen enthroned in the House of Lords,
the walls of which are decorated with the famous Armada tapestries. Here
the queen is attended by her ladies-in-waiting, heralds, officers of state and
pages. The House is in session: the temporal and spiritual peers are seated

FIG. 198
George Jones: *The Banquet
at the Coronation of George IV,
19 July 1821*, 1821

in their places around the chamber. The Lord Chief Justice is on the Woolsack and members of the House of Commons stand at the bar of the House.

A similar picture, possibly by John Wootton, illustrates the procession of George III to Parliament in 1762, the first time that the new Gold State Coach designed by Sir William Chambers was used (FIG. 197). Although there is a comparable painting in the Royal Collection showing Queen Anne processing to Parliament some half-century earlier, the reason for depicting George III's procession seems to have been the appearance of the coach as opposed to the event itself. The coach, however, is today more closely associated with the Coronation than with the State Opening of Parliament.

Coronations on the other hand have been depicted with increasing regularity as an official record since the time of George IV. The artist Benjamin Haydon felt that in the aftermath of the declaration of American Independence and the growth of the Reform movement in Britain 'the Coronation of George IV may be considered the setting sun of that splendid imposition – monarchy'.[34] George IV intended that his Coronation, held on 19 July 1821 and lasting five hours in intense heat, should offset such nascent republican sympathies, and the grandeur was not lost on Haydon, who witnessed the king arrive in Westminster Hall and later observed the Coronation Banquet. The Banquet, which was painted by George Jones (FIG. 198), followed the Coronation itself and involved the entry of the King's

FIG. 197
John Wootton (attributed
to): *George III's Procession to
the Houses of Parliament*, 1762

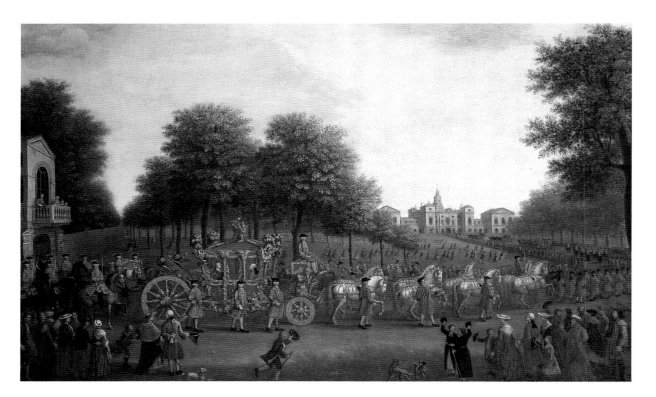

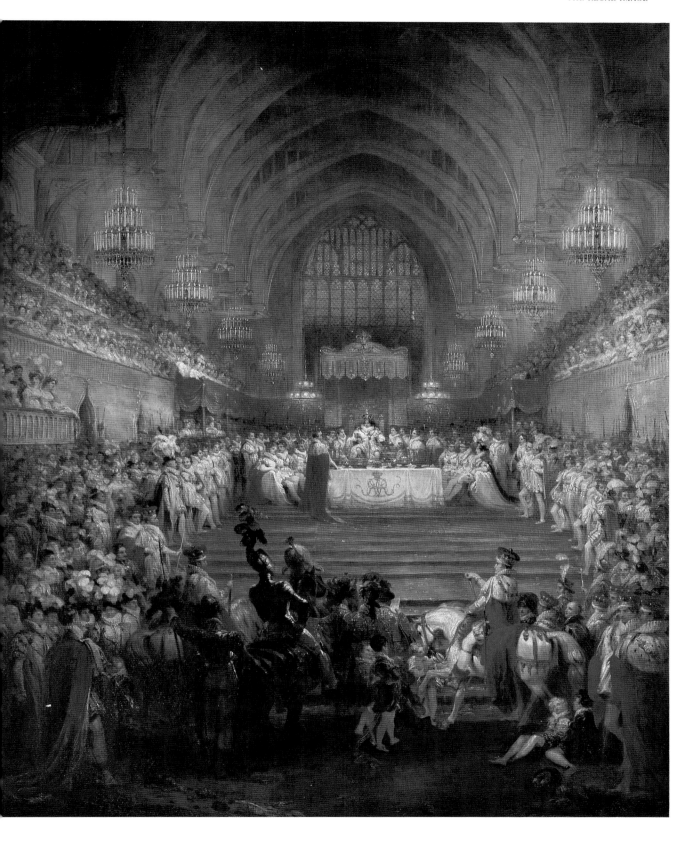

Champion, Henry Dymoke, mounted and in full armour. The Champion, accompanied by the Deputy Earl Marshal and the Duke of Wellington, in keeping with tradition challenged the 300 or so guests to impugn the king's right to the throne. This was acknowledged by the king, still wearing his robes and crown, seated on the throne under the south window of the Hall. At the table were seated the Dukes of York, Sussex, Gloucester, Clarence and Cambridge, and Prince Leopold of Saxe-Coburg. On the right was the royal box with members of the royal family and on the left the box for Foreign Ministers. Numerous peers and peeresses attended and spectators were admitted. Haydon's account of this scene – the last time that the Coronation Banquet was held – complements Jones's painting.

July 21. What a scene was Westminster Hall on Thursday last!

It combined all the gorgeous splendour of ancient chivalry with the intense heroic interest of modern times: everything that could effect or excite, either in beauty, heroism, genius, grace, elegance, or taste; all that was rich in colour, gorgeous in effect, touching in association, English in character or Asiatic in magnificence, was crowded into this golden & enchanted hall!

I only got my ticket on Wednesday at two, and dearest Mary & I drove about to get all I wanted. Sir George Beaumont lent me ruffles & frill, another a blue velvet coat, a third a sword; I bought buckles, & the rest I had, and we returned to dinner exhausted. After dinner with the playful, bewitching elegance of a beauty, she put on my coat & sword & marched about looking at herself. She staid up: I went to bed at ten, & arose at twelve, not having slept a wink. I dressed, I breakfasted, & was at the Hall Door at half-past one. Three Ladies were before me. The doors opened about four, & I got a front place in the Chamberlain's box, between the door and Throne, and saw the whole room distinctly. Many of the door keepers were tipsy; quarrels took place. The sun began to light up the old gothic windows, the peers began to stroll in, & the company to crowd in, of all descriptions; elegant young women tripping along in silken grace with elegant girls trembling in feathers & diamonds. Some took seats they had not any right to occupy, and were obliged to leave after sturdy disputes. Others lost their tickets. Every moment, as the time approached for the King's appearance, was pregnant with interest. The appearance of a Monarch was something [of] the air of a rising sun; there are indications which announce his approach, a whisper of mystery turns all eyes to the throne! Suddenly two or three run; others fall back; some talk, direct, hurry, stand still, or disappear. Then three or four of high rank appear from behind the Throne; an

interval is left; the crowds scarce breathe! The room rises with a
sort of feathered, silken thunder! Plumes wave, eyes sparkle, glasses
are out, mouths smile. The way in which the King bowed was really
monarchic! As he looked towards the Peeresses & Foreign
Ambassadors, he looked like some gorgeous bird of the East.

After all the ceremonies he arose, the Procession was arranged,
the Music played and the line began to move. All this was exceedingly
imposing. . . . The distant trumpets & shouts of the people, the slow
march, and at last the appearance of the king under a golden canopy,
crowned, and the universal burst of the assembly at seeing him
affected every body.

After the banquet was over, came the most imposing scene of
all, the championship & first dishes. Wellington, crowned, walked
down the Hall, & was cheered by the Officers of the Guards. He
shortly returned with Lords Howard & Anglesea, and rode
gracefully to the foot of the throne: they then backed out. Lord
Anglesea's horse became restive. Wellington became impatient, and,
I am convinced, thought it a trick of Lord Anglesea's to attract
attention. He backed on, & the rest of us were obliged to follow him.
This was a touch of character.

The Hall doors opened again, & outside in twilight a man in
dark shadowed armour against the shining light appeared. He then
moved, passed into darkness under the arch, & Wellington, Howard
& the Champion stood in full view, with doors closed behind them.
This was certainly the finest sight of the day. The herald read the
challenge; the glove was thrown down; they all then proceeded to the
throne. My imagination got so intoxicated that I came out with a
great contempt for the plebs, and I walked by with my sword. I got
home quite well, & thought sacred subjects insipid things. How soon
should I be ruined in luxurious society![35]

The Coronation of George IV was not all that it seemed, and behind the
scenes there was a fair amount of chaos. Prize fighters were hired to keep
the guests under control. The king ogled the ladies in Westminster Abbey
and was dressed in such a way that he 'looked too large for effect, indeed
he was more like an elephant than a man'.[36]

William IV, who talked through his brother's funeral and left early,
took little interest in his own Coronation on 8 September 1831, and the
only representation of it in the Royal Collection is the extensive pro-
cessional frieze painted by R. B. Davis, which is no more than a schematic
rendering, although David Roberts was on duty inside Westminster Abbey.

By contrast, there was considerable enthusiasm for the Coronation of

Queen Victoria on 28 June 1838. The queen was young and pretty: the public was fascinated. Even so, the ceremony was not without its defects: the Archbishop of Canterbury put the ring on the wrong finger and hurt the queen, the clergy were unrehearsed and concluded the service prematurely, the aged Lord Rolle tripped on his robes while paying homage to the queen and had to be helped to his feet, the choir sang inadequately, and Lord Melbourne had to be revived with wine in St Edward's chapel, having objected previously to the fact that the altar strewn with wine bottles and sandwiches resembled a cafeteria.[37] Yet this was the Coronation that established a pattern for later occasions, just as those of Queen Victoria's immediate successors, Edward VII and George V, set higher standards. The Coronation of Queen Victoria was accordingly depicted by

FIG. 199
Charles Robert Leslie:
*Queen Victoria Receiving the
Sacrament at her Coronation,
28 June 1838*, 1838–9

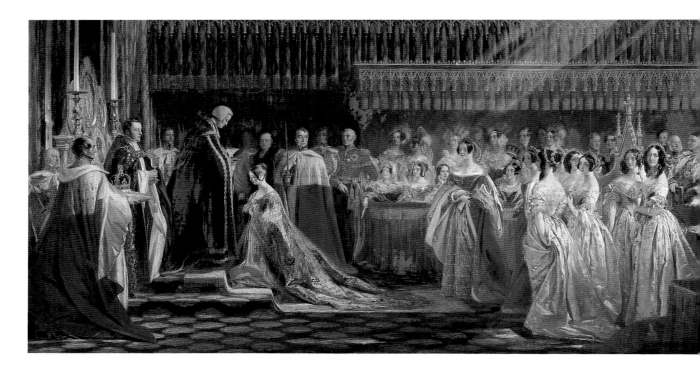

numerous painters: John Martin, Charles Robert Leslie (FIG. 199), and Sir George Hayter (FIG. 200) among others.

It was difficult for painters to determine which moment in the ceremony was the most momentous or the most characteristic – the crowning, the anointing, the taking of the sacrament or the paying of homage.

The depiction by Sir George Hayter is surely the most successful and has not been surpassed in its representation of the splendour and excitement – visual and otherwise – of the occasion. Hayter is situated by the altar looking towards the crossing of Westminster Abbey, where sections of the congregation are grouped in serried ranks. Unlike many such pictures, the work is not overwhelmed by its documentary basis. Even if the figures are accurately recorded, the architecture is not, and, although Hayter was painstaking in his preparatory sketches and worked on the canvas for two years, the composition remains visually convincing. Partly this conviction stems from the drama of the young queen herself, seated calmly on the Coronation chair, being invested with such great responsibilities, but it is also derived from the moment that Hayter has chosen to represent. It is the climax: the moment of the crowning, when all present exclaim several times 'God Save the Queen', after which the peers and peeresses replace their coronets. The raised arms, the open mouths, the fidgety pages, the toss of feathers on female heads, the glimpse of ermine robes offset by crimson cloth, the flash of jewels, diamonds and coronets,

FIG. 200
Sir George Hayter: *The Coronation of Queen Victoria, 28 June 1838*, 1839

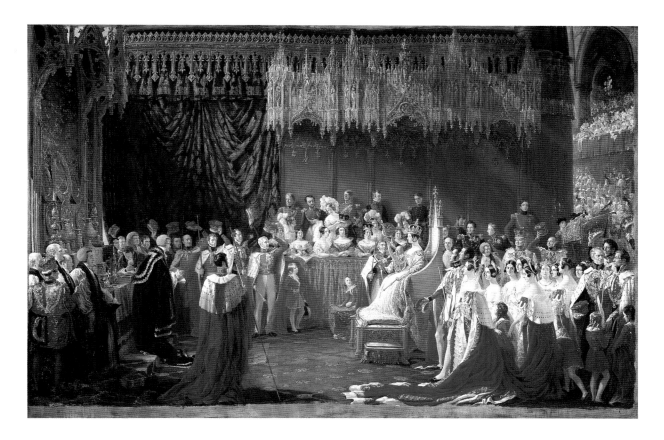

and the rich vivid colour, all impregnate the picture with lively, rippling rhythms that pullulate throughout in stark contrast with the still figure of the newly crowned queen. The internal rhythms suggest the vibrancy of the shouts of 'God Save the Queen' echoing around the Abbey and down the years.

Notes on the Text

CHAPTER 1: THE COLLECTORS

1 *Memoir of the Life of Colonel Hutchinson*, ed. C. H. Firth, London, 1885, Vol. I, pp. 119–20

2 'The Notebook and Account Book of Nicholas Stone', ed. A. J. Finberg, *The Walpole Society*, Vol. VII, 1918–19, p. 23

3 Quoted by Roy Strong, *Henry, Prince of Wales and England's Lost Renaissance*, London, 1986, p. 225

4 W. N. Sainsbury, *Original Unpublished Papers Illustrative of the Life of Sir Peter Paul Rubens*, London, 1859, pp. 354–5

5 *The Letters of Peter Paul Rubens*, ed. R. S. Magurn, Cambridge, Mass., 1955, pp. 101–2. Letter of 10 January 1625 to Palamyède de Fabri, Sieur de Valavez

6 G. Goodman, *The Court of King James the First*, London, 1839, Vol. 2, pp. 369–70. Letter dated 1625 (spelling modernised)

7 Sainsbury, *op. cit.*, p. 326. Letter of 12 May 1629 from Nys to Endymion Porter

8 Sainsbury, *op. cit.*, p. 325. Letter of 27 April 1628 from Nys to Endymion Porter

9 Sainsbury, *op. cit.*, p. 328. Letter of 23 January 1628 from Nys to Lord Dorchester

10 *The Letters of Peter Paul Rubens*, pp. 320 & 322. Letter of 9 August 1629 to Nicolas-Claude Fabri de Peiresc, repeating an opinion expressed the day before in a letter to Pierre Dupuy

11 C. V. Wedgewood, 'Two Painters' in *History and Hope*, London, 1981, p. 231

12 G. M. Trevelyan, *Clio, A Muse and other Essays*, London 1914, p. 26

13 W. M. Thackeray, *The Four Georges*, ed. G. Sainsbury, Oxford University Press, 1909, p. 783

14 *The Diary and Autobiography of John Adams*, ed. L. H. Butterfield, Cambridge, Mass., 1961, Vol. III, pp. 150–1, in a passage dated 8 November 1783

15 F. Haskell, *Rediscoveries in Art. Some aspects of Taste, Fashion and Collecting in England and France*, London, 1976, p. 27

16 W. Hazlitt, 'On the Pleasures of Painting' in *The Complete Works*, ed. P. P. Howe, London & Toronto, 1931, Vol. VIII, p. 14 (quoted in Haskell, *op. cit.*, p. 25)

17 G. F. Waagen, *Treasures of Art in Great Britain; Being an Account of the Chief Collections of Paintings, Drawings, Sculptures, Illuminated Manuscripts etc*, London, 1854, Vol. 1, p. 37

18 George Eliot, *Adam Bede*, Everyman ed., London, 1977, Book II, Chapter XVII, p. 173

19 Reported by Joseph Farington (see *The Diary of Joseph Farington*, ed. K. Cave, New Haven and London, 1983, Vol XI, January 1811–June 1812, p. 3919)

20 C. Hibbert, *George IV: Regent and King*, London, 1973, pp. 277–9

21 Hibbert, *loc. cit.*

22 *Journal*, 31 October 1842

23 *Journal*, 28 February 1838

24 *Journal*, 12 November 1847

25 *Journal*, 30 March 1839

26 *Journal*, 20 December 1846

27 *Journal*, 21 December 1846

28 *Journal*, 26 August 1843

29 *idem*

30 *Journal*, 31 December 1843

31 *Journal*, 20 May 1845

32 *Journal*, 20 August 1855

33 *Journal*, 3 May 1855

CHAPTER 2: THE GENIUS OF ITALY

1 *Boswell's Life of Samuel Johnson*, Everyman ed., London, 1960, Vol. II, pp. 25–6

2 C. Clough, 'Federigo da Montefeltro's Patronage of the Arts, 1468–1482', *Journal of the Warburg and Courtauld Institutes*, XXXVI (1973), pp. 29–30

3 *ibid*. p. 139

4 J. Burckhardt, *The Civilisation of the Renaissance in Italy*, trans. S. G. C. Middlemore, London, 1965, pp. 29–30

5 B. Castiglione, *The Book of the Courtier*, trans. G. Bull, London, 1976, p. 312

6 The quotation is from the inventory drawn up by Abraham van der Doort; see O. Millar, 'Abraham van der Doort's Catalogue of the Collections of Charles I', *The Walpole Society*, XXXVII (1958–60), p. 79 (14)

7 'The Notebooks of George Vertue', *The Walpole Society*, XVIII (1929–30), pp. 47 & 104

8 D. Garrard, *Artemisia Gentileschi: The Image of the Female Hero in Italian Baroque Art*, Princeton University Press, 1989, pp. 20–3. The trial testimony is Appendix B.

9 R. Wittkower, 'Inigo Jones – Puritanissimo Fiero' in *Palladio and English Palladianism*, London, 1983, pp. 67–70, trans. Edward Chaney, as given in *The Queen's Pictures*, 1991, pp. 30–1

10 *ibid.*

11 F. Haskell, 'Charles I's Collection of Pictures' in *The Late King's Goods*, ed. A. MacGregor, London & Oxford, 1989, p. 221

12 *idem*

13 *ibid.*, p. 222

14 *The Diary of John Evelyn*, ed. E. S. de Beer, Oxford, 1955, Vol. IV, p. 534

15 *idem*

16 *The Yale Edition of Horace Walpole's Correspondence*, ed. W. S. Lewis, London & New Haven, 1948, Vols. 13–14, p. 206. Letter to Richard West, written in Rome on 26 March 1740

17 These figures are from J. Pemble, *The Mediterranean Passion: Victorians and Edwardians in the South*, Oxford, 1987, p. 1

18 *Hamlet*, Act I, Scene IV, 59–80

19 Stanhope, Philip Dormer, fourth Earl of Chesterfield, *Letters To His Son*, ed. James Harding, London, 1973, p. 90. Letter of 15 May 1749

20 *ibid.*, p. 89. Letter of 19 April 1749

21 *ibid.*, p. 147. Letter of 8 November 1750

22 *Boswell on the Grand Tour. Italy, Corsica, and France 1765–1766*, eds. F. Brady & F. A. Pottle, New York, 1955, p. 6. In a letter to Jean-Jacques Rousseau, 3 October 1765

23 *ibid.*, p. 7

24 *ibid.*, p. 223. Letter written in Edinburgh, 10 August 1765

25 Walpole, *op. cit.*, Vol. 20, p. 240. Letter of 1 April 1751 to Horace Mann

26 *The Tour of His Royal Highness the Duke of York*, London, 1764, p. vi

27 *ibid.*, p. 9

28 J. W. Goethe, *Italian Journey* [1786–8], trans. W. H. Auden and E. Mayer, London 1970, p. 129

29 B. Connell, *Portrait of a Whig Peer*, London, 1957, p. 48

30 *Autobiography of Edward Gibbon as originally edited by Lord Sheffield*, Oxford, 1962, pp. 159–60

31 Goethe, *op. cit.*, p. 133

32 *ibid.*, p. 137

33 *ibid.*, p. 133

34 E. Gibbon, *The Decline and Fall of the Roman Empire*, The Chandos Classics, London [n.d.], Vol. IV, pp. 571–2

35 W. Hazlitt, 'Notes of a Journey through France and Italy' in *The Complete Works*, ed. P. P. Howe, London & Toronto, Vol. X, 1932, p. 232

36 *ibid.*, p. 211

37 See note 16 above

38 *Autobiography of Edward Gibbon*, cited at note 30 above, pp. 154–5

39 Oliver Millar, *Zoffany and his Tribuna*, London, 1966, p. 13

40 Walpole, *op. cit.*, Vol. 24, pp. 539–40. Horace Mann, in a letter to Horace Walpole, 10 December 1779

41 *ibid.*, Vol. 24, pp. 527–9. Letter to Horace Mann, 12 November 1779

42 *The Diary of Joseph Farington*, ed. K. Garlick & A. Macintyre, New Haven & London, 1979, Vol. VI, April 1803–December 1804, p. 2471

43 E. Wright, *Some Observations made in Travelling through France, Italy, etc in the years 1720, 1721 & 1722*, London, 1764, p. 45

44 *Boswell on the Grand Tour*, cited at note 22 above, p. 11. Letter of 3 October 1765 to Jean-Jacques Rousseau

45 *idem*

46 *The Complete Letters of Lady Mary Wortley Montagu*, ed. R. Halsband, London, 1956–7, Vol III, p. 127. Letter to Lady Bute, 13 May 1758

47 *ibid.*, Vol. III, p. 147. Letter to Lady Bute, 30 May 1757

48 Connell, *op. cit.*, pp. 50–1

49 Walpole, *op. cit.*, Vol. 18, p. 465. Letter to Horace Mann, 18 June 1744

50 Cited in Katherine Baetjer and J. G. Links, *Canaletto*, New York, 1989, no. 116, pp. 336–7

51 H. James, *Italian Hours*, New York, 1959, pp. 10–11

CHAPTER 3: THE KINGDOM OF NATURE

1 John Milton, *Paradise Lost*, Book IV, 246–68

2 The Book of Genesis, III: 1–7

3 *The Metamorphoses of Ovid*, Penguin Classics, ed. 1975, Book III, pp. 72–3

4 *ibid.*, Book III, pp. 77–80

5 *The Letters of Thomas Gainsborough*, ed. M. Woodall, 2nd ed., Ipswich, 1963, no. 56, p. 115

6 *ibid.*, no. 42, pp. 87, 91

7 K. Clark, *Landscape into Art*, London, 1986, p. 56

8 Saint Matthew, II:16, is the only gospel to recount the Massacre of the Innocents

9 W. H. Auden, *Musée des Beaux Arts* in *Collected Poems*, 1975, ed. Edward Mendelson, p. 173. The poem was written after a visit to the Musées Royaux des Beaux Arts in Brussels in December 1938. Edward Mendelson comments: 'Breughel's *The Fall of Icarus* – like the other paintings alluded to in the poem, *The Numbering at Bethlehem* and *The Massacre of the Innocents* – quietly points out that events of the greatest pathos and importance occur in settings that seem to be out at the edge of history, ordinary places where we pursue our normal unobservant lives. The poetic imagination that seeks out grandeur and sublimity could scarcely be bothered with those insignificant figures lost in the background, or in the crowd. But Auden sees in them an example of Christianity's great and enduring transformation of classical rhetoric: its inversion of the principle that the most important subjects require the highest style.' (*Early Auden*, London and Boston, 1981, p. 363)

10 The Book of Genesis, VI:17

11 *John Constable's Correspondence, VI. The Fishers*, ed. R. B. Becket, Ipswich, 1968, p. 74, and *John Constable: Further Comments and Correspondence*, eds. L. Parris, C. Shields and J. Fleming-Williams, Tate Gallery and Ipswich, 1975, p. 57

12 'Sketches of the Principal Picture Galleries in England' in *The Complete Works*, ed. P. P. Howe, London and Toronto, 1932, Vol X, p. 19

13 *idem*

14 C. Brown, 'Aelbert Cuyp's "River Landscape with Horseman and Peasants"', *National Art Collections Fund Review*, 1990, p. 88

15 Quoted from O. Millar, *The Tudor, Stuart and Early Georgian Pictures in the Collection of Her Majesty the Queen*, Oxford, 1963, no. 548

16 *The Correspondence of George, Prince of Wales, 1770–1812*, Vol. V, 1804–1806, ed. A. Aspinall, London, 1968, pp. 253–6 n. 3

17 D. Defoe, *A Tour through the Whole Island of Great Britain*, ed. P. Rogers, Harmondsworth, 1986, Letter 4, pp. 283–4

18 *Journal*, 31 July 1844, quoted in R. Ormond, *Sir Edwin Landseer*, Philadelphia and London, 1981, pp. 152–3

19 *Journal*, 10 January 1839

20 *Journal*, 26 August 1842. 'My principal present was Landseer's beautiful picture of a stag swimming through the water, & disturbing a number of wild duck – after having been hunted. This picture had already been purchased by old Mr Wells of Redleaf, but kindly gave it up to me.'

CHAPTER 4: THE SWORD AND THE SCEPTRE

1 K. Rose, *King George V*, London, 1983, p. 45

2 S. Anglo, *Spectacle, Pageantry and Early Tudor Policy*, Oxford, 1967, pp. 137–69; J. G. Russell, *The Field of the Cloth of Gold*, London, 1969; *Henry VIII: A European Court in England*, London, 1991, Part IV, pp. 50–3; C. Cruikshank, *Henry VIII and the Invasion of France*, Stroud and New York, 1991

3 *King Henry VIII*, Act I. Scene i, 19–36

4 Principally *Honda/Angel-cynnan or, A compleat View of the Manners, Customs, Arms, Habits etc of the Inhabitants of England* (1777–8), *A Complete View of Dress and Habits of the People of England* (1796–9) and *Sports and Pastimes of the People of England* (1801)

5 *Treatise on Ancient Arms and Weapons*, London, 1786

6 Jean Froissart, *Chronicles*, trans. Lord Berners, ed. G. Macaulay, London, 1895, Chapter CXLVI, p. 115

7 On history painting and the concept of chivalry, see R. Strong, *And When did you last see your Father? The Victorian Painter and British History*, London, 1988, and M. Girouard, *The Return to Camelot, Chivalry and the English Gentleman*, New Haven and London, 1981

8 Quoted from C. Woodham-Smith, *Queen Victoria, Her Life and Times 1819–1861*, London, 1972, p. 358

9 T. Martin, *The Life of His Royal Highness The Prince Consort*, 2nd ed., Vol. III, London, 1877, p. 255

10 Quoted from Woodham-Smith, *op. cit.*, p. 360. Letter of 1 September 1855 to Baron Stockmar

11 *The Letters of Queen Victoria, A Selection from Her Majesty's Correspondence Between the Years 1837 and 1861*, eds. A. C. Benson and Viscount Esher, Vol. III, 1854–61, London, 1907, p. 175

12 Martin, *op. cit.*, pp. 337–8; Woodham-Smith, *op. cit.*, p. 360; E. Longford, *Victoria RI*, London, 1964, p. 253

13 *The Letters of Queen Victoria, loc. cit.*

14 Quoted by M. Levey, 'Lawrence's Portrait of Pope Pius VII', *Burlington Magazine*, CXVII (1975), p. 203

15 D. Cooper, *Talleyrand*, London, 1932, p. 245

16 Quoted in O. Millar, *The Later Georgian Pictures in the Collection of Her Majesty the Queen*, Oxford, 1969, p. xxxiv

17 *ibid.*

18 Quoted by Levey, *op. cit.*, p. 204, from a letter to the artist David Wilkie (A. Cunningham, *The Life of Sir David Wilkie*, Vol. III, London, 1843, pp. 343–4)

19 J. Morris, *Pax Britannica, The Climax of an Empire*, London, 1979, p. 42, but see also p. 27, no. 2, where it is stated that in 1933, although in decline, the British Empire encompassed 13.9 million square miles with a population of 493 million people

20 Rudyard Kipling, 'The Widow at Windsor'. *A Choice of Kipling's Verse Made by T. S. Eliot*, London, 1963, p. 182 Jerome K. Jerome said of Kipling that '. . . his aggressive personality naturally made enemies. The critics and the public were more squeamish then. He was accused of coarseness and irreverence. The reason, it is said, that he was never knighted was that Queen Victoria would not forgive him for having called her "The Widdy of Windsor".' Quoted in *Kipling: Interviews and*

Recollections, ed. Harold Orel, London and Basingstoke, 1983, Vol. I, pp. 156–7

21 Quoted in O. Millar, *The Victorian Pictures in the Collection of Her Majesty The Queen*, Cambridge University Press, 1992, no. 186

22 J. Morris, *Heaven's Command, An Imperial Progress*, London, 1979, p. 435

23 *The Letters of Queen Victoria, Second Series. A Selection from Her Majesty's Correspondence and Journal between the Years 1862 and 1878*, ed. G. E. Buckle, Vol. II, 1870–1878, London, 1926, pp. 514–5

24 *The Times*, 23 June 1897

25 *The Letters of Queen Victoria, Third Series. A Selection from Her Majesty's Correspondence and Journal between the Years 1886 and 1901*, ed. G. E. Buckle, Vol. III, 1896–1901, London, 1930, p. 174

26 Quoted in Morris, *Pax Britannica*, p. 31

27 Morris, *Heaven's Command*, pp. 539–40

28 H. Walpole, *Memoirs of the Reign of King George II*, ed. J. Brooke, London, 1985, Vol. I, 1751–54, p. 116

29 C. Hibbert, *George IV: Regent and King*, London, 1973, pp. 78–80

30 J. Brooke, *King George III*, London, 1985, p. 88

31 Quoted in Millar, *op. cit.*, 1992, no. 771

32 *The Letters of Queen Victoria. A Selection from Her Majesty's Correspondence between the Years 1837 and 1861*, eds. A. C. Benson and Viscount Esher, Vol. III, 1854–1861, London, 1907, pp. 253–4. Letter of 21 July 1856 to Leopold, King of the Belgians

33 Quoted in Millar, *op. cit.*, 1992, no. 772. The fresco referred to on the main staircase at Osborne House is by William Dyce

34 Quoted in Millar, *op. cit.*, no. 768. Also see *The Letters of Queen Victoria, op. cit.*, Vol. III, p. 161. Letter of 22 May 1855 to Leopold, King of the Belgians

35 Livy, *History of Rome*, Book XVIII, but it is also recounted in detail by Silius Italicus in his *Punica*, Book VI, pp. 62–551 (see O. Millar, *The Later Georgian Pictures in the Collection of Her Majesty the Queen*, 1969, no. 1157)

36 Ancient historians such as Xenophon and Diodorus Siculus recount the episode, but West may have known it through *The Ancient History of the Egyptians, Carthaginians, Assyrians, Babylonians, Medes and Persians, Macedonians and Grecians* by Charles Rollins (1738–39), Eng. ed.; French ed. 1730–8

37 Pierre Terrail, Chevalier de Bayard (1473–1524), about whom biographies were written in 1760 and 1769 (H. von Erffa and A. Staley, *The Paintings of Benjamin West*, New Haven and London, 1986, no. 77)

38 J. Galt, *The Life, Studies and Works of Benjamin West*, London, 1820, Part II, p. 47

39 *ibid.*, p. 48

40 *ibid.*, p. 50. According to Galt, Reynolds said, 'I forsee that this picture will not only become one of the most popular, but occasion a revolution in the art.'

41 Quoted in O. Millar, *The Later Georgian Pictures in the Collection of Her Majesty the Queen*, Oxford, 1969, no. 762

42 There are many accounts of the incident: see the Marquess of Anglesey, *One Leg: The Life and Letters of Henry William Paget, First Marquess of Anglesey K. G. 1768–1854*, London, 1961, pp. 148–52

43 J. Ruskin, *Complete Works*. eds. E. J. Cook and A. Wedderburn, Vol. VII, p. 379, Vol. XII, pp. 369–70, Vol. XII, pp. 34, 47, 170

44 E. Butler, *An Autobiography*, London, 1922, pp. 46–7, quoted by P. Usherwood, and J. Spencer-Smith, *Lady Butler, Battle Artist, 1846–1933*, National Army Museum, London, 1987, p. 23

45 W. Holman-Hunt, *Pre-Raphaelitism and the Pre-Raphaelite Brotherhood*, London, 1905, Vol. II, p. 305

46 Quoted in Millar, *op. cit.*, 1992, no. 185

CHAPTER 5: PRIVATE VIEW

1 *The Times*, 15 July 1830. Quoted by C. Hibbert, *George IV: Regent and King*, London, 1973, p. 342

2 S. Schama, 'The Domestication of Majesty: Royal Family Portraiture, 1500–1850', *Journal of Interdisciplinary History*, XVII (1986), p. 183

3 S. Sitwell, *Conversation Pieces. A Survey of English Domestic Portraits and their Painters*, London, 1936, p. 28

4 Schama, *op. cit.*, p. 169

5 *ibid.*, p. 157

6 *ibid.*, p. 161

7 *ibid.*, p. 155

8 *The Letters of Charles Dickens*, eds. H. House, G. Storey and K. Tillotson, Vol. 3, Oxford, 1974, pp. 547–51. Letter to Cornelius Conway Felton dated 1 September 1843

9 See Chapter 1, p. 71 above

10 'Sketches of the Principal Picture Galleries in England', *The Complete Works*, ed. P. P. Howe, London and Toronto, 1932, Vol. X, p. 38

11 *The Diary of Samuel Pepys*, ed. R. Latham and W. Matthews, Vol. 5, *1664*, London, 1971, p. 209 and Vol. 6, *1665*, London, 1971, p. 172 and Vol 7, *1666*, London, 1972, p. 162. Also Vol. 10, *Companion*, London, 1983, p. 102

12 D. Defoe, *A Tour Through the Whole Island of Great Britain*, ed. P. Rogers, Harmondsworth, 1986. Letter 3, p. 183

13 C. Fiennes, *The Illustrated Journeys of Celia Fiennes c. 1682–c. 1712*, ed. C. Morris, London, 1982, p. 242

14 H. Fielding, *The History of Tom Jones, A Foundling*, Collins Classics, London, 1955, pp. 130–2

15 Quoted by R. Ormond and C. Blackett-Ord, *Franz-Xaver Winterhalter and the Courts of Europe 1830–1870*, National Portrait Gallery, London, 1987, no. 31

16 *Journal*, 23 December 1846. Quoted by Ormond and Blackett-Ord, *loc. cit.*

17 L. Colley in *Crown Pictorial. Art and the British Monarchy*, Yale Center for British Art, New Haven, 1990–1, p. 20

18 *Journal*, 8 January 1848

19 *Journal*, 8 September 1848, printed in *Leaves from the Journal of Our Life in the Highlands from 1848 to 1861*, 2nd ed., London, 1868, p. 101

20 C. Dickens, *All the Year Round*, 15 February 1868, p. 240

21 *Leaves from the Journal of Our Life in the Highlands*, p. 113

22 *Journal*, 17 September 1850

23 *Journal*, 19 September 1850

24 O. Millar, *The Queen's Pictures*, London, 1977, p. 173

25 G. D. Leslie, *Riverside Letters*, London, 1896, p. 199. Quoted in R. Ormond, *Sir Edwin Landseer*, Philadelphia and London, 1981, p. 163

26 Quoted in Ormond, *loc. cit.* Letter of 13 April 1870 from Landseer to William Russell

27 Letter of 27 September 1850 to the Duchess of Sutherland quoted by D. Millar, *Queen Victoria's Life in the Scottish Highlands depicted by her Watercolour Artists*, London, 1985, p. 47

28 Quoted in Ormond, *loc. cit.* Undated letter from Miss Marianne Skerret to the artist

29 M. Rogers, *Elizabeth II. Portraits of Sixty Years*, National Portrait Gallery, 1986, p. 11, where a similar comment made to Dame Laura Knight is reported: 'I love looking at the crowds gathering when I myself am out of sight.'

30 L. Gowing, *Vermeer*, London, 1952, p. 123

31 *ibid.*, p. 52

CHAPTER 6: THE REGAL IMAGE

1 Carel van Mander, *Het Schilder–Boeck*, Haarlem, 1604, as referred to in L. Campbell, *Renaissance Portraits, European Portrait Painting in the 14th, 15th and 16th Centuries*, New Haven and London, p. 84

2 A. Graham-Dixon, 'The Official Versions', *The Independent*, Tuesday 14 May 1991

3 *ibid.*

4 *ibid.*

5 M. Levey, *A Royal Subject: Portraits of Queen Charlotte*, National Gallery, 1977, p. 1

6 Graham-Dixon, *loc. cit.*

7 The Coronation portrait of Queen Mary was painted by Sir William Llewellyn

8 D. Hudson, *For Love of Painting: The Life of Sir Gerald Kelly, KCVO, PRA*, London, 1975, p. 43

9 Hudson, *op. cit.*, pp. 60–1

10 *ibid.*

11 The source for this is Sir Alan Lascelles (quoted by Hudson, *op. cit.*, pp. 64–6)

12 Graham-Dixon, *loc. cit.*

13 *ibid.*

14 Quoted by O. Millar, *The Victorian Pictures in the Collection of Her Majesty the Queen*, Cambridge University Press, 1992, no. 270

15 *The Times*, 14 May 1842, pp. 6–7

16 *Journal*, 1 May 1851

17 *ibid.*

18 H. Gutterman, 'Roberts on Royalty', *Turner Studies*, no. 10 (1990), p. 48

19 *ibid.*

20 W. Bagehot, 'The Income of The Prince of Wales', *The Economist*, 10 October 1874, reprinted in *The Collected Works of Walter Bagehot*, ed. N. St John Stevas, Vol V, London, 1974, p. 419

21 D. Cannadine, 'The Context, Performance, and Meaning of Ritual: The British Monarchy and the "Invention of Tradition", c. 1870–1977' in *The Invention of Tradition*, eds. E. Hobsbawm and T. Ranger, London, 1983, p. 116

22 Cannadine, *op. cit.*, p. 116

23 Cannadine, *op. cit.*, p. 140

24 Cannadine, *op. cit.*, pp. 139–40

25 Cannadine, *op. cit.*, p. 120

26 *idem*

27 Cannadine, *op. cit.*, p. 139

28 Cannadine, *op. cit.*, p. 157

29 J. Summerson, *Georgian London*, London, 1928, p. 22

30 Quoted by Millar, *op. cit.*, 1992, no. 650

31 Summerson, *op. cit.*, p. 25

32 Summerson, *op. cit.*, p. 26

33 Cannadine, *op. cit.*, p. 135

34 *Neglected Genius. The Diaries of Benjamin Robert Haydon 1808–1846*, ed. J. Joliffe, London, 1990, p. 132

35 *ibid.*, pp. 77–8

36 Cannadine, *op. cit.*, p. 117

37 For an account of Queen Victoria's Coronation see C. Woodham-Smith, *Queen Victoria, Her Life and Times 1819–1861*, London, 1972, pp. 154–60. For the queen's own account, see *The Girlhood of Queen Victoria. A Selection from Her Majesty's Diaries between the Years 1832 and 1840*, ed. Viscount Esher, Vol. I, London, 1912, pp. 356–64

Further Reading about the paintings in The Royal Collection

GENERAL

C. Lloyd (with an essay by Sir Oliver Millar), *The Queen's Pictures. Royal Collectors through the Centuries*, London, 1991

O. Millar, *The Queen's Pictures*, London, 1977

J. H. Plumb and H. Wheldon, *Royal Heritage. The Story of Britain's Royal Builders and Collectors*, London, 1977

J. H. Plumb and H. Wheldon, *Royal Heritage. The Reign of Elizabeth II*, London, 1981

CATALOGUES

L. Campbell, *The Early Flemish Pictures in the Collection of Her Majesty The Queen*, Cambridge University Press, 1985

M. Levey, *The Later Italian Pictures in the Collection of Her Majesty The Queen*, 2nd edn. Cambridge University Press, 1991

A. Martindale, *The Triumphs of Caesar by Andrea Mantegna in the Collection of Her Majesty The Queen at Hampton Court*, London, 1979

O. Millar, *The Tudor, Stuart and Early Georgian Pictures in the Collection of Her Majesty The Queen*, Oxford, 1963

O. Millar, *The Later Georgian Pictures in the Collection of Her Majesty The Queen*, Oxford, 1969

O. Millar, *The Victorian Pictures in the Collection of Her Majesty The Queen*, Cambridge University Press, 1992

G. Reynolds, *The Sixteenth and Seventeenth Century Miniatures in the Collection of Her Majesty the Queen*, The Royal Collection, 1999

J. Shearman, *Raphael's Cartoons in the Collection of Her Majesty The Queen*, London, 1972

J. Shearman, *The Early Italian Pictures in the Collection of Her Majesty The Queen*, Cambridge University Press, 1983

C. White, *The Dutch Pictures in the Collection of Her Majesty The Queen*, Cambridge University Press, 1982

R. Walker, *Miniatures in the Collection of Her Majesty The Queen. The Eighteenth and Early Nineteenth Centuries*, Cambridge University Press, 1992

OTHER TITLES

J. Roberts, *Royal Artists from Mary Queen of Scots to the Present Day*, London, 1987

The Late King's Goods. Collections, Possessions and Patronage of Charles I in the Light of the Commonwealth Sale Inventories, ed. A. MacGregor, London and Oxford, 1989

Carlton House. The Past Glories of George IV's Palace, The Queen's Gallery, Buckingham Palace, 1991

C. Lloyd and V. Remington, *Masterpieces in Little: Portrait Miniatures from the Collection of Her Majesty Queen Elizabeth II*, London, 1997

C. Lloyd, K. Barron, C. Noble and L. Whitaker, *The Quest for Albion: Monarchy and the Patronage of British Painting*, London, 1998

List of Illustrations

Anonymous

FIG. 90 *The Embarkation of Henry VIII at Dover, c. 1545*, oil on canvas, 168.9 x 346.7cms

FIG. 91 *The Field of the Cloth of Gold, c. 1545*, oil on canvas, 168.9 x 347.3cms

FIG. 127 *St. James's Park and the Mall, c. 1745*, oil on canvas, 104.1 x 138.4cms

FIG. 129 *The Family of Henry VIII, c. 1545*, oil on canvas, 169.5 x 356.9cms

FIG. 169 *Henry V, c. 1520*, oil on panel, 56.5 x 36.2cms

Jacques-Laurent Agasse, 1767–1849

FIG. 85 *The Nubian Giraffe, 1827*, oil on canvas, 127.3 x 102cms

FIG. 86 *White-Tailed Gnus, 1828*, oil on canvas, 127.3 x 102cms

Heinrich von Angeli, 1846–1925

FIG. 103 *Queen Victoria (Empress of India), 1885*, oil on canvas, 250.2 x 167cms

FIG. 176 *Queen Victoria in Mourning, 1899*, oil on canvas, 120 x 93.3cms

Pietro Annigoni, 1910–88

FIG. 186 *Queen Elizabeth II, 1954–5*, oil on canvas, 99 x 150cms (The Worshipful Company of Fishmongers, London)

Jules Bastien-Lepage, 1848–84

FIG. 143 *Albert Edward, Prince of Wales, 1879*, oil on panel, 43.2 x 34.9cms

Pompeo Batoni, 1708–87

FIG. 41 *Edward Augustus, Duke of York, 1764*, oil on canvas, 137.8 x 100.3cms

Louis-Gabriel Blanchet, 1705–72

FIG. 42 *Prince Charles Edward Stuart, 1737–8*, oil on canvas, 98.4 x 75.6cms

FIG. 43 *Prince Henry Benedict Stuart, 1737–8*, oil on canvas, 97.8 x 73cms

Jakob Bogdani, d.1720

FIG. 83 *Birds and Deer in a Garden, 1708–10*, oil on canvas, 194.3 x 280cms

Edward Bower, d.1667

FIG. 14 *Charles I at his Trial, 1648*, oil on canvas, 131.1 x 98.7cms

Jan Breughel the Elder, 1568–1625

FIG. 58 *Adam and Eve in the Garden of Eden, 1615*, oil on copper, 48.6 x 65.6cms

FIG. 59 *A Flemish Fair, 1600*, oil on copper, 47.6 x 68.6cms

Richard Brompton, 1734–88

FIG. 51 *The Duke of York with his Entourage in the Veneto, 1764*, oil on canvas, 122.5 x 161cms

Pieter Bruegel the Elder, active 1551, d.1569

FIG. 64 *The Massacre of the Innocents, c. 1565*, oil on panel, 109.2 x 158.1cms

FIG. 65 *The Fall of Icarus, c. 1550*, oil on panel, 73.5 x 112cms (Musées Royaux des Beaux-Arts de Belgique)

Elizabeth Thompson, Lady Butler, 1846–1933

FIG. 105 *The Defence of Rorke's Drift, 1880*, oil on canvas, 119.4 x 211.5cms

FIG. 126 *The Roll Call: Calling the Roll after an Engagement in the Crimean War, 1874*, oil on canvas, 92.7 x 183.3cms

Giovanni Antonio Canal, called Canaletto, 1697–1768

FIG. 44 *Rome: Ruins of the Forum looking towards the Capitol, 1742*, oil on canvas, 189.6 x 106cms

FIG. 45 *Rome: The Arch of Septimius Severus, 1742*, oil on canvas, 180.3 x 105.7cms

FIG. 46 *Rome: The Arch of Titus, 1742*, oil on canvas, 191.8 x 106cms

FIG. 47 *Rome: The Arch of Constantine, 1742, oil on canvas*, 185.4 x 105.7cms

FIG. 50 *Venice: The Bacino di S. Marco on Ascension Day, c. 1734*, oil on canvas, 76.8 x 125.4cms

FIG. 52 *Venice: A Regatta on the Grand Canal, c. 1734*, oil on canvas, 77.2 x 125.7cms

FIG. 53 *Venice: The Grand Canal from Campo S. Vio towards the Bacino, c. 1730*, oil on canvas, 47 x 79.1cms

FIG. 54 *Venice: The Piazzetta towards the Torre dell'Orologio, c. 1725–30*, oil on canvas, 172.1 x 134.9cms

FIG. 55 *Venice: The Piazzetta towards the Torre dell'Orologio, 1743*, oil on canvas, 60 x 95.6cms

FIG. 56 *A Caprice View with Ruins, c. 1740*, oil on canvas, 53 x 66.7cms

FIG. 57 *Interior of San Marco, c. 1735*, oil on canvas, 33 x 22.5cms

FIG. 193 *View of London: the Thames from Somerset House towards the City, 1750–1*, oil on canvas, 180 x 188cms

FIG. 194 *View of London: the Thames from Somerset House towards Westminster, 1750–1*, oil on canvas, 108 x 188.3cms

Andrea del Castagno, c. 1421–57

FIG. 98 *Pippo Spano, c. 1450*, fresco, 245 x 165cms (Uffizi, Florence)

John Charlton, 1849–1917

FIG. 106 *'God Save the Queen': Queen Victoria arriving at St. Paul's Cathedral on the occasion of the Diamond Jubilee Thanksgiving Service, 22 June 1897, 1899*, oil on canvas, 206.4 x 297.8cms

307

Gonzales Coques, c. 1614—84

FIG. 149 *The Family of Jan Baptista Anthonie, 1664*, oil on copper, 56.5 x 73.5cms

Aelbert Cuyp, 1620—91

FIG. 73 *An Evening Landscape, 1655—60*, oil on canvas, 101.6 x 153.6cms

Bernardo Daddi, c. 1300—48

FIG. 34 *The Marriage of the Virgin, c. 1335*, tempera on panel, 25.5 x 30.7cms

Arthur William Devis, 1762—1822

FIG. 120 *The Death of Nelson, c. 1807*, oil on canvas, 94.6 x 127.9cms

Denis Dighton, 1792—1827

FIG. 123 *The Battle of Waterloo: General advance of the British lines, 1816*, oil on canvas, 76.5 x 121.9cms

Domenichino, 1581—1641

FIG. 40 *St Agnes, c. 1620*, oil on canvas, 213.4 x 152.4cms

Alexandre-Jean Dubois Drahonet, 1791—1834

FIG. 108 *British Infantry. Night Rounds. Drummer William Cann, Scots Fusilier Guards, 1832*, oil on card, 34 x 24cms

Sir Anthony Van Dyck, 1599—1641

FIG. 1 *Charles I in Three Positions, 1635—6*, oil on canvas, 84.5 x 99.7cms

FIG. 11 *Charles I with Monsieur de St. Antoine, 1633*, oil on canvas, 368.4 x 269.9cms

FIG. 12 *Cupid and Psyche, 1639—40*, oil on canvas, 199.4 x 191.8cms

FIG. 13 *Thomas Killigrew and (?) William, Lord Crofts, 1638*, oil on canvas, 132.7 x 143.5cms

FIG. 130 *'The Greate Peece', 1632*, oil on canvas, 298.1 x 250.8cms

FIG. 145 *The Three Eldest Children of Charles I, 1635*, oil on canvas, 133.4 x 151.8cms

FIG. 147 *The Five Eldest Children of Charles I, 1637*, oil on canvas, 163.2 x 198.8cms

FIG. 178 *Charles I, 1636*, oil on canvas, 248.3 x 153.7cms

Sir Luke Fildes, 1843—1927

FIG. 181 *Edward VII, 1901—2*, oil on canvas, 280 x 182.9cms

FIG. 182 *George V, 1912*, oil on canvas, 279.4 x 182.9cms

William Powell Frith, 1819—1909

FIG. 29 *Ramsgate Sands: 'Life at the Seaside', 1852—3*, oil on canvas, 76.8 x 154.9cms

FIG. 134 *The Marriage of The Prince of Wales, 10 March 1863, 1863—4*, oil on canvas, 217.8 x 306.4cms

Thomas Gainsborough, 1727—88

FIG. 24 *John Hayes St Leger, 1782*, oil on canvas, 247.6 x 188cms

FIG. 61 *Diana and Actaeon, c. 1785*, oil on canvas, 158.1 x 188cms

FIG. 63 *Henry, Duke of Cumberland, with the Duchess of Cumberland and Lady Elizabeth Luttrell, 1783—5*, oil on canvas, 163.8 x 124.5cms

FIG. 135 *George III, 1781*, oil on canvas, 238.8 x 158.7cms

FIG. 136 *Queen Charlotte, 1781*, oil on canvas, 238.8 x 158.7cms

FIG. 142 *Mrs Mary Robinson, 1781*, oil on canvas, 76.2 x 63.5cms

FIG. 144 *Prince Edward, later Duke of Kent, 1782*, oil on canvas, 59 x 43.8cms

Orazio Gentileschi, 1563—1639

FIG. 38 *Joseph and Potiphar's Wife, c. 1632*, oil on canvas, 204.9 x 261.9cms

Artemisia Gentileschi, 1593—1652

FIG. 39 *Self-Portrait as the Allegory of Painting, c. 1630*, oil on canvas, 96.5 x 73.7cms

James Giles, 1801—70

FIG. 154 *A View of Balmoral, 1848*, oil on panel, 55.9 x 81.6cms

Sir Francis Grant, 1803—78

FIG. 189 *Queen Victoria Riding Out, 1839—40*, oil on canvas, 99.1 x 137.5cms

Jean-Baptiste Greuze, 1725—1805

FIG. 150 *Silence!, 1759*, oil on canvas, 62.5 x 50.8cms

Sir James Gunn, 1893—1964

FIG. 133 *Tea at Royal Lodge, 1950*, oil on canvas, 151.1 x 100.3cms (National Portrait Gallery, London)

FIG. 185 *Queen Elizabeth II, 1954—6*, oil on canvas, 244.5 x 152.9cms

The Monogrammist H. E., active 1560s

FIG. 172 *Elizabeth I and the three Goddesses, 1569*, oil on panel, 70.8 x 84.5cms

Benjamin Robert Haydon, 1786—1846

FIG. 28 *The Mock Election, 1827*, oil on canvas, 144.8 x 185.4cms

George Hayter, 1792—1871

FIG. 200 *The Coronation of Queen Victoria, 28 June 1838, 1839*, oil on canvas, 255.3 x 381cms

John Frederick Herring, 1795—1865

FIG. 82 *Tajar and Hammon, 1845*, oil on canvas, 55.9 x 76.2cms

Meyndert Hobbema, 1638—1709

FIG. 71 *Watermill beside a Woody Lane, 166(5 or 8)*, oil on panel, 53.4 x 70.5cms

FIG. 72 *Wooded Landscape with Travellers, 1668*, oil on panel, 62.2 x 89.5cms

William Hogarth, 1697—1764

FIG. 19 *David Garrick and his Wife, c. 1757*, oil on canvas, 133.3 x 104.1cms

Frank Holl, 1845—88

FIG. 153 *No Tidings from the Sea, 1870*, oil on canvas, 71.4 x 91.4cms

Melchior de Hondecoeter, 1636—95

FIG. 84 *Birds and a Spaniel in a Garden, c. 1680*, oil on canvas, 127.6 x 152.4cms

Gerrit van Honthorst, 1590–1656

FIG. 10 *Apollo and Diana, 1628*, oil on canvas, 357 x 640cms

Pieter de Hooch, 1629–84

FIG. 159 *Cardplayers in a Sunlit Room, 1658*, oil on canvas, 76.2 x 66.1cms

Alexander Hood, 1854–1937

Introduction FIG. IV *The Picture Gallery, Buckingham Palace, c. 1914*, photograph

Gerrit Houckgeest, c. 1600–61

FIG. 187 *Charles I, Queen Henrietta Maria, and Charles, Prince of Wales, Dining in Public, 1635*, oil on panel, 63.2 x 92.4cms

Jacob Huysmans, c. 1633–96

FIG. 139 *Francis Stuart, Duchess of Richmond, 1664*, oil on canvas, 127.6 x 104.1cms

Hieronymus Janssens, 1624–93

FIG. 188 *Charles II Dancing at a Ball at Court, c. 1660*, oil on canvas, 139.7 x 213.4cms

George Jones, 1786–1869

FIG. 121 *The Battle of Vittoria, 1822*, oil on canvas, 238.1 x 322.6cms
FIG. 122 *The Battle of Waterloo, c. 1824*, oil on canvas, 238.1 x 321.3cms
FIG. 198 *The Banquet at the Coronation of George IV, 19 July 1821*, oil on canvas, 109.2 x 89.8cms

Justus of Ghent, before 1440–c. 1480

FIG. 36 *Federico da Montefeltro, his son Guidobaldo and others, listening to a Discourse, c. 1480*, oil on panel, 130 x 212cms

Sir Gerald Kelly, 1879–1972

FIG. 183 *King George VI, 1938–45*, oil on canvas, 271.8 x 172.7cms
FIG. 184 *Queen Elizabeth, The Queen Mother, 1938–45*, oil on canvas, 271.8 x 172.7cms

Sir Godfrey Kneller, ?1646–1723

FIG. 140 *Margaret Cecil, Countess of Ranelagh, c. 1690*, oil on canvas, 232.4 x 143.5cms

Sir Edwin Landseer, 1803–73

FIG. 87 *Eos, 1841*, oil on canvas, 111.8 x 142.9cms
FIG. 88 *Isaac Van Amburgh and his Animals, 1839*, oil on canvas, 113 x 174.6cms
FIG. 89 *The Sanctuary, 1842*, oil on canvas, 61.3 x 152.7cms
FIG. 128 *Queen Victoria at Osborne House, 1865–7*, oil on canvas, 147.3 x 208cms
FIG. 131 *Windsor Castle in Modern Times, 1841–5*, oil on canvas, 113.3 x 144.5cms
FIG. 155 *Royal Sports on Loch and Hill, 1850*, oil on canvas, 42.9 x 76.5cms
FIG. 173 *Queen Victoria on Horseback, c. 1840*, oil on canvas, 52.1 x 43.2cms
FIG. 190 *Queen Victoria and Prince Albert at the Bal Costumé of 12 May 1842, 1842–6*, oil on canvas, 142.6 x 111.8cms

Sir Thomas Lawrence, 1769–1830

FIG. 16 *George IV, 1821*, oil on canvas, 289.6 x 200.7cms
FIG. 99 *Arthur Wellesley, First Duke of Wellington, 1814–15*, oil on canvas, 317.5 x 225.4cms
FIG. 100 *Matvei Ivanovitch, Count Platov, 1814*, oil on canvas, 269.2 x 179.1cms
FIG. 101 *Clemens Lothar Wenzel, Prince Metternich, 1818–19*, oil on canvas, 128.3 x 104.1cms
FIG. 102 *Pope Pius VII, 1819*, oil on canvas, 269.2 x 177.9cms
FIG. 137 *Queen Charlotte, 1789*, oil on canvas, 239.4 x 147.3cms (National Gallery, London)

Remigius van Leemput, d. 1675

FIG. 170 *Henry VII and Elizabeth of York, Henry VIII and Jane Seymour* (after Hans Holbein the Younger) *1667*, oil on canvas, 88.9 x 98.7cms

Frederick, Lord Leighton, 1830–96

FIG. 35 *Cimabue's Madonna being carried through the Streets of Florence, 1853–5*, oil on canvas, 231.8 x 520.7cms

Sir Peter Lely, 1618–80

FIG. 138 *Elizabeth Hamilton, Countess of Gramont, c. 1663*, oil on canvas, 125.1 x 101.6cms

Charles Robert Leslie, 1794–1859

FIG. 199 *Queen Victoria Receiving the Sacrament at her Coronation, 28 June 1838, 1838–9*, oil on canvas, 97.5 x 186.4cms

Claude Gellée called Le Lorrain, 1600–82

FIG. 60 *Coast Scene with the Rape of Europa, 1667*, oil on canvas, 134.6 x 101.6cms

Philip James de Loutherbourg, 1740–1812

FIG. 110 *Warley Camp: The Review, 1780*, oil on canvas, 121.3 x 183.5cms
FIG. 111 *Warley Camp: The Mock Attack, 1779*, oil on canvas, 121.9 x 184.1cms
FIG. 124 *The Glorious First of June, 1794, 1795*, oil on canvas, 266.5 x 373.5cms (National Maritime Museum, London)

Nicholas Maes, 1634–93

FIG. 165 *The Listening Housewife, 1655*, oil on panel, 74.9 x 60.3cms

Andrea Mantegna, c. 1430/1–1506

FIG. 9 *The Triumphs of Caesar, c. 1485–94*, tempera on canvas, each approx 268 x 279cms

William Marlow, 1740–1813 & Sawrey Gilpin, 1733–1807

FIG. 76 *The Duke of Cumberland visiting his Stud, c. 1764*, oil on canvas, 106 x 139.7cms

Benjamin Marshall, 1768–1835

FIG. 80 *Curricle with a Huntsman, c. 1794*, oil on canvas, 86.4 x 101cms

John Martin, 1789–1854

FIG. 66 *The Eve of the Deluge, 1840*, oil on canvas, 142.9 x 218.4cms

Rudolf Swoboda, 1859–1914

FIG. 107 *Waiting for the Train, 1892*, oil on canvas, 90.5 x 55.9cms

David Teniers the Younger, 1610–90

FIG. 162 *Peasants dancing outside an Inn, c. 1645*, oil on canvas, 135.3 x 205.1cms

Gerard Terborch, 1617–81

FIG. 167 *The Letter, c. 1660*, oil on canvas, 81.9 x 68cms

George Thomas, 1824–68

FIG. 112 *Queen Victoria and the Prince Consort at Aldershot, 1866*, oil on canvas, 86.4 x 127.6cms
FIG. 113 *The Presentation of Crimean Medals by Queen Victoria on 18 May 1855, 1857–8*, oil on canvas, 99.1 x 177.8cms

Peter Tillemans, 1684–1734

FIG. 196 *Queen Anne at the House of Lords. c. 1710*, oil on canvas, 139.7 x 122.2cms

Titian, 1487/90–1576

FIG. 62 *The Death of Actaeon, 1570–75*, oil on canvas, 178.4 x 198.1cms (National Gallery, London)

Girolamo da Treviso, active 1524, d. 1544

FIG. 37 *A Protestant Allegory, c. 1542–4*, oil on panel, 68 x 84.4cms

Joseph Mallord William Turner, 1775–1851

FIG. 125 *The Battle of Trafalgar, 21 October 1805, c. 1823*, oil on canvas, 261.5 x 368.5cms (National Maritime Museum, London)

Laurits Regner Tuxen, 1853–1927

FIG. 132 *The Family of Queen Victoria, 1887*, oil on canvas, 165.7 x 226.1cms
FIG. 192 *The Queen's Garden Party, 28 June 1897, 1897–1900*, oil on canvas, 167.3 x 228.3cms

Jan Vermeer, 1632–75

FIG. 168 *A Lady at the Virginals with a Gentleman, c. 1665*, oil on canvas, 73.3 x 64.5cms

Elizabeth-Louise Vigée-Lebrun, 1755–1842

FIG. 20 *Charles-Alexandre de Calonne, 1784*, oil on canvas, 149.9 x 128.3cms

Edward Matthew Ward, 1816–79

FIG. 95 *The Investiture of Napoleon III with the Order of the Garter, 18 April 1855, 1860*, oil on canvas, 96.8 x 175.6cms
FIG. 96 *Queen Victoria at the Tomb of Napoleon, 24 August 1855, 1860*, oil on canvas, 94.9 x 175.3cms

James Ward, 1769–1859

FIG. 81 *Nonpareil, 1824*, oil on panel, 80 x 111.1cms

Benjamin West, 1728–1820

FIG. 93 *Edward III Crossing the Somme, 1788*, oil on canvas, 137.2 x 149.9cms
FIG. 94 *The Burghers of Calais, 1789*, oil on canvas, 100 x 153.3cms
FIG. 109 *George III, 1779*, oil on canvas, 255.3 x 182.9cms

FIG. 115 *The Departure of Regulus, 1769*, oil on canvas, 229.9 x 304.8cms
FIG. 116 *The Death of Epaminondas, 1773*, oil on canvas, 222.2 x 179.4cms
FIG. 117 *The Death of Chevalier Bayard, 1772*, oil on canvas, 221.6 x 179.1cms
FIG. 118 *The Death of Wolfe, 1771*, oil on canvas, 153.7 x 245.1cms

Charles Wild, 1781–1835

Introduction FIG. I *The Blue Velvet Room, Carlton House, c. 1818*, watercolour over etched outlines published in W. H. Pyne's *The History of the Royal Residences (1819)*, 21.1 x 24.8cms
FIG. 92 *The King's Audience Chamber, Windsor Castle, 1817*, watercolour over etched outlines published in W. H. Pyne's *The History of the Royal Residences (1819)*, 21.1 x 24.8cms

Sir David Wilkie, 1785–1841

FIG. 27 *The Defence of Saragossa, 1828*, oil on canvas, 94 x 141cms
FIG. 30 *The First Council of Queen Victoria, 1838*, oil on canvas, 151.8 x 238.8cms
FIG. 161 *The Penny Wedding, 1818*, oil on panel, 64.4 x 95.6cms

Franz Xaver Winterhalter, 1805–73

FIG. 31 *The Family of Queen Victoria, 1846*, oil on canvas, 260.2 x 316.9cms
FIG. 32 *The First of May, 1851*, oil on canvas, 106.7 x 129.5cms
FIG. 33 *Queen Victoria, 1843*, oil on canvas, 65.4 x 53.3cms
FIG. 148 *Albert Edward, Prince of Wales, 1846*, oil on canvas, 127.3 x 88.3cms
FIG. 174 *Queen Victoria, 1859*, oil on canvas, 241.9 x 157.5cms
FIG. 175 *Prince Albert, 1859*, oil on canvas, 241.9 x 158.1cms

Richard Caton Woodville, 1856–1927

FIG. 104 *Khartoum: Memorial Service for General Gordon, 1899*, oil on canvas, 132.7 x 199.1cms

John Wootton, 1686?–1764

FIG. 74 *A View of Park Place, c. 1742–3*, oil on canvas, 90.2 x 153cms
FIG. 75 *A View of Henley-on-Thames, c. 1742–3*, oil on canvas, 101 x 156.2cms
FIG. 114 *The Siege of Lille, 1742*, oil on canvas, 311.2 x 490.3cms

John Wootton (attributed to)

FIG. 197 *George III's Procession to the Houses of Parliament, 1762*, oil on canvas, 90.2 x 135.9cms

Philips Wouwermans, 1619–68

FIG. 22 *Cavalry at a Sutler's Booth, 1650–60*, oil on panel, 49.5 x 44.4cms

Michael Wright, 1617–1700?

FIG. 171 *Charles II, 1661*, oil on canvas, 283.2 x 225.4cms

Johann Zoffany, 1733/4–1810

FIG. 17 *Queen Charlotte at her Dressing Table, c. 1765*, oil on canvas, 112.4 x 129.2cms
FIG. 49 *The Tribuna of the Uffizi, 1772–80*, oil on canvas, 123.5 x 154.9cms
FIG. 141 *Queen Charlotte, 1771*, oil on canvas, 163.8 x 137.5cms
FIG. 146 *George, Prince of Wales, and Frederick, later Duke of York, c. 1765*, oil on canvas, 111.8 x 127.9cms

Permissions

All pictures, watercolours, engravings and photographs from The Royal Collection are reproduced © 1992 by gracious permission of Her Majesty The Queen.

Paintings not in The Royal Collection are acknowledged in the List of Illustrations.

The author and publishers are grateful to the following:

The *Independent*, for permission to quote an extract from 'The Official Versions' by A. Graham Dixon, first published in the *Independent*, Tuesday 14 May 1991.

Cambridge University Press: for permission to quote from 'The Context, Performance, and Meaning of Ritual: The British Monarchy and "The Invention of Tradition", c.1870–1977' in *The Invention of Tradition*, eds. E. Hobsbawm and T. Ranger.

Faber and Faber Ltd: for permission to quote an extract from 'Musée des Béaux Arts' by W. H. Auden in *Collected Poems*; and an extract from *Unquiet Landscape: Places and Ideas in 20th Century English Painting* by Christopher Neve.

John Murray Ltd: for permission to quote from *Landscape into Art* by Kenneth Clark.

George Weidenfeld & Nicolson Ltd: for permission to quote from *The Queen's Pictures* by Sir Oliver Millar.

Every effort has been made to trace the holders of copyrights. Any inadvertent omissions of acknowledgement or permission can be rectified in future editions.

Index